Your FINANCIAL FUTURE
A Guide to Personal Finance

Steven D. Harrop

Kendall Hunt
publishing company

Cover image © Shutterstock, Inc.

www.kendallhunt.com
Send all inquiries to:
4050 Westmark Drive
Dubuque, IA 52004-1840

Copyright © 2015 by Kendall Hunt Publishing Company

ISBN 978-1-4652-4974-6

All rights reserved. No part of this publication may be reproduced,
stored in a retrieval system, or transmitted, in any form or by any means,
electronic, mechanical, photocopying, recording, or otherwise,
without the prior written permission of the copyright owner.

Printed in the United States of America

Contents

Introduction vii

FINANCIAL PLANNING 1

Chapter 1   **The Personal Finance Process........3**
- The Cycles of Life 4
- To There........................... 5
- Financial Goals...................... 5
- Alternative Paths to "There".......... 7
- Choosing Your Path.................. 7
- Get It Done 8
- Habits.............................. 9
- Those Other Influences.............. 9
- Life's Situations..................... 9
- The Economy 11
- The Value of Money................ 12
- Looking Forward—Future Value..... 13
- The Compounding Mechanism...... 15
- Present Value 15
- Knowledge Is Power 16

Chapter 2   **Financial Planning Instruments.... 21**
- Your Pond 23
- The Balance Sheet 23
- The Income Statement............. 26
- The Budget Statement 29
- A Brief Examination 31
- Where Do the Savings Go.......... 31
- Budgeting Methodologies........... 33
- Interpreting the Data............... 34
- Mitigating that Tug-of-War 36
- Documentation 37

Chapter 3   **Your Career....................... 41**
- The Value of Competence........... 43
- Employment Opportunities 44
- Interests and Aptitudes 45
- The Definition of Success 48
- Career Opportunity Costs 49
- Your Resume—An Advertisement 50
- A Better Resume................... 51
- Job Search 54
- Internships 55
- Networking....................... 55
- Meeting with the Employer 57
- Compensation 59
- Indirect Compensation............. 59

Chapter 4   **Taxes............................. 63**
- Cost of Government 65
- Taxes on Purchases 65
- Taxes on Property 67
- Payroll Taxes...................... 68
- Gift and Estate Taxes 69
- Income Taxes 70
- The Federal Income Tax Return 72
- A Thirty Minute Job................ 75
- Some Common Mistakes 77
- Capital Gains and Losses 77
- Reducing Your Income Tax 79
- The Audit Procedure 80
- Sources of Assistance............... 82

CASH & DEBT MANAGEMENT 85

Chapter 5   **Cash Management & Banking 87**
- Managing Your Cash............... 88
- Services Offered by Financial Institutions 88
- Payment Services 90
- Electronic Banking 92
- Savings........................... 93
- Borrowing........................ 95
- Costs, Always To Be Considered 96
- Accessing Your Money 97
- Online Financial Management....... 97
- Types of Financial Institutions....... 99
  - Commercial Banks 99
  - Savings and Loan Associations ... 99
  - Mutual Savings Bank............ 99
  - Credit Unions.................. 99
  - Investment Companies.......... 100
  - Life Insurance Companies 100
  - Finance Companies............. 100
  - Payday Loans 100
  - Title Loans 101
  - Tax Refund Loans 101
  - Pawnshops 101
- Consumer Protection for Deposit Accounts...................... 102

Chapter 6   **Establishing Credit................ 103**
- Consumer Credit: What Is It? 104
- Credit and Our Economy 105
- Types of Credit 105

Closed Ended Credit.......... 106	Research Who You Are Going to Purchase the Vehicle From...... 154
Open Ended Credit............ 106	Buying a Car from a Private Party................... 155
The Four or Five Cs.............. 108	Some Things to Remember if Buying a Used Car from a Private Party................... 156
Character 108	Research the Vehicle that You are Thinking of Buying........... 157
Capacity 108	Research What a Vehicle Should Cost You to Purchase and How Much It Would Cost You to Finance that Purchase..... 158
Capital...................... 108	1. Price...................... 158
Collateral................... 109	2. Trade-ins.................. 162
Conditions 110	3. Financing 164
Credit Reporting 110	4. Additional Products or Services Offered........... 165
Credit Scoring Models............ 110	5. Timing of Your Purchase 166
Credit Scoring Factors............. 111	Slow the Process Down........... 167
Credit Report and Scoring Guidelines................... 111	

Chapter 10	**The Housing Decision........... 169**
A Note on Credit Scoring and the Effects of Different Actions 114	Some Primary Considerations...... 171
Cards, Cards, Cards............... 114	1. Life Stage.................. 171
Credit Cards................. 114	2. Financial Capacity........... 171
Debit Cards..................... 116	3. Financial Advantages 173
Gift Cards 116	4. Stability................... 179
Travel & Entertainment Cards (T&E Cards)................. 116	The Steps in Buying a Home........ 179
How Much Credit Can I (or Should I) Use? 117	1. Know What You Can Afford ... 179
Some Closing Thoughts 117	2. Neighborhood Selection....... 181

Chapter 7	**Borrowing & Debt Management .. 119**
A Lesson from History 121	3. Pick a Real Estate Agent....... 182
When is Borrowing Not a Good Idea 121	4. Find Your Home 183
What Does It Mean When We Borrow 123	5. Purchase Negotiation and Inspection Reports 184
The Cost of Debt 124	When It's Time to Sell 185
Better Access to Borrowings........ 127	Effective Presentation of Your Home 187
Special Types of Consumer Loans... 129	
Danger Signals 130	**INSURANCE............................189**
When We Face Financial Difficulties 130	
Bankruptcy..................... 131	

Chapter 11	**Property & Casualty Insurance.... 191**
A Word of Caution................ 133	The Nature of Insurance 192
BETTER BUYING..........................135	How Much is Enough 194

Chapter 8	**Smart Buying.................... 137**
Is it Need or Want 138	Property & Casualty Coverage...... 195
Opportunity Costs................ 139	Liability 195
A Game Plan for Buying........... 139	Umbrella Insurance............... 196
Changing Buying Patterns 142	Automobile Insurance............. 197
A Few Tips to Save You Money 143	Keeping Automobile Insurance Premium Low................. 199
Unit Pricing..................... 146	Homeowners Insurance 200
The Pantry Plan 146	Property Coverage................ 202
Understanding the Terms.......... 147	Insuring the Contents 202
Resolving Disappointments 149	Homeowners Liability Coverage 204

Chapter 9	**The Automobile Decision 151**
Should You Own a Vehicle......... 153	Keeping Home Insurance Premiums Low............... 204
The Car Buying Process 154	

	When You Have a Loss 205		Diversification 256
	No-Fault Insurance 207		The Allocation Process 257
			Investment Information 258
Chapter 12	**Health & Disability Insurance..... 209**		
	Health Insurance 211	**Chapter 15**	**Investment Securities 261**
	Staying Well 212		Investment Securities 263
	Private Sources of Health Insurance		Trading Investment Securities 263
	and Health Care................ 213		Investment Strategies.............. 266
	Health Maintenance Organization		A Certificate of Ownership......... 267
	(HMO) 213		Dividends 268
	Preferred Provider Organization		Preferred Stock.................... 269
	(PPO) 213		Dissecting Stocks 270
	Exclusive Provider Organization		Stock Market Indexes 271
	(EPO) 214		A Few Analytical Considerations ... 272
	High Deductible/Catastrophic		A Certificate of Indebtedness....... 274
	(HSA) 214		Who Issues Bonds 275
	Government Health-Care Programs. 215		Corporate Bonds 276
	Medicare..................... 215		Municipal Bonds 276
	Medicaid..................... 215		Treasury Bonds.................... 277
	Disability Insurance................ 216		Early Redemption Provisions....... 278
	Long Term Care 220		Current Yield and Yield to Maturity . 279
	What We Want When		Ratings......................... 280
	We Get Sick 223		
	Politics and the Economy of Health	**Chapter 16**	**Mutual Funds.................... 283**
	Care 223		What is a Mutual Fund 285
			Why Choose a Mutual Fund 286
Chapter 13	**Life Insurance 225**		Net Asset Value................... 288
	Life Insurance..................... 227		Open-End versus Closed-End 289
	Determining the Proper Amount of Life		The Costs of a Mutual Fund 290
	Insurance 228		Specialty Mutual Funds............ 291
	Types of Life Insurance 229		Grading of Mutual Funds 293
	Term Life........................ 230		Researching a Mutual Fund 294
	Permanent Insurance.............. 231		Gains and Taxes 296
	Whole Life....................... 232		Total Return 297
	Universal Life 232		
	Variable Universal Life 233	**Chapter 17**	**Real Estate and Commodities 299**
	Mutual versus Stock Company...... 233		Real Estate Investing 301
	Buy Term and Invest the Difference . 233		Nine Truths of Investing........... 302
	Buying Life Insurance 234		Three Investment Lessons from
	Settlement Options 235		the Stock Market 304
	Annuities........................ 236		What Kind of Investor Are You 305
			There are Three Broad Ways to
INVESTMENTS 239			Invest in Real Estate 307
			Who Should Use the Stock Market to
Chapter 14	**Fundamentals of Investment 241**		Invest in Real Estate 308
	Earned Income................... 242		When Should You Join a Group
	The Goal of Savings 244		(LP, LLC, TIC, etc.) to Invest in
	Your Investor Profile 246		Real Estate..................... 309
	The Broker....................... 247		When Should You Go it Alone and
	Which Club Should I Choose....... 248		Directly Invest in Real Estate 311
	Income versus Appreciation........ 250		1—Competitive Advantage
	Safety versus Risk................. 252		(Lynch's Rule)................ 311
	The Classic Investment Con........ 252		2—Real Estate Skills 312
	Risk 253		Types of Direct Real Estate
	Liquidity 253		Investment 312
	The Right Club 254		How To Begin.................... 313

When Is Real Estate Right for You... 314
What Is a Commodity?............ 314
The Commodity Futures
    Contract 317
An illustration into Commodities
    Trading 317
How to Invest in Commodities 318

Chapter 18   **Entrepreneurial Investment Opportunities** 321
Risk and Reward 323
The Value of Investments in
    Entrepreneurship............... 323
The Life Cycle of Entrepreneurial
    Ventures 324
Investment and Funding Sources at
    Various Life Cycle Phases........ 327
    Self-Funding.................. 329
    Crowdfunding 330
    Government Programs.......... 330
    Angel Investors 330
    Venture Capital 331
    Initial Public Offering.......... 332
    Mergers and Acquisitions........ 333
    Debt versus Equity.............. 333
Uniqueness of "Start-up" or
    Development Stage Investing..... 333
Rapid-Growth-Stage Investors...... 334
Return on Investment (ROI):
    Liquidity and Monetizing Events . 335
Who Should Be an Investor in
    Entrepreneurial Ventures? 336
How to Attract Capital to
    Entrepreneurial Ventures........ 336
    Business Plan 336
    Markets and Marketing.......... 337
    Team 338
    Resources 338

RETIREMENT............................. 339

Chapter 19   **Retirement** 341
What Are the Demographics? 342
Prerequisites to a Successful
    Retirement 343
    Prerequisite No. 1: Be Debt Free .. 344
    Prerequisite No. 2: Have a Plan ... 344
    Prerequisite No. 3: Prepare
        Financially 346

Social Security 346
Employer Retirement Programs 347
Savings and Investments........... 350
Insurance and Annuities........... 352
Reverse Annuity Mortgage......... 353
The Inflation Monster 354
The Bottom Line.................. 355

Chapter 20   **Your Legacy** 357
Legacy Planning & Estate Planning.. 358
Three Important Legacy Planning
    Warnings..................... 360
    Warning #1: The cost of not having a
        legacy plan far exceeds the value of
        an investment in a legacy plan.. 360
Why Plan Your Legacy Now?....... 363
    Warning #2: We never know when an
        emergency will hit, where we will
        be when it happens, and what the
        actual result will be 364
    Warning #3: A Will isn't the only
        tool that will protect your assets
        and your family in case of death or
        incapacity 366
Three Legacy Planning Myths 367

APPENDIX I: ADDITIONAL READINGS & CASE STUDIES 375

Chapter 8:	Article 8:1 — How a Family of Four Manages To Live Well On Just $14,000 Per Year.............. 376
Chapter 9:	Article 9:1 — Car Buyers Burned by Negative Equity......... 379
Chapter 14:	Article 14:1 — Risk Profile Questionnaire................... 380
	Article 14:2 — Suitability 383
	Article 14:3 — A State of Mind 386
Chapter 15:	Article 15:1 — Growth Versus Value 389
	Article 15:2 — In Search of Alpha... 392

APPENDIX II: APPLICATION WORKSHEETS.... 395

APPENDIX III: GLOSSARY 445

Introduction

As we push ourselves up the learning curves of life, there may be times when we pursue a subject simply for the sake of increasing our awareness of that subject. There may be times when we say, "I don't think I will ever use this knowledge again" . . . and occasionally we are right. Personal Finance is not that subject. The management of our financial affairs is a reality that every adult faces virtually every day of their life. The only question is, do I have the knowledge that will enable me to do it right—the awareness to know what is needed—the moxie to understand what is happening.

Personal Finance is Cash Management 101, Career Planning 101, Banking 101, Smart Buying 101, Insurance 101, Investments 101, and Estate Planning 101. It is a host of considerations, which will define one's financial future. Today, more than ever, it is important that we have a handle on these subjects, so as to successfully navigate our course through an increasingly complex world.

It has been said that "experience is the best teacher." While that may be true much of the time, in your personal financial world, stumbling through in "trial and error" mode can be expensive . . . or worse. In these contexts, it may be better to learn from other people's experience—and thereby chart a course that will enable you to steer your financial ship around the shoals that wreck so much havoc on so many people.

This book was prepared to help chart that course. A Board of Contributors has been assembled, each specializing in a given realm of personal finance. These individuals have spent decades focusing on their respective area of expertise, and their respective chapters would pass that knowledge on to you, to better enable you to "get it right."

The following chapters cover a range of topics, each of which addresses an aspect of personal finance. Taken together, they provide a library designed to coach you in the basics of many of the financial aspects of your life. While each chapter is intended to be a stand-alone treatment of that subject, it is our intention that, taken together, they provide a reservoir of knowledge that you can refer to again and again as these topics occur in your life.

Allow us to introduce the Board of Contributors.

Robert J. Eagleston carries on a family tradition started in 1965, of helping clients establish peace of mind through the proper implementation of insurance. Representing the second generation in managing a leading insurance provider, Mr. Eagleston has practiced in virtually all areas of insurance and risk management. As a member of the Million Dollar Round Table, he is licensed in and has clients in every state. With 15 years of insurance acumen, he is involved in developing imaginative solutions for the insurance needs of his clients. Mr. Eagleston holds a bachelor's degree in business.

Steven D. Harrop served as an investment analyst and portfolio manager for 26 years, before joining a university faculty as executive in residence. Mr. Harrop was involved as an analyst and portfolio manager for both private account and mutual fund portfolios. These portfolios invested in stocks, bonds, and money market funds; over his 26-year career, portfolios under his management earned a total of 24 Lipper Awards (Lipper Analytical Services recognition of No. 1 portfolio in category). When he transitioned into teaching, he was managing approximately $5 billion in Mutual Fund assets. As a university professor for 15 years, Mr. Harrop taught both undergraduate and graduate courses in investments, strategic management, and personal finance. Mr. Harrop is a certified financial analyst (CFA). He holds a bachelor's degree in business and a master's degree in finance and marketing.

Ken R. Hart has extensive experience applying his financial acumen in a number of contexts. Mr. Hart has been an auditor with a national accounting firm; has served on the staff of a U.S. Senator in Washington, DC; has held the position of chief operating officer and chief financial officer for a Chapter of the American Red Cross; and has held the position of chief financial officer for a multiple-dealership auto group. He is currently vice-president of operations for a major regional medical center. Mr. Hart is a certified public accountant (CPA). He holds a bachelor's degree in business administration and a master's degree in political science.

Craig E. Isom served as a small business partner and consultant for 26 years, before joining a university faculty as executive director of its Business Resource Center. Employed by a national accounting firm, Mr. Isom's experience in public accounting was focused primarily on small business, where he was involved in the policy making, operation, and reporting functions. His transition into teaching includes his role as lecturer in entrepreneurship on a university level, and as executive director of the University Business Resource Center. In addition, he is the director of the State's Regional Small Business Development Center. The Center provides a wide range of consulting services to area small businesses in various stages of their life cycle. Mr. Isom is a certified public accountant (CPA). He holds a bachelor's degree and a master's degree in accounting.

Ryan O'Shea is a full-service financial planner and wealth strategist. Mr. O'Shea is the owner and chief executive officer of a registered investment advisory firm and an insurance agency. Licensed as a financial advisor, and as a life, disability, and health insurance representative, he is qualified to work with individuals, couples, and business owners. He has a decade of experience in financial services, evaluating and advising both personal and institutional clients as to their unique financial planning needs. Mr. O'Shea is an investment advisor and wealth strategist, and holds a bachelor's degree in business administration and a master's degree in business.

John W. Packer has more than 40 years of real estate experience. After 30 years with institutional real estate companies, he currently buys, manages, and develops real estate as a general partner and for his own account. Mr. Packer has been involved in real estate analysis, acquisitions, lending, and property management. He has been on both sides of the real estate business, participating in asset management as well as commercial lending. He has worked on hundreds of real estate transactions totaling billions of dollars on most property types in most major markets in the United States. Mr. Packer is a California real estate broker and has been a member of the Appraisal Institute. He holds a bachelor's degree in business management and a master's degree in business administration.

Denton S. Whitney is an attorney focusing on mediation and legacy planning, and a college professor teaching classes in communication and conflict management, business law, and negotiation. Mr. Whitney is the founder of Whitney Mediation & Legal Counsel, providing training on legacy planning, collaboration, and conflict management. He is regularly involved in issues of personalized estate and business planning, negotiation, and conflict management. He has been an invited speaker and consultant for multiple international organizations, including the World Bank. He has decades of faculty experience at three Universities. Mr. Whitney holds a certificate in dispute resolution, a bachelor's degree in economics and english, a master's degree in business administration, and a degree in law.

This book has been prepared with only one goal in mind—to help you better manage your financial future. To that end, we dedicate this book to you . . . the student. Per aspera ad astra!

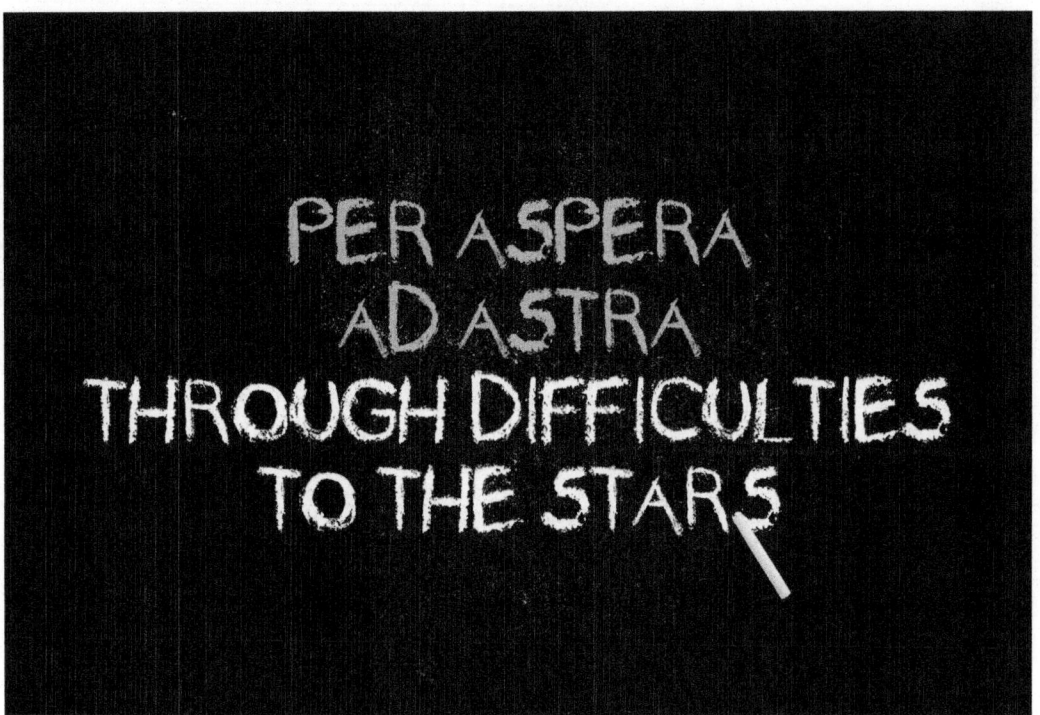

Financial Planning

Chapter 1
The Personal Finance Process

> # Chapter Objectives
>
> 1. Understand the five steps of the Financial Planning Process.
> 2. Identify four critical elements in the setting of personal financial goals.
> 3. Develop your own personal financial goals; short-term, intermediate-term, and long term.
> 4. Be aware of external influences that may impact your efforts to chart your financial future, including influences stemming from your life situation and personal values, and those stemming from economic factors.
> 5. Explain the Time Value of Money, and assess the four different contexts for its application.
> 6. Be able to calculate Future Value and Present Value scenarios using the Time Value of Money Tables.

The Cycles of Life

It would be an easy matter if we could prepare a template that would enable you to chart your financial future simply by filling in the blanks. Unfortunately, there is no single template that is applicable to everyone, at every stage in their life. Some of you are single, others are married. Some are young whereas others are older. Some of you are struggling to put your lives back together again after a serious setback, others have yet to face such challenges. Whatever your life situation, you are unique in many ways, and a "one size fits all" approach would not be individualized enough to always be relevant. We recognize your individuality, and have tried to accommodate it in two ways.

First, the following pages deal in processes more than formulas, in concepts more than recipes. We recognize that some of the topics we will be pursuing may apply to you today, whereas others won't appear on life's road until later. It is important to understand that preparation for each of these topics is vitally important, and we should not wait until the time has arrived to begin thinking about it. We invite you to apply each subject to your situation, and make it relevant in your own life. Second, to aid you in so doing, we have included a number of Application Worksheets, to be found in Appendix II. These worksheets are designed to get you into the water . . . to help you learn how to swim as you apply the knowledge to your own unique circumstance. Each chapter has several Application Worksheets that relate to that topic, which will help make that chapter more relevant to you.

Figure 1:1 Whatever your life situation, you are unique in many ways.

To There

The paragraphs above have put a spotlight on the first step in any planning process: Where are you. To really understand your current situation, can be illuminating. How old are you and how is your health. How much money do you make, do you have savings, do you have debts. What is your education, what skills do you possess, what kind of career are you pursuing. What do you want out of life, what is really important to you, what are your values, your relationships. No doubt, as you examine these kinds of questions, you find satisfaction on some points, and have a desire to improve on others. As you consider where you are, and where you want to go, you have put yourself on the path of the Planning Process.

Some of these considerations have little to do with money. A desire to get into better shape by working out or losing weight, though extremely important, is not really a financial issue. Getting a better grade in a class, or improving a relationship with someone else, may be worthwhile objectives, but are usually separate from your financial well-being. We acknowledge the importance of these other considerations, but in this book we are going to focus more closely on your financial situation. And so, let us state one of the prime lessons which underscore our efforts here: The only way most of us will ever improve our financial situation, is by earning more than we spend. Sorry to be the one to break it to you, but you will not win a lottery. A financial windfall that will leave you rich is unlikely . . . you are going to have to do it yourself.

So, as you examine your financial situation, you are at the beginning of the Financial Planning Process. There are, no doubt, some thoughts that enter your mind as to where you would like to be. You may be "here" today, but you would like to be "there" tomorrow. Good for you. You have already advanced to the next step in your financial plan, and that is Where Would You Like To Be . . . the "there."

Financial Goals

Financial goals are extremely important, as they become the compass that will guide our future efforts. Not having a goal is like walking out on the golf course with no idea where the cup is. Swing away—Good luck. It is only when we know where the cup is, and make an effort to move in that direction, that we can be successful. Similarly, if we establish a financial goal . . . knowing what we want . . . and move in that direction, we can be successful. To be relevant, a financial goal must be comprised of at least four elements.

Figure 1:2 Not having a goal is like walking out on the golf course with no idea where the cup is.

1. First, it must be a realistic point on the horizon, which is written down. A goal that is not realistic and not written down, is a wish or a dream, and of impractical utility.
2. Second, the goal must have a time element associated with its accomplishment. If the goal is to save for a car or to pay off a debt, for example, it must have a "when" so that we can steer in that direction with confidence. Short-term goals can usually be accomplished within a year or so. Intermediate goals might require several years. Long-term goals are those that are more than 5 years out on the horizon.
3. Third, if you are like most of the rest of us, this process will result in more goals than you have money to achieve them. Welcome to the club. We would all like to achieve much, but our limited finances most often dictate the pace. So, it will be necessary to prioritize your goals by assigning some of them first, or second, or third place rankings. Here, a word of caution is in order. It may be tempting to prioritize first those goals that are the shortest term, that is, those that need to be reached soonest. Although some goals may be pushing us more than others, don't neglect the longer-term goals. Though they may be further out on the horizon, they are not less important, and need to be attended to sooner rather than later.
4. Fourth, consistent with your prioritization in step three, be prepared to allocate some financial resources for their accomplishment. The goal must be fed if it is to live. We will talk more about financial allocation in Chapter 2. Application Worksheet 1:1—Goals is available in Appendix II.

As you wrestle with the third and fourth elements of goal setting, you will probably feel that many of your goals are equally important, and you don't like to push one off, or reduce the amount you are allocating to it, to have enough money to keep the other goals alive. You have discovered an important concept in the allocation process, and that is Opportunity Cost. Opportunity cost is what you give up, to obtain something else. It is the trade-off of every decision, the path we turn from to walk down the path we have chosen. Such trade-offs are not always easy, and we sometimes struggle wishing we could have it all. As that is not possible, it is best to view the opportunity cost objectively, as part of the decision process. Weighing that trade-off is a part of many decisions, and as we become better at evaluating the opportunity cost, we become better decision makers.

Exhibit 1:1 Goals

	Target Date	Priority	Allocation
Short-Term Goals			
Example: Next Semester Tuition	January 1	1	$357 Mo
_____	_____	_____	_____
_____	_____	_____	_____
Intermediate-Term Goals:			
_____	_____	_____	_____
_____	_____	_____	_____
Long-Term Goals:			
_____	_____	_____	_____
_____	_____	_____	_____

It is not uncommon for our money problems to come from poor planning, or weak financial habits, or the persuasive effects of advertising. Setting and following goals will help mitigate each of these goblins, and put control of your Financial Future in your hands—where it belongs.

> **Summary & Review**
>
> 1. Name four critical elements in the setting of personal financial goals.
> 2. Why is it important to prioritize your goals? On what basis would you set your own goal priorities?
> 3. What is Opportunity Cost? How does an understanding of Opportunity Cost affect the planning of your goals?

Alternative Paths to "There"

The above discussion of opportunity costs, suggests that many of our goals may have alternative paths to reach them. Educational goals or career advancement goals, goals relating to the purchase of a car or a house, or acquiring adequate insurance protection, or investment goals, certainly have a number of alternatives that may take you to where you want to be. As you evaluate the alternative approaches, you are at the third stage in the financial planning process, and that is the consideration of Alternative Means of Achieving that Goal.

It is important that this stage not be hampered by too much critical thought. Like the imaginative folks at the animated studio Pixar, let the creative juices flow. Allow yourself to brain storm on the options you may have, and see if you can identify a number of alternatives for achieving that goal. Here, let us suggest seven words that could help frame your thinking. The words are these: "What Would It Take for Me to _____".

These seven words accomplish two things. First, there is a goal identified as you fill in the _____, and second, you are looking for a potential means of reaching that goal—What Would It Take. If you live within the confines of those seven words for a while, inspiration will come and you will have options to consider.

Figure 1:3 Many of our goals may have alternative paths to reach them.

Choosing Your Path

In Stage 3, we urged you not to be too critical of the ideas you place on the table. This will enable you to consider alternatives that may, at first glance, sound a bit absurd, but which may, on further analysis, prove feasible. That is as it should be. However, in Stage 4, you need to make a decision. Now, in Stage 4, get out a pencil and list the pros and cons, the costs and benefits; and consider which alternative is most likely to succeed. This is the Selection Stage. There are opportunity costs associated with Step 4, and a careful evaluation of what you are giving up as you choose which path to take, may help you make the best decision.

At this stage, each of us wish we could catch a glimpse of the path ahead, and know with certainty which alternative is the best one. If you can find a way to see into the future, would you share it with the rest of us, because the rest of us are trying to make the best decision we can in the midst of uncertainty. That is all we can do. However, if you carefully implement the process of (1) evaluating where you are, (2) carefully and specifically drawing a bead on where you want to be, (3) gathering alternative means of reaching that goal, and (4) carefully weighting each alternative as you select the means most likely to succeed, you have given yourself a much better chance of success, than if you had simply acted on impulse or reacted to the needs of the moment.

Get It Done

The fifth stage is simply to get it done. Here you want to implement the selection you made, roll up your sleeves, and make it happen. It may be as simple as allocating funds to that goal, as illustrated in Exhibit 1:1. Or it may be more complex, such as working to get the education you need to put yourself on the career path you want. Whatever the decision, it is time to put doubts aside and go to work.

As you push down the path you have selected, you will get the best kind of education—experience. You will find that the goal is coming closer to your reach, or perhaps, that other factors are impacting your efforts and you face headwinds that you were not expecting. Such headwinds are frequent on the oceans of life, and you may need to adjust your sails to maintain your course in the face of such obstacles. Don't be easily dissuaded—man the braces and tack your way to your goal. However, if, in the process of the education you are receiving, you find that you are not where you want to be, and that the course you are steering is not likely to get you there, you have come full circle back to the first stage in the planning process; you are evaluating where you are.

So you see, the process is a circular one. If you are not where you want to be, and the course you are on is unlikely to get you there, you face the stages of reevaluating or possibly resetting your goals; brain-storming what actions might take you to your goals, selecting the course most likely to succeed and heading out on that course. It is a process you will engage in over and over, and it will become second nature to you. And that is an object we have in mind as we prepared this text.

Exhibit 1:2 Financial Planning Process

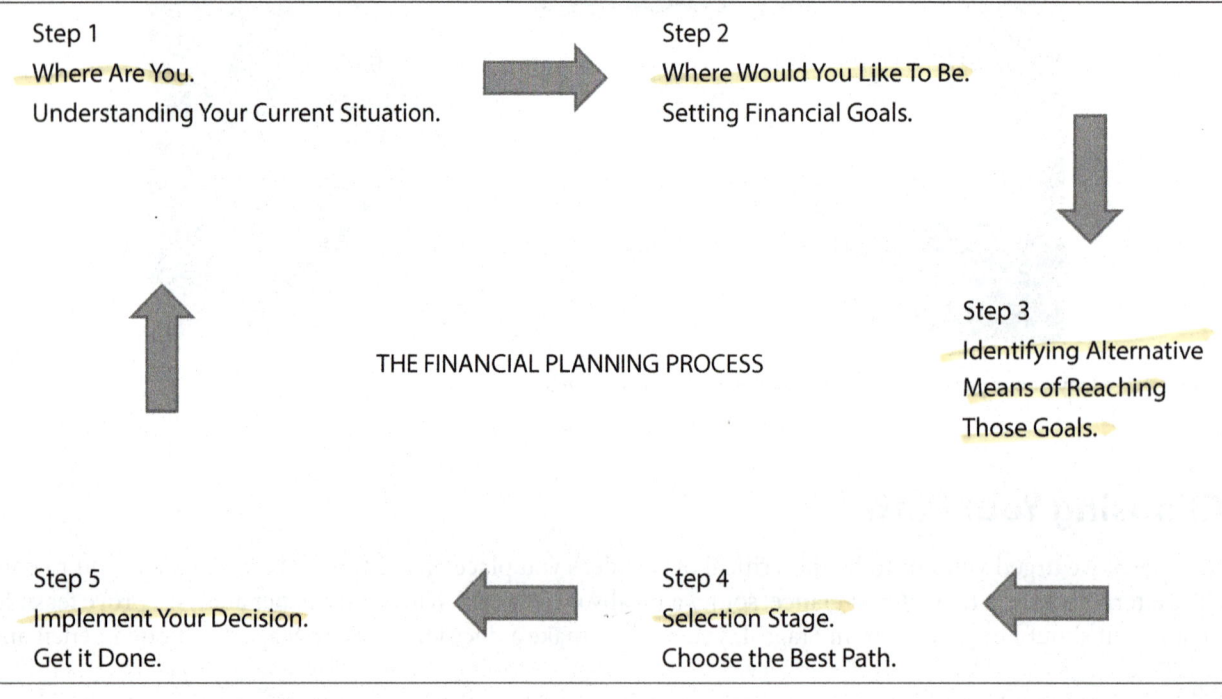

Habits

In high school, as you visited with your counselor about a range of life's issues, your counselor probably said something like this: "Your destiny is in your hands . . . you can be anything you want to be." Actually, none of us are in control of our destiny. We are in control of our habits, and then our habits control our destiny. As you move through the pages of this text, look for those processes and concepts that you can turn into habits. By so doing, this will be more than an intellectual exercise for you; it will make you a better manager of Your Financial Future. After all, isn't that the reason you are reading these pages?

> ### Summary & Review
> 1. What are the five steps of the Financial Planning Process?
> 2. Why is it so difficult to write a step by step manual instructing you at each stage in the Financial Planning Process?
> 3. What do you do if your planned course of action does not take you to where you want to be?

Those Other Influences

There is another reason why it is sometimes difficult to achieve everything we would like too, and that is those outside influences that are often pushing and pulling us in other directions. Maybe it's the demands of family, possibly resulting from illness or death. Maybe it's our values, our choice of activities, or the demands of our job. Maybe the economy has gone into the tank, or interest rates are soaring, or prices are rising. Whatever the reason, most of us feel the impact of factors we cannot control. Perhaps, we should take a minute and examine some of these influences, and see if we can prepare ourselves for their impact on our Financial Future.

Perhaps an illustration would help. Let's say that you are devout in your religion—and regular participation in your faith holds a high place in your set of values. You give generously of both your time and money in support of your faith. The fellow who works right next to you on the job is not particularly religious, does not participate in any faith, and tends to change the subject whenever religion comes up. One day, he drives up in a brand new luxury car, saying that he thought it was time to upgrade his transportation. He makes the same money you do—maybe you should buy a brand new car too. Can you see the dilemma?

Each of you have a different set of values, a different definition of what is important. If you were to try and spend your financial resources keeping up with him, while maintaining your own life's objectives, you would very quickly find your income strained to the limit. As noted earlier, each of us are unique, with unique lives and situations. Although it is important to acknowledge those outside influences that would move us in a different direction, to try and keep up with all of the joneses around us would be impossible.

The two outside influences that most regularly impact our financial pathway are our own Life's Situation and Economic Factors.

Life's Situations

The example above illustrates one of those Life's Situations. This one happened to be of our own choosing, and many of the situations we find ourselves in are the result of our choices. For the most part, we choose our values and our education. We choose our friends, our hobbies, and much of our daily activities. We choose how we will spend our time and our money, how we will cultivate our interests, and how we will respond to life's challenges. Perhaps William Ernest Henley said it best in his poem "Influence."

Figure 1:4 I am the master of my fate: I am the captain of my soul.

"I am the master of my fate: I am the captain of my soul."

Although it is important for us to take command of our own lives, it is also important to recognize that there are situations that are the result of factors we do not control. For example, we can do little to change our age, and those conditions that are a function of our age. Exhibit 1:3 illustrates some of the influences that normally accompany us at a different age in our life cycle.

No doubt you can add your own unique considerations to this list, which serves to underline the point. We are all impacted by circumstances that affect our financial planning, over which we have little direct control.

Exhibit 1:3 Our Life Cycle

As a Young Adult	Concerned with transitioning into a level of independence. Gaining an education, or establishing oneself in a career. Dating and developing long-term relationships.
Young Couple or Single Parent	The care of someone else impacts our life's choices. Looking to improve our education or career potential. Responsibility prompts us to mitigate risks—insurance.
Midlife	Older children may mean college, weddings, obligations. Career considerations important—maintain life style. Health issues increasingly force themselves into the picture.
Retirement	Retirement issues include financial support and living conditions. Review will and estate planning. Health considerations important—long-term care issues.

The Economy

The second influence that affects virtually all of us in one way or the other is the economy. After the Second World War, Germany lay in shambles, and the German currency, the Deutschmark, was virtually worthless. It would literally take a wheelbarrow full of deutschmarks to buy a loaf of bread. Depending on your currency, its value may rise or fall over time . . . prices of goods and services may go up or decline . . . jobs may be plentiful or unavailable . . . and the list goes on.

For most of us, there are a handful of economic factors that regularly affect our financial future. Being aware of those influences will aid us in the decision making process. If the U.S. dollar is your currency, then Exhibit 1:4 identifies some of the more important economic considerations. If the U.S. dollar is not your currency, there will, no doubt, be other statistics unique to your monetary unit, which will reveal similar kinds of conditions for your economy. Application Worksheet 1:2 in Appendix II, gives you the opportunity to track these important economic indices.

Figure 1:5 The second influence that affects virtually all of us in one way or the other is the economy.

12 Financial Planning

Exhibit 1:4 Economic Factors

Interest Rates	Short-Term interest rates in the United States are largely influenced by the Federal Reserve (The central bank of the United States), which sets the Discount Rate and targets the Fed Funds Rate. Long-Term interest rates are set by the market, typically measured by long-term mortgage rates or by the 10-year Treasury Bond. Higher interest rates means the cost of borrowing is higher.
Inflation	Inflation in the United States is measured by the CPI—the Consumer Price Index. There are a number of indexes, with many focused on specific products or services. The broadest measure of inflation would be the CPI-U—U.S. Urban Average—All items, which is a measure of price changes among all products including food and energy. This number is released monthly. Higher inflation rates means that the value of the currency is declining at a faster pace.
Unemployment	The U.S. unemployment rate is calculated by the Bureau of Labor Statistics, and is the percentage of adults who are actively seeking work, who have not found a job. It does not include those under 16, full-time students, or stay-at-home adults. This statistic is released monthly. Higher unemployment rate means there are more job-seeking adults who are out of work.
Gross Domestic Product	Gross Domestic Product or GDP is the sum total value of all goods and services produced in a given time period. It is reported Quarterly by the U.S. Department of Commerce, as the percent change (on an annualized basis) over the previous quarter. A higher GDP means that the economy is expanding at a higher pace, typically giving rise to more jobs.
Consumer Confidence Index	The Consumer Confidence Index is a measure of the attitude of the American consumer. It is an index number, with 1,985 comprising the base of 100. This statistic is released monthly. A high Consumer Confidence Index means a positive attitude on the part of the average consumer, which typically signals a better economy.

Summary & Review

1. What are the two principal influences on your financial planning process?
2. One of the Life Situations that impacts our financial planning is our personal values. Can you name other Life Situations that makes your own financial plan unique?
3. How does your age in the life cycle affect your financial plans?
4. What economic factors to you regard as most impacting you at the moment?

The Value of Money

If you were asked the question: "Do You Respect Money?" it is likely that you would answer; "Yes." Yet, if asked whether you would stop and stoop down to pick up a penny lying on the floor of a busy shopping mall, what would be your answer? Would you stop for a nickel, a dime, a quarter? If not, do you really respect money? One secret known to many people who have achieved success in the management of their money is this: It doesn't matter how large the amount is—every transaction should be accorded careful respect. As the old proverb reminds us: "Watch your pennies, and the dimes will grow."

Like a seed, money has the capacity to grow more money. The amount of money that can be grown is a function of three factors.

- The Amount
- The Rate
- The Term

Figure 1:6 Like a seed, money has the capacity to grow more money.

The Amount of money that can be planted will be a function of the savings you have accumulated—that amount which is not spent. Here is an obvious opportunity cost; if you spend it, you can't save it. The larger the amount saved and planted, the more dollars of interest you can earn.

The Rate is that return which can be realized from our plantings. The rate varies quite a lot, depending on economic factors and on the specific ground in which the money is planted. Lower rates of return will come from something like a passbook savings account, whereas higher rates of return can often be obtained from investments in bonds or stocks or real estate. The higher the rate realized, the more dollars of interest you can earn.

The Term is the period that is allocated to the growth of that money. Money that is needed in a short period has little time to grow, and the amount realized will be less. Conversely, if we reinvest the proceeds and allow more time to pass, the amount of money realized can be much larger.

Summary & Review

1. What does it mean to respect money?
2. What are the three factors that impact the return of an investment?
3. How does Term affect the growth of money?

Looking Forward—Future Value

Considering these three factors, let's ask the question: "If I had $1,000 of savings to allocate to one of my goals, say a trip to Tahiti that I would like to take five years from now, and I could plant that money into a Certificate of Deposit that earns 3% and matures in 5 years, how much money would I have at the end of those 5 years?" Here we have provided all three of the factors required:

Amount:	$1,000
Rate:	3%
Term:	5 years

We could calculate the sum that would be available in 5 years by multiplying $1,000 by 1.03, and do that five times. However, such calculations have already been done, and the results are displayed in the Time Value of Money Tables, which are provided as Exhibit 1:5 at the end of this chapter. If we go to Table A, we see that this table is the Future Value of $1.00 (Amount), given a range of possible Rates and possible time periods (Term). Given our example rate of 3%, and our term of 5 years, we can identify the factor of 1.15927 in the body of the table. This means that for every dollar of money planted, we would have $1.15927 at the end of 5 years. Since we planted $1,000, we would have 1.15927 x $1,000 or $1,159.27 five years from now.

There is a second way in which we might accumulate the funds needed, and that is to plant a regular amount of money in each and every year. Instead of simply putting $1,000 into an investment, we might put $200 at the beginning of year 1, add another $200 at the beginning of year 2, followed by another $200 at the beginning of year 3, and so on. This series of payments is called an Annuity, and it means that we are making a series of regular payments. If we make these payments over 5 years, we will have set aside the same $1,000, but the net effect of those systematic deposits will be different. Consulting the second Time Value of Money Table—Table B, we see that this table is the Future Value of $1.00 invested at the beginning of each period over a number of time periods (an annuity), again given a range of possible rates and possible time periods. Using a 3% rate for 5 years, we find a factor of 5.3091 at the end of 5 years for each dollar planted. As we planted $200 at the beginning of each year, we would have 5.3091 x $200 or a total of $1,061.82 five years from now.

Examining the results of these two future value calculations, we find that, even though we used the same interest rate over the same period of time, and even though we ended up planting $1,000 in each case, the future value at the end of 5 years of that $1,000 planted at the beginning of the term was $97.45 more than

Figure 1:7 This confirms the notion that the greater the amount available to earn interest, the greater the amount of interest earned.

had we spread that $1,000 over regular installments of $200 each year. This is because the entire $1,000 was available to earn interest in every year, whereas the annuity made available only $200 to earn interest in year 1, $400 in year 2, $600 in year 3, and so on. This confirms the notion that the greater the amount available to earn interest, the greater the amount of interest earned—assuming the same rate and same term.

The Compounding Mechanism

It should be noted that every time an interest rate is quoted, it is an annualized rate. That is, it represents the interest rate that is paid or received over a 12 month period. That is standard protocol, and if you are interested in a monthly rate or a quarterly rate, you will need to divide that number by 12 or 4 to get the shorter approximation.

Now you may be doing a little math in your head and concluding that a 3% return on $1,000 is $30. Moreover, if you get $30 per year over a 5 year period, you would have interest of $150. Yet, the Time Value of Money factor shows that you have $159.27 in accumulated interest over the 5-year term, which is $9.27 more. This additional amount is the interest earned on the previous interest earned. At the end of the first year, (assuming you left the interest earned that year in the account), the total money you have is $1,030.00—and it is that amount that is now earning your interest rate. The interest earned on previously earned interest is called Compound Interest, and it is a little-recognized miracle. Simply put, if you leave the interest earned to earn more interest, you eventually reach the point where you have more interest working for you than principal. Obviously, the more frequent the compounding the better the results, with daily compounding earning more than monthly or annual compounding.

Present Value

There may be another viewpoint that you would like to have as you contemplate your financial future, and that scenario could go something like this. Yes, I would like to go to Tahiti in 5 years, and I know that I will need $1,000 at that time to accomplish that goal. If I can find a Certificate of Deposit with a 5-year maturity (which dovetails nicely into my goal), and that CD pays 3% interest, how much money would I need to invest today to have $1,000 in 5 years. In other words, you would like to know the Present Value of $1,000, given a 3% return over 5 years.

Again, it might save you some calculating time if you go to the Time Value of Money Tables at Exhibit 1:5. In Table C, you find the present value $1.00 (Amount) to be received at the end of a period of time (Term), given a range of rates and time periods. Given our example of a 3% rate over 5 years, we find a factor of 0.86261 in the body of the table. This means that if we invest 86.261 cents at the beginning of that period, by the end of year five we will have $1.00. As we wish to have $1,000 by the end of year five, we should invest 0.86261 × $1,000 or $862.61 now to realize that goal.

To complete our examination of Time Value of Money concepts, we need one more viewpoint, and that is the present value of a series of payments, or the present value of an annuity. Let's pursue a different example. Let's say that you would like to place some funds with an institution to provide for the care of a loved one. The institution can arrange to invest those funds at 3%, and will draw on that investment at the end of each year to meet the needs of that individual. If the annual draw is $1,000, how much money do you need to give that institution today to pay for that program over a 5-year term? In effect, you are asking for the present value of a series of payments or an annuity, and that calculation is available in Table D of the Time Value of Money Tables. Again, assuming a 3% rate and a 5-year time horizon, we find the factor of 4.57971 in the body of the table, meaning that we need to place $4.57971 into the fund today, to accommodate the withdrawal of $1.00 each year for the next 5 years. As we actually need to accommodate a $1,000 withdrawal each year, we will need to place 4.57971 × $1,000 or $4,579.71 into the fund. This is less than the $5,000 that will be withdrawn over 5 years, but the interest accumulated over that time frame will make up the difference, and at the end of year 5 we will have exactly $1,000 left to withdraw.

Knowledge Is Power

As you can see, these four applications provide a range of answers to help us define how much we need to feed each of our goals. Future Value computations answer the questions: If I deposit a given amount today, how much will it be worth tomorrow. Or, if I am able to contribute regularly to a savings or investment program, how much will that annuity be worth at a given point down the road. Present Value computations answer the questions: How much do I need to set aside today to have a given amount tomorrow? Or, if I have an ongoing need down the road such as my daughter's college education, how much do I need to set aside today to meet that need?

Again, we emphasize that if you start sooner, time is on your side. Even though rates may be low, much can be accomplished given the impact of compounding over a longer period of time. Spend a moment perusing the Time Value of Money Tables. Look again at Table A. Note how that $1.00 you invested at the beginning grows over time, given different rates. If you are earning a 3% rate, your $1.00 will double in 24 years and triple in 38 years. If you are earning a 4% rate, it will take only 18 years to double, 29 years to triple, and by year 36, you will have earned over $3.00 in compound interest for every $1.00 you invested. Application Worksheet 1:3—Time Value of Money Calculations, found in Appendix II, provides the opportunity for you to apply these concepts to your own unique circumstance.

Figure 1:8 Again, we emphasize that if you start sooner, time is on your side.

Summary & Review

1. In the context of the Time Value of Money, what does Future Value mean?
2. How would you describe an Annuity?
3. When we talk about Compound Interest, what do we mean?
4. Why is it, that a Present Value factor will always be less than 1?

Exhibit 1:5 Time Value of Money Tables

Table A Future Value of $1

$$FV = \$1(1+i)^n$$

n/i	1.0%	1.5%	2.0%	2.5%	3.0%	3.5%	4.0%	4.5%	5.0%	5.5%	6.0%	7.0%	8.0%	9.0%	10.0%	11.0%	12.0%	20.0%
1	1.01000	1.01500	1.02000	1.025000	1.03000	1.03500	1.04000	1.04500	1.05000	1.05500	1.06000	1.07000	1.08000	1.09000	1.10000	1.11000	1.12000	1.20000
2	1.02010	1.03022	1.04040	1.05063	1.06090	1.07123	1.08160	1.09203	1.10250	1.11303	1.12360	1.14490	1.16640	1.18810	1.21000	1.23210	1.25440	1.44000
3	1.03030	1.04568	1.06121	1.07689	1.09273	1.10872	1.12486	1.14117	1.15763	1.17424	1.19102	1.22504	1.25971	1.29503	1.33100	1.36763	1.40493	1.72800
4	1.04060	1.06136	1.08243	1.10381	1.12551	1.14752	1.16986	1.19252	1.21551	1.23882	1.26248	1.31080	1.36049	1.41158	1.46410	1.51807	1.57352	2.07360
5	1.05101	1.07728	1.10408	1.13141	1.15927	1.18769	1.21665	1.24618	1.27628	1.30696	1.33823	1.40255	1.46933	1.53862	1.61051	1.68506	1.76234	2.48832
6	1.06152	1.09344	1.12616	1.15969	1.19405	1.22926	1.26532	1.30226	1.34010	1.37884	1.41852	1.50073	1.58687	1.67710	1.77156	1.87041	1.97382	2.98598
7	1.07214	1.10984	1.14869	1.18869	1.22987	1.27228	1.31593	1.36086	1.40710	1.45468	1.50363	1.60578	1.71382	1.82804	1.94872	2.07616	2.21068	3.58318
8	1.08286	1.12649	1.17166	1.21840	1.26677	1.31681	1.36857	1.42210	1.47746	1.53469	1.59385	1.71819	1.85093	1.99256	2.14359	2.30454	2.47596	4.29982
9	1.09369	1.14339	1.19509	1.24886	1.30477	1.36290	1.42331	1.48610	1.55133	1.61909	1.68948	1.83846	1.99900	2.17189	2.35795	2.55804	2.77308	5.15978
10	1.10462	1.16054	1.21899	1.28008	1.34392	1.41060	1.48024	1.55297	1.62889	1.70814	1.79085	1.96715	2.15892	2.36736	2.59374	2.83942	3.10585	6.19174
11	1.11567	1.17795	1.24337	1.31209	1.38423	1.45997	1.53945	1.62285	1.71034	1.80209	1.89830	2.10485	2.33164	2.58043	2.85312	3.15176	3.47855	7.43008
12	1.12683	1.19562	1.26824	1.34489	1.42576	1.51107	1.60103	1.69588	1.79586	1.90121	2.01220	2.25219	2.51817	2.81266	3.13843	3.49845	3.89598	8.91610
13	1.13809	1.21355	1.29361	1.37851	1.46853	1.56396	1.66507	1.77220	1.88565	2.00577	2.13293	2.40985	2.71962	3.06580	3.45227	3.88328	4.36349	10.69932
14	1.14947	1.23176	1.31948	1.41297	1.51259	1.61869	1.73168	1.85194	1.97993	2.11609	2.26090	2.57853	2.93719	3.34173	3.79750	4.31044	4.88711	12.83918
15	1.16097	1.25023	1.34587	1.44830	1.55797	1.67535	1.80094	1.93528	2.07893	2.23248	2.39656	2.75903	3.17217	3.64248	4.17725	4.78459	5.47357	15.40702
16	1.17258	1.26899	1.37279	1.48451	1.60471	1.73399	1.87298	2.02237	2.18287	2.35526	2.54035	2.95216	3.42594	3.97031	4.59497	5.31089	6.13039	18.48843
17	1.18430	1.28802	1.40024	1.52162	1.65285	1.79468	1.94790	2.11338	2.29202	2.48480	2.69277	3.15882	3.70002	4.32763	5.05447	5.89509	6.86604	22.18611
18	1.19615	1.30734	1.42825	1.55966	1.70243	1.85749	2.02582	2.20848	2.40662	2.62147	2.85434	3.37993	3.99602	4.71712	5.55992	6.54355	7.68997	26.62333
19	1.20811	1.32695	1.45681	1.59865	1.75351	1.92250	2.10685	2.30786	2.52695	2.76565	3.02560	3.61653	4.31570	5.14166	6.11591	7.26334	8.61276	31.94800
20	1.22019	1.34686	1.48595	1.63862	1.80611	1.98979	2.19112	2.41171	2.65330	2.91776	3.20714	3.86968	4.66096	5.60441	6.72750	8.06231	9.64629	38.33760
21	1.23239	1.36706	1.51567	1.67958	1.86029	2.05943	2.27877	2.52024	2.78596	3.07823	3.39956	4.14056	5.03383	6.10881	7.40025	8.94917	10.80385	46.00512
25	1.28243	1.45095	1.64061	1.85394	2.09378	2.36324	2.66584	3.00543	3.38635	3.81339	4.29187	5.42743	6.84848	8.62308	10.83471	13.58546	17.00006	95.39622
30	1.34785	1.56308	1.81136	2.09757	2.42726	2.80679	3.24340	3.74532	4.32194	4.98395	5.74349	7.61226	10.06266	13.26768	17.44940	22.89230	29.95992	237.37631
40	1.48886	1.81402	2.20804	2.68506	3.26204	3.95926	4.80102	5.81636	7.03999	8.51331	10.28572	14.97446	21.72452	31.40942	45.25926	65.00087	93.05097	1469.77160

Table B Future Value of an Ordinary Annuity of $1

$$FVA = \frac{(1+i)^n - 1}{i}$$

n/i	1.0%	1.5%	2.0%	2.5%	3.0%	3.5%	4.0%	4.5%	5.0%	5.5%	6.0%	7.0%	8.0%	9.0%	10.0%	11.0%	12.0%	20.0%
1	1.0000	1.0000	1.0000	1.0000	1.0000	1.0000	1.0000	1.0000	1.0000	1.0000	1.0000	1.0000	1.0000	1.0000	1.0000	1.0000	1.0000	1.0000
2	2.0100	2.0150	2.0200	2.0250	2.0300	2.0350	2.0400	2.0450	2.0500	2.0550	2.0600	2.0700	2.0800	2.0900	2.1000	2.1100	2.1200	2.2000
3	3.0301	3.0452	3.0604	3.0756	3.0909	3.1062	3.1216	3.1370	3.1525	3.1680	3.1836	3.2149	3.2464	3.2781	3.3100	3.3421	3.3744	3.6400
4	4.0604	4.0909	4.1216	4.1525	4.1836	4.2149	4.2465	4.2782	4.3101	4.3423	4.3746	4.4399	4.5061	4.5731	4.6410	4.7097	4.7793	5.3680
5	5.1010	5.1523	5.2040	5.2563	5.3091	5.3625	5.4163	5.4707	5.5256	5.5811	5.6371	5.7507	5.8666	5.9847	6.1051	6.2278	6.3528	7.4416
6	6.1520	6.2296	6.3081	6.3877	6.4684	6.5502	6.6330	6.7169	6.8019	6.8881	6.9753	7.1533	7.3359	7.5233	7.7156	7.9129	8.1152	9.9299
7	7.2135	7.3230	7.4343	7.5474	7.6625	7.7794	7.8983	8.0192	8.1420	8.2669	8.3938	8.6540	8.9228	9.2004	9.4872	9.7833	10.0890	12.9159
8	8.2857	8.4328	8.5830	8.7361	8.8923	9.0517	9.2142	9.3800	9.5491	9.7216	9.8975	10.2598	10.6366	11.0285	11.4359	11.8594	12.2997	16.4991
9	9.3685	9.5593	9.7546	9.9545	10.1591	10.3685	10.5828	10.8021	11.0266	11.2563	11.4913	11.9780	12.4876	13.0210	13.5795	14.1640	14.7757	20.7989
10	10.4622	10.7027	10.9497	11.2034	11.4639	11.7314	12.0061	12.2882	12.5779	12.8754	13.1808	13.8164	14.4866	15.1929	15.9374	16.7220	17.5487	25.9587
11	11.5668	11.8633	12.1687	12.4835	12.8078	13.1420	13.4864	13.8412	14.2068	14.5835	14.9716	15.7836	16.6455	17.5603	18.5312	19.5614	20.6546	32.1504
12	12.6825	13.0412	13.4121	13.7956	14.1920	14.6020	15.0258	15.4640	15.9171	16.3856	16.8699	17.8885	18.9771	20.1407	21.3843	22.7132	24.1331	39.5805
13	13.8093	14.2368	14.6803	15.1404	15.6178	16.1130	16.6268	17.1599	17.7130	18.2868	18.8821	20.1406	21.4953	22.9534	24.5227	26.2116	28.0291	48.4966
14	14.9474	15.4504	15.9739	16.5190	17.0863	17.6770	18.2919	18.9321	19.5986	20.2926	21.0151	22.5505	24.2149	26.0192	27.9750	30.0949	32.3926	59.1959
15	16.0969	16.6821	17.2934	17.9319	18.5989	19.2957	20.0236	20.7841	21.5786	22.4087	23.2760	25.1290	27.1521	29.3609	31.7725	34.4054	37.2797	72.0351
16	17.2579	17.9324	18.6393	19.3802	20.1569	20.9710	21.8245	22.7193	23.6575	24.6411	25.6725	27.8881	30.3243	33.0034	35.9497	39.1899	42.7533	87.4421
17	18.4304	19.2014	20.0121	20.8647	21.7616	22.7050	23.6975	24.7417	25.8404	26.9964	28.2129	30.8402	33.7502	36.9737	40.5447	44.5008	48.8837	105.9306
18	19.6147	20.4894	21.4123	22.3863	23.4144	24.4997	25.6454	26.8551	28.1324	29.4812	30.9057	33.9990	37.4502	41.3013	45.5992	50.3959	55.7497	128.1167
19	20.8109	21.7967	22.8406	23.9460	25.1169	26.3575	27.6712	29.0636	30.5390	32.1027	33.7600	37.3790	41.4463	46.0185	51.1591	56.9395	63.4397	154.7400
20	22.0190	23.1237	24.2974	25.5447	26.8704	28.2797	29.7781	31.3714	33.0660	34.8683	36.7856	40.9955	45.7620	51.1601	57.2750	64.2028	72.0524	186.6880
21	23.2392	24.4705	25.7833	27.1833	28.6765	30.2695	31.9692	33.7831	35.7193	37.7861	39.9927	44.8652	50.4229	56.7645	64.0025	72.2651	81.6987	225.0256
30	34.7849	37.5387	40.5681	43.9027	47.5754	51.6227	56.0849	61.0071	66.4388	72.4355	79.0582	94.4608	113.2832	136.3075	164.4940	199.0209	241.3327	1181.8816
40	48.8864	54.2679	60.4020	67.4026	75.4013	84.5503	95.0255	107.0303	120.7998	136.6056	154.7620	199.6351	259.0565	337.8824	442.5926	581.8261	767.0914	7343.8578

The Personal Finance Process   19

Table C Present Value of $1

$$PV = \frac{\$1}{(1+i)^n}$$

$ needed now to have $1 later

n/i	1.0%	1.5%	2.0%	2.5%	3.0%	3.5%	4.0%	4.5%	5.0%	5.5%	6.0%	7.0%	8.0%	9.0%	10.0%	11.0%	12.0%	20.0%
1	0.99010	0.98522	0.98039	0.97561	0.97087	0.96618	0.96154	0.95694	0.95238	0.94787	0.94340	0.93458	0.92593	0.91743	0.90909	0.90090	0.89286	0.83333
2	0.98030	0.97066	0.96117	0.95181	0.94260	0.93351	0.92456	0.91573	0.90703	0.89845	0.89000	0.87344	0.85734	0.84168	0.82645	0.81162	0.79719	0.69444
3	0.97059	0.95632	0.94232	0.92860	0.91514	0.90194	0.88900	0.87630	0.86384	0.85161	0.83962	0.81630	0.79383	0.77218	0.75131	0.73119	0.71178	0.57870
4	0.96098	0.94218	0.92385	0.90595	0.88849	0.87144	0.85480	0.83856	0.82270	0.80722	0.79209	0.76290	0.73503	0.70843	0.68301	0.65873	0.63552	0.48225
5	0.95147	0.92826	0.90573	0.88385	0.86261	0.84197	0.82193	0.80245	0.78353	0.76513	0.74726	0.71299	0.68058	0.64993	0.62092	0.59345	0.56743	0.40188
6	0.94205	0.91454	0.88797	0.86230	0.83748	0.81350	0.79031	0.76790	0.74622	0.72525	0.70496	0.66634	0.63017	0.59627	0.56447	0.53464	0.50663	0.33490
7	0.93272	0.90103	0.87056	0.84127	0.81309	0.78599	0.75992	0.73483	0.71068	0.68744	0.66506	0.62275	0.58349	0.54703	0.51316	0.48166	0.45232	0.27908
8	0.92348	0.88771	0.85349	0.82075	0.78941	0.75941	0.73069	0.70319	0.67684	0.65160	0.62741	0.58201	0.54027	0.50187	0.46651	0.43393	0.40388	0.23257
9	0.91434	0.87459	0.83676	0.80073	0.76642	0.73373	0.70259	0.67290	0.64461	0.61763	0.59190	0.54393	0.50025	0.46043	0.42410	0.39092	0.36061	0.19381
10	0.90529	0.86167	0.82035	0.78120	0.74409	0.70892	0.67556	0.64393	0.61391	0.58543	0.55839	0.50835	0.46319	0.42241	0.38554	0.35218	0.32197	0.16151
11	0.89632	0.84893	0.80426	0.76214	0.72242	0.68495	0.64958	0.61620	0.58468	0.55491	0.52679	0.47509	0.42888	0.38753	0.35049	0.31728	0.28748	0.13459
12	0.88745	0.83639	0.78849	0.74356	0.70138	0.66178	0.62460	0.58966	0.55684	0.52598	0.49697	0.44401	0.39711	0.35553	0.31863	0.28584	0.25668	0.11216
13	0.87866	0.82403	0.77303	0.72542	0.68095	0.63940	0.60057	0.56427	0.53032	0.49856	0.46884	0.41496	0.36770	0.32618	0.28966	0.25751	0.22917	0.09346
14	0.86996	0.81185	0.75788	0.70773	0.66112	0.61778	0.57748	0.53997	0.50507	0.47257	0.44230	0.38782	0.34046	0.29925	0.26333	0.23199	0.20462	0.07789
15	0.86135	0.79985	0.74301	0.69047	0.64186	0.59689	0.55526	0.51672	0.48102	0.44793	0.41727	0.36245	0.31524	0.27454	0.23939	0.20900	0.18270	0.06491
16	0.85282	0.78803	0.72845	0.67362	0.62317	0.57671	0.53391	0.49447	0.45811	0.42458	0.39365	0.33873	0.29189	0.25187	0.21763	0.18829	0.16312	0.05409
17	0.84438	0.77639	0.71416	0.65720	0.60502	0.55720	0.51337	0.47318	0.43630	0.40245	0.37136	0.31657	0.27027	0.23107	0.19784	0.16963	0.14564	0.04507
18	0.83602	0.76491	0.70016	0.64117	0.58739	0.53836	0.49363	0.45280	0.41552	0.38147	0.35034	0.29586	0.25025	0.21199	0.17986	0.15282	0.13004	0.03756
19	0.82774	0.75361	0.68643	0.62553	0.57029	0.52016	0.47464	0.43330	0.39573	0.36158	0.33051	0.27651	0.23171	0.19449	0.16351	0.13768	0.11611	0.03130
20	0.81954	0.74247	0.67297	0.61027	0.55368	0.50257	0.45639	0.41464	0.37689	0.34273	0.31180	0.25842	0.21455	0.17843	0.14864	0.12403	0.10367	0.02608
21	0.81143	0.73150	0.65978	0.59539	0.53755	0.48557	0.43883	0.39679	0.35894	0.32486	0.29416	0.24151	0.19866	0.16370	0.13513	0.11174	0.09256	0.02174
24	0.78757	0.69954	0.62172	0.55288	0.49193	0.43796	0.39012	0.34770	0.31007	0.27666	0.24698	0.19715	0.15770	0.12640	0.10153	0.08170	0.06588	0.01258
25	0.77977	0.68921	0.60953	0.53939	0.47761	0.42315	0.37512	0.33273	0.29530	0.26223	0.23300	0.18425	0.14602	0.11597	0.09230	0.07361	0.05882	0.01048
28	0.75684	0.65910	0.57437	0.50088	0.43708	0.38165	0.33348	0.29157	0.25509	0.22332	0.19563	0.15040	0.11591	0.08955	0.06934	0.05382	0.04187	0.00607
29	0.74934	0.64936	0.56311	0.48866	0.42435	0.36875	0.32065	0.27902	0.24295	0.21168	0.18456	0.14056	0.10733	0.08215	0.06304	0.04849	0.03738	0.00506
30	0.74192	0.63976	0.55207	0.47674	0.41199	0.35628	0.30832	0.26700	0.23138	0.20064	0.17411	0.13137	0.09938	0.07537	0.05731	0.04368	0.03338	0.00421
31	0.73458	0.63031	0.54125	0.46511	0.39999	0.34423	0.29646	0.25550	0.22036	0.19018	0.16425	0.12277	0.09202	0.06915	0.05210	0.03935	0.02980	0.00351
40	0.67165	0.55126	0.45289	0.37243	0.30656	0.25257	0.20829	0.17193	0.14205	0.11746	0.09722	0.06678	0.04603	0.03184	0.02209	0.01538	0.01075	0.00068

Financial Planning

Table D Present Value of an Ordinary Annuity of $1

$$PVA = \frac{1-\frac{1}{(1+i)^n}}{i}$$

Take out # to have $1.00 each year start amount

n/i	1.0%	1.5%	2.0%	2.5%	3.0%	3.5%	4.0%	4.5%	5.0%	5.5%	6.0%	7.0%	8.0%	9.0%	10.0%	11.0%	12.0%	20.0%
1	0.99010	0.98522	0.98039	0.97561	0.97087	0.96618	0.96154	0.95694	0.95238	0.94787	0.94340	0.93458	0.92593	0.91743	0.90909	0.90090	0.89286	0.83333
2	1.97040	1.95588	1.94156	1.92742	1.91347	1.89969	1.88609	1.87267	1.85941	1.84632	1.83339	1.80802	1.78326	1.75911	1.73554	1.71252	1.69005	1.52778
3	2.94099	2.91220	2.88388	2.85602	2.82861	2.80164	2.77509	2.74896	2.72325	2.69793	2.67301	2.62432	2.57710	2.53129	2.48685	2.44371	2.40183	2.10648
4	3.90197	3.85438	3.80773	3.76197	3.71710	3.67308	3.62990	3.58753	3.54595	3.50515	3.46511	3.38721	3.31213	3.23972	3.16987	3.10245	3.03735	2.58873
5	4.85343	4.78264	4.71346	4.64583	4.57971	4.51505	4.45182	4.38998	4.32948	4.27028	4.21236	4.10020	3.99271	3.88965	3.79079	3.69590	3.60478	2.99061
6	5.79548	5.69719	5.60143	5.50813	5.41719	5.32855	5.24214	5.15787	5.07569	4.99553	4.91732	4.76654	4.62288	4.48592	4.35526	4.23054	4.11141	3.32551
7	6.72819	6.59821	6.47199	6.34939	6.23028	6.11454	6.00205	5.89270	5.78637	5.68297	5.58238	5.38929	5.20637	5.03295	4.86842	4.71220	4.56376	3.60459
8	7.65168	7.48593	7.32548	7.17014	7.01969	6.87396	6.73274	6.59589	6.46321	6.33457	6.20979	5.97130	5.74664	5.53482	5.33493	5.14612	4.96764	3.83716
9	8.56602	8.36052	8.16224	7.97087	7.78611	7.60769	7.43533	7.26879	7.10782	6.95220	6.80169	6.51523	6.24689	5.99525	5.75902	5.53705	5.32825	4.03097
10	9.47130	9.22218	8.98259	8.75206	8.53020	8.31661	8.11090	7.91272	7.72173	7.53763	7.36009	7.02358	6.71008	6.41766	6.14457	5.88923	5.65022	4.19247
11	10.36763	10.07112	9.78685	9.51421	9.25262	9.00155	8.76048	8.52892	8.30641	8.09254	7.88687	7.49867	7.13896	6.80519	6.49506	6.20652	5.93770	4.32706
12	11.25508	10.90751	10.57534	10.25776	9.95400	9.66333	9.38507	9.11858	8.86325	8.61852	8.38384	7.94269	7.53608	7.16073	6.81369	6.49236	6.19437	4.43922
13	12.13374	11.73153	11.34837	10.98319	10.63496	10.30274	9.98565	9.68285	9.39357	9.11708	8.85268	8.35765	7.90378	7.48690	7.10336	6.74987	6.42355	4.53268
14	13.00370	12.54338	12.10625	11.69091	11.29607	10.92052	10.56312	10.22283	9.89864	9.58965	9.29498	8.74547	8.24424	7.78615	7.36669	6.98187	6.62817	4.61057
15	13.86505	13.34323	12.84926	12.38138	11.93794	11.51741	11.11839	10.73955	10.37966	10.03758	9.71225	9.10791	8.55948	8.06069	7.60608	7.19087	6.81086	4.67547
16	14.71787	14.13126	13.57771	13.05500	12.56110	12.09412	11.65230	11.23402	10.83777	10.46216	10.10590	9.44665	8.85137	8.31256	7.82371	7.37916	6.97399	4.72956
17	15.56225	14.90765	14.29187	13.71220	13.16612	12.65132	12.16567	11.70719	11.27407	10.86461	10.47726	9.76322	9.12164	8.54363	8.02155	7.54879	7.11963	4.77463
18	16.39827	15.67256	14.99203	14.35336	13.75351	13.18968	12.65930	12.15999	11.68959	11.24607	10.82760	10.05909	9.37189	8.75563	8.20141	7.70162	7.24967	4.81219
19	17.22601	16.42617	15.67846	14.97889	14.32380	13.70984	13.13394	12.59329	12.08532	11.60765	11.15812	10.33560	9.60360	8.95011	8.36492	7.83929	7.36578	4.84350
20	18.04555	17.16864	16.35143	15.58916	14.87747	14.21240	13.59033	13.00794	12.46221	11.95038	11.46992	10.59401	9.81815	9.12855	8.51356	7.96333	7.46944	4.86958
21	18.85698	17.90014	17.01121	16.18455	15.41502	14.69797	14.02916	13.40472	12.82115	12.27524	11.76408	10.83553	10.01680	9.29224	8.64869	8.07507	7.56200	4.89132
25	22.02316	20.71961	19.52346	18.42438	17.41315	16.48151	15.62208	14.82821	14.09394	13.41393	12.78336	11.65358	10.67478	9.82258	9.07704	8.42174	7.84314	4.94759
30	25.80771	24.01584	22.39646	20.93029	19.60044	18.39205	17.29203	16.28889	15.37245	14.53375	13.76483	12.40904	11.25778	10.27365	9.42691	8.69379	8.05518	4.97894
40	32.83469	29.91585	27.35548	25.10278	23.11477	21.35507	19.79277	18.40158	17.15909	16.04612	15.04630	13.33171	11.92461	10.75736	9.77905	8.95105	8.24378	4.99660

Chapter 2
Financial Planning Instruments

"You are, without a doubt, the most disorganized person I've ever met!"

© 2013 The Atlantic Media Co., as first published in The Atlantic Magazine. All rights reserved. Distributed by Tribune Content Agency, LLC

Chapter Objectives

1. Understand the Balance Sheet, together with its component parts of assets, liabilities, and net worth.
2. Identify the importance of liquidity as a key measure in the balance sheet.
3. Be familiar with the Income Statement or Cash Flow Statement, together with its component parts of income, fixed expenses, and variable expenses.
4. Understand the Budget Statement, and the expansion of the Budget Statement called the Budget and Spending Log. Explain how the Budget and Spending Log can track both the expected cash flows and the actual cash flows, flagging variances that may occur.
5. Be aware of those ingredients that will improve the usefulness of the Budget document, including savings and expense accruals, as well as tracking the accumulated cash available at the beginning and at the end of the period.
6. Be aware of some of the ratios used in interpreting the Balance Sheet, Income Statement, and Budget.
7. Spending decisions can often cause conflict where more than one adult shares a given set of resources. Be aware of the means by which this conflict can be minimized.
8. Identify the more desirable methodologies for keeping records.

Your Pond

Imagine that your financial resources are like a pond of water. You are concerned with several issues, including the flow of water into your pond, the integrity of your pond at holding the water it has, and controlling any flow out of your pond. You want to make sure that the available water is used for the specific purposes intended, and not lost or wasted. This is the nature of Money Management—those daily financial activities by which we allocate our limited resources to achieve economic satisfaction and security.

Figure 2:1 Imagine that your financial resources are like a pond of water.

Clearly, there are trade-offs involved in each money management decision. Money that is spent cannot be saved. Funds used for one purpose, are not available to be used for another. Money that is borrowed to meet a current expenditure must be repaid—with interest—at a later date, thereby reducing the amount of money we have available in the future. Such opportunity costs should be evaluated carefully, so that the best decisions can be made. This chapter deals with some of the instruments that can be used to measure and control the water in your pond.

The Balance Sheet

The first instrument we want to examine is called a Balance Sheet, and it serves to measure three things. First, it measures the quantity of water in your pond. Second, it is a measure of who owns it. And third, it measures how available or how liquid is the water in your pond. (If the water is frozen, it may not be readily available.)

The first point to make as we examine the balance sheet is that it is a snapshot of a point in time. It may be accurate today, but tomorrow it is already obsolete. That's OK. It is intended to do just that, and it is not a problem that things have changed tomorrow. Another thing to remember in producing a balance sheet is that it is a summary of what you own, and what you owe. Although you may feel that you own all the water in your pond, if you have debts, you in fact owe some of your resources to someone else. (We will be talking about debts and credit management in a later chapter.)

Most balance sheets are presented with a left side and a right side, as shown in the example following. The left side shows what you own—called Assets, and the right side shows what you owe—called Liabilities. There are a couple of important protocols in preparing a balance sheet that should always be followed. The first one is this: Always list the most current asset or liability first. How do you know which is the most current? It is usually that asset which is easiest to spend, that is, which is the most Liquid—such as cash or savings, and that liability which is due soonest, such as this month's car payment. Many balance sheets have a separate section at the top of each side, where the most liquid assets and liabilities are summarized as Current Assets and Current Liabilities.

Figure 2:2 The left side shows what you own—the right side shows what you owe.

Then, as you move down the page, list those assets that are increasingly more difficult to spend—which must be sold and converted into cash to spend their value, and those liabilities that are due further and further down the road. This way, you have a glimpse at which assets are the easiest to convert into cash, and which are more difficult, and which liabilities are due just around the corner, as opposed to debts that may be due at a later time. This is an important distinction, as we will discuss in a moment.

In the course of listing current liabilities, don't list current living expenses such as rent or your car insurance premium. Although these items are liabilities, they do not constitute indebtedness in the traditional sense of the word. If you decide to move, or if you sell your car, these expenses cease. Accordingly, there is another context in which we will examine such items, and you do not need to include them in your balance sheet.

The second protocol is this: Always list both assets and liabilities at their current market value. This rule creates a bit of a disparity, because many assets depreciate in value over time, whereas liabilities don't. For example, if you buy a brand new car and take out a loan to finance part of the purchase price, you would list the car as an asset at its current market value, which no doubt declined the moment you drove it off the lot. However, there is no concurrent decline in the money you owe on the loan. The result is that the left hand side of the balance sheet—or asset—declines over time with depreciation, whereas the right hand side of the balance sheet—or liability—declines only when we have paid that liability. (That fact is a revelation in itself.)

Now, you can total up all of your assets and all of your liabilities. Here, another important principle needs to be observed. The left hand side of the balance sheet should always equal the right hand side … exactly. That is why they call it a balance sheet. But, you say, that is impossible. My assets and my liabilities don't equal one another. Therefore, there needs to be another entry to bring about the balance, and that entry is called <u>Net Worth</u>. Simply put, net worth is the difference between everything you own, and what you owe to others. The net worth entry is placed on the right hand side of the balance sheet, directly under your liabilities. If your assets exceed your liabilities, your net worth number will be positive. If your assets are less than your liabilities, you have a negative net worth, (which is not unusual for a struggling college student.) As you can see, from the standpoint of the calculation, we back into the net worth number by subtracting total liabilities from total assets. It is simply that number necessary to make the right side of the balance sheet equal to the left side. More to the point, it is the net ownership you have in your combined assets, after subtracting the amounts you owe to others.

Figure 2:3 If you assets exceed your liabilities, your net worth number will be positive.

If your net worth increases over time, you have added more assets than liabilities, or you have paid down your liabilities. This is a good thing, and one of your goals should be to increase your net worth as you move ahead in life. Now, take a look at the sample balance sheet following, and tell me what you see.

One of the first things you might notice is that total assets exceed total liabilities, resulting in a positive net worth. In fact, about half of everything this person owns belongs to him alone—his debts are only half of his total assets. So far so good. However, another observation you might make is that the current assets are quite a bit lower than the current liabilities. This is not so good, and requires immediate attention. Here is the problem you have flagged by that observation. If you examine individual bankruptcies, you will note that much of the time the dilemma leading up to the bankruptcy was not too few assets, but too few current assets. There are simply not enough liquid assets to meet current liabilities. For example, a rancher may have property and equipment worth $5 million, but if he doesn't have the money to meet the current mortgage payment due on the property, he is in danger of losing it all. The comparative level of current assets to current liabilities is an important measure.

Exhibit 2:1 Balance Sheet

Assets		Liabilities and Net Worth	
Cash and Checking	$335	Current Car Payment	$282
Savings	1,542	Money Owed Sister	1,900
Total Current Assets	1,877	Total Current Liabilities	2,182
CD's, Stocks and Bonds	2,003	Balance Car Loan	5,500
Furniture	1,250	Balance Student Loan	2,948
Car	12,400	Total Liabilities	$10,630
Coin Collection	3,727	Net Worth	$10,627
Total Assets	$21,257	Total Liabilities and Net Worth	$ 21,257

As you examine the balance sheet, you might conclude that the best way for him to raise the additional funds needed to meet his current liabilities is to sell some of his stocks and bonds, as they would be the next most liquid asset that he holds. That is a reasonable consideration, assuming that he does not have additional funds coming his way in the form of income. Application Worksheet 2:1 in Appendix II gives you the opportunity to prepare your own balance sheet; list those assets and liabilities and net worth that apply to your circumstance.

> **Summary & Review**
>
> 1. What is an Asset? In the preparation of a Balance Sheet, in what order should your assets be listed?
> 2. What does Liquidity mean? How is it identified in a balance sheet?
> 3. What is a Liability: Again, in what order should your liabilities be listed?
> 4. What is Net Worth, and how is it presented on a Balance Sheet?

The Income Statement

This brings us to the next important instrument, and that is the Income Statement, also sometimes called the Cash Flow Statement. Unlike the balance sheet, which is a snapshot of a point in time, the income statement is a movie, chronicling the flow of funds in and out over a given period. It is a measure of how much has gone into your pond, versus how much has gone out of your pond … and where did it go.

It is not unusual for a person to wonder where their money went. If you asked someone how much they spent on groceries last week, or what gasoline cost them last month, they might not be able to give you the answer. The income statement does. It is simply a listing of inflow and outflow, typically over a months' time. There is no magic in using a month. You could use a week or a year. But many of our expenses, such as rent, debt payments, and utility bills, occur on a monthly basis.

The income statement always begins with income—from whatever source. Whether the income is from a job, a regular check from home, an insurance settlement, or alimony, it is all listed at the top of the income statement. If the income is not from a regular source, perhaps a tax refund or some other nonrecurring and irregular amount, it is still listed as an income item for the period it was received.

Most income statements then list the expenses incurred for the period. Here, it may be useful to divide expenses into two types, fixed expenses and variable expenses. Fixed expenses are those that typically occur in the same amount each month. Your rent payment or car loan payment are examples of fixed expenses. Clearly, fixed expenses are easiest to list, because we know what they are from month to month.

However, don't be complacent in your attitude toward fixed expenses. Sometimes we have the notion that, because it is a fixed expense, we can't control it. Nothing could be further from the truth.

Get Real

The author was visiting with a member of the United States Congress some time ago. This Congressman was wringing his hands over the number of expenses that they could not control … which were fixed. He cited the interest on the Federal Debt as one such expense. "That amount," he said, "is a function of the size of the debt and interest rates. We don't have any control over either of those items."

"Nonsense," I responded. "You are the political body which is in charge of the Federal Budget. If you don't control it … who will? Just because it's a fixed charge, does not mean you don't have any control. Don't cop out on us – you can control it if you want to."

All that is meant by the label "fixed" charge is this: It will occur unless you do something to change it. That is different from a variable charge, which will not occur unless you do something to incur it. For example, we may list rent as a fixed charge. And indeed it is. It will occur month after month … unless you move. You will face the same car loan payment each month … unless you sell the car and pay off the loan. The reality is that there is no such thing as a fixed expense. Each of us can … and should … exercise control over our fixed expenses.

Exhibit 2:2 How Americans Spend Money

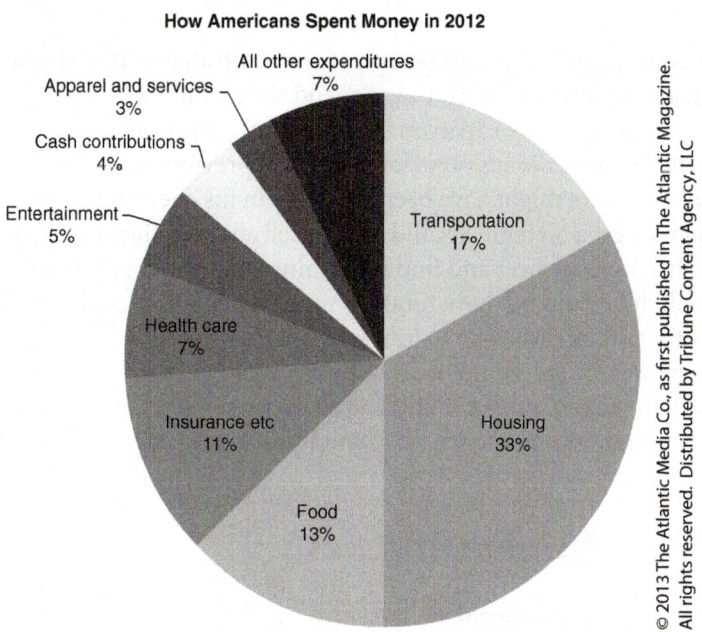

Variable expenses are those that will not happen unless you do something to incur them. You have to go to the store to buy clothing, or to the restaurant if you're going to eat out. These expenses vary from month to month, and include the amount spent for food, clothing, or gasoline. Variable expenses are a bit tougher to get a handle on, and may require keeping a log of sorts so that you know what has been spent in a given category. Following is a sample monthly income statement.

Looking at this income statement, you might conclude that this is a single person with few expenses. Yet, it appears that he has spent more in the course of this month than he took in. The result is a deficit for the month.

Exhibit 2:3 Income Statement

Income:	
Wages (Net of Taxes and Withholdings)	$567
Check from Home	450
Birthday Gift	25
Total Income	$1,042
Fixed Expenses:	
Rent (Including Utilities)	$250
Car Loan Payment	282
Auto Insurance Payment (6 Months)	264
Variable Expenses:	
Cell Phone	$97
Food	189
Gas and Oil	62
Clothing	57
Entertainment	29
Total Expenses	$1,230
Surplus (Deficit)	$(188)

Here is an important concept that needs to be considered, and that is this: There is no such thing as deficit spending. The very idea is an oxymoron. You can't spend what you don't have. As in this example, he did not have the income necessary to meet the expenses for the month, there are only three options available to him.

First, if there was sufficient water in his pond left over from previous months, he might be able to simply draw down the level of the pond. There might have been a surplus in his checking account, or perhaps savings that he can draw on when expenses get a bit high. Second, he can sell an asset, thereby raising some funds. Here, he may need to dip down into his balance sheet and find something that he can sell, to produce the liquidity necessary to meet his need for cash. If he does not have funds to meet his expenses, and if he does not sell an asset to raise those funds, the only other option available to him is to borrow. He must tap someone else's pond for the water necessary to pay his expenses. There are no other options. Again, he can't spend what he doesn't have.

Here, it might be well to suggest a slight modification to the usual income statement to allow you to monitor the level of your pond from month to month. That modification is simply to add, at the very top of a monthly income statement, the entry:

    Accumulated Cash Balance—Beginning of Month $ x x x x

And at the very bottom of the income statement, the entry:

    Accumulated Cash Balance—End of Month $ x x x x

This will indicate whether the first option, that of drawing down the accumulated level of the pond, is feasible. Of course, the income received in the month is then added to your cash balance, and the expenses incurred in the month are then subtracted, resulting in a net cash balance at the end of the month. If this number continues to decline month after month, it is a sure indication that you will eventually come to the point where your pond is dry, and then options two or three are your only recourse.

> ## Summary & Review
>
> 1. How is tracking the flow of individual funds into and out of an Income Statement useful; what information does it provide?
> 2. What is the difference between Fixed Expenses and Variable Expenses?
> 3. Name the three options available to anyone who finds that he has spent more than he has taken in.
> 4. How does the entry "Accumulated Cash Balance" aid in evaluating one of the options noted under 3) above.

.The Budget Statement

Both the Balance Sheet and the Income Statement report what has occurred in your financial situation. They are historical numbers. Wouldn't it be nice to get ahead of the flow to anticipate the financial events before they occur, and thereby direct the flow of water more deliberately into those areas desired. Often, when someone looks at their income statement, they are surprised at how much money is spent in one area or another, and they resolve that they would like to allocate funds in a direction that is more meaningful, instead of the black holes they have been dumping their dollars into. Well, the Budget Statement is the device that accomplishes that. The budget is the sluice gate that can be raised and lowered to allocate just that amount of water needed for a particular purpose. Moreover, the control occurs in advance of the flow, with the positioning of the sluice gate the result of thought and planning.

Figure 2:4 The budget is the sluice gate that can be raised and lowered to allocate just that amount of water needed for a particular purpose.

The budget document may look much like the income statement, with the income items posted first, followed by the expenses—both fixed and variable. However, again note that your budget is prospective; that is, it anticipates the income and expense items that will occur in the course of a month. This feature gives you the opportunity to include in your budget, items that are scheduled to occur, such as an increase in the level of support from home or the proceeds of a student loan. It also gives you the opportunity to include certain items that should occur in your income statement, but which often do not occur without planning.

For example, we all know that we should save a portion of our income to increase our financial security. Yet, many times, we simply hope that something will be left over at the end of the month that we can put toward savings. This is an inadequate provision. A savings goal should be at the top of your budget statement, ahead of any expenses. (For a delightful commentary on the importance of savings, you might enjoy reading "*The Richest Man in Babylon*" by George Clason. First published in 1924, this short book is available free on the web at Wikipedia.) We will discuss the importance of savings later.

In addition, we have noted above the limited options you have when you end up spending more in the course of a month than you made. Unfortunately, those months occur more often than we would like. Occasions when we overspend are typically the result of an unplanned expense that creeps around the corner. Maybe the breaks on the car went out, or perhaps the water heater in your home started leaking and had to be replaced. In life, those events are not "if," they are "when." Such things happen to all of us, and they happen often. Rather than face the need to sell an asset, or worse, borrow the funds necessary to deal with these issues, wouldn't it be better if you had accumulated an "emergency fund" designed for just such occasions. Maybe you could call this emergency fund a SOOD fund—an acronym for "Stay Out Of Debt." If you had a SOOD fund accrual provision in your budget, and built it up over a period to some desirable level, you would have the water necessary to pay for those events when they occur, without having to borrow.

Another provision that you should have in your budget is an accrual for those expenses that do not occur on a monthly basis. In our example Exhibit 2:3, it appears that he had a semiannual car insurance payment of $264 that had to be made in the current month. Wouldn't it be easier on his budget if he saved a little each month toward that expense? If you are in school, you might have a tuition payment due on a semester basis. Whatever the expense, it is real and the wherewithal should be accumulated to meet it when it is due. The best way to make sure that the water will be there would be to allocate resources each month as part of your monthly budget.

A well-designed budget will make provision for savings, for emergencies—will provide a regular accrual for those costs that occur on an irregular basis, and will meet both your fixed and variable expenses. There is one thing more that needs to be included in your budget. We spent a lot of time talking about this in Chapter 1—and that is your Goals. Remember our discussion of Financial Goals—Short-Term, Intermediate-Term, and Long-Term. Remember how you struggled to prioritize your goals, and then provide a level of funding that would bring those goals to life. Now, take that level of funding and make it a part of your budget. Life is not just about food, clothing, and shelter. Life is about

Figure 2:5 A well-designed budget will make provision and will meet both your fixed and variable expenses.

dreams—those ambitions that we have that make life worthwhile. Don't forget to include those aspirations in your budget.

Now that you have an idea of what needs to be included in your budget planning, let's do something kind-of neat. Let's combine your Budget Statement, with your Income Statement (or Cash Flow Statement), and produce one document that does three thing. First, it allocates your limited resources as per your budget. Second, it tracks your income and expenses as they actually occur in the course of the month. Third, it measures the budget allocation against the actual expenditure, to see if you achieved what you wanted. If the actual expense was as planned, you are on track. If it was not—if the actual was higher or lower than planned—you have a red flare that might need reviewing. We could call this instrument a Budget and Spending Log. The process of combining these two statements can be done by simply adding three columns to each line item. Let's not forget to also include the cumulative level of water in our pond—the Accumulated Cash Balance. An illustration of what this Budget and Spending Log might end up looking like is shown in Exhibit 2:4.

A Brief Examination

This individual knew before the month ever began, that he would be spending more than he was making. He added the proceeds from a student loan to his income, thereby supplementing the water in his pond with some borrowing. His budget anticipated an inflow of $1,360 and an outflow of $1,741, resulting in a deficit of $381. Although he may have been expecting to draw down the cash balance he had available to him at the beginning of the month, as the month unfolded, it looks like he became increasingly nervous over the situation, and began reining in costs. He skipped adding to his coin collection this month, he pared back his summer vacation funding goal. He also tightened his belt in most of the variable expense categories. As a result, his spending was reduced and the number at the end of the month was not as negative as he was budgeting.

Still, the water in his pond has been reduced substantially, and he cannot draw down anywhere near the same amount next month. If his income and expenses remain as they are, he will be forced to either sell an asset or borrow to raise the funding necessary to meet his expenditures in the coming months. Application Worksheet 2:2 in Appendix II provides you the opportunity to apply these concepts to your own unique situation.

Where Do the Savings Go

There are a number of provisions at the top of the expense categories, which allocate water to savings, to the emergency or SOOD fund, and to accruals for insurance, tuition, and goals. This is all water that needs to be collected in various buckets for future use. If it is not collected now, there will come the time when payment is due, but the resources don't exist to meet the payment. That puts us continually behind the curve—and in the red. It is much better to set the resources aside ahead of the need. Question: What do those collection buckets look like?

Actually, they may vary depending on the nature of the expense item you are accruing. Those items that you will be paying in a short period, such as the SOOD fund, the automobile insurance, or tuition, should be kept in a very safe and liquid bucket—such as a passbook savings account. This way, they are readily available to be drawn on a moment's notice. Those items that will occur further down life's road, such as your savings, a vacation, or maybe the down payment on a house, could be put in a bucket, which is a little less liquid, but which earns a little more interest—such as a Certificate of Deposit. Your financial institution can explain the various savings options that they have available, and we will be talking more about saving and investing in later chapters.

As we raised the prospect of placing some of our accruals in a liquid account, you may have been reminded that the first asset category in your balance sheet are your liquid accounts—your current assets. As you begin to grow these various accruals, you will be adding to your current assets or, if the accrual bucket you are using is less liquid, perhaps you will be adding to your longer-term assets. Either way, you see that the process is a cycle ... that adding an accrual to your budget also adds an entry to your balance sheet. Your documents are linked, and that is as it should be.

Exhibit 2:4 Budget and Spending Log

	Budget	Monthly Actual	Variance	Cash Balance
Accumulated Cash Balance				$435
Income:				
Wages	$560	$567	$7	
Check From Home	450	450	0	
Student Loan	350	350	0	
Birthday Gift	___	25	25	
Total Income	$1,360	$1,392	$32	$1,827
Savings:	$50	$50	$0	
SOOD Fund:	25	25	0	
Accruals:				
Auto Insurance	44	44	0	
Tuition	357	357	0	
Goals:				
Coin Collection	25	0	−25	
Summer Vacation	100	75	−25	
Home Down Payment	150	150	0	
Fixed Expenses:				
Rent	$250	$250	0	
Car Loan Payment	282	282	0	
Variable Expenses:				
Cell Phone	93	97	4	
Food	200	189	−11	
Gas and Oil	70	62	−8	
Clothing	60	57	−3	
Entertainment	35	29	−6	
Total Accruals and Expenses	$1,741	$1,667	−74	$160
Surplus (Deficit)	$ (381)	$ (275)	$106	___
Accumulated Cash Balance				$ 160

Figure 2:6 It is much better to set the resources aside ahead of the need.

Budgeting Methodologies

It is one thing to understand the usefulness of a budget in allowing control over your resources … it is another thing to be able to actually exercise that control. Once you have designed and completed your budget and spending log, the question remains; can I stick to it? The numbers that are posted in the Actual column, and the size of the numbers in the Variance column, will be able to answer that question. Don't be too hard on yourself if everything doesn't go off like clockwork the first time. Managing a budget is a learning experience, and it may take a few months for you to begin to feel comfortable. If the budgeted numbers are unreasonable, you might consider revising them in subsequent months. Make your budget flexible enough to be able to respond to your needs, but not so flexible that it fails to serve its purpose of allocating your money properly. Remember, this tool puts you in charge ahead of the flow. As has been pointed out earlier—it is building the habit that we are concerned with.

If you can manage the budget discipline from your checkbook, simply by referring to your budget numbers and allocating your resources accordingly—great! If you would like another suggestion as to how you might manage the allocation process, consider the envelop method. Many people have a stack of envelopes in a secure place, each labeled with a budget line item such as rent, food, gas and oil, clothing, or entertainment. Then, when the income arrives, they simply put the budgeted amount in cash in each of the envelopes. Presto ... they have the resources necessary to meet that expense properly allocated.

From a budgeting perspective, it is important to identify the difference between our needs and our wants. This is often easier said than done. Yet, if we can get a handle on our budget to where overspending and borrowing is reduced and savings is increased, we can keep our lives on a track that will result in less financial stress and more financial rewards.

> ### Summary & Review
>
> 1. What is the purpose of the Budget? How is that purpose accomplished?
> 2. What kinds of things might be included in a budget, which do not appear in last months' income statement?
> 3. How might we expand a standard budget, into what we have called the Budget and Spending Log? Identify the additional information that is available from the Budget and Spending Log.
> 4. Explain the budgeting methodology that works best for you.

Interpreting the Data

As we study the three documents detailed above, we see a wide assortment of numbers. What do they mean? Sometimes, it is easiest to interpret a number by comparing it with another number—by creating a ratio. If you were to apply for a loan, the loan officer would do just that. He would look at the numbers provided in these documents, and he would create ratios that would help him understand your current financial position. Let's take a look at some of the more important ratios, and the story they tell.

Current Ratio: Current Assets/Current Liabilities
In our example above: $1,877/$2,182 = 0.86

As we discussed the balance sheet, we noted how important it was that you have enough current or liquid assets to meet your current liabilities. The ratio of current assets to current liabilities is called the current ratio, and the higher the number, the better. If the current ratio is below 1.00, as it is in our example, it is a red flat—a problem waiting to happen. Remember, as you add accruals to your budget, you are adding to your current assets. Or, if the accrual is placed in a longer-term savings device, such as a certificate of deposit or other investment, you are adding to your longer-term assets.

Survival Ratio: Current Assets/Monthly Living Expenses
In our example above: $1,877/$1,230 = 1.5 Months

What if something were to happen tomorrow that stopped all of the water flowing into your pond—there was simply no more income. How long could you live on the water remaining at your current level of fixed and variable expenditure? These assumptions might seem extreme, but if your only source of income is wages, and if you are injured and can't work, the scenario could become very real very fast. If this were to happen, you may discontinue adding to savings or accruals for a time as you button down the hatches and simply try to survive. In our example above we have done that, and the monthly living expenses exclude savings and accruals, but do include the car insurance premium he paid. You may wish to modify these assumptions to suit your own circumstance, but the question remains, how many months can you meet your expenses given your current outflow, on what is currently in your liquid accounts.

Debt Ratio: Total Liabilities/Total Assets

In our example above: $10,630/$21,257 = 50.5%

The debt ratio addresses the question as to how much debt you have taken on. There are two ways of looking at the magnitude of debt. First, is the dollar amount of debt when compared with your total assets. This is the ratio we are examining here. As your liabilities are, by definition, funds that you owe someone else, we have taken the total liability figure as the amount of debt outstanding. At just over 50% of total assets, debt is a little on the high side. As you get older, this percentage should decline—with the goal being to reach near 0% by the time you retire.

The second way of looking at the magnitude of debt is to measure your ability to meet the debt service payments (interest and principal repayments) required. This ratio is called the debt payment ratio.

Debt Payment Ratio: Debt Payments/Income

In our example above: $282/$1,392 = 20.3%

Any debt you have incurred is a lien on your future income. This ratio asks the question; what proportion of your future income have you promised to someone else? In our example, the only debt that is being repaid at the moment is a car loan, which is costing $282 per month or 20.3% of each months expected income. This is not altogether accurate though, because he also has a student loan that he has recently received, which he must begin repaying on graduation. Although those payments do not impact his current Debt Payment Ratio, they will be a factor down the road, and should be noted as such.

Figure 2:7 This ratio asks the question; what proportion of your future income have you promised to someone else?

Savings Ratio: Savings/Income

In our example above: $50/$1,392 = 3.6%

This ratio addresses the question as to how much of your income you are saving. It might be argued that the emergency fund or SOOD fund is savings, and that money set aside for vacation and the down payment on a home constitutes savings, or even that the accrual for auto insurance and tuition is a kind of savings. Although it is true that money set aside for a SOOD fund, or for a vacation or a down payment is saving targeted for a specific purpose or goal, the money set aside for insurance or tuition is an expense that has simply not happened yet. You are wise to accrue the funds to meet those expenses, but it would be a stretch to call that savings. In our example, we have identified savings as those funds that are not associated with a specific goal or expense. If this definition seems too restrictive, you should define savings in the way that is most useful to you. In the book "*The Richest Man in Babylon*" referenced earlier, his savings goal was 10% of income. Although that may seem ambitious when you are young, it would be an appropriate goal as you grow older and your income increases.

> ### Summary & Review
>
> 1. Explain how the current ratio is calculated. What does it mean?
> 2. Why would someone be interested in the Debt Payment ratio? Why would a lender be concerned if this ratio is high and rising?
> 3. What other ratios can you devise to measure and interpret the financial statements discussed above?

Mitigating that Tug-of-War

We all know that money is power. Many times, we think that only the rich have power. In reality, every time we exercise control over our money, we are exercising power. Even if we only have enough to take a friend to lunch, we have power.

This can create a problem when two of us are linked to the same pond, and we each would like to exercise control over those resources. This can lead to a domestic tug-of-war with unhappy consequences. There is little doubt that arguments over money are a major reason for marital strife, and a primary cause of divorce. Is there a way that we might minimize this tug-of-war, and reduce those occasions when an argument over money strains a relationship? Consider the following four part plan.

First, recognize that a union between two people is the birth of a new entity—the Jones Family, for example. Once they are formed, there is a new organization that must be managed, and the Jones' are the board of directors of this new organization. What does a board of directors do? To begin with, they are responsible for the policy decisions—the broad guiding strategies that would steer this new entity down life's road. One of those policy decisions is the allocation of resources to various purposes. Does that sound familiar? It is up to the board of directors to determine how much money will be budgeted for what purposes. In effect, they sit down and have a budget meeting and determine where their limited resources will be directed. The budget is written down, and is regarded as policy.

Second, the board of directors must make some decisions as to who will do what. They hire a president, who in turn will appoint individuals to manage the various tasks of this new entity. So, the Jones' determine who will be responsible for each of the tasks that this new organization will undertake. Who will do the cooking, who will take care of the car … and so forth. It is important to know who leads in a given area.

Third, once an individual has been delegated the responsibility in a given area, they should also be delegated the budget in that area. It is illogical to ask someone to do something, and then withhold the resources necessary for them to carry out their task. Too many times, we expect one of us to do something, but we want them to come to us to get the money to do it. This is a problem waiting to happen. The budget has been set by the board. Now, give the individual assigned the task that portion of the budget, so they may have the resources necessary to perform that task.

Fourth, and most important, once the budget has been prepared and the tasks assigned, and the person delegated with a task has the money (read, the power) to carry it out, that money belongs to them. Leave it alone.

Figure 2:8 Is there a way that we can minimize this tug-of-war?

If they happen to spend less in one area in a given month than was budgeted—good for them; they saved some money. Don't ask for it back ... that savings is theirs. It is true that the Board may wish to have another budget meeting and allocate less to one category and more to another, but that is up to the Board, not to each individual. And, as you remember, a budget is prospective ... it applies to tomorrows spending plan, not yesterdays. By delegating both the responsibility and the resources to each employee, we have empowered that employee to do their best to discharge that responsibility within, or maybe even below, the budgeted amount. That is simply good management, and should not be undone if that employee is successful.

In this way, there is seldom occasion to argue over who gets what in terms of the water in the pond. Those decisions were made, and the resources allocated.

1. What is the emotional or psychological factor that sometimes gives rise to arguments over the way we spend money?
2. Summarize the four-part plan for mitigating such conflicts.
3. What do you regard as the key to the success of this plan?

Documentation

We have introduced three documents that provide information and give control over your pond. How is the best way to maintain and preserve these documents? Any documents that you need regular access to should be maintained in a file that is readily available. This might include a file drawer in a desk, or on a computer. The key is user-friendly accessibility. This applies not just to these documents, but to other documents that you will access on a regular basis.

Of course, there are a number of documents that should be secured in a safer location than a desk drawer or on a computer. Such documents are the ones that are hard to replace. For example, replacing your original Social Security card can be a lengthy and difficult process. Such papers need to be placed in a fireproof safe, or possibly in a safety-deposit box at your financial institution.

Exhibit 2:5 Accessible Record Keeping

- Financial Records (Balance Sheet, Budget and Spending Log, Checkbook, Savings)
- Employment Records (Time Logs, Benefit Information, Resume)
- Tax Records (Tax Deductible Expenses, Prior Tax Returns)
- Credit Records (Debt Documents, Credit Card Documentation, Credit Reports)
- Automobile Records (Purchase or Rental Documents, Maintenance Warranties)
- Housing Records (Purchase or Rental Documents, Maintenance Log, Instructions)
- Insurance Documents (Insurance Policies, Payment Information, Claim Information)
- Investment Records (Brokerage Account Information, Research Information)
- Retirement Planning Records (Pension Reports, IRA Reports, Social Security Reports)
- Estate Planning Records (Will, Living Will, Letter of Instruction, Trust Information)

Figure 2:9 Any documents that you need regular access to should be maintained in a file that is readily available.

Exhibit 2:6 Secured Record Keeping

- Identification Documents (Birth Certificate, Citizenship Papers, Social Security Card)
- Event Documentation (Marriage Certificate, Adoption Papers, Military Documents)
- Ownership Documentation (Titles, Deeds, Documentation of Expensive Items)
- Valuables (Bearer Bonds, Collectibles—Coins, Stamps, etc.,)

It is important, as a matter of practice, to shred any documentation or records that you are throwing away, which may include your account information, account numbers, or other tidbits that someone might use in the course of identity theft. This would include receipts that you no longer need, monthly billing notices, or regular account statements. Application Worksheet 2:3 in Appendix II invites you to list those records and documents that you would like to maintain, and then determine what protocol you would use in maintaining them.

Summary & Review

1. Explain why certain documents should be kept in a readily accessible location.
2. List some of the documents that should be maintained in a readily accessible location.
3. What documents would you want to store in a safe place? Why?

Chapter 3
Your Career

Chapter Objectives

1. Understand the importance of acquiring those skills and abilities that better position you to make a contribution—thereby increasing your value in the employment marketplace. Note the difference between IQs and EQs, and how each is obtained.
2. Be aware of the difference between interests and aptitudes, and be able to integrate these two considerations. Perhaps you will want to pursue a personal evaluation from one of several interests and aptitude evaluation sources.
3. Know the five yardsticks of career success, and weigh each according to your own priorities.
4. Gain an understanding of what a Resume is, and the ways in which you might prepare your best resume.
5. Develop familiarity with some of the numerous avenues available in researching job opportunities. Consider the value of an internship in assessing career potential.
6. Understand the process of Networking, and how the web can be useful in your networking efforts.
7. Know the three levels of job interviews, and how to prepare for your best job interview.
8. Be aware of the different types of compensation available in the employment marketplace, including direct and indirect compensation formulas.

The Value of Competence

It is no secret that, all other things being equal, the more education a person has, and the more qualified he is, the more money he will make in his career. When we talk about getting an education, there are a couple of paths that a person might follow. They may pursue a liberal arts degree that is available from a college or university. An education from a college or university is focused toward a broad level of mental development, combined with an expansion of knowledge in a particular field or discipline. Or, the person may opt to focus exclusively on the expansion of knowledge in a particular field or discipline, and will attend a trade or vocational school to acquire training and skills in that field.

Whether the schooling is at a college or university, or whether it is conducted at a trade or vocational school, the goal is to improve competence. The world will pay for competence, and your job security is enhanced if you can perform in your chosen avocation better than others. Perhaps we may regard this credential as your Intelligence Quotient or IQ—as it measures your ability to perform the tasks inherent in your job. It is important to obtain such competence, and it is equally important to maintain it over the course of your career. Reflecting back on our analogy where we compared your wealth and resources to a pond of water—your career produces the income that flows into your pond. It is the means by which the pond is filled.

Yet, we all know people who are very smart . . . who are very competent, but who don't seem to be able to function well in the job. They seem to lack something—and sometimes it's hard to know just what that something is. The "something" is often those characteristics, which enable us to function well around other people, or which enable us to function in a rapidly changing environment that requires adaptability. These other characteristics might be called your EQ or Emotional Quotient, and they are equally important to your career. Consider the relevance of the following EQs to almost any career one might pursue.

Exhibit 3:1   Emotional Quotient

- The ability to work well with other people.
- An understanding of how to motivate and direct others.
- An awareness of group interaction, commonality of goals, and team coordination.
- Insights in seeing problems unfolding, anticipating issues, and visualizing conditions.
- A desire to tackle problems and work toward a solution.
- The willingness to cope with conflict and, where necessary, adapt to change.
- The development of good interpersonal communication skills.
- The determination to stick with a task until it is accomplished, and accomplished well.
- The willingness to put other considerations ahead of your own—to sacrifice to achieve a higher purpose.
- Being able to graciously accept criticism or correction, and implement self-improvement.
- The ability to persuade others, to negotiate or compromise without offense.
- Maintaining a sense of candor, acknowledging realities, and inviting input from others.

No doubt, you can add additional characteristics to this list. The point is there is more to our qualifications than simply IQs. And, there is more to our career success than schooling.

It cannot be stressed enough, the importance of not only gaining, but of maintaining a level of competence that will position you for continued career growth and job security. Virtually every field has seen substantial changes in both the nature of the work, and in the requirements necessary to do the job. Once you have obtained the position, the work of preparing yourself is not over. Most employers will train you in the specifics of the job, and coach you in the various process and functions. However, it is up to you to maintain that edge that will put you near the front of the class; that will help insure your job security. If your employer ever asks for volunteers to attend a seminar or other educational or training event, your answer should always be: Yes!

Figure 3:1 There is more to our qualifications than simply [IQ's]

Employment Opportunities

Although employment opportunities vary from country to country, and even from region to region, there are certain sectors within the economy ,which have experienced strong growth over the last several decades, and where the outlook is bright over the foreseeable future. Among these sectors are:

- Information Technology—Including computer applications, networking technology, data maintenance, website development, and communication.

- Health Care—Providing health-care services and administration, as well as research, laboratory technology, and a host of related clinical, home health, and therapy services.

- Business Services—Those products and services that are sold to business or that business outsources, such as human resources, accounting, public relations and communication, and security.

- Travel, Entertainment, and Food Services—Including cruise and resort operation, food service, and event management.

- Social Services—Especially those that relate to child care or the care of the elderly, and including counseling, administration, and program management.

Figure 3:2 There are certain sectors within the economy, which have experienced strong growth over the last several decades, and where the outlook is bright over the foreseeable future.

> ## Summary & Review
>
> 1. What is the role of education in preparing for a desired career? What are the two alternative paths to education—how are they different?
> 2. Describe the difference between Intelligent Quotient (IQ) and Emotional Quotient (EQ). How is each obtained?
> 3. If you were to focus on improving your EQ in just one area, what would that be?

Interests and Aptitudes

When you were in high school, and you were visiting with a counselor about vocational interests, he probably said something like: "What is it you enjoy doing?" Your Interests are important to be sure, but by no means a deciding factor. You may enjoy playing golf, but if there are already a large number of very good PGA golfers competing for jobs at golf courses or for spots on the circuit, your interest alone may not be enough.

Consider also your Aptitudes: What it is that you are good at. Sometimes we are aware of the talents we have ... functions or characteristics, which set us apart from most other people. Sometimes, these strengths lie dormant in our character, and we simply don't realize how unique we are. Benjamin Franklin may have said it best.

"Hide not your talents. They for use were made. What's a sundial in the shade?"

Certainly, the ideal career would be one, which combines our interests with our abilities; one in which we enjoy what we do, and we do it well. One, without the other, would make for a very long day on the job.

> ## Get Real
>
> In high school, I enjoyed drawing architectural plans. The process of allocating space and function appealed to some inner need for organization, and in my spare time I would draw blueprints for houses and buildings of all kinds. I concluded that I wanted to be an architect. The education leading to that career was in two parts. First, I would pursue an engineering degree—which typically takes 5 years, and then I would get a Master's degree in Architecture. That was the plan.
>
> In my freshman year of college, I was sitting in my first drafting class when the professor lifted a large opaque object onto the table in the front of the room, and invited us to take out our sketching pads and draw the object. I was in the process of trying to do just that, when the professor came around behind me, took a long look at my efforts, and asked me what I was doing. I told him that I was trying to draw the object on the table. He paused for a moment, studied my sketch intently, and announced: "You need a new major."
>
> The reality is that I was not an artist. While I enjoyed putting a ruler to paper in producing a floor plan, I could not draw what that building should look like. Even now, my people are stick figures—it is not an aptitude I possess. I may have the interest, but I did not have the aptitude, to be an architect.

There are a number of assessment tools that try to provide a handle on your interests as well as the identification of those areas where you appear to have some natural abilities. These evaluations may be available from your school career center or, if you prefer, they can be pursued online for a fee.

One such evaluation is called the Myers-Briggs Career Assessment, and it is available online at "mbticomplete.com." The Myers-Briggs evaluation identifies certain characteristics that you might have, namely:

Extraversion versus Introversion

Sensing versus Intuition

Thinking versus Feeling

Judging versus Perceiving

Once the assessment has identified your characteristics, they provide a list of those avocations that appear consistent with those characteristics.

Another evaluation program is called Strength Finder, and it is available at "gallupstrengthscenter.com." This program is also available as a book titled *StrengthsFinder 2.0* by Tom Rath. The book is well written, and includes such insightful comments as:

"From the cradle to the cubicle, we devote more time to fixing our shortcomings than to developing our strengths."

The Strength Finder program utilizes what are called Holland Codes or Holland Occupational Themes. Named after psychologist John L. Holland, the Codes indicate certain personality types, namely:

- Realistic—(Doers)
- Investigative—(Thinkers)
- Artistic—(Creators)
- Social—(Helpers)
- Enterprising—(Persuaders)
- Conventional—(Organizers)

Figure 3:3 Sometimes strengths lie dormant in our character, and we simply don't realize how unique we are.

A simple ordering of a person's resemblance to each of the six characteristics provides the possibility of 720 different personality patterns. To the extent that the choice of vocation is an expression of personality, the results of this assessment could prove helpful. Once again, the assessment provides a listing of those professions that appear to be consistent with a persons' evaluation. The U.S. Department of Labor/Employment and Training Administration has been using the RIASEC model in the "Interests" section of its online database. Another program that also uses the Holland Codes is the Strong Interest Inventory, available at "takeinterestinventory.com." This assessment reports the RIASEC evaluation as a General Theme, and then further breaks down the results into 30 Specific Interests, including:

Culinary Arts	Human Resources and Training	Office Management
Social Sciences	Religion and Spirituality	Performing Arts
Nature and Agriculture	Counseling and Helping	Law
Management	Marketing and Advertising	Science
Taxes and Accounting	Teaching and Education	Entrepreneurship
Protective Services	Writing and Mass Communication	Sales
Medical Science	Politics and Public Speaking	Military
Finance and Investing	Mechanics and Construction	Athletics
Research	Programming and Information Services	Health-care Service
Visual Arts and Design	Computer Hardware and Electronics	Mathematics

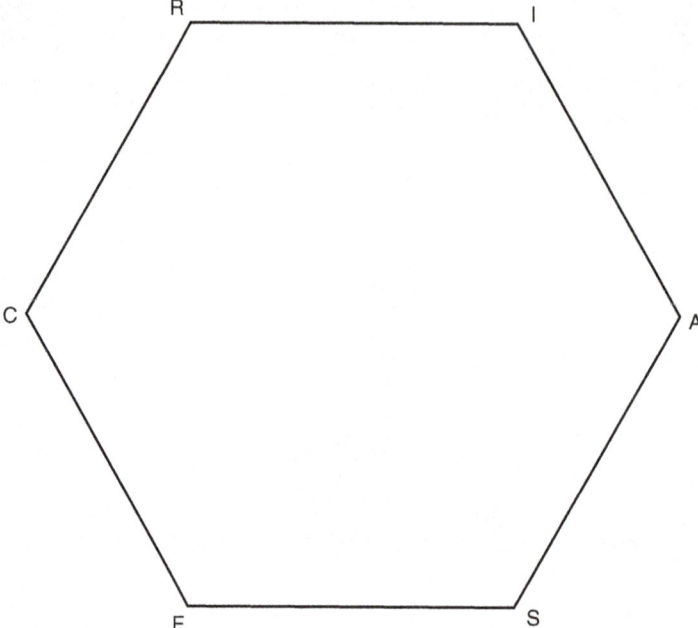

Figure 3:4 RIASEC Diagram

The Definition of Success

How might different people measure career success?

We have delved into the issue of identifying a career that is compatible with your interests and aptitudes. These considerations are intended to help identify a profession that you are good at, and you can enjoy. Having done that, you are still faced with a number of alternatives from which to choose.

Your career will dominate the waking hours of most of your life. If there is a single factor that impacts your life style the most, it will be your job. Therefore, it might be well for us to consider the yardsticks by which career success might be measured. The following diagram illustrates the primary considerations that are weighted by most people in their definition of career success.

Exhibit 3:2 Yardsticks of Career Success

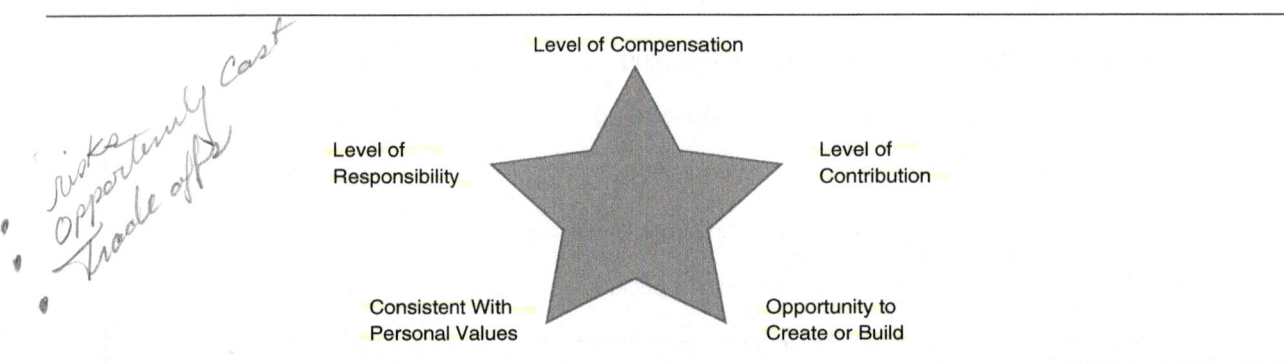

These five yardsticks of career success each play a role in our level of satisfaction. Some play a larger role, whereas others are secondary considerations. But each is important. Moreover, the relative weight given to these five factors shifts over time. Although one might be important early in life, another might be found to be more important later on.

Clearly, the amount of money you make is a common yardstick of career success. The more water that flows into your pond, the larger your pond and the more financial options you have when it comes to allocating your resources to your various financial goals. The nature of compensation can be a bit complex, with formulas that vary from emphasizing direct wages and salaries, to formulas that emphasize indirect benefits. (We will spend more time discussing these differences later on.) Many people chose careers where the income may be less, because they may weigh other factors as more important.

One of these other yardsticks, which often outweighs money in a persons' definition of career success, is the Level of Contribution that might be made to society. Teaching, law enforcement, a religious avocation—are examples of careers that typically rank high in terms of the contribution we may make. As a result they may offer a higher level of social prestige, as society often views these professionals as "givers." It is not uncommon for money to rank high early in one's life, and for the Level of Contribution to rank higher as we grow older.

As every entrepreneur knows, there are long hours and low income in the early stages of building a new business. Yet, the satisfaction of creating something, of building an enterprise, often outweighs other considerations. To that person, success comes from giving his idea wings, and seeing it grow and succeed over time.

It is not unusual for a person to turn down a job because it takes too much time away from his family, or because it is not in the location where he wants to live. For him, the definition of success is the assertion of those personal values first and foremost, and a career is successful only to the extent that it supports those values.

The Level of Responsibility is certainly a determiner of employment success. If you are effective, you are often promoted, and promotions to higher positions are often seen as a reward for good performance. Higher levels of responsibility don't always come with higher salaries, particularly in certain marketing positions. Yet, the satisfaction that comes from being the boss is certainly one measure of job success.

Figure 3:5 It might be well for us to consider the yardsticks by which career success might be measured.

Career Opportunity Costs

In Chapter 1, we introduced the concept of Opportunity Cost: the identification of what we give up—the trade-off—which comes when we chose a course of action. The career decision carries significant opportunity cost, and a careful evaluation of the trade-offs will help improve the quality of the decision process.

It may be useful to note that much of the opportunity cost evaluation is simply a matter of weighting those yardsticks of career success outlined above. To the extent that you emphasize one measure of success over another, you have identified and weighted the accompanying opportunity cost. Such trade-offs are seldom easy, but they accompany every decision—especially those relating to your career path. Being aware of the opportunity costs can help bring confidence to the employment decision.

> **Summary & Review**
>
> 1. How do your interests and your aptitudes affect your career choice?
> 2. In the event you are unsure of your interests and abilities, name one or two interest and aptitude assessment programs that might help reveal those characteristics.
> 3. What are the five yardsticks of career success? How does being aware of those yardsticks help in your evaluation of the opportunity costs associated with your career decision?

Your Resume—An Advertisement

Once you have identified your preferred career, and have invested the time and effort necessary to become qualified in your avocation, you are ready to present yourself to the world. The job search will be most effective if you open as many doors as possible. That may begin with an internship, which we will discuss in a moment. It will certainly involve networking. If you are geographically flexible, there will be more potential opportunities, than if you confine yourself to a limited locale. Whatever job you are seeking, you will need a means of introducing yourself to potential employers. That introduction typically begins with a resume.

A Resume is a factual, honest, results-oriented summary that says who you are and what you can do. It is fundamentally an advertisement for a product—and that product is you. Like advertising toothpaste or jeans, it is intended to draw the attention of the reader to you—the product. To be an effective advertisement, you want your resume to convey to the reader why they should consider you for a job position. To do this well, you need to present certain facts about your goals, experience, and qualifications, which convey to the reader your desire and ability to meet the demands of that position better than anyone else they are considering. In effect, you need to look like a square peg that fits well into that square hole they are trying to fill.

Figure 3:6 Whatever job you are seeking, you will need a means of introducing yourself to potential employers.

Virtually no one ever gets hired solely on the basis of their resume. But it is the first step . . . the ticket that gets you in the door. Based on the strength of your resume, you may be invited to an interview; which is what you want. It is the interview that will result in you getting the job—or not.

There are typically two kinds of resumes.

The Chronological Resume is a summary of your experience, presented in reverse chronological order. That is, when listing your education or your past jobs, it lists the most recent first, and then lists the one before that, and the one before that. This is the most common type of resume, and most individuals will start with a chronological resume. There are typically five sections to a Chronological Resume.

1. Personal Data: Name and contact information.
2. Career Objective or Profile: This can be either a brief statement of your career goals, or, a handful of bullet points summarizing your qualifications.
3. Education: A listing of the education you received since high school, including dates, schools attended, and degrees or certificates earned.
4. Experience: A listing of your employment, again including dates, employers, and a brief summary of your duties and responsibilities.
5. Related Information: This might include skills, interests, recognitions received, participation in other activities, or anything else that might set you apart for the employment opportunity considered.

The Functional Resume focuses more on what you have accomplished. It is used by authors, engineers, research specialists, or others who wish to highlight achievements in their career as opposed to where they have been and what they have done. The functional resume may not account for all periods per se, but does summarize the results of your efforts. The functional resume also has five sections.

1. Personal Date: Including contact information.
2. Career Objective or Profile: This can be either a brief statement of career goals, or, a handful of bullet points summarizing your qualifications.
3. Education: A summary of the education you received since high school, focusing on the qualifications and skills obtained.
4. Accomplishments: A summary of activities and accomplishments, highlighting what was achieved in each endeavor.
5. Related Information: Including skills, interests, recognitions received, participation in other activities, etc.

Perhaps it would be well to look at a typical resume, and then we could comment on how it might be improved. The following page is a sample of a Chronological Resume.

The reality is, most resumes are not read. The reader will most likely scan the document, starting at the top and moving down, until he finds a reason to stop. At that point, the reading stops. Therefore, your job is to keep him reading . . . to put those features in this ad that will capture and hold his attention. Remember, he is looking for a square peg. Can you see how difficult it would be to design a generic resume that would interest a multitude of readers looking to fill a variety of positions? How can you make yourself look like that square peg?

A Better Resume

The generic—one size fits all—resume, is going to face serious obstacles as it tries to look like a square peg. Does that mean you need to produce a separate resume for each job opportunity? Only if you want the job!

The practice of customizing a resume to fit a particular job opportunity is not as onerous as it sounds. Let's start with some improvements to the basic resume presented on page 50.

First, from the standpoint of readability, the basic resume shown is a good start. Resumes should be limited to 1 page, or roughly 250 words. It is important that all time since high school be accounted for. If you leave out a 2-year span of time, the reader may think that you were backpacking in Europe or perhaps in jail.

As we are trying to get everything onto a single page, it seems that we are wasting a lot of space by centering the contact information in half a dozen top lines in the top-middle of the page. Perhaps we can spread this information across the page, thereby taking only a couple of lines, as illustrated on page 51.

Exhibit 3:3 Chronological Resume

	JOHN DOE
	123 Main Street
	Albany, New York 12345
	(123) 444-5555
Objective:	A position in environment consulting.
Education:	
2012–2016	State University, Albany, New York
	Bachelor of Science—Major: Environmental Science
	Major GPA 3.6
Experience:	
2014–Present	Research Assistant to Dr. Steven R Jones
	State University, Albany, New York
	Documented studies on effect of pollution in ground water.
Summer 2013	Field Intern, College of Living Sciences
	State University, Albany, New York
	Gathered water samples from various locations across New England.
Summer 2012	Warehouse Assistant
	Johnson & Company, Environmental Consultants, Albany, New York
	Maintain and distribute supplies and equipment from the warehouse.
Skills:	Proficient in computer applications.
Interests:	Enjoy hunting, fishing, backpacking, and canoeing.
References:	Available Upon Request

Figure 3:7 How can you make yourself look like that square peg?

JOHN DOE

123 Main Street (123) 444-5555
Albany, New York 12345 johndoe@gmail.com

Now we come to an important part of the resume—the Objective or Profile. If you choose to list your objective, as is done in the sample resume, this refers to your career objective and can be done in a line or two. However, you would go a long way toward looking like a square peg if you chose instead to assemble a profile of some of those qualifications that strengthen your candidacy for the job you are pursuing. For example, let's suppose that the Environmental Protection Agency is trying to fill a position out of Salt Lake City, which would monitor the Great Salt Lake and surrounding wetlands. Knowing what it is that the EPA desires, you might replace the phrase "Objective" with the phrase "Profile," and approach this section with a few strong bullet points, such as:

Profile:	* Strong background in environmental research
	* Experienced in gathering, evaluating, and documenting water quality
	* University education specific to environmental studies and management
	* Strong GPA in core classes
	* Career goal to be involved in wetlands' studies and management

You haven't changed your own career objective, but you look a lot more like a square peg now than you did before.

When you reference your education, go ahead and report your GPA if it is above a 3.0. (If it is not, it would be better not to reference it.) In addition, as you list your educational achievements, it might be well to list those classes you have taken that are particularly applicable to the current job opportunity. If you received any special honors or recognition at school, if you participated in any extracurricular organizations, or if you supported yourself financially for a major proportion of your schooling—those typically add points to a resume.

Similarly, when you talk about your job experience, highlight those tasks you have performed that may touch on the tasks inherent in the job you are seeking. Normally, it is not necessary to report education or experience prior to college. However, if you had a high school job that is relevant to the opportunity at hand, go ahead and list it.

Should you decide to draw the readers' attention to particular skills you possess or experiences you have had, you can further target your resume by drawing from a Qualifications Bank. The qualifications bank is simply a summary of particular education, experiences, skills, knowledge, and accomplishments that help mark who you are. It is prepared on a page away from the resume, which you can access and add to the resume if it is appropriate. For example, your qualifications bank may include a reference to your computer proficiency or possibly a leadership conference you were invited to attend. Let's say that you reached the Rank of Eagle in the Boy Scouts of America, and that your Eagle Project was building birdhouses along a river near your home. (You never though you would use that experience again . . . did you.) Yet, as you read through your qualifications bank, it is just the thing to add under skills to make yourself look more and more like a square peg. With a couple of key strokes, you can add it to your resume.

In the resume cited above, John Doe listed under "Interests" a number of hobbies or sports pursuits. Although this is interesting, does it contribute to the level of professionalism that you want on your resume? Perhaps, instead, you could change that line to Service, and list those occasions when you served. If you volunteered at the local hospital, or spent time in the Peace Corps or other service endeavor, this would be the place to include that. This provides the added benefit of giving you a chance to account for any time that were spent in service, which are not otherwise accounted for under education or experience.

One last observation; don't list references on your resume. The reader knows he can ask you for references, you don't need to remind him. That will save you a line to use elsewhere.

Application Worksheet 3:1 is a framework for a functional resume. Penciling in your own information can give you a start in preparing your resume.

One more way in which you might target your resume, and set it apart from most others, is to include a brief cover letter. The cover letter should not repeat what you have already summarized on your resume. Rather, you want to use it to accomplish two things. First, you want to reference the employment opportunity being offered—assert your interest in and fit for this opportunity. Second, you want to provide just one or two reasons why you are qualified for their consideration. Perhaps it is your education, or your experience. Just a couple or three lines pointing out your strongest points relative to the job would be sufficient. This would give them some incentive to read the resume, as opposed to putting it in the pile with the rest of them. It would also further the goal of making you look like a square peg.

> ### Summary & Review
> 1. Name the two kinds of resumes. How are they different?
> 2. Many people prepare a generic resume that is offered to any and all potential employers. What are the limitations in this approach?
> 3. What is a Qualifications Bank? How may it be used to help target your resume?
> 4. In what other ways might you target your resume?

Job Search

At the time you are preparing your resume, you are no doubt looking to make those contacts and get those introductions, which will give your job hunt some vitality. Perhaps you may have already done some of that, and may not realize it. In the course of your summer jobs or other part time employment, you no doubt gained experience along with some contacts. If you still have ways to go in your education, perhaps you should consider a part-time opportunity in your field. This would serve the dual purpose of seeing if you have both an interest and an aptitude in that field, and gaining some valuable experience, which will move you closer to the job you want. It may also provide you with a contact or two, which could be helpful when you are ready for that full-time position.

Figure 3:8 Give your job hunt some vitality.

Another avenue that will help you gain experience and contacts is volunteer work.

There are many opportunities for volunteer work on a campus or other community outreach initiative, within a religious context, an educational organization, or youth-centered program. There is considerable variety in terms of the context of volunteer work, including organizing and coordinating, speaking and presenting, planning and supervising, and managing and reporting.

Both part-time employment and volunteer work will help bridge the gap that often occurs when a potential employer wants to know if you have any experience. Though you may be fresh out of school, these kinds of opportunities do provide a level of experience that is typically regarded positively.

When you are ready to search for that desired full-time position, there are a number of resources that may help identify job opportunities. If you are in school, and if your school has a career center, they can be very helpful in your job search.

Another resource is the Department of Workforce Services or similar agency. These agencies are State sponsored, and include a library of job opportunities within the state. Their website typically includes a tab titled Occupational Explorer, where you access information by typing in your desired occupation. The information available at this site includes employment potential, wages, and the educational or certification requirements necessary to enter that field. At most sites, you can identify job opportunities by job title and by location.

"Onetonline.org" is a well-established career explorer site, which provides detailed descriptions of the world of work. One of their categories is: "I want to be a . . . ," in which you can type in the occupation you are considering, and receive all kinds of information on that occupation.

Internships

Often, the best way to get your foot in the door is to have already worked in the field—perhaps part-time or as a volunteer or intern. An Internship is an opportunity to serve as an apprentice or trainee within an organization, and in a capacity that gives you the opportunity to gain a level of experience. Your career center may have a few ideas when it comes to finding internship opportunities. Many internships pay a small wage; however, others expect you to serve at your expense as a means of gaining experience.

There are a number of websites that are helpful in learning about internship opportunities. One is called "indeed.com," which is basically a library of jobs advertised on the web. As you access this site, note that it invites you to type in "What" options and "Where" options. Although this is a good site for accessing any and all kinds of job opportunities, it is unique in that you can type in Internship, or, if you prefer, a specific kind of internship such as Engineering Internship. Once you have identified the What, then you can identify the Where, and the site will tell you how many positions fit your What in that particular Where. You can then gather specific information about each position, including contact information.

Another possible resource, if you know what company you want to work for, is to simply Google that company and reference Internships. For example, Monsanto—Internships, may, depending on the company, provide information on any opportunities they may have.

Networking

Sometimes we ponder the question: "Is it who you know, or what you know, that gets you the job?" The answer is "Yes." It may seem unfair at times, but the realities are that people will often hire the people they know, or the people who have been recommended to them by people they know. Networking is the process of making and using individual contacts to further your opportunities. If done right, it can be a major aid in your efforts to find and get that job you want.

In the past, networking meant a prolonged task of letters and telephone calls. Today, thanks to the web, making contacts is much quicker. For example, if you have attended school, either a college or university or a vocational school, there is a network of alumni who have graduated ahead of you and who are already positioned in the workforce. This is a natural networking channel, as you share the same educational institution. This alumni network can be contacted through your career center or directly on the web by posting the name of your institution and the words Alumni Network.

Another networking resource, which has developed a strong following over the years, is LinkedIn. You can join LinkedIn simply by creating a profile for yourself. There is no charge for the non-premium level. Once you have registered, this site will identify other subscribers of LinkedIn who share a connection with you. These shared connections could be:

> Where They Live
>
> What They Studied
>
> Where They Work

Figure 3:9 Networking is the process of making and using individual contacts to further your opportunities.

What They Do

What Their Skills Are

For example, you may wish to locate contacts who work for the American Cancer Society in the Human Resource area. You can use this site to network Where They Work: American Cancer Society—What They Do: Human Resources. Given the information you provided in your own registration, the website will look for any shared connections. This is where the networking begins. LinkedIn also has a jobs directory by Region, by Title, and by Company.

The purpose of all this is to identify those employment opportunities that fit with your career goals. The broader you cast your net, the more opportunities you could identify. You should plan on spending at least as many hours a week looking for a position, as you expect to spend in that position. To send out a handful of resumes, and then wait by the phone, simply will not produce the kind of results you need. Each individual you speak with becomes a potential introduction. Though they may not have the position you seek, ask them for the names of other individuals who might be able to help. Then contact each of those, who in turn may know other individuals that they might be willing to introduce you too. In the end, it is the opportunity to interview that you want. The interview brings you face to face with a potential employer.

Summary & Review

1. There are many ways in which you might identify a potential job opportunity. Name several of them.
2. What is an Internship? How might it be a helpful part of your career plan?
3. What is Networking? Cite several methods you might use to instigate the networking process.

Meeting with the Employer

There are several levels at which an interview occurs. The first level typically takes place the first time you meet with a prospective employer. This level can be called an Informational Interview, and it is a get-acquainted session. This may occur at a job fair, where you pull up a chair and chat with a representative, or it may occur as you respond to an ad and find yourself in the company of dozens of other people who are similarly responding to the ad. It is designed as an information exchange, where the employer learns something about you and you learn something about them. There is no commitment on the part of either of you, just an effort to see if this is an opportunity you wish to pursue, or if you are a candidate they wish to pursue.

Figure 3:10 There are several levels at which an interview occurs.

If the answer to that question is yes, you may be invited to sign up for a Screening Interview. This session is a serious exploration of the possibilities of employment. If you attend a college where the career center is active in bringing employers onto campus, you may be able to sign up for a half-hour interview session where you can sit down with the employer and examine the possibilities of employment. You might be invited to meet with a recruiter at their place of business. From both your perspective and their perspective, the screening interview is designed to reduce the number of candidates or companies under consideration, to a short list.

If you are on their short list, and they are on your short list, a Selection Interview, sometimes called an in-depth interview, is arranged. At this stage, you will probably be invited to meet a number of people, as the hiring of the final candidate is almost always a joint decision. You may be asked to take some kind of evaluation exam, or make a presentation, so they can determine first hand your skills and abilities. It is possible that the selection interview process may take more than 1 day, as they try to judge your fit with their organization and your potential to make the contribution they are seeking. You need to be making the same kind of evaluation of them; what level of responsibility will you assume—can you make the contribution they are expecting—are you a fit with their organization—how do your career goals fit with their needs—will you be happy there?

In both the screening interview and the selection or in-depth interview, there are a few rules of thumb that will help you to be successful.

First, plan on arriving at least 15 minutes early. The extra time will allow you to fill out any paperwork, collect your thoughts, and be ready when they are. To dash in late with the excuse that you couldn't find a parking place, will usually result in a short interview and an end to that prospect.

Second, dress one notch better than they do, in neat, comfortable, and simple styling. If they are open collared, put on a tie. If they wear a tie, put on a coat. The reason; you can always come down if invited to, you can never go up. If they say; "take off your coat, we are pretty informal here," you don't have a problem. But if you show up in tennis shoes and they wear ties, you can never make up the lost ground.

Third, come with a purpose. Have several copies of your resume, and possibly a typed list of references, in a nice binder or satchel. Don't forget to bring paper and pen, together with a listing of the questions you might have about their organization or this opportunity. If you have done some research on the company, and are prepared to converse and ask questions about them, you will be judged a much more serious candidate.

And fourth, take a deep breath, and be yourself. Recognize that the interview is a time to toot your own horn. Do it truthfully and sincerely . . . and convey confidence. Know what points you want to make, and do it positively. Do not say anything negative. If asked to discuss an unpleasant subject such as a failed project or an unpleasant supervisor, put it in a positive light such as—what did you learn. If you are uncomfortable with questions about yourself, you might wish to conduct mock interviews with a friend, so you will be better prepared to field those questions when they come.

No matter how well prepared you are for the interview, if you are like the rest of us, there will no doubt be a time when your response was a bit clumsy or incomplete. On the way home, you may shake your head and wish that you had answered that particular question in another way. Don't despair, there is one more opportunity for you to make yourself look like a square peg, and correct that response at the same time. A targeted letter sent a day or two after the interview, can strengthen your position as a candidate. In that letter, express thanks for the opportunity to meet with them, and restate your interest and fit for that position. Now you have the chance to turn around that clumsy or incomplete impression, and provide a strong, positive answer.

Application Worksheet 3:2, in Appendix II, provides a template to help you prepare for your interview.

Summary & Review

1. Name the three levels or types of interviews.
2. If invited to comment on a previous experience that did not go very well, such as: "Why were you employed with another company for only 6 months?" how would you respond.
3. Summarize the kinds of preparations that would make your interview successful.
4. What additional step could you take after the interview to make a positive impression and keep your name in front of the employer?

Get Real

While visiting family in Nebraska over the Christmas holidays, I took the opportunity to meet with a number of potential employers. A family friend was kind enough to make a number of calls, introducing me to several potential employers. At one firm, one of the vice-presidents was available to meet with me, and we sat down to a conversation. He mentioned that they were looking for an analyst to join their Investment Department, and I left him a copy of my resume. After returning home to Michigan, I wrote the kind of follow-up letter that has been discussed above. In that letter, I thanked him for his time, again expressed interest in the opportunity we had discussed, and boldly declared that—while I knew they were interviewing other individuals for that position, no one would work as hard as I would. He called me a week later, and pointed out that my level of interest and commitment to hard work had impressed him . . . and offered me the job.

Compensation

Although the level and nature of compensation is only one of the five yardsticks of career success, it is an important consideration, and may come in several forms. There are basically two types of compensation that an employee receives—direct and indirect.

Exhibit 3:4 Types of Compensation

Direct Compensation	Indirect Compensation
Wages and Salary	Health Insurance
Performance Bonus	Other Benefits (Parking, Discounts, etc.)
Profit Sharing	Pension Program

Wages is the term used to describe hourly compensation, typically paid based on a time card that evidences the hours worked in a given week. Wages may vary from week to week depending on the hours on the job. Salary is the term used to describe an annual compensation amount, usually paid in semimonthly installments. A salary presupposes a given number of hours per week on the job, though it is not reduced if the worker takes time off for a doctors' appointment or other tasks away from work. Moreover, a salary generally continues during the employees vacation time (with a specified number of days per year allocated to vacation leave), and during the time an employee may be away from work due to illness, whereas wages are not typically paid during such absences.

If a Performance Bonus is offered, it is usually on the basis of specified criteria, and paid only if the criteria are met. A proportional performance bonus may be paid at different junctures in the specified criteria, with a smaller amount due at lower levels of performance and a higher amount due at higher levels. Profit Sharing is a type of bonus based on the profits of the enterprise, and may be paid proportional to the wage or salary level of each employee. Profit sharing is usually paid annually.

Since the early 1940s, all types of direct compensation paid in the United States are taxed under the "pay-as-you-go" Federal tax laws. This means that employers are required to withhold a portion of each employee's direct compensation to be paid in Federal employment taxes on a regular basis. (Individuals who are self-employed are similarly required to pay a portion of their income on a quarterly basis under the "pay-as-you-go" system.) Even those individuals who may not be subject to withholdings for Federal Income Tax, do face withholding for other Federal employment taxes—including FICA (Social Security) and Medicare taxes. A W-2 form (wage and tax statement) prepared by the employer and given to the employee at the end of each calendar year, reports the total direct compensation received by the employee, together with the withholdings for Federal Income Tax, Social Security, and Medicare. This form is filed with the employee's federal, state, and, where applicable, city income tax returns. A sample W-2 firm is shown below.

Indirect Compensation

Sometimes we make the mistake of underestimating the value of indirect compensation. For many careers, the value of the indirect compensation can be substantial. In addition, most indirect compensation received is not subject to employment taxes, giving you more value for the dollar.

Perhaps the most common forms of indirect compensation are what we sometimes call "fringe benefits." These benefits may be presented in a so-called Cafeteria-Style program, which allows the employee to choose among a number of alternative benefits. These may include health insurance, life insurance, lunch programs, day care assistance, parking allowance, discounts for company products or services, and other benefits.

The way it typically works is this. Depending on the employees' job or grade level, he is allocated a certain number of points. Each of the potential benefits carries a price in terms of the number of points required to receive it. The employee then allocates his points to those benefits that are most useful for him. For example, if

Exhibit 3:5 W-2 Form

d Control No 1295	1 Wages tips other compensation 58643.28	2 Federal income tax withheld 9203.25
OMB No 1545-0000	3 Social securty wages 58643.28	4 Social security tax withhold 2463.02
	5 Medlcare wages and tps 58643.28	6 Modicare tax withheld 850.33

Employers name address and ZIP node

7 Social security tps	8 Allocated tips	9
10 Dependont care benofits	11 Nonqualited plans	12a Code see Insl for box 12 C 75.24
12b Code DD 11045.28	12c Code	12d Code

b Employer identification number (EIN)	a Employee's social security number

13 Statutory empl.	Rellrement plan X	Third-party sick pay	14 Other

a Employee's name, address, and ZIP code

2012 38-2099803	15 State Employer's ID number UT	16 State wages, tips, etc 58643.28
W-2 Wage and Tax Statement Copy 2-To Be Flled With Employee's State, City, or Local Income Tax Return,	17 State income tax 2932.17	18 Local wages, tips, etc
	19 Local Income tax	20 Locality name

Department of the Treasury - Internal Revenue Service

---

he is married with children, and if his spouse also works, he may opt to spend some of his points on life insurance or child care. Once his points have been allocated, he receives those benefits that he has chosen.

For most of these benefits, the employer pays the majority, if not all, of the costs. One way to measure the value of these programs is to determine what each would cost if the employee had to pay for them directly. Of course, in the calculation of that cost, don't forget to add an amount equivalent to your tax bracket to the cost of the program. This is because, if you had to pay for it yourself, you would be paying from your direct compensation, which faces a tax bill before you can use it to meet the cost of the respective benefit. For example, if you were pricing life insurance, and you found that the life insurance policy you wanted would cost $250 per month, and you are paying employment taxes equivalent to 19% of your direct compensation, you would need to earn $297.50 ($250 × 1.19) to be able to make the $250 monthly premium payment. If you elect life insurance as a fringe benefit, your employer would pay the monthly premium and you would not have to pay employment taxes on that benefit. The importance of such fringe benefits should not be underestimated.

Other types of indirect compensation may include a pension program designed to help the employee prepare for retirement. There are different types of pension programs, but in most instances the employer contributes a portion—if not all, of the amount set aside for retirement. (We will devote an entire chapter to this important benefit later on.)

Figure 3:11 For many careers, the value of indirect compensation can be substantial.

Summary & Review

1. Name the two general types of compensation.
2. How does the "pay-as-you-go" Federal tax system affect the amount of money the employee actually receives under his direct compensation formula.
3. Cite those "fringe benefits" that you would regard as most important as you consider various cafeteria-style benefit options.v

Chapter 4
Taxes

"Today we are introducing a new simplified tax code: Send us all of your money and we'll send back whatever we don't use."

Chapter Objectives

1. Gain an understanding of the scope and size of taxes, and of the five major kinds of taxes that are currently assessed by different levels of government.
2. Understand the two kinds of taxes on purchases, and how they affect the cost of virtually every transaction.
3. Become aware of the three stage approach in levying property taxes, and of the impact of each approach on the welfare of the community.
4. Consider the nature of payroll taxes, and of the role of FICA assessments.
5. Identify the scope of gift and estate taxes, and the reason for their application.
6. Understand the protocol for calculating the income tax, and become familiar with the income tax preparation and filing requirements.
7. Be aware of some of the most important characteristics of the income tax code. Identify the three general means by which the income tax bill might be reduced—exclusions, deductions, and credits—and explain the characteristics of each.
8. Consider the nature of capital gains, and the tax advantages associated with long-term capital gains.
9. Cite the three levels of a tax audit, and explain the nature of each level.
10. Identify those resources that are available to help with the income tax preparation and filing procedure.

Cost of Government

Thomas Payne—the American revolutionary who wrote the pamphlet *"Common Sense"*—observed that government is a "Necessary Evil." Depending on your political philosophy, you may choose to put the emphasis on the first of those two words, or the second. The reality is that government plays a major role in each of our lives, and certainly impacts our personal finances on a number of fronts ranging from regulations to taxes. In this chapter, we will be looking at the levies government assesses to raise the money it requires.

The principal means governments use to raise money is through taxes. It is estimated that government taxes take approximately one-third of the income of the average American. In other countries, this burden may be more or less, depending on the size and scope of their respective government. Did you realize that government costs so much? A very good question would be whether the benefits provided by government are equal to the costs incurred.

Figure 4:1 It is estimated that government taxes take approximately one-third of the income of the average American.

In the United States, there are typically five major kinds of taxes assessed by different levels of government.
Taxes on Purchases: Including sales tax and excise tax.
Taxes on Property: Consisting primarily of real estate taxes and certain other taxes on automobiles, boats, trailers, and farm equipment.
Payroll Taxes: Assessed on both the employee and the employer.
Gift and Estate Taxes: Sometimes referred to as death taxes, these are taxes paid on the transfer of assets.
Income Taxes: Applied on the income of both individuals and institutions. Includes capital gains taxes.

Taxes on Purchases

Every time you purchase something, whether it is a meal at a restaurant or a pair of socks, there is a tax added to the cost of that good or service. For many products, there is more than one purchase tax added.

Federal, state, and local governments are each involved in the assessment of Excise Taxes, which is a tax levied on particular products or services. At the present time, excise taxes are levied on gasoline, liquor, airline tickets, firearms, tires, cigarettes, cell phones, and many other products. Unlike the sales tax, the excise tax is typically not broken out, but remains "hidden" in the price of the product or service. As a result, we usually don't know the amount of excise tax we are paying. For example, excise tax currently constitutes most of the retail cost of a pack of cigarettes. There are two kinds of excise tax. Ad Valorem tax is a percentage of the value of the item being taxed. It is added to the price of the product and paid by the merchant. A Specific tax is a fixed dollar amount, which is similarly added to the cost of the product and paid by the merchant. Again using cigarettes as an example; the federal government currently assesses a flat $1.01 per pack excise tax on all cigarette sales in the United States. In addition, States levy an excise tax ranging from $0.17 per pack in Missouri to $4.35 per pack in New York.

State and local governments assess another kind of purchase tax, called a Sales Tax, on the retail price of most goods and services. The sales tax is an ad valorem tax, and is broken out separately from the cost of the product and paid by the purchaser. Most of the time there are multiple sales taxes charged, with the state, county, city, and occasionally other local agencies, each assessing a sales tax on the same purchase. Products that carry an excise tax are typically also charged a sales tax at the time of purchase. One fairly aggressive form of the sales tax—which is used in much of Europe—is called a Value Added Tax or VAT. Whereas the cumulative sales taxes in the United States may range from 6% to 15% of the purchase price depending on the locale, the VAT averages 20% in many countries and is as high as 27% of the purchase price in Hungary.

Both the sales tax and the excise tax have been criticized for being regressive—that is, having a disproportionate impact on low-income individuals. This is because lower-income individuals spend a much higher proportion of their income on basic purchases, and therefore, pay proportionally more in purchase taxes than higher income individuals. In many jurisdictions, this impact is mitigated by reducing sales taxes on certain commodities such as rent or food.

Figure 4:2 The sales tax is an ad valorem tax, and is broken out separately from the cost of the product and paid by the purchaser.

Chapter 6
Establishing Credit

Contributed by Ryan O'Shea. Copyright © Kendall Hunt Publishing Company.

Chapter Objectives

1. Understand the factors that affect your credit from both a credit reporting and scoring basis.
2. Obtain a general knowledge regarding the various scoring models.
3. Develop the ability to track and manage your own credit report and scores through the major credit bureaus.
4. Describe each of the four Cs and understand how each is important when interpreting an individual's creditworthiness.
5. Know the three major credit bureaus in the United States.
6. Understand the difference between Open ended and Closed ended lines of credit.
7. Know the major credit scoring models and which credit bureaus are responsible for them.

Consumer Credit: What Is It?

The use of credit permeates the entire American economy and our personal financial lives. Using credit in some situations can vary from unnecessary, to advantageous, to an outright necessity. The use of credit throughout one's lifetime is inevitable; being responsible and careful when using credit is essential.

At its heart, <u>Credit</u> is the idea that a purchase is financed, meaning that the purchase can happen today and the payment can happen at some time in the future. When discussing <u>Consumer Credit</u>, we refer to the use of credit for personal goods and services. This excludes both business credit and a mortgage on one's home. This, however, does not mean that a home mortgage and business credit cannot impact a person's ability to borrow, as well as their credit reporting and scoring as discussed later in the chapter.

To understand how prevalent credit is in our society, it is useful to describe some common and sometimes overlooked examples of credit. The most common form of credit is the "credit card," but most individuals use credit on a daily basis whether they engage in the use of credit cards or not. Most individuals have conveniences such as mobile phones, electricity, natural gas, Internet connections, television, and many other similar services which, in most cases, are provided before they are paid for. This is the use of credit in its most basic form. When payment is made, it is actually for the service provided in the prior month. As these services were not paid for in advance, the company that provided the service has extended credit to the consumer.

When it comes to paying for goods and services there are several options available to consumers. We have the ability to pay for a service with our current income, our cash or investment savings, or utilize our future earnings and credit rating to secure credit.

Credit and Our Economy

To understand how prevalent the use of credit is—the following chart from the Federal Reserve shows actual consumer debt outstanding in the United States. It is easy to see the upward trend over time as more and more people choose to use credit to finance their lives. With consumer debt on the rise, the proper and responsible use of credit becomes more important. The simple fact that credit is in many cases easy to use, does not make it wise nor responsible in many cases.

Exhibit 6:1 Total Consumer Debt Outstanding in the United States

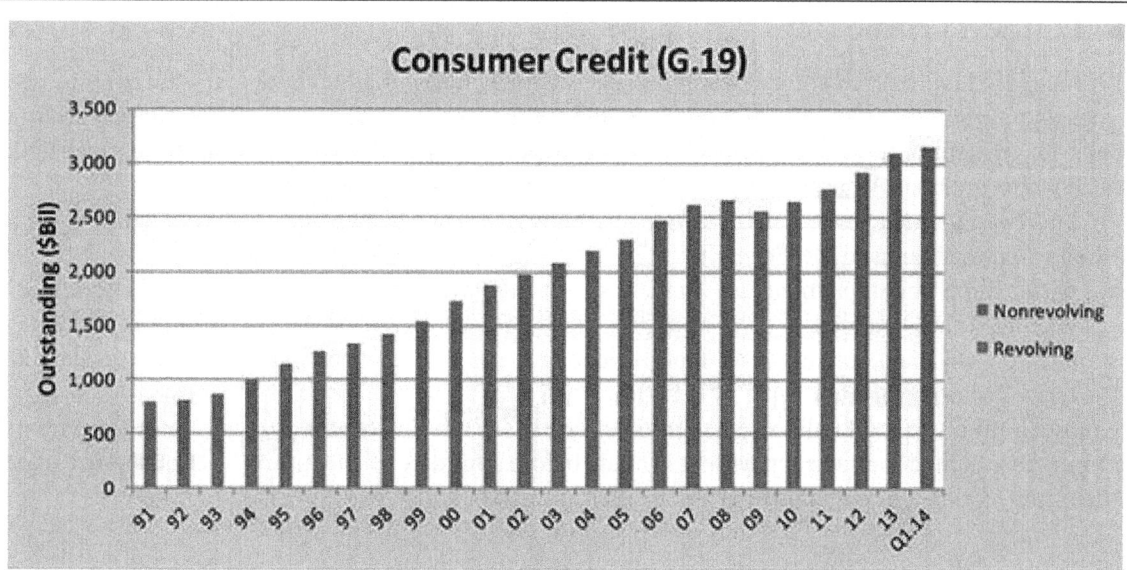

Summary & Review

1. What is Credit? Why is it important for you to establish positive credit—especially in today's marketplace?
2. Do you think that credit is an important factor in our economy?
3. What kinds of limitations would you face if you did not have access to credit?

Types of Credit

The basic types of Credit are <u>Closed Ended Credit</u> and <u>Open Ended Credit</u>.

Figure 6:1 The basic types of credit are Closed Ended Credit and Open Ended Credit.

Closed Ended Credit

When using closed ended credit, a specific purchase is usually being made. These loans are used to purchase items such as automobiles. In most cases, closed ended credit requires a down payment in some amount by the consumer. Repayment of these loans has two different structures that are typical. These repayment structures are typically referred to as <u>Amortized Payment</u> schedule and <u>Balloon Payment</u> schedule.

In an amortized loan, payments are made in set amounts over a predetermined period, with the frequency established when the loan is made. See Exhibit 6:2 for an example of this type of loan.

Loans with a lump-sum repayment are what are sometimes referred to as balloon payments or single lump-sum repayments. These loans are usually repaid in full by a predetermined date in the future. In some cases interest on the loans is paid during the term of the loan and in other cases the interest accrues until repayment (thus the term "balloon" for these types of loans).

The most common types of balloon payment loans are those offering 60–90 day loans or other similar offers where a purchase is made and the repayment is made before a set date in the future. These loans are often seen in the furniture, appliance, and consumer electronics industries.

Open Ended Credit

Sometimes referred to as "revolving" lines of credit, open ended credit is most commonly associated with credit cards. This type of credit typically has a preset limit and the individual can utilize any amount, at any time, up to the limit. Your credit limit is typically referred to as your <u>Line of Credit</u>. When using the line of credit, an individual has the freedom to use any amount up to the limit, without prior authorization from the lender.

In the event that any borrowings under the line of credit remain outstanding beyond the current billing period, <u>Interest</u> must be paid for the use of this service. The interest charge varies widely throughout the industry. This is the price one pays for the use of credit and the option to repay the debt at a later date.

Exhibit 6:2 Closed Ended Credit—Repayment Schedule

Auto Loan Summary

On an auto loan of $30,000.00, with an interest rate of 5% for 60 months, your monthly payment is **$566.14**. At the end of your term, you will have paid **$30,000.00** in principal and **$3,968.22** in interest for a total payment of **$33,968.22**.

Amortization Schedule

Payment	Principal	Interest	Balance	Payment	Principal	Interest	Balance
1	$441.14	$125.00	$29,558.86	31	$499.74	$66.39	$15,434.60
2	$442.98	$123.16	$29,115.89	32	$501.83	$64.31	$14,932.77
3	$444.82	$121.32	$28,671.07	33	$503.92	$62.22	$14,428.85
4	$446.67	$119.46	$28,224.39	34	$506.02	$60.12	$13,922.84
5	$448.54	$117.60	$27,775.86	35	$508.13	$58.01	$13,414.71
6	$450.40	$115.73	$27,325.45	36	$510.24	$55.89	$12,904.47
7	$452.28	$113.86	$26,873.17	37	$512.37	$53.77	$12,392.10
8	$454.17	$111.97	$26,419.01	38	$514.50	$51.63	$11,877.60
9	$456.06	$110.08	$25,962.95	39	$516.65	$49.49	$11,360.95
10	$457.96	$108.18	$25,504.99	40	$518.80	$47.34	$10,842.15
11	$459.87	$106.27	$25,045.12	41	$520.96	$45.18	$10,321.19
12	$461.78	$104.35	$24,583.34	42	$523.13	$43.00	$9,798.06
13	$463.71	$102.43	$24,119.64	43	$525.31	$40.83	$9,272.75
14	$465.64	$100.50	$23,654.00	44	$527.50	$38.64	$8,745.25
15	$467.58	$98.56	$23,186.42	45	$529.70	$36.44	$8,215.55
16	$469.53	$96.61	$22,716.89	46	$531.91	$34.23	$7,683.64
17	$471.48	$94.65	$22,245.41	47	$534.12	$32.02	$7,149.52
18	$473.45	$92.69	$21,771.96	48	$536.35	$29.79	$6,613.17
19	$475.42	$90.72	$21,296.54	49	$538.58	$27.55	$6,074.59
20	$477.40	$88.74	$20,819.14	50	$540.83	$25.31	$5,533.76
21	$479.39	$86.75	$20,339.75	51	$543.08	$23.06	$4,990.68
22	$481.39	$84.75	$19,858.36	52	$545.34	$20.79	$4,445.34
23	$483.39	$82.74	$19,374.97	53	$547.61	$18.52	$3,897.73
24	$485.41	$80.73	$18,889.56	54	$549.90	$16.24	$3,347.83
25	$487.43	$78.71	$18,402.13	55	$552.19	$13.95	$2,795.64
26	$489.46	$76.68	$17,912.67	56	$554.49	$11.65	$2,241.15
27	$491.50	$74.64	$17,421.17	57	$556.80	$9.34	$1,684.36
28	$493.55	$72.59	$16,927.62	58	$559.12	$7.02	$1,125.24
29	$495.61	$70.53	$16,432.01	59	$561.45	$4.69	$563.79
30	$497.67	$68.47	$15,934.34	60	$563.79	$2.35	$0.00

Summary & Review

1. What are the primary differences between closed ended credit and open ended credit?
2. When might a consumer pursue closed ended credit, and when might open ended credit be more desirable?
3. Why do you think open ended credit is such a challenge for many people in today's society? What affect does open ended credit have on a person's budget?

The Four or Five Cs

Depending on which reference source you use, there are a number of guiding principles lenders use to make decisions as to when to extend credit, and how much credit to extend. Some references call them the "Four Cs" whereas others call them the "Five Cs." These principles are the same except for the addition of Conditions to the five Cs model. They are as follows:

Exhibit 6:3 The Cs of Creditworthiness

Character	Character
Capacity	Capacity
Capital	Capital
Collateral	Collateral
	Conditions

Character

Character refers to the financial history of the borrower, which in the view of a lender can be used to estimate future financial responsibility (or lack thereof). There are many factors that go into an individual's financial history. Some important factors are:

- Total Debt
- Delinquent Accounts
- Available Credit
- Late Payments

In general, the fewer the issues on a person's credit history the higher their credit score will be. The reason they call this "Character" is it describes how a person has interacted with their past and current creditors, and establishes a trend in borrower behavior.

Capacity

This term refers to one's ability to make payments on debt. (See "Debt-to-Income Ratio" elsewhere in the chapter.) The amount of income a person receives is directly related to the amount of money they can borrow and the monthly payments on those debts that is sustainable on an ongoing basis. This calculation refers to one's capacity for debts.

Different financial institutions have limits on how much of a person's income can be dedicated to debt payments. These limits can and will vary based on the type of debt or loan, credit history, regulatory environment, and other factors. Limits have been placed on this ratio in the past through government intervention.

Capital

Capital simply refers to the amount of cash reserves (or other liquid assets) a borrower has to repay debts. Such resources can be used as a down payment, to cover costs associated with borrowing such as closing costs or appraisals, or as a "backup plan" if the borrower is unable to make debt payments from their income.

Collateral

When borrowing, it is a common practice to use an asset as Collateral with the lender. A collateralized position gives the lender a claim against the property, which claim can be asserted and the asset recovered by the lender, in the event the loan is not repaid as agreed. The most common collateral is the actual asset a person is borrowing to purchase. In the case of purchasing a home, the lender most often has a Lien against the property. When purchasing an automobile on credit, the lender is similarly listed as a lienholder on the Title to the automobile, holding a lien against the car as collateral until the auto loan is repaid.

Collateral, when valuable enough, can make borrowing money easier because the lender has a clearly defined legal recourse if the loan is not repaid. The amount of collateral required for any particular loan can also vary based on credit history, credit score, lending company, government regulations, and other factors.

Figure 6:2 In the case of purchasing a home, the lender most often has a lien against the property.

Summary & Review

1. Which of the Cs of credit do you regard as most important? Which one do you think points to your strongest financial characteristic? Which one points to your weakest financial characteristic?
2. When does Collateral enter into the borrowing and lending decision? How does it make a loan easier to obtain?
3. Conditions refer more to the lender's status than yours. It includes the state of the economy as a whole and the state of the individual lender. How can you address this final C as you consider your credit status?

Conditions

The structure of the debt also has an impact on the decision a lender makes. This includes the interest rate, amount of principal on the loan, length of loan, and many other factors. These factors, when combined, help to guide the lender as to whether lending money in a given instance is a sound business decision.

Credit Reporting

Credit reporting and scoring is designed to be a way that any lender or potential lender can judge the ability of a borrower to repay their debts. It also allows them to gauge the likelihood of a default if they lend money to the individual. All reporting and scoring is designed with these things in mind. When the consumer is aware of this fact, they can then build their own credit history in such a way as to become more "predictable" to creditors. In general, when an individual mindfully builds their credit to be stable and predictable, it will inevitably lead to better credit reports and scores.

There are three major credit bureaus in the United States. These organizations are Equifax, Experian, and Transunion. Although much of the data contained in their reports are typically very similar, it is important to review reporting from each agency when examining your credit reports.

A consumer has the ability to review their own credit report for free once per year. You may access your credit report at: annualcreditreport.com. This service is provided as a protection to consumers, so that you have the ability to see what your creditors can see regarding your financial life. Consumers are also entitled to a free credit report when they apply for credit. They can typically request the report from the bureau or bureaus who shared information with the potential lender.

Data contained in these reports include name, address, credit accounts—which includes revolving lines of credit, loans, mortgages, and repayment history, and credit inquiries, and other pertinent information. These data are used to evaluate someone's creditworthiness. With all of this information available, it is very important that consumers regularly review these reports for accuracy and awareness of their current credit data.

Aside from the availability of free reports annually, there is a multitude of other outlets to view one's credit report and scores. These services vary in price, so it is left up to the consumer to research an appropriate outlet to view the information they would like to see regarding their own financial situation. Each of the three credit bureaus offers its own credit reporting format, with many options regarding the features and inclusions.

Credit Scoring Models

Several scoring models exist in the marketplace to help lenders and consumers interpret their credit report. These models assign a number indicating the creditworthiness of the individual. The most well-known scoring model is the FICO scoring model, which is designed by Equifax. VantageScore, which is designed by Experian, is the second most well-known scoring model. Each model can have different versions, which are updated from time to time by the companies who designed the models. These models can change from time to time; another reason for consumers to continually monitor their credit reports and scores.

In general, there are several factors that can affect a person's credit score in either a negative or positive manner regardless of the scoring model being viewed. Some of these factors include:

- Length of Credit History
- Payment History
- Line of Credit Utilization Rate
- Frequency of Credit Inquiries
- Variety of Credit Utilized
- Derogatory Marks

Credit Scoring Factors

With the credit bureaus changing the credit scoring models on a regular basis, there are few hard and fast rules regarding your credit scores. There are, however, some general guidelines that can help an individual when building and maintaining their credit. Most of the factors used in calculating an individual's credit score can be attributed to the following categories.

Categories:

- Payment History
- Amounts Owed
- Length of Credit History
- New Credit
- Types of Credit Used

Within each of these categories, a person has a specific history that is either helping or hurting their score. The compilation of these factors, along with the weight of the particular category, gives the overall score within the specific scoring model. The importance and exact weighting of these factors to one's score can vary by model and can often change.

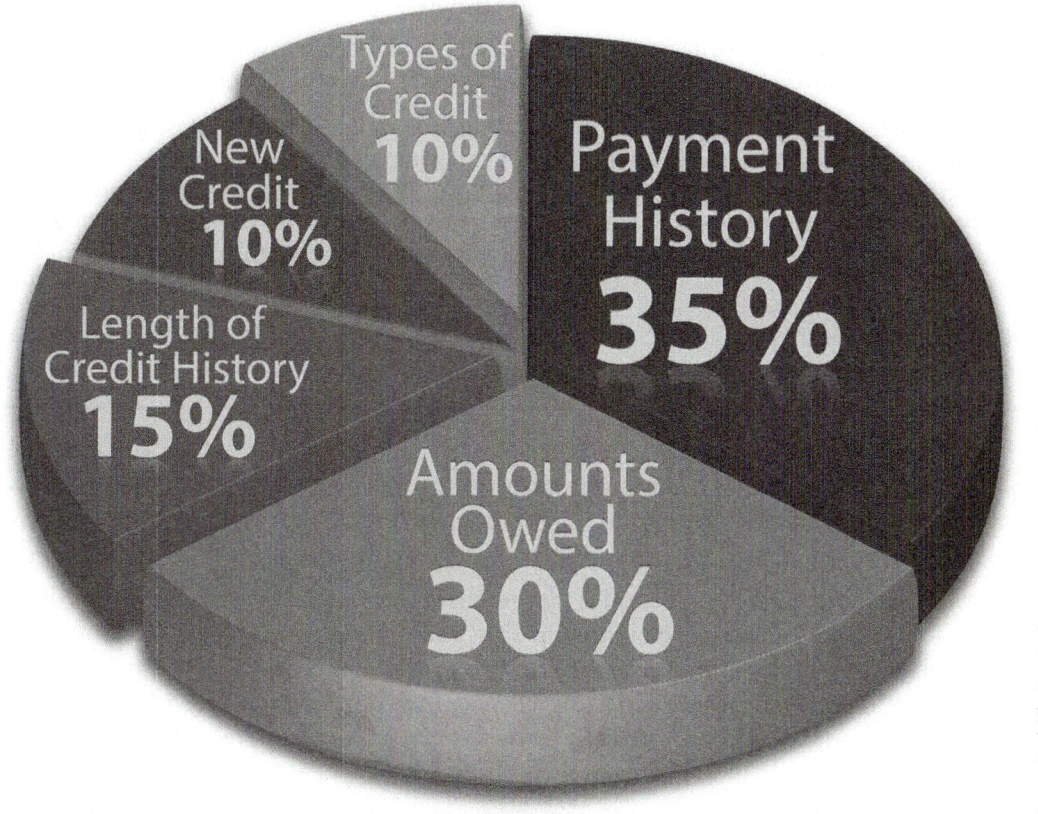

Figure 6:3 Most of the factors used in calculating an individual's credit score can be attributed to these categories.

Credit Report and Scoring Guidelines

There are several general rules that consumers may follow to optimize their credit scores.

Get Real

I have a friend, we will call him Chad. My friend grew up in a family with wealth. They paid cash for their cars, did not carry much debt, and even paid for their first home with cash. In fact, the only debt my friend carried was his monthly American Express bill, which was also paid in full every 30 days when he received the bill.

When my friend and his family of four were ready to purchase a larger home, they were able to pay cash but decided instead to keep some of their cash and take out a mortgage on the home. When Chad went to his bank to borrow money to purchase the home he ran into some issues. Even though he had enough cash to purchase the home outright, the bank was unwilling to lend him the money for the home without even more collateral than the home itself. He was even planning on a 50% down payment on the home, but the bank was still asking for more collateral and wanted him to pledge some of his cash as collateral. This would completely defeat the purpose of borrowing to purchase the home if he had to pledge his cash as collateral rather than keeping it for himself.

The bank cited two reasons for their uncertainty. One seemed fairly normal to Chad, the other was a complete surprise. The home was worth several million dollars, so the fact that the bank was categorizing the loan as atypical was not a surprise to him. The other factor they pointed to was his lack of credit history, and the fact that he had never borrowed a large sum of money. He explained to the bank that the reason he had not borrowed was his ability to pay in full for most items, but this did not sway the bank. When my friend began to look into his credit report, it quickly became apparent to him that his 700 FICO credit score was not as good as he would like. The reason: he only had one credit card on his history and a few other small items from long ago.

Chad learned quickly how important it is to properly manage your credit. In this case, not borrowing was actually a detriment, which was completely foreign to him. Using credit and using it responsibly are both important.

Eventually Chad paid cash for his home, and took out an auto loan for $10,000 against a car that he already owned free and clear. After a period in which he paid his car loan consistently and on time, the bank was willing to revisit the mortgage decision. His credit score and history had improved and they were willing to lend him the money with only his home as collateral. This was a great lesson in the fact that sometimes, what may actually seem like the best thing you could do financially may not be the best thing you can do for your credit report and score.

If you are planning on making a major purchase utilizing borrowed funds, it is always wise to manage your personal credit accordingly.

- **Utilization Rate:** This term refers to how much of the available credit is currently being used—in general the less available credit used the better. It is important for an individual to use their available lines of credit to keep them active, but a high utilization rate represents an over usage of their available credit.
- **Available Credit:** Many individuals consider the fact that they have no debt as a positive. Although it may be positive for your personal finances, it is often a negative for your credit score. To prove to lenders that a person is able to use credit responsibly, you must have available credit to use. Although this may seem strange to many, it shows that credit reporting agencies can only judge an individual on the information they have, and in many cases it can hurt an individual to not have enough records available for interpretation by the credit agency.
- **Sunset on Items:** Most items will stay on your credit report for 7 years. Some negative items such as repossession, bankruptcy, etc. will stay on your credit report for 10 years. If something negative is on your credit report for longer than it should be, make sure you dispute it as too old and have it removed.
- **Recent History:** The last 2 years of your credit history are more important than previous years. This can work for you or against you depending on what your most recent 2 years include.

- **Credit Cards:** Having credit cards from large reputable institutions is very important. Rather than holding many cards from department stores and other retail stores, it is better to have one or two cards from large institutions that have the potential to offer larger credit limits over time. This will allow an individual to maximize their available credit while only having a few credit cards.
- **Joint Credit:** Many people stumble and have a negative mark on their credit report due to cosigning or taking out joint credit with someone and then having something negative happen on the account. When choosing whom to open a line of credit with or who you are willing to help as a personal guarantor, it should be approached with caution. If having a credit account under an individual's name rather than jointly is a possibility, then it could be the best option to keep credit "personal" and not have joint credit accounts.

Figure 6:4 Many people stumble and have a negative mark on their credit due to cosigning or taking out joint credit.

- **Errors:** Many individuals have errors on their credit reports. Depending on which statistics you read, 20% to 90% of individuals have an error on their credit report. These errors are sometimes simple and have no negative effect—such as having the incorrect home address—but in other cases it could be an error in reporting incorrect late payments or an account that does not even belong to the individual. In extreme cases, errors could cause a person to be declined for a line of credit, when they in fact were more than eligible to receive the credit account. Errors should be reported to the credit reporting agency.
- **Diversity of Credit:** It is very important to have a diverse credit history including revolving credit (credit cards), installment loans, and real estate loans. By showing the ability to responsibly use different types of credit without any "black" marks on your credit, it decreases the likelihood a borrower will default in the future, which typically increases an individual's credit score.

A Note on Credit Scoring and the Effects of Different Actions

One of the most difficult things to understand and evaluate regarding credit and the scoring models is the fact that to improve one's credit it may be necessary to actually do something that temporarily lowers one's credit score. A great example of this is opening a new credit card. In the short term, it will shorten the overall length of a person's credit history and will show a new inquiry on their report. Both of these will negatively affect the score in most models. What will happen longer term though is that the individual will have more credit available, a more diverse credit history, and another account showing their ability to pay on time and use credit responsibly.

The best way to understand how this works is to use one of the many credit reporting sites that offer credit score simulation as part of their offering. This allows a person to go through many hypotheticals without unintentionally hurting their credit. Then, as a consumer, the decision can be made in an educated manner with knowledge of any consequences to one's actions. There are several simulation sites that can be accessed on the web, including: myfica.com, Equifax.com, Experian.com, and creditkarma.com. Application Worksheet 6:1, in Appendix II, provides an opportunity to actually walk through a credit score simulation.

Summary & Review

1. Although a credit bureau maintains a detailed file on your credit history, most use a single number to summarize your creditworthiness. What are the pros and cons of this practice? Why do credit bureaus use scoring?
2. What is the single most important consideration used in most scoring models?
3. In the event that you find an error in your credit file, can you do anything about it? What?
4. What are some things you can do to improve your credit score?

Cards, Cards, Cards

With so many cards to choose from and use, it is important to highlight and understand the distinctive groups of cards and their characteristics. Knowledge of how each works, their benefits, and drawbacks, will help you to choose which card(s) is best for you.

Credit Cards

Credit cards have grown in popularity since their inception. Most households carry at least one card if not multiple credit cards. As with any credit, responsible use can be a beneficial financial tool. Many individuals use their cards often but pay off their balance in full each month. These users enjoy the convenience, protection, and other features of their cards, without getting into serious debt.

In general, purchases made with these cards are the most protected. Often, if a purchase is made fraudulently, the card issuer will immediately refund the amount of the purchase and simply send a replacement card to the consumer. The most popular credit card brand names are Visa, MasterCard, Discover, and American Express, though small competitors do exist. Financial institutions such as large banks tend to affiliate with one of these card companies and use their branding along with their own to market and service credit cards. Card usage is replacing traditional forms of payment such as checks and cash.

Banks and credit card companies spend astronomical amounts of money annually on marketing to encourage consumers to sign up and use their cards. The industry touts characteristics such as fraud protection, financial flexibility, and even ego to encourage use of their cards. These driving market forces make responsible use even more important when you choose to use a credit card as a form of payment.

Establishing Credit 115

Figure 6:5 Credit cards have grown in popularity since their inception.

Exhibit 6:4 Trends in Noncash Payments by Number and Type of Transaction

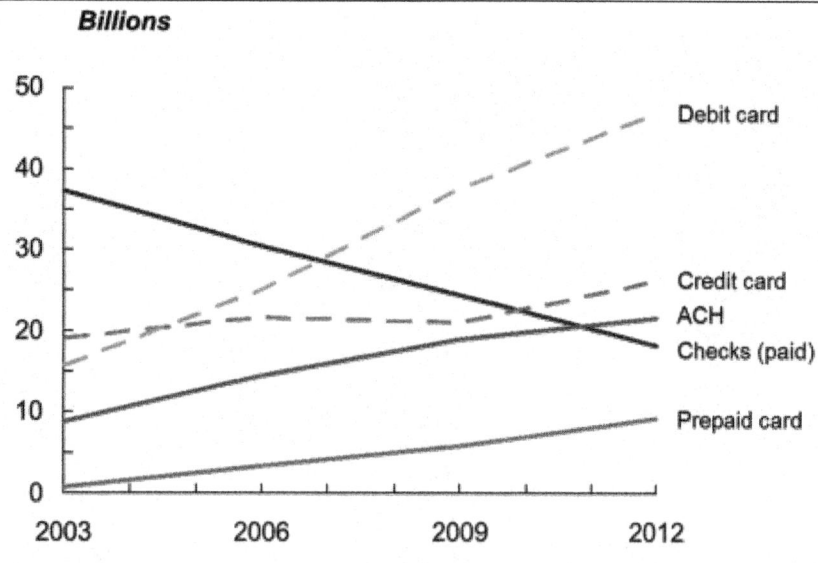

Debit, credit, and prepaid card trends include general-purpose and private-label payments.

Debit Cards

These types of cards are typically issued by banks and are directly related to an account with a financial institution. As with credit cards, the consumer is not typically responsible for fraudulent purchases when they are properly reported to the issuer of the card.

These cards are also often affiliated and cobranded with a company such as Visa or MasterCard, though their use is directly related to the money on deposit in an account with a financial firm. As implied by their name, these cards take the amount of a purchase made and debit it directly against the funds on deposit with the financial institution, typically a bank or credit union.

Gift Cards

Often referred to as "stored value cards" or "prepaid cards," Gift Cards are a way of storing prepaid value on a card similar to a debit or credit card. These cards are issued by most popular retailers and the amount of money stored on the card can be exchanged for goods and services at the participating retailer.

The money put on these cards can be redeemed in many ways. Gift Cards can be purchased like other goods at a retail store and used to buy goods at either that particular store, or in some cases, at many stores. These cards are also often branded with Visa, MasterCard, American Express, or another card brand.

There is risk in using these types of cards. If the card is issued by a company that later becomes insolvent, the value may be characterized as debt owed by the company. If you hold a card from a company that becomes insolvent, you then become a creditor of the company and the value stored on the card would then be subject to the laws dictating liquidation of a failing company.

Travel & Entertainment Cards (T&E Cards)

The most popular Travel & Entertainment cards in the marketplace are the Diners Club International and American Express cards. These cards, although often associated with credit, are in fact a form of payment that must be repaid in full at the end of each month.

Figure 6:6 Travel & Entertainment cards are in fact a form of payment that must be repaid in full at the end of each month.

American Express also issues credit cards, but the first cards issued by American Express were cards that were to be fully repaid each month.

> ### Summary & Review
> 1. What are the four major types of cards available in today's marketplace?
> 2. Which type of card makes the most sense for you? Why?
> 3. Why do you think cards are becoming such a popular means of payment? Can you see any downside to their popularity?

How Much Credit Can I (or Should I) Use?

Often referred to as one's credit capacity, the amount a person is qualified to borrow from financial institutions is very important. The two most used measures involved in this qualification are the Debt-to-Income Ratio and the Debt-to-Equity Ratio. These are used by potential lenders to evaluate how much an individual can borrow.

These calculations can also be useful to consumers trying to measure or limit their debts. The formulas for both ratios are as follows:

- Debt-to-Income Ratio: Divide total required monthly debt payments by total monthly income
- Debt-to-Equity Ratio: Divide total liabilities by net worth

In some cases, mortgages and the value of personal residences are not included in these ratios, whereas in other cases they may be included

Although most of this chapter is devoted to personal credit, it is important to note that both of these ratios are also used in evaluating a business's ability to borrow and repay their debts.

Some Closing Thoughts

As this chapter describes, credit management can be a complex and daunting task. It is always important to begin with the knowledge of how your actions affect your credit. Remember the 4 (or 5) Cs when considering borrowing and consider how a potential lender will look at you long before actually applying to borrow.

By being proactive about building a credit history and improving credit scores, an individual can ensure that, at the various stages in life, they have the ability to borrow when needed and at the levels they wish to borrow. Responsible use of credit can put you in the upper tier of potential borrowers by making you much more attractive to financial institutions. These factors will help when borrowing money, but will also affect a number of other aspects of your personal financial well-being, including such things as auto insurance rates, access to online markets, even job prospects.

> ### Summary & Review
> 1. Explain how the debt-to-income ratio is calculated? What does this measure?
> 2. Explain how the debt-to-equity ratio is calculated? What does this measure?
> 3. What condition is evidenced by a rising debt-to-income ratio? By a rising debt-to-equity ratio?
> 4. Why is building positive credit so important?

Chapter 7
Borrowing & Debt Management

Contributed by Ryan O'shea. Copyright © kendal Hunt Publishing Company

Chapter Objectives

1. Be aware of those times when borrowing may be desirable, and those times when it is not desirable.
2. Develop an appreciation of the importance of debt management, not only to a persons' personal financial plan, but to his individual well-being.
3. Understand what it means when we borrow, and how we sometimes underestimate the impact of borrowings on our budgeting efforts and our credit profile.
4. Know the various components that affect the cost of credit. Be aware of the three ways in which interest may be calculated on closed ended credit.
5. Know the three ways in which interest may be calculated on open ended credit.
6. Cite various ways that might enable a person to lower their cost of borrowing.
7. Be aware of various sources of borrowing, including those sources that are likely to be the lowest cost and those sources that represent higher cost alternatives.

Chapter Objectives

8. Understand the warning signs of over-indebtedness, and what might be done in the event one or more of those warning signs appear on your radar.
9. Be familiar with current bankruptcy laws, including the differences between Chapter 7 and Chapter 13 bankruptcy petitions.
10. Understand the risks and rewards associated with borrowing and debt management.

A Lesson from History

Toward the end of World War II when the Allies were closing in on Germany—the Soviet Union from the east and the United States, Great Britain, and their allies from the West—entire countries were being overrun as Germany collapsed in on itself. Where the Soviet Union overran a country, it quickly set up a puppet government and began to establish control over that country. As a result, a number of nations found themselves within the Soviet Block, including Albania, Bulgaria, Czechoslovakia, East Germany, Hungary, Poland, Romania, and Yugoslavia. Soviet influence over these countries was not just political, but was economic as well, and a brand of Communist Socialism was imposed.

Under socialism, their economies were subject to planning by the government, and all levels of production and distribution were under government control. Although the alleged goal of socialism was to spread economic well-being equally among all of the people, the actual result was an ongoing failure to provide even a modest standard of living for most citizens.

Initially, this failure was obscured by substantial borrowings from the Soviet Union. Later, when the Soviet Union was unwilling to continue to bankroll these countries, they turned to Western banks for loans. The borrowings were used to buy goods and services that would help bridge the gap between what the socialist economies could actually produce and what was being provided to the people. Margaret Thatcher, former Prime Minister of Great Britain, once remarked that: "Socialism is a wonderful idea . . . everyone loves it . . . until the money runs out." Finally, in 1989, a wave of revolutions swept across the Eastern Bloc nations, and the political and economic landscape of Europe was changed.

Most historians point to the Ronald Reagan administration stance of "negotiation from a position of strength," and to the Mikhail Gorbachev administration position of Glasnost and Perestroika (openness and economic restructuring) as prime reasons for the change. And those factors certainly played a vital role. But the reality of it was that these countries were simply broke. They had no money left . . . the banks would not lend them anymore . . . and the peoples' standard of living under socialism was going from bad to worse.

When is Borrowing Not a Good Idea

As we begin our discussion of Credit Management, it is important to understand that there are times when borrowing may be a good idea.

- If borrowings are used to expand the means of production, or increase return through careful use of leverage, such borrowing may enhance future capability and profitability.
- If borrowings are used to improve educational capability and expand vocational credentials, such borrowing may position a person for better economic potential over the course of their life.
- If borrowings are used to procure a major asset such as a home or a car, which will provide shelter and transportation needs while the asset is being repaid, such borrowings may allow an improved standard of living on a longer-term basis, and an even better standard of living once such borrowings are repaid.

122   Cash & Debt Management

Figure 7:1 Finally, in 1989, a wave of revolutions swept across the Eastern Block nations, and the political and economic landscape of Europe was changed.

However, as our lesson from history reminds us, there are times when borrowing is definitely not a good idea.

- If borrowings are used to fund current expenditures, resulting in higher levels of accumulated debt with nothing to show for it, such borrowings should be avoided. This is not only true of individuals, but should be an abiding tenant of businesses and governments as well.
- If borrowings are used to permit us to "keeping up with the Joneses," fostering a standard of living that is beyond our current ability to produce, such borrowings encourage us to live a lie and should be avoided.
- If borrowings are used to repay other borrowings, with the end result that we have not reduced overall indebtedness but simply stirred things around a bit, such borrowings should be avoided. A notable exception to this is when we refinance a higher interest loan into a lower interest loan. But be careful, sometimes the end result is that the process simply opens up borrowing capacity—inviting us to borrow more not less.

Get Real

I am often asked if it wouldn't be a good idea to maintain a mortgage on a persons' home, which is often at a relatively low rate of interest, rather than paying it off. After all, the interest portion of any mortgage payment is tax deductible, and the money that would have gone to paying off the mortgage might be invested in the stock market or other attractive securities, producing a positive spread.

Although there is some appeal to this argument, I have chosen to pay off my mortgage rather than use those funds for investing. There are three major considerations to this decision.

First, the tax advantage cited applies only as far as a persons' tax bracket. For example, if someone is in the 25% tax bracket, the tax benefit amounts to only 25% of the interest paid. They are still paying 75% of the interest expense out of pocket.

Second, the notion that the money can be better invested in the stock market or some other security assumes that the investment selected will perform better than the interest rate being paid on the mortgage. In this case,

> they are literally betting the ranch that this will be true. Sometimes such investments perform as expected … other times they do not. Remember, the chosen investment must perform better than the interest rate being paid on the mortgage, or the spread is negative.
>
> Third, in my case a certain peace of mind comes with knowing that my home is paid; that my family will have that asset no matter what. That assurance goes a long way toward providing a level of certainty in the face of volatile markets and fortunes.

It certainly comes as no surprise when we review statistics on the contributing causes of debt default, to learn that the number one cause of default is excessive use of credit. This is a much more common contributor than other factors, such as loss of employment or medical issues.

Figure 7:2 It certainly comes as no surprise when we review statistics on the contributing causes of debt default, to learn that the number one cause of default is excessive use of credit.

Summary & Review

1. What lessons can we learn from the history of Eastern European countries under Soviet control, as to the role of government borrowings in a nations' economy?
2. When might debt be useful to a personal financial plan?
3. On what occasions should we avoid debt?
4. As part of your personal financial plan, do you anticipate buying a home and paying off the mortgage, or do you expect to have a mortgage payment your entire life?
5. What is the number one cause of debt default?

What Does It Mean When We Borrow

In the United States today, borrowing has been made easy. It has been estimated by one advertising firm that the number of credit card solicitations that are sent in the mail amount to 11 per year for every man, woman, and child in this country. Furniture stores tout that you don't have to pay anything for 12 months, and merchandizers of all kinds announce that: "your credit is good here." The theme seems to be "buy now and pay later," and perhaps we will be more inclined to purchase their product if we can delay payment. And therein is the problem!

Any borrowing is a claim on your future income. That claim comes in two parts. First, the cost of the good or service needs to eventually be paid. Even if a store tells you they won't start charging interest until some later date, or you pledge to pay your credit card in full with the next billing—the principal is still due. Second, most of the time there is a charge for the money borrowed. This is called interest, and it can be relentless. Interest never sleeps, does not take weekends off, and knows no vacation. If you are paying interest, it is typically added to the cost of your purchase, resulting in an increase in the total cost over time. Sometimes we fall under the notion that we should buy now while the item is on sale, thereby saving us some money. Yet, if we have to borrow to effect the purchase, the interest cost of that borrowing may well offset any savings.

As your borrowings effectively reduce the amount of future income that you have discretion over, lenders are careful to note how much of tomorrows check you have already promised to someone else. Credit Bureaus monitor your debt, as well as your repayment history, as was discussed in Chapter 6. To the extent you have little or no debt, you have more discretion over how you will use your future income. As you add debt, and the debt payment and interest cost requirements, you reduce your discretionary income.

The Cost of Debt

The Truth in Lending Law of 1969 requires lenders to disclose the cost of credit in both a dollar amount and as a percentage. The dollar amount is typically referred to as the Finance Charge, which is the total dollar amount paid to use credit. This includes the interest amount paid on borrowings, and also includes any service charges, credit insurance premiums, or other related costs. The percentage is typically referred to as the Annual Percentage Rate or APR, and represents the percentage cost of credit on an annual basis. When you are shopping around for the best borrowing terms, these two numbers—the Finance Charge and the Annual Percentage Rate—can give you a good basis for comparisons.

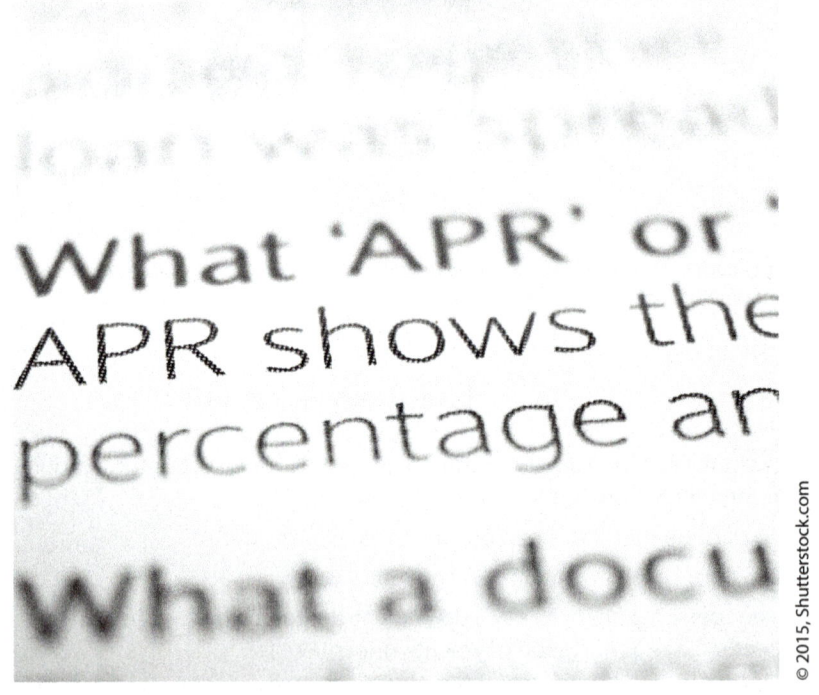

Figure 7:3 The percentage is typically referred to as the Annual Percentage Rate or APR, and represents the percentage cost of credit on an annual basis.

In Chapter 6, we noted the two broad kinds of credit: Closed Ended and Open Ended. Both kinds of credit calculate interest by considering the same three variables we introduced in Chapter 1.

The Amount: The Quantity or Principal of Money Borrowed.
   Higher Amounts Mean More Interest Paid/Lower Amounts Mean Less Interest Paid.

The Rate: The Percent Return or Yield.
   Higher Rates Mean More Interest Paid/Lower Rates Mean Less Interest Paid.

The Term: The Length of Time the Borrowing is Outstanding.
   Longer Term Means More Interest Paid/Shorter Term Means Less Interest Paid.

Put simply, how much are you borrowing; what interest rate are you paying; and how long will your borrowings remain outstanding. For purposes of our examples following, let's assume that you wish to borrow $1,000, the lender is quoting an Annual Percentage Rate or APR of 6%, and you expect to be able to repay your borrowings in 1 year.

Amount (A) = $1,000
Rate (R) = 6%
Term (T) = 1 Year

If you are borrowing under a Closed Ended Credit facility, there are three ways in which the cost of credit may be calculated.

1. <u>Simple Interest</u> is the Rate computed on the Amount borrowed for the Term outstanding, or Amount × Rate × Time.

   Given our example: $1,000 × 0.06 × 1 = $60

2. <u>Simple Interest on the Declining Balance</u> is often used when more than one payment is made on the loan. Sometimes referred to as the <u>Declining Balance Method,</u> the calculation is still Amount × Rate × Time, but it is on the balance outstanding after the previous payment is made. If you are paying down the amount by $100 each month, at the end of month two you will have only $800 in principal outstanding.

   Accordingly: $800 × 0.06 × 1/12 = $4 of interest will be due in the ensuing month instead of $5 each month, because you have repaid a portion of the original amount.

   In practice, most Closed Ended Credit that involves a series of payments will calculate a payment schedule with regular equal payments. The result is that the amount of principal being paid rises each month as the amount of interest assessed declines.

3. <u>Add-on Interest</u> is a method of calculating credit cost, which does not give allowance for repayments made. Given our example and assuming that, at a repayment schedule of $100 per month, this loan would be repaid in 10 months, the Add-on Interest formula would be Amount × Rate × Time.

   $1,000 × 0.06 × 10/12 = $50

   You would be paying $50 in interest over a 10-month period, even though you are making regular payments to principal of $100 per month. The Add-on Interest formula is not uncommon. If you think it unfair that you would not be given credit for principal payments made, you may want to make sure that your lender does not use this method.

If you are borrowing under an <u>Open Ended Credit</u> facility, there are also three ways in which the cost of credit may be calculated.

1. The <u>Adjusted Balance Method</u> is a simple interest calculation where interest is assessed after subtracting payments made during the billing period. The calculation is:

   Amount Due – Payments Made = Net Amount Outstanding × Rate × Time

2. The <u>Previous Balance Method</u> is similarly a simple interest calculation, but here interest is assessed on the entire amount borrowed, without giving credit for payments made during the billing period. The calculation is:

   Amount Borrowed × Rate × Time

3. The <u>Average Daily Balance Method</u> applies simple interest to the average daily balances for the billing period. The calculation is:

   Average Daily Balances × Rate × Time

In the event that you do not pay off the entire balance by the due date, most Open Ended Credit facilities will calculate proportional finance charges from the date the credit was extended, not from the date when payment is due. This means that unless the balance is repaid on or before the due date, the interest clock dials back to the date you signed the charge, providing the lender with upward of a months' worth of interest.

Figure 7:4 Unless the balance is repaid on or before the due date, the interest clock dials back to the date you signed the charge, providing the lender with upward of a months' worth of interest.

There has been a change in the law regarding minimum payment due. Previously, it was not unusual for credit card companies to charge a minimum payment that was less than the interest assessed for the month. This meant that if an individual habitually paid only the minimum, he would actually find the total balance due increasing over time as the interest charged each month exceeded his payment. Now, credit card companies are required to collect a "reasonable" portion of the principal, together with total interest accrued, as the minimum requirement each month. Still, if an individual pays only the minimum requirement, it will take a very long time to repay any borrowings.

Summary & Review

1. In what two ways must lenders disclose the cost of borrowing? How can this information benefit a potential borrower?
2. Name the three methods of calculating interest charges on a Closed Ended Loan? As the borrower, which one would you prefer?
3. Name the three methods of calculating interest charges on an Open Ended Loan? Which one would you prefer?
4. As an Open Ended Borrower, why is it particularly advantageous for you to repay your charges—in full—by the date due?

Better Access to Borrowings

In the previous chapter, we discussed the importance of maintaining good credit to maximize your credit score and insure a favorable reception in the event you needed to borrow. Are there other things you might do that would improve the likelihood of a favorable reception and keep the costs of borrowing at a minimum? Consider the following:

Exhibit 7:1 Reducing Lender Risk

- ☐ Increasing the size of the down payment will reduce the credit risk to the lender, and make the loan more secure from his standpoint.
- ☐ Reducing the term of the loan generally results in a lower interest rate, as the risks inherent in longer-term lending are minimized.
- ☐ Providing security such as collateral will give the lender a viable fallback in the event that you fail to repay the loan as promised.
- ☐ Applying for a variable rate loan, which gives the lender a chance to adjust interest rates in the event market rates increase substantially, will provide an avenue to reduce his interest rate risk. (We do not recommend this approach when applying for a mortgage loan.)

If you find you need to borrow, consider first the least expensive loans: Those that may be obtained from parents or family members; those that may be fully secured by cash or other assets; and those that may be cosigned by an individual having stronger credit. A brief word on cosigning. If you decide to approach someone to cosign a loan for you, or if you are ever asked to be a cosigner, remember that approximately 75% of all cosigners are eventually asked to repay the loan. This would be bad news if you were the borrower, but even worse news if you had cosigned for someone else. Before you do this, make sure that you can repay the loan . . . and that the indebtedness will not unduly hurt the credit standing of the cosigner.

> ### Get Real
>
> A number of years ago, with several members of the family borrowing heavily as they struggled through doctoral programs, it was suggested that the family establish its own bank . . . call it a Family Bank. This entity could make loans to family members for such things as schooling, at a reduced rate of interest, and under terms that might be more favorable than available from conventional financing sources. An agreement was prepared, and with the first deposit of $20, a Family Bank was born. That was about 40 years ago, and today the Family Bank is alive and well and helping its members with their financial needs.
>
> If you think that such an institution might benefit you and your family, consider the following essential ingredients.
>
> First, it makes no sense for everyone to line up at the borrowing window if there is no money in the till. There will be need of members of the family who are in a position to make deposits into the Family Bank. Those individuals are entitled to a return, and whatever rate of interest is charged to the borrowers should serve as a return to the depositors.
>
> Second, you will need a manager. This would be someone inside the family who is both willing and capable of providing loan statements, audits, tax returns, and generally overseeing the ongoing operations of the institution. In our case, we requested and received an Internal Revenue Service EIN (Employer Identification Number), so that we could report the results of the Family Bank separate from the income tax return of any of the family members. Each year, the collective earnings of the Family Bank are reported, and then dispersed to the depositors in proportion to the size of their deposits. The Family Bank itself does not pay taxes, as any income flows through to the depositors.
>
> Third, you need a collection of individuals within the family who will regard any indebtedness to the Family Bank as an absolute economic imperative. If their version of integrity is something like: "Oh, it's only a debt to

Continued

the family . . . they will understand if I miss this payment," then you will have a problem. In this instance, the Family Bank has the potential to be a destructive force within the family, rather than the unifying and strengthening force it is meant to be.

In our case, we limited membership in the Family Bank to two generations, inviting the third generation to form their own family banks if they wanted to. This way, the number of individuals involved was relatively small, and their relationships stronger.

Standard loans might be obtained from commercial banks and credit unions. To be eligible to receive loans from these institutions, you generally need a FICO Score in the 700 range, though you might be able to work with a lower score if the loan is strengthened by a larger down payment or collateral.

Figure 7:5 To be eligible to receive loans from commercial banks and credit unions, you generally need a FICO Score in the 700 range.

For those with lower scores, loans are available from finance companies, pawn stores, certain retailers, and banks, but these loans will be more expensive. Consumer Finance Companies specialize in personal installment loans and second mortgages.

Summary & Review

1. Name several things you might do to reduce lender risk and improve the likelihood that you will get the desired loan on more favorable terms.
2. Do you think that the concept of a Family Bank makes sense for you and your family at the present time? Why?
3. What sources of credit do you use? What is the rate that you pay for your sources of borrowing?

Special Types of Consumer Loans

Student Loans are a special type of unsecured loan with relatively low, federally subsidized interest rates, which are available to individuals pursuing a post high school degree. The two most popular student loans are Federal Direct/Stafford Loans and the PLUS Direct/PLUS Loans. The structure of student loans varies widely, and is being revised frequently by both the government and lenders. In most cases, the lender is either the college or a financial institution such as a bank, and the borrower is either the student themselves or the parents of a student. The majority of student loans do not require repayment to begin until after the student graduates—generally 6 or 12 months following graduation. A few student loans require cosigners.

Home Equity Loans are a special type of secured loan that utilizes the equity in your home as collateral for the loan. Home equity loans are a type of second mortgage on your home, and become a lien on your house just like a mortgage. Like the mortgage, the interest payment under a home equity loan is tax deductible up to certain limits. Although the intent of a home equity loan is to provide a source of funding for home repairs and upgrades, the loan proceeds can, in fact, be used for any purpose. The home equity loan is a closed ended loan, and specific repayment terms begin immediately.

Figure 7:6 Home Equity Loans are a special type of secured loan that utilizes the equity in your home as collateral for a loan.

Payday Loans are a short-term advance extended to individuals who need funds before their paycheck arrives. Such loans are extended for a period of days or weeks, against repayment from the anticipated paycheck. The cost of these loans comes in the form of a fee, which may seem nominal but in reality is anything but that. For example, if an individual has the need of funds a week before payday, and agrees to pay $25 for a $500 advance, consider the effective rate of interest being paid. The $25 fee amounts to 5% . . . for a week! That works out to approximately 260% per annum. Obviously, payday loans should be avoided.

Danger Signals

Warning signs of over-indebtedness come long before a collision with creditors. Exhibit 7:2 presents some of those warning signs.

Exhibit 7:2 Warning Signs of Over-indebtedness

		Yes	No
1.	Are you borrowing to pay for items you used to pay for with cash?		X
2.	Is an increasing percentage of your income going to pay debts?		X
3.	Are you paying bills with money earmarked for something else?	X	
4.	Are you tapping your savings to pay current bills?	X	
5.	Is your savings cushion (which should be at least three months' take-home pay) inadequate?		X
6.	Can you make only the minimum payments on your open ended credit?		X
7.	Are you extending repayment schedules; paying in 60 days bills you once paid in 30?		X
8.	Are you near or at the limit on your lines of credit?		X
9.	Do you take out a new loan to pay off an existing loan?		X
10.	Are you unsure about how much you owe?		X
11.	Are you chronically late in paying your bills?		X
12.	Are you being threatened with repossession or cancellation of your credit cards?		X

If you answered yes to any of questions 1 through 5, it is time to put on the breaks. If you answered yes to any of questions 6 through 10, there is a serious squall on the horizon and you should take steps to change course. Discontinue credit use and revise your budget to include significant debt repayments. A yes answer to questions 11 or 12 points to serious trouble. Credit counseling help may be essential at this point.

> **Summary & Review**
>
> 1. What advantages and disadvantages do you see in a Home Equity Loan?
> 2. As you review the warning signs of over-indebtedness, do you find that you have answered yes to any of the questions? Which ones? What are you going to do about it?
> 3. How can a person avoid having debt problems in their personal financial plan?

When We Face Financial Difficulties

Sometimes our financial condition goes sour; we may feel trapped and long for a way out of the morass. When our debt burden becomes unmanageable, or we face unemployment, a medical emergency has sapped our net worth, or we are involved in a costly divorce, we may feel destitute. If that should ever happen, and you are feeling overwhelmed, consider the option of credit counseling.

Figure 7:7 When our debt burden becomes unmanageable, consider the option of credit counseling.

There are many credit counseling organizations, some of which are nonprofit. (This does not mean that they don't charge a fee—only that they do not expect to make a profit at the end of the day.) One of the most notable credit counseling services is Consumer Credit Counseling Service, which is a local nonprofit organization affiliated with the National Foundation for Consumer Credit. Counseling services are also available from universities, churches, military bases, banks, and credit unions.

Credit counseling can help in several ways. First, they can help cut through the cloud that may be building in your mind, pointing out where the problems lie and suggesting ways of resolving them. Second, they can contact your lenders and try to work out a modified payment plan. In the event that you find yourself behind in payments, it is always a good idea to contact the lender before they contact you. This initiative on your part will evidence good faith, and go a long way toward encouraging them to work with you rather than taking a hard-nosed tact against you. If you wait until the creditor has contacted you, they will already be in a bad mood, and less willing to work with you. Third, they can suggest ways in which you might structure your finances to avoid continued problems in the future.

Bankruptcy

You have probably seen those ads offering to handle a bankruptcy filing for you, which promise a fresh start financially. Actually, nothing could be further from the truth. Bankruptcy is a legally sanctioned renouncement of your debt . . . and the promises of repayment you made when you incurred that debt. Financial institutions do not view Bankruptcy as a fresh start, but as a major black spot on your character.

Most information on your credit report can be reported for 7 years. A bankruptcy can be reported for at least 10 years—so it is very serious. Moreover, a bankruptcy does not occur automatically with the legal filing,

132 **Cash & Debt Management**

but is a decision that a bankruptcy judge must make. Bankruptcy proceedings are under the exclusive jurisdiction of Federal Courts, which administer the U.S. Bankruptcy Code.

Figure 7:8 Bankruptcy proceedings are under the exclusive jurisdiction of Federal Courts, which administer the U.S. Bankruptcy Code.

Bankruptcy laws in the United States do change from time to time. It seems that there is a pendulum that may swing toward more lenient allowances one year, only to swing back to stricter allowances a few years later. At the moment, bankruptcy laws make it more difficult to wipe out certain types of debt, especially for middle and upper income households. Most households earning more than their state's median income level now have to file under Chapter 13 of the U.S. Bankruptcy Code. The court will apply a strict means test to determine who is eligible to file under Chapter 7. Nevertheless, more than 70% of Americans who file for bankruptcy do so under Chapter 7 of the U.S. Bankruptcy Code.

Under Chapter 7, a petitioners assets are forfeited to the court (with certain exceptions), which then sells those assets and repays creditors from the proceeds. Though creditors are seldom paid in full, an order is then issued preventing a creditor from seeking additional monies from the debtor. Under Chapter 13, which a debtor may pursue only if he has regular income, the debtor is allowed to keep his property and his debts are repaid under a court ordered repayment plan over an extended period of time—usually 3 to 5 years. However, failure to make the debt payments as ordered under Chapter 13 can result in foreclosure and repossession.

Under both Chapter 7 and Chapter 13, there are a number of requirements that a debtor must satisfy in the filing process.

First, under changes to the law effective October, 2006, debtors are required to receive credit counseling at their own expense 6 months before filing. The goal is to encourage consumers to pay back debts rather than simply walk away. The revisions to the law also require consumers to take a financial management course (Personal Finance?) after filing for bankruptcy.

Second, the petition filed by the debtor must include:

- Schedule of assets and liabilities
- Schedule of income and expenditures
- Schedule of financial affairs—including all debts and creditors
- Certain other financial information including pay stubs, tax returns, and leases
- Certificate of Credit Counseling including any debt repayment plan derived from the credit counseling
- Payment of Filing Fees that typically total $300–$500

Once the filing has been received, the court will appoint a Case Trustee who is responsible for administering the discovery phase of the proceeding and making a recommendation to the court as to disposition. In approximately 21–50 days after appointing the Case Trustee, a meeting is held between the debtor and the creditors, in which the debtor is placed under oath and questioned by the Case Trustee and the creditors. Creditors are able to review all items filed, and are able to challenge any discrepancies.

The Case Trustee then makes a recommendation to the bankruptcy court, and a federal judge rules on the petition. As you can see, the process is not a simple one, and the end result can be difficult.

Summary & Review

1. In the event that you find yourself in financial difficulty, credit counseling may be an option to consider. What can credit counseling offer?
2. Individuals filing for bankruptcy may petition under Chapter 7 or Chapter 13 of the U.S. Bankruptcy code. What are the primary differences between these two Chapters?
3. A bankruptcy petition involves a filing with a U.S. Federal Court. What information must be included in a bankruptcy filing?
4. What is the role of the Case Trustee in a bankruptcy proceeding?

A Word of Caution

You might characterize our attitude toward borrowing as one of caution. Although there are circumstances when incurring debt may be a reasonable decision, the financial landscape is littered with those who took on more debt than they could service, and found themselves unable (or unwilling) to live up to the promises they made when they borrowed money. When that happens credit scores fall, the credit report is tarnished, and it may take years to recover financially.

You have spent a great deal of time and effort preparing a budget that will allow you to meet your obligations and reach your goals. You have carefully structured your finances so as to successfully manage this important aspect of your life. Be careful not to let over-indebtedness compromise all of that. From the standpoint of deliberate management, Closed Ended Credit, with its specified repayment terms, is easier to account for in a budget than Open Ended Credit, with its more variable repayment terms.

Figure 7:9 You might characterize our attitude toward borrowing as one of caution.

With respect to Open Ended Credit especially, be careful when you pull out the plastic that you have the wherewithal to meet the ensuing indebtedness. There is in the mind of many people a misconception that needs to be addressed here. You have probably gone out to dinner with someone who paid for the meal with a credit card, maybe commenting as they pulled out the card that they would pay for it. Actually, a credit card pays for nothing. It only borrows money to meet a current obligation. Payment comes later when the statement is received. Nothing can be more damaging to your finances than a credit card, which can all too easily pull an end run around your budget. Can we say that again. Nothing can be more damaging to your finances than a credit card, which can all too easily pull an end run around your budget.

Better Buying

Chapter 8
Smart Buying

"It's hard to call it a 'smart watch' when I feel stupid for buying it."

Chapter Objectives

1. Understand the difference between needs and wants, and the difference between deliberate purchasing designed to satisfy a need, and shopping "for the fun of it."
2. Be aware of the opportunity costs—the trade-offs—involved in the buying decision. Understand the nature of impulse buying, and its attendant hazards.
3. Identify the five steps involved in any purchase, and how each step can contribute to the overall success of this aspect of your financial program.
4. Be aware of changing buying patterns throughout society, and the emerging role of catalogs and the Internet. Understand the advantages and disadvantages of various buying mediums.
5. Note the telltale signs of scams, particularly in web-based purchasing.
6. Consider various ideas for price efficient purchasing, including an understanding of unit pricing. Be aware of a methodology by which larger quantities can be purchased at lower cost per unit—the Pantry Plan.
7. Understand the nature of guarantees—including the explicit warranty and the implicit warranty. Note the usefulness of the service contract that may be offered as part of a purchase.
8. Identify the steps involved in resolving a dispute with a seller. Be aware of the difference between a mediator and an arbitrator, and when it may be appropriate to involve a third party in a dispute.
9. Be able to describe the protocol for bringing a complaint in small claims court.

Is It Need or Want

When the subject of buying comes up, most of us are quick to put on our shopping shoes. This knee-jerk reaction underscores two very separate and distinct contexts to the buying decision. In the first place, we recognize that there are occasions when we purchase something to satisfy a need or solve a problem. In this context, buying something is the quickest, or the easiest, or the surest way to resolve a situation, and so we embark on a deliberate effort toward making the best purchase possible.

However, there is an entirely separate context for the buying decision, and that is the emotionally fulfilling activity of shopping. Some people will say that they don't enjoy shopping, but name a product or service that they are into, and they are as willing to put on their shopping shoes as anyone else. In this context, it doesn't even matter that there is no pressing need or problem to solve . . . it is enough that we can shop around and maybe buy something just because it strikes our fancy. Can you see a potential problem in this activity?

Actually, there are a couple of potential dangers. The first is financial. To the extent that shopping for nonessentials—just for the fun of it—occurs more and more often, it is likely to result in a strain on our budget. Such shopping is not limited to stores, but might include going to restaurants—which is increasingly cited by consumer research studies as a significant source of overspending, or entertainment expenditures.

The second potential danger is emotional. Researchers have found that across cultures around the world, being able to obtain such basics as food, clothing, and shelter produces high levels of long-term satisfaction. Spending money beyond those basic needs, however, does not generally increase the level of long-term satisfaction. For example, one study reported that the average life-satisfaction level for the Inughuit people of northern Greenland was virtually indistinguishable from that of American billionaires, despite the enormous difference in material possessions and wealth. How could that be?

Research has consistently shown that when we purchase something we want but don't really need, we generally experience a short-term feeling of satisfaction (a chocolate high), followed by a relatively swift return to our earlier satisfaction level. In other words, just about everything we buy that we do not really need is rapidly taken for granted. Living on such a consumer treadmill, with its short-term highs, can actually run counter to our longer-term emotional well-being.

Evidence from studies in positive psychology strongly suggests that in contrast to getting caught up in the culture of wanting it all, the practice of simplifying our lives can lead to greater financial stability and emotional satisfaction. One researcher summed it up by saying that when there are too many competing demands on our time, our attention, or our finances, our ability to be present "in the moment" is diminished—and with it our ability to appreciate and enjoy the experience. We are like the Greyhound race dog chasing the mechanical rabbit around the track. We have this notion that when we finally catch the rabbit we will be happy. The problem is . . . we never catch the rabbit.

Figure 8:1 We have this notion that when we finally catch the rabbit we will be happy. The problem is . . . we never catch the rabbit.

Opportunity Costs

We have discussed the concept of opportunity costs before. There are several trade-offs associated with every buying decision that might be considered. Perhaps Exhibit 8:1, reflecting the pros and cons of a number of different considerations, will help frame those opportunity costs.

Keeping in mind the various trade-offs involved, can help you make a better buying decision. Of course, many of us give in to Impulse Buying from time to time—those unplanned purchases that occur on a whim. Although the occasional shirt or candy bar will probably not break the bank, be aware that repeated impulse buying, particularly for larger ticket items, can be a destructive behavior pattern with negative financial and emotional consequences.

A Game Plan for Buying

This chapter deals with smart buying. Accordingly, let's explore a specific game plan that can help you to be more successful in this important aspect of personal finance.

Exhibit 8:1 Opportunity Costs of Buying

	Advantage	Disadvantage
Higher Price for Quality	Better Made – Longer Lasting	Budget Constraints
Paying Lower Price	More Affordable	Quality Issues
Buying on Credit	Obtain now when Needed	Higher Cost—Overspending
Unknown Brands	May Be an Improvement	Unknown Quality
Foreign Brands	Competitive Merits	Service/Repair Issues
Buying by Mail/Internet	Lower Prices	Difficult To Return/Service
Comparison Shopping	Seek Out Better Deals	Involves Time and Effort
Store Selection	Better Service or Pricing	Time and Distance Involved

1. **Define Your Problem.** We pointed out earlier that purchasing something is often done to satisfy a need or solve a problem. If this is true, perhaps the place to begin is in defining the problem you are trying to solve. For example, if you define the problem as getting from point A to point B, it is easier to examine the issues than simply jumping to the conclusion that you need a car. Most people in the world don't have a car. In fact, there are a great many Americans who don't own a car—and they get from point A to point B every day. How do they do it? If you begin by taking a look at the need, rather than jumping right into your shopping shoes, you have the opportunity to view the situation in an entirely different context—with entirely different options.

    It may be that the problem is already defined. If you are at the grocery store looking for food, it may be assumed that you have not grown the food yourself, and there are few options aside from making a purchase. Here, the problem is one of making a choice among various alternatives. This takes us to step 2.

2. **Look at Alternative Means of Solving the Problem.** Here, you want to do a little brainstorming. You want to look at options . . . you want to let your imagination join up with your ingenuity and come up with alternatives. It may be that owning a car is one alternative—but it is only one. What are the other options—how do other people solve this problem? Let's not be too critical at this stage. Instead, let's be creative.

    In our western culture today, more and more food options are prepared at the plant, then packaged for ready eating. All we have to do is open the box or warm it up. Yet there are alternatives even here. If we learn how to cook using basic ingredients—which are much cheaper and healthier than prepared foods—we may eat better on less money. The prepared foods are a convenient alternative—but it is only one alternative.

3. **Examine the Alternatives for the Best Option.** Once you have your options in view, you can examine each of them. Now is the time to judge which option is best. The criteria for judging each alternative identified in step 2 will include whether the option is feasible to implement, whether it is the most cost effective, and whether it will solve the problem the best. A consideration of pros and cons may help visualize the relative merits of each choice, and bring any opportunity costs into focus.

4. **Implement Your Choice.** The result of step 3 will be a choice; step 4 is to put that choice into action. Perhaps the decision is to make a purchase, or a different kind of purchase from the one you initially had in mind. There may be times when you find that the best solution does not involve a purchase after all. If you follow this deliberate game plan, you will be surprised how many times the chosen option takes you in a direction you were not initially anticipating.

5. **Storage and Maintenance Issues.** Once you have implemented your choice you may feel that you have solved your problem—and hopefully you have. But there is usually one more step to take once you get home, and that involves the storage and care of your purchase. It has been said that we don't own our stuff . . . our stuff owns us. Consider where you should store your purchase to provide the best security and care; whether you should maintain packing, instructions, or warranty information; whether there is

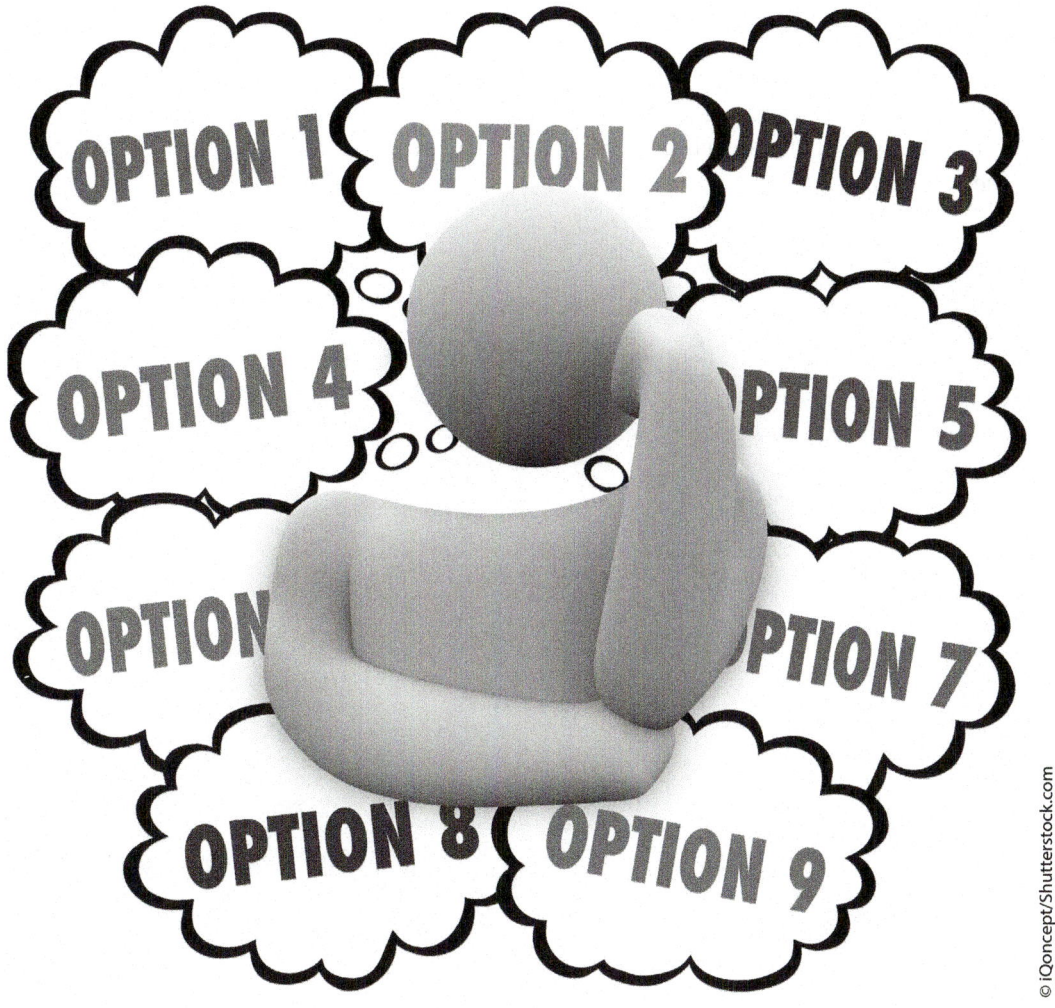

Figure 8:2 You want to let your imagination join up with your ingenuity and come up with alternatives.

assembly or installation involved; whether your purchase is substantial enough to require insurance; and what additional items may be needed to interact with or maintain your purchase. The care and feeding of your stuff is important if you want to keep it in good working order for an extended period.

Does this game plan look familiar? It is similar to the Personal Financial Process discussed in Chapter 1. Can you see a pattern in all this? Hopefully by now you have come to realize that your financial future is a do-it-yourself thing. And the best way to do it yourself is to have a strategy that will help you to do it successfully.

Summary & Review

1. There are two very separate and distinct contexts to the buying decision. What are they?
2. What are the dangers in the practice of shopping "just for the fun of it?"
3. Why is it important to be able to distinguish between our wants and our needs?
4. What are some of the opportunity costs associated with our buying decisions?
5. Cite the five steps in the game plan for buying.
6. In examining alternative means of solving a problem, what criteria would you use to judge which option is best?

Changing Buying Patterns

Over the past hundred years, buying patterns around the world have been changing. In the middle of the last century, if you wanted to purchase something, you generally went to the store where that item was sold. Accordingly, merchants struggled to get the best location, and paid top dollar to position their stores on Main Street or in the best malls.

Figure 8:3 Over the past hundred years, buying patterns around the world have been changing.

Then along came catalogs. The use of catalogs was not new—Sears and Montgomery Wards had sold through catalogs for years. But the use of that merchandising medium grew rapidly in the latter half of the twentieth century. Consider the dilemma for the retailer operating out of expensive storefront space with significant costs in brick and mortar facility and inventory. Catalogs don't require an expensive location . . . and may not require any location at all. All they need is a printer, an address book, and inventory. If the catalog merchandiser forward orders directly to the manufacturer, and if the manufacturer can respond to those orders on a timely basis, the catalog merchandiser may not even need inventory. This is steep competition for the retail store.

Then along comes the web. If you are a merchandiser who lists your products on the web, you don't even need a catalog . . . or an address book. Suddenly, two of the greatest costs of the catalog merchandiser are omitted. Moreover, you can provide more information, including pictures and demonstrations, than can be provided in a catalog. Today, we have all three types of merchandisers operating together. Exhibit 8:2 summarizes some of the strengths and weaknesses of each.

Please note that the above evaluation is a generalization, and there are certainly exceptions. Moreover, the marketing challenge faced by each of these mediums is likely to evolve over time, resulting in changes to their approach.

The emergence of the large chain stores has brought challenges to the smaller locally owned merchandisers. For example, the local shoe store, with the attentive shoe salesman who helps measure your feet for the perfect fit, is virtually gone. In its place are regional and national chains that may specialize in shoes, and the "big box" stores that carry a multitude of household items—including shoes. These superstores have an advantage in terms of their buying power, helping them keep costs low. The reality is that you will find a greater selection in these larger stores than in smaller retailers.

Exhibit 8:2 Types of Merchandisers—Evaluated on a Scale of 1 (Best) to 5 (Worst)

	Retail Store	Catalog	Web
Convenient Access	4	1	1
Breadth of Selection	3	4	1
Sample—Try-On	1	5	4
Lowest Price	3	3	2
Additional Charges	1	5	5
Return and Refund	1	4	5
Known Reputation	2	3	4
Resolve a Problem	1	3	4

The competition that comes from the catalog and web-based merchandisers is not without their own disadvantages. These new mediums compete in a market that is impersonal and often transient. As a result, there have been a growing number of scams, particularly on the Internet, which you should be aware of. Although the following flags do not always signal a scam, a combination of these factors should sound a warning to any buyer.

1. Have you received any e-mail from a source you didn't recognize?
2. Was the e-mail's return address anonymous? For example, did it look anything like 1234@anon.penet.fit?
3. Did the e-mail involve a solicitation of any kind?
4. Did it use the Honest-John approach, saying something like: "This is not the same as . . . ?"
5. Did it use uncheckable references, such as: "Before he died, Liberace himself endorsed this product?"
6. Did the message use urgent-sounding CAPITAL letters?
7. Was the body of the message addressed to someone else, as if you had accidentally received the e-mail?
8. Did it seem as if the sender of the message was revealing inside information on a product or service?

A Few Tips to Save You Money

All of us pat ourselves on the back if we can save some money by shopping smarter. Going back to our earlier analogy that your money is like a pond of water; you have the opportunity to allocate that water in such a way that it will meet your needs and help you reach your goals. Given the limited resources each of us has, it only makes sense to spread those funds as far as they can go, and not waste it by dumping it into a prairie dog hole where it is dissipated away. Paying less for something gives us a little more water to use somewhere else. In Appendix I, there is an article (Article 8:1) about how a family of four manages to live well on just about $14,000 per year. Sound impossible—read the article. It contains a number of tips on how to make your resources go further.

In addition, consider the following ideas that might help spread your precious water a little bit further.

- Buy out of season. We all know that Christmas wrap and Easter candy is available at half price in the days after Christmas and Easter. In addition, coats go on sale in the spring, and bathing suits can be purchased for much less in the fall. A little planning can put these items in your shopping cart at big discounts.
- Buy in bulk. The larger box of breakfast cereal is usually cheaper per ounce, and the bigger bag of potatoes costs less per pound. We will talk about unit pricing in a moment. There is a condition associated with this savings; however, and it is that you are able to use up the larger quantity before it goes bad. If half the

Figure 8:4 Going back to our analogy that your money is like a pond of water; you have the opportunity to allocate that water in such a way that it will meet your needs and help you reach your goals.

potatoes in the larger bag spoil before you get around to using them—maybe buying the big container was not such a savings after all.

- Consider the store brand. We have talked about the broader selection available in the "big box" stores. Take this one step further, and note that most national chains have their own brand of many products. From breakfast cereal to cold remedies, most large retailers have a brand that competes with the advertised well-known brands located right next to them on the shelf. Next time you are looking for a flavored drink mix, for example, take a look at the store brand. Chances are, it is made by the same manufacturer that makes the nationally recognized brand, and the price is lower. If your response is: "It only saves me a nickel . . . it's no big deal," consider that you are saving a nickel with each purchase you make—for the rest of your life! If you prefer the nationally known brand for whatever reason, then go back to it. Nothing is lost.

- There are three "nevers" when it comes to grocery shopping. Never go grocery shopping when you are hungry; never go grocery shopping without a shopping list; and never run to the grocery store for just an item or two. There is a reason why the grocery store puts the milk in the back, and it is because they know that you will walk the length of the store to get there—past a number of other items that you may pick up along the way. Instead, try this approach. Come up with a menu for each meal you will be preparing. Write it down by day and by meal. Then prepare a shopping list from your menu. Put on your list the things you will need for each meal—checking to see what you might already have in stock. Now, when you go to the store, shop from your list. This will minimize the extra expense that comes from impulse spending, redundant spending, and spending for something you won't use. In addition, fewer trips to the store mean you have more time and more gas to use for something else. We have included an Application Worksheet 8:1 in Appendix II, which provides a weekly menu planner form and accompanying shopping list. If you are not already doing this—give it a try.

- Both coupons and price discount sales are designed to increase awareness of the merchandiser and boost volume sells. Studies have shown that you can indeed save money by using coupons and watching for the discounted sales price. However, there is a catch. Studies have also shown that using coupons and shopping the sales leads many consumers to purchase items they would not normally buy—simply to take advantage of a sales price. In other words, the coupon or sales price becomes an inducement to

Figure 8:5 Never go grocery shopping when you are hungry; never go grocery shopping without a shopping list; and never run to the grocery store for just an item or two.

bring you in, with the likelihood that you will make additional purchases once you get there. The merchandiser knows this, and it is the reason he uses coupons and sales prices to bring you in his direction. A good rule of thumb is to limit your use of coupons and participation in sales events to those items you would have purchased anyway—thereby, saving your money instead of increasing your spending.

Summary & Review

1. How have buying patterns changed over the past hundred years? What additional buying options are available to today's consumer?
2. The newer merchandising channels are often impersonal and transient, especially when compared with the local store. How can you protect yourself from unscrupulous catalog or Internet sales?
3. Which of the ideas designed to help spread your money a little further do you find most applicable to your current situation?

Unit Pricing

We have previously pointed out how the purchase of a larger quantity of something might result in a per unit savings. There is often a volume discount, in addition to savings in packaging and shipping costs. To determine how much you are saving by purchasing the larger quantity, you need to look at the price per unit you are paying. Many times the store will perform the Unit Pricing calculation for you, and reflect it on the pricing label that appears on the shelf. If they do not, it is a fairly simple calculation that you can do yourself.

First, consider the measurement unit that applies to this product. It might be ounces, gallons, sheets, or simply a unit count as in the number of eggs in a carton or the number of pills in a bottle.

Next, divide the price of that product by the number of measurement units it contains. For example, a 16-ounce bottle for $1.93 is: $1.93/16 = $0.12 per oz. On the other hand, the same product in a 12-ounce bottle for $1.69 is: $1.69/12 = $0.14 per oz.

Finally, compare the various sizes available per measurement unit, to see where the better deal might be found. If the 16-oz. bottle sells for 12 cents per oz. and the 12-oz. bottle sells for 14 cents per oz., you are paying 2 cents per oz. less when you buy the larger size. Although this might seem insignificant, if you are buying this product often, over a long period, it can add up.

There are a couple of qualifiers that should be considered. As has been mentioned previously, if you buy the larger quantity but can't use it up before it goes bad, there is no savings. Buy what you will use in the time available before the product spoils. Second, as your budget must cover a lot of ground, it may put a strain on your spending to buy bigger amounts all at once. If you are suddenly filling your pantry with larger quantities, will your spending stay below the level you have allocated?

The Pantry Plan

One way to address this dilemma is to establish a goal of building up the quantity of basic needed items over a period. You can allocate some additional dollars into your budget for the express purpose of buying larger quantities—and beefing up your pantry in the process. Let's call this approach the Pantry Plan. It may seem that you are spending more money to do this—not less. But that is only in the beginning; while you are stocking your pantry. Once your pantry is stocked, and you begin dipping into this resource and using items that you have purchased at a reduced unit cost, you will find that your regular budget is more than ample to replace the pantry stockpile as it is being used. Once you reach this point, you can discontinue the additional expense of expanding your pantry, and rely on your regular budget for the purchase of perishable items, and for those purchases that will replace items drawn out of the pantry. The net result is that you have increased your supplies by purchasing greater quantities at a lower unit cost, and you are now maintaining that level of consumption for less than you were spending previously.

Of course, this can only apply to items that have an extended shelf life. It is hard to build a stockpile of lettuce, for example. Those things that store well and have an almost unlimited shelf life include flour, sugar, salt, oatmeal, pasta, pinto beans, powdered milk, and honey, to name a few. Today's packing gives a fairly long shelf life to canned goods, syrup, peanut butter, cereals, bakery mixes, powdered desserts, powdered drink mixes, first aid supplies, most over-the-counter medicines . . . well, the list goes on and on. Perhaps the bigger constraint will be the shelf space you have available to store these items.

Summary & Review

1. Unit pricing is the practice of knowing how much you are paying per measurement unit. How is unit pricing calculated? Why is this knowledge important?
2. Most of the time, purchasing larger quantities will result in less cost per measurement unit. What are some of the drawbacks to purchasing larger quantities of perishable items?
3. How does the Pantry Plan concept facilitate the purchase of larger quantities?
4. Let's say that you are currently renting, and there is little space to initiate the Pantry Plan. Is there an adaptation of this concept that will allow you to purchase larger quantities at reduced prices? If so, how can you make it work?

Figure 8:6 One way to address this dilemma is to establish a goal of building up the quantity of basic needed items over a period.

Understanding the Terms

Most of the regular everyday items we purchase come at a price that is not subject to negotiation. This is not to say that we can't get it for less if there is a coupon or a sale, or if the item is dated or damaged in some way. But for the most part, we do not expect to negotiate the price at the grocery store counter.

However, there are many items where a level of price negotiation is expected. The automobile and the house are prime examples, and we will be discussing these important purchases in the following two chapters. In addition, most furniture stores expect a level of price negotiation, and the salesman may have the authority to offer a discount to close the sale. Other merchandisers where price negotiation often occurs include home improvement stores, jewelry stores, and resorts. When considering purchasing from one of these merchandisers, it is not uncommon to ask for a discount. If a discount price is quoted, make sure that you understand both the price, and what is included at that price. If the purchase involves shipment or installation, be sure that the costs of these additional services are quoted up front, to avoid any surprises later on.

Most products come with some guarantee of quality or performance—a Warranty. An Explicit Warranty is always in writing. It details the extent of the warranty both in terms of the coverage offered and the length of time it applies, together with any exceptions to the warranty. As to exceptions, it may stipulate what the consumer must do to maintain the warranty, such as maintenance requirements. Many times, the warranty does not contain exceptions, but simply states that if you are unhappy with the product for any reason, simply return it for replacement or refund.

Even though there may be no explicit warranty, there is inherently an Implied Warranty, which is understood to mean that the product will perform the task intended. The implied warranty is not in writing and may be voided by two words: "As Is." If a consumer purchases a product "As Is" he understands that there

Figure 8:7 Most products come with some guarantee of quality or performance—a warranty.

may be certain defects or other conditions that may interfere with the products intended performance. As with the pricing, make sure that any warranty protection is clearly understood, together with any costs and limitations.

Many times, the seller will offer a <u>Service Contract</u>, which is intended to supplement the normal warranty in terms of the extent of coverage and/or the length of coverage. For this reason, service contracts are sometimes called extended warranties. In actuality, the service contract is not a warranty at all, but is a type of insurance policy that, for a fee, insures the buyer against the cost of certain repairs. Most service contracts are very limited in terms of the extent of their coverage, and end up being quite expensive as an addendum to the warranty.

Get Real

On one of those rare occasions when I bought a brand new car, I paid $2,000 for a service contract that was purported to include items not covered by the manufacturers' warranty and, in addition, extend the life of this protection to 100,000 miles. My thinking was to protect myself from anything that could go wrong with my automobile investment.

During the next 10 years, as I racked up 100,000 miles, I had several occasions to take the car to the dealer for repairs of one kind of another. Not once, in those 10 years and 100,000 miles, did the service contract cover anything. There were simply too many exclusions and exceptions. That was an expensive lesson on the limitations of service contracts.

Resolving Disappointments

It is unlikely that you will always be completely satisfied with every purchase you make. On those occasions, what can you do? First, give some thought to the nature of your disappointment, and which of the three Rs you wish to pursue. The three Rs are Repair . . . Replace . . . or Refund.

Figure 8:8 If you haven't visited a small claims court as an observer, it may be worthwhile to attend for an hour so you can understand their procedures.

The majority of disappointments can be resolved by returning the product to the place of purchase. This may be more difficult if you purchased online or from a catalog, but even in these instances there is usually a protocol for returning the item. If you purchased your item from a local merchant, they are typically anxious to resolve any problems you may have. They are not going anywhere—and they want you to be satisfied to the point where they not only keep you as a customer, but where you will refer your friends and neighbors to them as well.

If the local merchant does not offer a solution, and if they are part of a regional or national chain, you may wish to take your complaint to their corporate headquarters. This can be done with a phone call, but is usually better communicated in a letter, where you point out what you purchased and where, when you purchased it, and why you are dissatisfied. Providing this information in a letter or e-mail gives the recipient the chance to pass it to the appropriate officer who may be able to help you. The website of most major companies can provide you with their contact information.

If you are still not satisfied, and if the merchant refuses to work with you, you have the option of turning up your grievance by involving a third party. Here, you have several choices to involve another party, which may be helpful.

A Mediator is an outside party that tries to resolve the issue by negotiation. The mediator has no authority, and cannot make either party do anything. They will approach the issue by trying to clear up any miscommunication, by helping both you and the merchant see each other's position, and by trying to find a common ground that each of you can agree on. The Better Business Bureau (BBB) is an example of a mediator. They exist in larger communities, and can be found in the phone book.

An Arbitrator is an outside party that resolves the issue by decree. The arbitrator has the authority to settle the dispute, and the terms of any such settlement are spelled out by them. Although many governmental regulatory agencies can be arbitrators, most of the time your best approach is to file a complaint with the courts. If the dispute involves a relatively modest sum of money—in most states the maximum ranges from $3,000 to $10,000—the small claims court is likely to be the least expensive approach. The small claims court is a state court that has limited jurisdiction among private litigants. Most of the time you can represent yourself... you don't need a lawyer.

If you haven't visited a small claims court as an observer, it may be worthwhile to attend for an hour so you can understand their procedures. In most instances, you can file a claim in small claims court for a relatively modest filing fee of $15–$150, depending on the amount in dispute. A filing document will be required in which you provide your contact information, the defendants contact information, the amount in dispute, and a description of the problem. It would be well to include with your filing document any related documents that would support your claim, such as receipts, warranty information, or repair invoices. The defendant will be notified of your claim by the court and invited to file a written response.

You will then be given a court date when you will be invited to present your case. The defendant will also be notified of the court date. You will be most effective at the hearing if you avoid any emotional approach. Instead, present your case in a clear and concise manner—using evidence, witnesses, or other documentation where possible. The more concise your case, the easier it will be for the judge to render a decision. Anticipate the response the defendant will use, and be ready with a reply.

Remember, that if you receive a favorable judgment, you still must collect the funds. Courts will not collect the funds for you. However, if payment is not made, it is possible that a "contempt of court" action might follow, which would increase the costs to the defendant substantially.

Summary & Review

1. Cite the differences between an Explicit Warranty and an Implied Warranty? Under what conditions would you expect to receive an explicit warranty?
2. If you are unhappy with a purchase, what is the first step in resolving your concern?
3. What is the difference between a Mediator and an Arbitrator? Under what conditions would you seek the assistance of either?
4. There are certain limitations in using the auspices of a small claims court to resolve a dispute. What are they?

Chapter 9
The Automobile Decision

"We have developed a revolutionary new car that is powered by magnets. But there's just one problem — it sticks to your refrigerator door."

Contributed by Kenneth Hart. Copyright © Kendall Hunt Publishing Company

Chapter Objectives

1. Consider the alternatives to owning a car, and the pros and cons of other options available in solving your transportation needs.
2. Become aware of the various steps in the car-buying process, and the importance of each step in reaching a successful transaction.
3. Know how you can "check-up" on a dealership to determine the level of confidence and trust you might place in them. Know how you can "check-up" on a vehicle you might consider purchasing from a private party.
4. List those features that are important to you as you consider your next car. Be able to prioritize those features so you can increase the likelihood that you will be happy with your purchase.
5. Understand the nuances of car pricing, and the importance of focusing on the total price of the vehicle as opposed to the monthly payment. In this regard, be able to determine what you can afford to spend for your car purchase.
6. Consider the value of any trade-in as it impacts the vehicle purchase process. Know the methodology for selling your car yourself, versus offering it as a trade-in.

Chapter Objectives

7. Understand the alternative means of financing your automobile purchase, and the relative costs of each. Know about the lease option in financing your automobile.
8. Be aware of the merits of those additional products and services that the dealership will offer you, including extended warranties, protection applications, insurance products, and service plans.
9. Note the merits of timing your purchase to coincide with various dealership incentives and deadlines.
10. Recognize that the automobile purchase decision is too often an impulse buy, be aware of the merits of slowing the process down to a pace that allows you to do your research and negotiate effectively.

Should You Own a Vehicle

Owning a car is expensive. Many people spend more on their vehicle than on any other purchase except housing. Be aware that buying a car is only the tip of the iceberg as far as the total cost of owning and maintaining a car. Insurance, taxes and licensing, gas, maintenance, tires . . . the list goes on and on. Clearly, the initial cost of purchase is only the beginning, and it is important that your budget be able to handle all of the expenses surrounding your vehicle. Moreover, the value of a car declines as the years pass and the mileage on the vehicle increases. As with any well thought out purchase, remember that you are trying to solve a problem . . . in this case getting from point A to point B. Before you turn on the car shopping app on your phone and decide that a vehicle is the only option available to you, consider other transportation alternatives.

In many other countries, owning a vehicle is the exception rather than the rule. Most people throughout the world walk, or own bicycles, or rely on public transportation to get from point A to point B. Depending on where you live and the distances involved, these might be feasible alternatives. Carpooling, especially among individuals who live in the same house or in proximity to one another, could reduce the number of cars owned and the expenses that go along with car ownership. As you approach this topic, look at the problem you are trying to solve and the alternative means of solving that problem. Then, if you decide that a vehicle is the best solution, you can be satisfied that you have at least considered the other options as well.

Figure 9:1 Most people walk, or own bicycles, or rely on public transportation.

The Car Buying Process

Buying a car is one of the first major financial decision that many people make in their lives next to deciding how they will finance their college education. Although the decision about your education is more important in the long term than your car purchase decision, this choice is usually more emotional and fun, even if the conventional wisdom is that buying a car is expected to be an unpleasant experience. The key to any major decision is to educate yourself ahead of time and find a trusted partner to work with.

This chapter outlines the recommended key steps in your car buying experience:

- Research who you are going to purchase the vehicle from.
- Research the vehicle that you are thinking of buying.
- Research what that vehicle should cost you to purchase and how much it would cost to finance that purchase.
- Slow the process down—if you are not comfortable with the speed of the process or you need more time to do your research; a good and reputable dealership and salesperson will honor that and give you the time you need.

Research Who You Are Going to Purchase the Vehicle From

Trust is not something that comes to mind when thinking about going to a car dealership or a used car lot, but building trust with the seller is important to getting the best result out of your car shopping experience. According to a November 2012 Gallup poll, car salesmen were seen as very trustworthy by only 8% of respondents, two percentage points lower than Members of Congress. So to make sure you build that level of trust, do some research ahead of time. This is not research about the car—this is research about who and where you will purchase the vehicle.

Be open minded when you approach the car buying experience—especially when you have a level of trust with the salesperson and dealership. Car sales staff have a great deal of knowledge that can be helpful to your purchase experience if you allow them to assist you.

Figure 9:2 Car sales staff have a great deal of knowledge that can be helpful.

The most important decision you can make before you purchase a car is finding a reputable dealership to do business with. This is especially important if you purchase a used car.

> ### Get Real
>
> During my days in the dealership business I had friends approach me and say they found a great car for their daughter similar to a used car on our lot, but for $1,500 less at this other lot. In this case, the other lot had been open for less than a year and did not have an in-house service department. I would see what we could do to get a better price and often get within $750 of the other car lot. I would argue with my friend that if they purchased a car from the other lot and had a mechanical problem in the future—what was that dealership prepared to do to rectify the problem? A great deal on the purchase price of a car can be reversed quickly with a significant mechanical repair bill. At our dealership—which had been in the community for three generations and over 50 years—we would stand behind our cars and work with a customer if an issue arose in the future. Trusting a major purchase such as a car to a car lot with an unknown reputation is a gamble that you may not be able to afford.

A similar argument can be made for purchasing a car from a private party as compared to a dealership. At all major car buying websites, those sites state that you will be expected to pay more for a used car at a dealership versus a private party. Once the check clears with a private party car purchase, your recourse—if there is a mechanical or other problem with the car—is very minimal.

How can you find out about the reputation of a dealership that you are going to purchase from:

- Go online and see what other customers have said about the dealership in online reviews. Most dealerships take every customer comment very seriously and some even pay sales staff a bonus based on how favorable their customer reviews are.
- Determine if the dealership has a service department. If there are issues with your vehicle it is a significant benefit if the dealership has its own service department to assist with addressing mechanical issues. It is also a benefit if the used car you purchase is the same make as the dealership new car sales (i.e. purchase a used Chevrolet from a new Chevrolet dealership). Most dealerships will usually take those cars that come in on trade that their mechanics can't work on easily to auction and trade them for this very reason. (Don't buy a Ferrari from a golf cart dealership and expect the golf card dealership to be able to fix any issues that might arise). If you do buy an off-brand car, make sure there are local mechanical experts to assist with repairs if an issue arises in the future.
- The most important source of recommendations comes from family and friends. Knowing that a friend had a great buying experience from dealership is worth a great deal. A good salesperson will be able to work on referrals only if they do a good job of taking care of their customers and their customers' friends and families. Use your network of friends to find out what they think about a dealership before you ever step on the lot.

Buying a Car from a Private Party

As was noted before, you will usually pay a higher amount if you purchase a used car or truck from a car dealership as compared to a private party. The example below highlights this point (the following is based on Kelly Blue Book, www.kbb.com, for a 2010 Ford Expedition with 65,000 miles):

Purchase price at a dealership	$26,821
Purchase from a private party	$23,918

In this example, you would pay an additional $2,903 for this car by purchasing from a dealership versus trying to purchase this vehicle from a private listing in the paper or on the Internet. It is this reason why many people decide the savings is worth buying a used car directly from the public.

When buying a car or truck from a private party it is difficult to determine the trustworthiness of the person you are buying from, unless you have known this person for some time or were referred to this person by a friend. Even if you know the person well, it is still important to do some research on the car you are thinking about buying from this person. Although you may have some recourse against a business that sells you a vehicle with mechanical issues—your options under a private party transaction are more limited (which is a part of the reason for the difference in what you will pay between a dealership and a private party).

There are a number of websites that you can use to research the service and title of the vehicle you are thinking of buying. Sites such as AutoCheck and CARFAX will provide a vehicle history report, which note such items as how many previous owners the vehicle has had as well as service records and if there has been any issues with the title of the vehicle. It is recommended that you always run this type of report before you buy a car (whether buying from a dealership or someone in the public—even if it is someone you know). Although your friend may have taken very good care of the vehicle during the time they had it, they may not know the history of the vehicle before they took possession of it. Buying a car from a friend with unknown mechanical issues is an easy way to damage a good friendship.

Some Things to Remember if Buying a Used Car from a Private Party

- First step is to research with your local Department of Motor Vehicles (online or in person) what type of paperwork is needed to purchase a car or truck from a private party in your area. (Don't leave this up to the seller—you as the buyer need to be informed as well.)
- Find the car (or a number of cars) that fit your needs and budget, and contact the seller(s).
- Take someone with you to look at the car either at the seller's location or meet the seller in a public place like a mall parking lot.
- It is important to test drive the car and ask if you can take the car to a mechanic to have it inspected. (Some areas have services that will inspect cars for a fee or if you have a relationship with a local mechanic that will do a quick look to spot issues that an untrained eye may not see such as oil leaks, body damage, or uneven wear on the tires.)
- Take the seller's information including the VIN (vehicle identification number) of the vehicle so that you can run the car through a vehicle history report. (You can even do this step immediately on many smartphones).
- You can also use this information to conduct a title search to make sure the seller owns the vehicle, or if it is partly owned by a bank or other third party.
- Once you feel comfortable about the price and condition of the vehicle, you are ready to complete the sale.
- Paying with a check is a great way to show a paper trail of the transaction. If the seller would prefer cash—offer to meet them at your bank so that the transaction can be documented and the bank can verify your check is good or even cash the check there at the bank.
- If you are paying with cash it is important that you get possession of the vehicle and the signed title of the vehicle at that time.
- If at any time before you complete the purchase of the vehicle you begin to feel uncomfortable—don't hesitate to slow the process down and take the time you need. Never feel pressured to finish a transaction that you are not comfortable with. Don't worry—there are plenty of cars out there.

> ## Summary & Review
>
> 1. What are the key steps in a successful car buying experience?
> 2. How can you assess the reputation of a car dealership? Why do you think this is the first step in the car buying experience?
> 3. What are some of the advantages and disadvantages of buying a car from a private party?
> 4. Explain some of the things to remember when buying a used car from a private party?

Research the Vehicle that You are Thinking of Buying

Now that you have a good idea from whom and where you will purchase your vehicle, spend some time researching the vehicle that you think you want to purchase. There are many websites that will give you reviews on the positives and negatives of each vehicle. As noted previously, Autocheck and CARFAX are two websites that can give you a handle on various aspects of the car you are thinking of buying. Make a list of the key attributes of the car or truck you desire, including:

- Gas mileage
- Seating
- Ease and cost of repair
- Towing capacity
- Front wheel drive, rear wheel drive, all-wheel drive, four-wheel drive
- Price range (either in total or how much a month are you willing to spend). We will discuss later the importance of not focusing too much on monthly payment to the exclusion of total price.
- Future trade-in value

Figure 9:3 Make a list of the key attributes of the car or truck that you will look at.

Now that you have fully researched the car or truck you think you want to buy—be ready to be open minded about looking at a different vehicle once you get on the dealership lot. In my years working in the dealership environment, I was amazed at how many people came into our dealerships to buy one car or truck and ended up leaving with a completely different vehicle. A good salesperson will interview their customer to find out what it is that they are looking for (great gas mileage, good car to drive in bad winter weather, reliable, and affordable to maintain). Based on your interview you might find that the dealership has an alternative that might fit your needs just as well or better. Warning—an unscrupulous salesperson might listen to your top priorities and still steer you in the wrong direction to benefit themselves. (For example, trying to get you to buy a car that will pay them a large bonus but not what is right for you and your circumstances.)

Summary & Review

1. What are the important attributes of the vehicle you would like to purchase? Why is it important to prioritize these attributes?
2. The web is an important independent source of information on vehicle types and histories. Name a couple of websites that may help you get a handle on the car you are thinking of buying.
3. How can a good salesman help you in finding the right car for your needs and budget?

Research What a Vehicle Should Cost You to Purchase and How Much It Would Cost You to Finance that Purchase

Once you think you have the car choice narrowed down, I would suggest that you determine what you are willing to pay for the vehicle.

1. Price

For new vehicles this is fairly straightforward. Sites such as Edmunds, Kelley Blue Book, and TRUE Car give you very accurate information about what you should pay for a new car. This information is readily available and takes much of the mystery out of the new car buying experience.

The used car purchase price can be more subjective and not as easy to determine. When you are buying a new car, there is a good chance that you could find a number of other dealers within a reasonable distance that have exactly the same car you want—making the purchase more generic. (Remember your economic class about price and elasticity of demand.) If you are trying to compare what you would pay for a used 2009 Ford F150 4X4 with 80,000 miles on it, there is a less likely chance that there are similar units just like it within a reasonable distance from you. New cars are all in the same condition—they are all new. Used cars vary greatly depending on how they look, drive, previous maintenance records, etc. It is safe to say that depending on the condition of a car or truck, the value of a vehicle could swing 25% to 35% depending on this information for the otherwise same vehicle (age and mileage).

Walking into a dealership with printed price information is a great way to establish a strong negotiating position with a dealership. Showing the salesperson that you are well prepared will help you get the best price that you can.

IMPORTANT NOTE: Never talk monthly payment

When a customer walks into a car lot or dealership and mentions a monthly payment, it is music to a salesperson's ears, and not good for the customer. A salesperson can adjust almost any vehicle to meet the expressed monthly payment regardless of the profit on the specific vehicle. Below is a good example to prove this point:

Mary walks into a car dealership and says she is looking for a low mileage Mini Cooper and doesn't want her monthly car payment to exceed $230 per month. The salesperson says, "Mary, this is your lucky day (and he thinks to himself, my lucky day as well) because I have just the perfect car for you." The salesperson shows Mary a cute little green number with racing stripes and notes that the monthly payments are only $233 a month—well within your range. Are you getting a good deal? Maybe:

Figure 9:4 Pay attention to how much the car costs—not how much your monthly payments are.

Example A:	
Mini Cooper Cost	$13,000
Dealer mark-up	3,000
Retail price	$16,000
Monthly payment	$233.74
Number of months	84
Interest rate	6%
Total payments	$19,634
Example B:	
Mini Cooper Cost	$13,000
Dealer mark-up	1,000
Retail price	$14,000
Monthly payment	$264.20
Number of months	60
Interest rate	5%
Total payments	$15,852

In example A, you are getting the monthly car payment you want—but paying $3,000 over the dealer cost for the vehicle. This lower payment is due to the fact that you are making payments over 7 years or 84 months.

In example B, you are only paying $1,000 over cost and at a lower annual interest rate of 5% versus 6%. As the monthly payments are over 60 months (or 5 years) you end up paying nearly $30 more per month—but you are getting a much better deal for exactly the same car. In example A—with the lower monthly payment—you would be paying 24% more for the vehicle or $3,782 over the life of the payments. Pay attention to how much the car costs—not how much your monthly payments are.

Like many people you are more than likely going to need to make a monthly car payment to pay for your purchase. There are several different websites (such as Edmunds.com noted below) that will help you determine how much you can spend on a car based on how much you want to pay each month and how much you are willing to put down on a loan.

Exhibit 9:1 Sample Debt Payment Calculation

How much car can I afford?
Calculate your ideal price range for buying a car

Financing

1. Your Target Monthly Payment ? 150
2. Loan Term (months) 60 months
3. Market Finance Rate ?

Trade-In and Down Payment

1. Select a vehicle for your Trade-In to receive the most accurate calculation. Select TradeIn
2.
    1. Specify ○ New ● Used
    2. Model Year Select Year
    3. Vehicle Make Select Make
    4. Vehicle Model Select Model
    5. Style Select Trim
    6. Update Vehicle Reset
3. Value of Your Trade-In ? 0
4. Amount Owed on Your Trade-In ? 0
5. Cash Down Payment ? 0

Calculate

Results

1. Total Down Payment (with net trade-in) $2,000
2. Sticker Price Range $5,100 - $8,100
3. Maximum TMV® Price (Don't pay more than this amount) $6,600

It is important to find a calculator that allows you to enter in the level of payment that you would be comfortable with and an estimated interest rate. At Edmunds.com (noted above) you can type in what you can afford for a monthly payment and select a number of months for loan payments and interest rate as follows:

What monthly payment can I afford?	$150
Loan term in months	36 months
Market rate finance	5.0%
Cash down payment	$2,000
Maximum price	$6,600

If you adjust your loan term to 48 months and can afford a little more each month at $175, your revised maximum price would change to $9,000.

Take some time and try different combinations of payments, loan terms, and interest rates to see what the possibilities are. Most important is to make this decision before you get to the dealership. Stick with your decision and don't allow the excitement of the moment result in your agreeing to spend more per month than you can afford.

Figure 9:5 Take some time and try different combinations of payments, loan terms, and interest rates.

Now that you have established what price you will pay for the vehicle, there are still four more areas that you might need to research prior to stepping on to the lot:

- How much will the dealership pay you for your trade-in.
- What interest rate will you pay on the loan to finance the purchase of the vehicle?
- What additional products or services you might purchase from the dealership (warranties, insurance products, service contracts, and other purchased services)?
- The timing of your purchase.

Your ability to pay a fair price or get a fair price in each of these four additional areas is impacted by the research you do prior to walking on the lot.

Summary & Review

1. Why is it more important to focus on the total price of the vehicle, instead of the monthly payment requirement?
2. In the example discussed above, Mary found a car priced near her monthly budget constraints. Why was this transaction not the best deal for her?
3. It is recommended that you determine the price you are able to pay for your vehicle before you begin shopping. Why is this important? How can you determine this price?

2. Trade-ins

Trading in a vehicle is also a very emotional part of any car transaction—especially if you have any amount of attachment for the vehicle. Do your research first and get a good idea of what you can realistically get for your car if you trade it or sell it. I have seen many good car deals go bad because a customer has an unrealistic expectation of what their car is worth. When a customer states, "I know I could get $2,000 more for the vehicle if I sold it myself on eBay," many salesman will say under their breath—then why don't you take the time to sell it and come back to see us.

The same websites that you explore to give you a good indication of what you should pay for a car, will also let you know what you can expect to get for your vehicle as a trade. If asked about your desire to trade in your existing car at the beginning of the negotiation for the car purchase, one should not be predicated by the other. The amount you pay for a new or used car should be the same regardless of whether or not you have a trade-in. Make that decision later once you have settled on a price for the new vehicle.

If you have the time and talent to sell your trade-in, you will almost always do financially better to take that route—but for most of us that is not something that we want to spend our time doing.

Get Real

Recently my mother was in the market for a new car and she knew she would need to either trade-in her car at a dealership or sell it to a private party. She researched the expected trade-in value of her car on the Kelly Blue Book site (www.kbb.com). The trade-in value is determined by loading in the year, mileage, options, and condition of the car you want to trade-in. The result was a range in the amount she could expect to receive if she traded in the car—and the site also gave her a range of what she could expect to get if she sold the car on her own. According to the site she could expect to get around $2,000 as a trade-in at a dealership as compared to $3,500 to $4,000 if she sold her car herself. We took the printout from our Internet research to the dealership and they confirmed they would give her $2,000 for her car. A friend of hers had heard she was getting a new car and asked if she was willing to sell her car to them. The friend drove the car and they agreed on a sale price of $3,500. Because of the close connection with the buyer—my mom got the benefit of an additional $1,500 toward her new car purchase and she did not need to go through most of the process of selling the car to the public. The dealership she was buying the new car from even helped guide her through the process of selling her car and got her the legal forms she would need to finalize the transaction with the other person (now that is great customer service!).

Figure 9:6 If you have the time and talent to sell your trade-in, you will almost always do financially better to take that route.

On occasion, there are special new car purchase rebates that are specifically tied to a trade-in. (As an example: a $500 additional rebate if you trade in a Chevrolet truck and buy a new Ford truck—this is referred to as a Conquest Rebate). Search the manufacturer websites for these types of rebates. Sometimes they are unintentionally missed by sales staff and can benefit you in your decision to buy a certain make of new car.

As noted earlier—a person will usually get much more for their old car if they are willing to sell it themselves as compared to trading it in at a dealership. The following notes the estimated difference a person would get for trading in their 2009 Ford Focus as compared to selling it to the public (the example below is based on Kelly Blue Book, www.kbb.com, for a 2009 Ford Focus with 85,000 miles):

| Trade-in value at a dealership | $6,179 |
| Expected sale prices from a private party | $7,724 |

For many people the additional $1,545 they could potentially get by selling their old car themselves is worth the time and energy to take on the task. But for the majority of us, it may not be worth the effort—and we are happy to let the dealership get the trade and take care of the paperwork.

If you do decide to sell your old car yourself, here are some key steps:

- Do the research on your car that any good buyer would do. See what the online sites recommend someone will pay for your vehicle based on its condition and miles.
- Obtain your own vehicle history report and make it available to any potential buyers. You should put this fact in your ad and share the information you have with the potential buyer. Hopefully the information is positive or you should be ready to discount your asking price if it is not.
- TIP: get your car Detailed by a local detail shop before you sell it. The $100 to $200 you will spend is often well worth it. (It might even result in a decision to keep your car, now that it is cleaned up and looks like new again!). At a minimum wash and vacuuming the car yourself—you must put your best foot forward to get the most from the car sale.
- Research at your Department of Motor Vehicles the proper forms that you and the buyer will need to fill out—including signing over the title to the buyer. (If you still owe money on the car you will need to get a "pay-off" amount from the bank that holds the loan and more than likely holds the title to the vehicle.)
- Depending on your area you will need to determine how best to market your car (newspaper, campus bulletin board, online sites).
- If you receive a check for the vehicle it is important that you verify the funds are in the account or wait until the check has cleared the bank before you sign over the title to the car. Should there be an issue with the check it will be very difficult to take action against the buyer if you have already released the vehicle and title to them.
- Finally, it is important to think about the timing of selling your car and buying its replacement. It is seldom a good situation if you must buy a car in a short period—it limits your options and can weaken your negotiating position when buying the replacement car.

Summary & Review

1. How is the best way to affect a trade-in? Will trading in your old vehicle get you the best price?
2. Under what conditions might you be willing to try and sell your vehicle yourself, versus trading it in at the dealership?
3. Whether you sell your existing car yourself or trade it in, there are a few things you should do to maximize the value and help make the process smoother. What actions should you take prior to offering your vehicle for sale?
4. Why is it risky to accept a check, and sign over title, at the same time?

3. Financing

Dealerships have a number of relationships with banks or car finance companies to help with financing your vehicle purchase. If you purchase a new car or truck, there may also be financing available from the manufacturer. As noted, how well you do in negotiating financing for your purchase or lease will depend on how much research you do beforehand.

Know your Credit Score and try to get a commitment to get car financing from a local bank or credit union before you go on to the dealership lot. There are also many websites that will give you guidelines on what you should expect to pay based on your credit score. If you have poor credit, expect to pay a much higher interest rate to purchase a vehicle, if you can get financing at all.

Financing a vehicle is another profit center for a car dealership. Many times the amount made financing a car purchase for the customer will exceed the profit made on the car sale itself. This profit is made based on the interest rate that the dealership is able to get from a bank and what you ultimately agree to pay. For example, you might be eligible for an interest rate of 6.5% directly from the lender and the dealership will sign you up for 7.0%. This practice is legal and is allowed as a service to be provided by a dealership; however, each state is different in how they regulate what a dealership can do as it relates to financing income.

Why is it important to know what interest rate you could get if you arranged your own financing? In the example above, if you knew that you could get a loan for 6.75% from your local credit union directly, you could inform the dealership of that. The dealership can then decide if it wants to match that interest rate or have you arrange your own financing. If the dealership is willing to match the interest rate you found elsewhere, it is often easier to allow them to provide that service for you as part of the car purchase.

Figure 9:7 How well you do in negotiating financing for your purchase will depend on how much research you do beforehand.

Another form of financing a car is through a Lease. Although there are a number of banks or leasing companies that will lease a car for you—it is usually the manufacturers that offer the most attractive lease options on their own vehicles. Manufacturers will do this to entice you to lease their vehicle and hopefully gain you as a future loyal customer of their brand. The primary difference between a lease and a loan to obtain a car or truck is that in a loan situation you will own the vehicle at the end of the term of the loan. When you lease you return the car to the leasing company or dealership at the end of the term of the lease.

Some positive aspects of the lease option include:

- Leases can result in lower monthly payments and a lower down payment.
- A lease may result in being able to lease a more expensive car than you could afford if you took out a loan on the same vehicle.
- Lower repair costs as the factory warranty covers most repairs in the first 3 years that is the usual lease term.
- You don't need to worry about a trade-in at the lease term end because you don't own the car.
- You only pay sales tax (if your state has a sales tax) on the portion of the car you are financing.

Some disadvantages to leasing include:

- You don't own the car at the end of the lease.
- It can be expensive to try to end the lease early (before the stated lease term ends). With a loan you can sell the car at any time—however, the sale proceeds may not be enough to pay off the car loan especially if you try to sell the car in the first few years of ownership.
- The amount of miles you can drive each year is limited depending on your lease agreement (usually 12,000 to 15,000 miles a year). You can face a substantial penalty if you exceed the miles agreed to in your lease agreement.

If you can stay within the mileage restrictions of a lease and are not sure of your willingness to stay with one car for more than 3 years—a lease might make sense. At the end of the lease you have the option of buying the car if you think it is in your best interest (i.e. you have enjoyed the car and the resale value of the car is still good), or simply hand the keys back to the leasing company and walk away. If you have purchased the car instead of leasing it, and at the end of 3 years you find that you don't like the car and the resale value is not good, you may be stuck in a situation with a car that you don't like and may find hard to sell for a reasonable price.

If you are buying a new car, as you are finalizing the car purchase process, ask the dealership to present a lease option along with a financing option for the car you are wanting to buy and ask the dealership staff to explain the differences to you. You might find that leasing a new car makes more sense for you at the end of the day.

Summary & Review

1. Why is it a good idea to get a loan commitment from your local bank or credit union before accepting the financing provided by a dealership?
2. Leasing has become an increasingly popular method of financing your vehicle. What are the pros and cons of leasing as opposed to a loan?
3. It has been noted that a lease may be a better approach especially for more expensive vehicles. Why do you think this is true?

4. Additional Products or Services Offered

There are a number of other services and products that you will be offered at the end of the car purchase experience. Once again, this is another opportunity to make some additional profit on the car deal for the dealership—which is OK. After all, they are a business and need to make some money in this process. Do some research to see what you think is a reasonable amount to pay for these services. If there is something you have an interest in and you are armed with good data, the dealership should be willing to negotiate on these items as well. Additional products may include:

- Extended warranties
- Exterior and interior protection applications (i.e. protection against damage to the vehicle's paint, damage to interior and seats)

- Insurance products
- Service plans (to pay for routine maintenance of the vehicle)
- Windshield replacement plans

Each state has different laws about how a dealership can present this information to you, and in some cases regulates how much profit can be made on each item.

The Warranty is an area where everyone usually has a strong opinion (they never buy them, or they have had good luck when buying a warranty). It is safe to say that if you have the resources to maintain and fix any mechanical issues with your car without buying a warranty, it is statically a better option not to purchase an extended warranty policy. However, if you are not comfortable being able to come up with a large sum of cash, or like the peace of mind of knowing most future issues will be covered for repairs, a warranty (if priced appropriately) might be well worth the additional amount of money. To offset the concern about significant repair bills, more and more new vehicle manufacturers are including service plans and longer-term warranties in the price of the car purchase upfront.

Figure 9:8 It is statistically the better option not to purchase an extended warranty option.

5. Timing of Your Purchase

Finally, the time of the month does matter in purchasing both new and used cars.

- New Cars—buying at the end of the month does matter
  - Like all companies, the monthly sales volumes are very important to show growth in sales from the prior month or the prior year. If the dealership that you are working with is close to hitting a specific

target from the manufacturer they may be more willing to make a deal to get one more new truck sale for the end of this month.
  - Many manufacturers award dealers "stair step" money for hitting certain volume targets. An example is that for every fifth new car sold the manufacturer may offer the dealer an extra $200 for every vehicle sold that month—so if you are the 30th new car sold that month it could mean $6,000 in bonus money for the dealership ($200 × 30). Being the 30th new car sold that month is worth a great deal for that dealership and hopefully results in the dealership making you a better deal.

- Salesman bonus plans
  - Although some dealerships tout that they pay on salary and not commission, many dealerships continue to pay on commission. Often times a salesman's pay is based on a percentage of the gross sales or net gross of all car deals for the month. Many times this percentage is impacted based on how many cars or trucks they sell that month (i.e., they get paid 6% of gross sales if they sell 10 cars for the month but that percentage increases to 9% once they hit 11 cars for the month). So if you are lucky enough to be the salesperson's 11th customer to purchase that month they have an additional incentive to make a deal with you.

- Other volume incentives
  - There are many other monthly volume incentives that could impact what the dealership and salesman highlight during your purchase. Some of these may not be to your advantage i.e., pushing a service maintenance plan aggressively because of a bonus for selling a certain amount each month. Dealerships often have relationships with financing sources (banks, car finance companies) that may include volume incentives for the Finance and Insurance (F&I) staff or dealerships. Being well informed about what a reasonable interest rate would be for you based on your credit score is important to make sure you are getting the best deal possible for financing your car.

Do not wait until the weekend that you must buy a car or truck to start looking. If you have waited until your old car has been towed in for repairs to look for that replacement vehicle you are in a much weaker negotiating position with the dealership. Exercise discipline in your car purchase effort and you will end up with a much better car purchase decision.

Slow the Process Down

In a situation where you are not fully informed, you are in a weaker position when it comes to negotiating the final sales price and terms of a vehicle purchase. If you begin to feel unprepared you should be comfortable in telling the salesperson that you need to go home and do some additional research. A good salesman will do all that they can to not let you leave the lot (in car sales lingo this would be allowing you to leave on the "be back" bus). That is not good for the salesperson when they explain to their manager why they let you leave. However, if you are honest with the salesperson about your reason for slowing down the purchase decision, they will honor your wishes. They are counting on the fact that they have built a good rapport with you and you will return to them to finish your purchase once you have done your additional research.

Being a well-informed shopper (and seller if you are trading in your old car) is the most important thing you can do to ensure you have a good car buying experience. Good professional salespersons and reputable car dealerships will not be afraid of you if you have your facts and figures in order before you step on the lot. Find a dealership that you feel comfortable with and a salesperson you enjoy and the rest of the car experience will take care of itself. Remember—it is OK for the dealership to make some money on your transaction, and if you are well informed you can ensure it is a reasonable amount.

Figure 9:9 Being a well-informed shopper is the most important thing you can do to ensure that you have a good car buying experience.

Summary & Review

1. When you sit down to close your purchase, the dealership will usually offer a number of other products and services at additional cost. What approach should you take toward these other products?
2. Does it matter what time of month you choose to purchase your vehicle?
3. What does it mean to "Slow the Process Down"?

Chapter 10
The Housing Decision

Chapter Objectives

1. Understand the four primary factors to be considered in your decision to buy or rent your housing.
2. Be aware of your own life stage, and importantly, of the life stage you believe you are about to enter.
3. Note your financial capacity for owning a home. Be able to calculate your financial ability to buy a home in today's market.
4. Identify the financial advantages of home ownership.
5. Summarize the five steps to buying a home.
6. Understand some of the considerations in identifying the best neighborhood, and the reasons why this is so important.
7. Cite the game plan for selecting a real estate agent, and for finding your home.
8. Identify some of the factors that will strengthen your negotiating position. Understand the importance of the inspection report.
9. Outline those considerations that accompany your decision to sell your home.
10. If you are looking to sell your home, be aware of steps you might take to improve the presentation of your house.

Some Primary Considerations

Buying a home is the largest financial decision most people make. In addition to the financial effects, this decision has significant effects on quality of life issues such as friends, schools, discretionary income, and discretionary time. There are four primary factors to consider in deciding to buy or rent:

1. Life Stage

Your life stage is a key driver in the home buying decision. Here are typical life stages and associated housing desires:

Young Single: Typically prefer rental housing for lower initial costs, lower time commitment, and flexibility to relocate.

Couple, no children: Typically prefer rental housing for lower initial costs, lower time commitment, and flexibility to relocate.

Couple, with children at home: Rental housing becomes less attractive as the desire for more control over the housing environment increases. Other advantages include tax benefits and equity build-up.

Single, children at home: Very similar needs as couple, with children at home, but the lower cost and time commitment of rental housing are also very important.

Couple, children not at home: The decision is usually whether to downsize and possibly relocate or keep the larger home for family gatherings. Financial needs for retirement are an important factor to possibly downsize. Health is a major factor. The time commitment to maintain the larger home is also a factor. Where the children and grandchildren live is another factor.

Single, children not at home: Very similar needs as couple, with children not at home, but the lower cost and time commitment of rental housing become more important.

Owning your home has the advantages of greater privacy and control (pride of ownership). Rental living has the advantages of more flexibility with a month-to-month or a 1-year time commitment, less financial commitment, and someone else to do the maintenance. Rental living also can come with more recreational amenities such as a pool and fitness center. Having more space is not a reason to own because you can usually find large homes to rent in most neighborhoods. However, at some point in life, most people want to "put down roots" and "live the American dream of home ownership" and the privacy and control advantages tip the scale to make ownership more attractive. According to the U.S. Census Bureau, home ownership in America peaked in 2002 at nearly 70% and in 2013 was 65%—a more historical average. For most people, the rent versus buy decision is not primarily driven by finances, it is primarily driven by emotions. It is a lifestyle decision.

2. Financial Capacity

The government encourages home ownership by allowing home mortgage interest and real estate taxes to be tax deductible. Our culture encourages us to own our own home. Many homeowners have enjoyed great financial returns from home ownership. However, as proven by the last housing down cycle, if you lack the financial capacity to meet the demands of home ownership, owning a home can be a financial disaster.

A good rule of thumb is that your monthly housing costs (mortgage interest + mortgage principle + property taxes + home owners insurance + mortgage insurance) should not exceed one-third of your monthly income before taxes.

If household income is $3,000 a month, you should not spend more than $1,000 on monthly housing. In most areas of the United States, this means you will need to rent unless you have a large down payment to lower your monthly expenses below $1,000. If household income is $6,000 a month, you can spend up to $2,000 on monthly housing. In most areas of the United States, you can afford a typical home for $2,000 a month.

The 2007–2012 housing down cycle caused record levels of home owner mortgage loan defaults and foreclosures. Here are some lessons learned:

1. Your income needs to be secure and at least three times the monthly housing cost
2. Do not include occasional bonus income in this affordability calculation
3. Do not finance your home with interest rates and payments that step up in the first 5 years and make sure any increase in payments after 5 years is clearly understood and affordable

Figure 10:1 Your life stage is a key driver in the home buying decision.

4. <u>Fixed Rate Fully Amortizing Loans</u> are the safest loans—the interest rate is unchanged for 30 years and the loan is paid in full at the end of 30 years
5. <u>Down payments of at least 20% are safer than 10% down payment loans</u> that require private mortgage insurance and higher interest rates. Avoid no money down loans.

Do not let aggressive real estate agents and mortgage loan brokers talk you into stretching to buy a home you cannot afford. It is better to buy a more affordable home or rent for another year or two. You will be happier being able to comfortably pay all your bills than owning a home that leaves you financially stressed.

Summary & Review

1. The first consideration in the housing decision is your life stage. What life stage are you currently in . . . and importantly, what life stage do you think you will enter next?
2. As you consider the second consideration in the housing decision—your financial capacity—why is it important to be conservative in the calculation of the cost of housing you can afford?
3. A good rule of thumb is that your monthly housing costs should not exceed what proportion of your monthly pretax income?
4. What lessons can be learned from the 2007–2012 downturn in housing?
5. What is the safest kind of mortgage loan? Why is this kind of mortgage loan safe?

Figure 10:2 Your income needs to be secure and at least three times the monthly housing cost.

3. Financial Advantages

A third factor in deciding to own versus rent is the potential financial advantages of home ownership. There are three primary financial advantages of home ownership:

1. *Tax Savings.* Home mortgage interest and real estate taxes are tax deductible. Owning a home can lower your tax liabilities
2. *Forced Savings Plan.* Most people have a difficult time saving money, but a portion of each monthly mortgage payment pays down the loan balance; so over the life of the loan you have a significant amount of forced savings
3. *Home Appreciation.* Home values usually, but not always, increase over time. The increase is primarily due to inflation, but if the local employment market is very strong, home values can increase more than inflation. Where the local employment market is weak, home values can decrease.

Let's track the U.S. housing market over the last 10 years to see what history can teach us:

Exhibit 10:1 10-Year U.S. Home Cost and Mortgage Rate History

	2001	2002	2003	2004	2005	2006	2007	2008	2009	2010	Average
Average U.S. Home Price (1)	$213,200	$228,700	$246,300	$274,500	$297,000	$305,900	$313,600	$292,600	$270,900	$272,900	$271,560
% Change from prior year	3.0%	7.3%	7.7%	11.4%	8.2%	3.0%	2.5%	-6.7%	-7.4%	0.7%	2.5%
30 Year Mortgage Interest Rate (2)	7.3%	6.8%	6.3%	5.8%	5.8%	6.4%	6.6%	6.4%	5.5%	4.7%	6.2%
% Change from prior year	-8.7%	-6.8%	-7.4%	-7.9%	0.0%	10.3%	3.1%	-3.0%	-14.1%	-14.5%	

(1) Source: www.census.gov/const/uspriceann.pdf
(2) Source: mortgage-x.com/trends.htm

Exhibit 10:2 Own vs Rent—Years 2001–2010

Cost of Home Owning	Beg. 2001	End 2001	End 2002	End 2003	End 2004	End 2005	End 2006	End 2007	End 2008	End 2009	End 2010	
Purchase Price (1)	$213,200											
Purchase & Finance Costs @ 3%	$6,396											
Total Purchase Cost	$219,596											
Sales Price (1)											$272,900	$59,700 Gross Appreciation
Broker and Sale Costs @ 9%											$24,561	$30,957 Buying and Selling Costs
Year End Mortgage Loan Amount (4)	$175,677	$173,993	$172,182	$170,234	$168,139	$165,886	$163,463	$160,857	$158,054	$155,041	$151,799	
Net Sale Proceeds											$96,540	$28,743 Net Appreciation
Down Payment @ 20% Total Purchase Price	$43,919											
Mortgage Loan Interest Payment @ 7.3% (2)		$12,769	$12,642	$12,505	$12,358	$12,200	$12,030	$11,847	$11,650	$11,439	$11,211	
Mortgage Loan Principle Payment (3)		$1,684	$1,811	$1,948	$2,095	$2,253	$2,423	$2,606	$2,803	$3,014	$3,242	$23,879 Mortgage Paydown
Total Mortgage Loan Payment (3)		$14,453	$14,453	$14,453	$14,453	$14,453	$14,453	$14,453	$14,453	$14,453	$14,453	$144,527
Property Taxes @ 1.5% of Value + 3% infl.		$3,198	$3,294	$3,393	$3,495	$3,599	$3,707	$3,819	$3,933	$4,051	$4,173	$36,661
Property Insurance @ 0.4% of Value + 3% inflation		$853	$878	$905	$932	$960	$989	$1,018	$1,049	$1,080	$1,113	$9,776
Home Maintenance Cost @ 2% of Value + 3% infl.(5)		$4,264	$4,392	$4,524	$4,659	$4,799	$4,943	$5,091	$5,244	$5,402	$5,564	$48,882
Home Owner's Association Fees @ $200 a month+3% inflation		$2,400	$2,472	$2,546	$2,623	$2,701	$2,782	$2,866	$2,952	$3,040	$3,131	$27,513
Tax Benefits of Home Ownership (6)		-$3,992	-$3,984	-$3,974	-$3,963	-$3,950	-$3,934	-$3,916	-$3,896	-$3,872	-$3,846	-$39,327
Total Annual Home Ownership Cost (7)	$43,919	$21,176	$21,505	$21,846	$22,198	$22,563	$22,940	$23,330	$23,735	$24,153	-$71,953	$228,033 Total Monthly Occupancy Costs
Cumulative Total Home Ownership Cost	$43,919	$65,095	$86,600	$108,446	$130,644	$153,206	$176,146	$199,476	$223,211	$247,365	$175,412	

(continued)

Exhibit 10:2 Continued

Cost of Home Owning	Beg. 2001	End 2001	End 2002	End 2003	End 2004	End 2005	End 2006	End 2007	End 2008	End 2009	End 2010	
Home Rental Cost (8)		$17,568	$18,095	$18,638	$19,197	$19,773	$20,366	$20,977	$21,606	$22,254	$22,922	$201,394
Rental Security Deposit @ 1 month's rent	$1,464		$0	$0	$0	$0	$0	$0	$0	$0	-$732	$732
Renters Insurance @ 1.4% of rent		$246	$253	$261	$269	$277	$285	$294	$302	$312	$321	$2,820
Total Annual Home Rental Cost	$1,464	$17,814	$18,348	$18,898	$19,465	$20,049	$20,651	$21,270	$21,909	$22,566	$22,511	$204,945
Cumulative Total Home Rental Cost	$1,464	$19,278	$37,626	$56,524	$75,990	$96,039	$116,690	$137,960	$159,869	$182,435	$204,945	
												Ownership Savings
Cumulative Cost Savings of Owning	-$42,455	-$45,817	-$48,974	-$51,922	-$54,654	-$57,167	-$59,456	-$61,516	-$63,342	-$64,930	-$23,088	$29,534
Present Value of Savings at a 8% Discount Rate	-$42,455	-$42,424	-$45,130	-$47,470	-$49,478	-$51,189	-$52,631	-$53,833	-$54,820	-$55,614	$29,534	-$11,859

(1) Source: www.census.gov/const/uspriceann.pdf
(2) Source: mortgage-x.com/trends.htm
(3) Source: www.amortization-calc.com
(4) Mortgage Loan Amount begins at 80% of the original Total Purchase Price and then decreases by the Mortgage Loan Principle Payment.
(5) 2% annual costs assumes a 50-year life. Some components such as foundation and walls should last more than 50 years, but components such as furnace, water heater, appliances, floor coverings, etc. will be replaced multiple times in 50 years. If you are buying a house over 20 years old, consider a higher maintenance cost, maybe 3%.
(6) Mortgage Loan Interest and Property Taxes are tax deductible. Assumes 25% tax rate.
(7) Down Payment + Total mortgage Loan Payment + Property Taxes + Property Insurance + Home Maintenance Cost, less Net Proceeds form Sale
(8) Source: www.zillow.com. According to Zillow, the average U.S. home price is currently $169,000 and the average month home rent is $1,310 (0.8% of home price).
In higher price markets like Los Angeles the monthly rent to home value decreases to 0.5% ($2,356 avg. rent/$503,400 value). In lower price markets like Dayton, Ohio monthly rent to home value increases to 1.0% ($954 avg rent/$96,400 value). In this example, 0.8% is used.
Utility Costs – this comparison assumes that the owner and the renter pay all utilities. If rent includes water, sewer, and trash, then deduct this savings from rent.

Over this 10-year period, home prices peaked in 2007 and dropped in 2008 and 2009. The average home increased 2.5% a year—about the increase in inflation. During this same period, interest rates decreased from 7.3% to 4.7% and averaged 6.2%. Assuming you bought a home in 2001 and sold it 10 years later at the end of 2010, your home ownership costs, as compared to home rental costs, are reflected in Exhibit 10:2.

Using historic data and reasonable assumptions, home ownership in this example costs $29,534 less than renting a comparable home. This home ownership savings is almost $250 a month. However, this does not include opportunity costs for investing the down payment and renting savings in years 1–9. If you assume an 8.0% return on your money (typical average return of the stock market over the last 50 years), the ownership savings becomes an ownership loss of $11,859 ($99 a month). Using a 5.0% return on your money, the ownership loss drops to $701 over 10 years. Does this mean that for most people buying a home is a poor financial decision? The answer is no for two reasons:

1. Most people are not good savers. It is highly unlikely that a couple who chose to rent, using the data in Exhibit 10:2, would have saved each month's savings for 120 months. Also most people's investment results underperform the stock market. For these reasons, lifetime renters who turn 65 are much less likely to be able to retire at 65 than a lifetime home owner. Employee Benefit Research Institute reports that one in three workers have less than $1,000 in savings. Sixty percent report they or their spouse have less than $25,000 when they reach retirement. The forced savings from paying down a mortgage, month after month, year after year becomes a significant portion of most retiree's savings. Because most people are not good savers, renters have a harder time being financially prepared for retirement.

2. Interest rates today are near historic lows, which make home ownership more attractive. Using similar assumptions as Exhibit 10:2, here is what to expect:

Exhibit 10:3 Own versus Rent—Years 2014–18

Cost of Home Ownership	Beg, 2014	End 2014	End 2015	End 2016	End 2017	End 2018		
Purchase Price - house you saw last week	$300,000							
Purchase & Finance Costs @ 3%	$9,000							
Total Purchase Cost	$309,000						$47,782	Gross Home Appreciation
							$40,300	Buying and Selling Costs
Sales Price - assume 3% appreciation						$347,782	$7,482	Net Appreciation
Broker and Sale Costs @ 9%						$31,300		
Year End Mortgage Loan Amount (4)	$247,200	$243,212	$239,041	$234,678	$230,115	$225,342		
Net Sale Proceeds						$91,140		

Exhibit 10:3 Continued

Cost of Home Ownership	Beg, 2014	End 2014	End 2015	End 2016	End 2017	End 2018		
Down Payment @ 20% Total Purchase Price	$61,800							
Mortgage Loan Interest Payment @ 4.5% (today's rate)		$11,042	$10,859	$10,667	$10,467	$10,257		
Mortgage Loan Principle Payment (3)		$3,988	$4,171	$4,363	$4,563	$4,773	$21,858	Mortgage Paydown
Total Mortgage Loan Payment (3)		$15,030	$15,030	$15,030	$15,030	$15,030		
							$75,152	
Property Taxes @ 1.5% of Value + 3% inflation		$4,500	$4,635	$4,774	$4,917	$5,065	$23,891	
Property Insurance @ 0.4% of Value + 3% inflation		$1,200	$1,236	$1,273	$1,311	$1,351	$6,371	
Home Maintenance Cost @ 2% of Value (5) + 3% inflation		$6,000	$6,180	$6,365	$6,556	$6,753	$31,855	
Home Owner's Association Fees @ $200 a month + 3% inflation		$2,400	$2,472	$2,546	$2,623	$2,701	$12,742	
Tax Benefits of Home Ownership (6)		-$3,886	-$3,874	-$3,860	-$3,846	-$3,831	-$19,296	
Total Annual Home Ownership Cost (7)	$61,800	$25,245	$25,680	$26,129	$26,592	-$64,070	$130,714	Total Monthly Ownership Costs
Cumulative Total Home Ownership Cost	**$61,800**	**$87,045**	**$112,724**	**$138,853**	**$165,445**	**$101,374**		

Exhibit 10:3 Continued

Cost of Home Renting	Beg, 2014	End 2014	End 2015	End 2016	End 2017	End 2018		
Home Rental Cost (8)		$24,000	$24,720	$25,462	$26,225	$27,012	$127,419	
Rental Security Deposit @ 1 month's rent	$2,000		$0	$0	$0	-$1,000	$1,000	
Renters Insurance @ 1.4% of rent		$336	$346	$356	$367	$378	$1,784	
Total Annual Home Rental Cost	$2,000	$24,336	$25,066	$25,818	$26,593	$26,390	$130,203	Total Monthly Rental Costs
Cumulative Total Home Rental Cost	$2,000	$26,336	$51,402	$77,220	$103,813	$130,203	-$511	Total Monthly Ownership Savings
Cumulative Cost Savings of Owning	-$59,800	-$60,709	-$61,322	-$61,633	-$61,632	$28,829	$28,829	Cumulative Cost Savings of Owning
Present Value of Savings at a 8% Discount Rate	-$59,800	-$56,212	-$56,738	-$56,984	-$56,984	$4,582		

(1) Source: www.census.gov/const/uspriceann.pdf
(2) Source: mortgage-x.com/trends.htm
(3) Source: www.amortization-calc.com
(4) Mortgage Loan Amount begins at 80% of the original Total Purchase Price and then decreases by the Mortgage Loan Principle Payment.
(5) 2% annual costs assumes a 50-year life. Some components such as foundation and walls should last more than 33 years, but components such as furnace, water heater, appliances, floor coverings, etc. will be replaced multiple times in 50 years. If you are buying a house over 20 years old, you should use a higher maintenance cost, maybe 3%.
(6) Mortgage Loan Interest and Property Taxes are tax deductible. Assumes 25% tax rate.
(7) Down Payment +Total mortgage Loan Payment + Property Taxes + Property Insurance + Home Maintenance Cost, less Net Proceeds form Sale
(8) Source: www.zillow.com. According to Zillow, the average U.S. home price is currently $169,000 and the average month home rent is $1,310 (0.8% of home price).
In higher price markets like Los Angeles the monthly rent to home value decreases to 0.5% ($2,356 avg. rent/$503,400 value). In lower price markets like Dayton, Ohio monthly rent to home value increases to 1.0% ($954 avg rent/$96,400 avg. value). In this example, 0.8% is used.
Utility Costs - this comparison assumes that the owner and the renter pay all utilities. If rent includes water, sewer, and trash, then deduct this savings from rent.

In this final example, using a 4.50% interest rate, the cost of home ownership is $28,829 less than the cost of renting ($480 a month). However, this does not include opportunity costs for investing the down payment and renting savings in years 1–4. If you assume an 8.0% return on your money (typical average return of the stock market over the last 50 years), the ownership savings is reduced to $4,582 ($76 a month).

There are three other lessons that can be learned from the example in Exhibit 10:3:

First, stay in your home as long as possible. Home ownership of less than 5 years is usually a bad financial decision. In this 5-year example, the home value increases by $47,782, but the costs to buy and sell the home total $40,300. The buy/sell costs offset all but $7,482 of the value increase. The small gain becomes a loss with a 4-year ownership period. Moving into a bigger home every 5 years as your income increases is great deal for the real estate agent and loan broker, but a bad deal for you.

Second, the monthly home ownership cost, not including the initial down payment, with today's low interest rates is about the same as renting. In this 5-year example, the monthly cost of ownership totals averages about $9 a month more than the monthly cost of renting. If you can afford to rent, you can afford to own—if you have a down payment.

Third, 76% of the financial benefits of home ownership in this example come from the mortgage pay down of $21,858 over the 5 years.

For you to determine if the cost of home ownership is higher or lower than renting, you need help from a good real estate agent to give you prices, rents, interest rates, tax rates, insurance rates, closing costs, and other assumptions to create your own comparison. To aid you in this effort, consider Application Worksheet 10:1 in Appendix II. Make sure you are comparing similar size homes in similar locations. Comparing the cost of renting a two-bedroom apartment close to work to the cost of owning a four-bedroom home far from work is not a reasonable comparison.

We have all heard stories of big profits from owning homes and many of those stories are true, but most homes go up in value at about the inflation rate. The major financial reason to buy a home is the forced savings from paying down your mortgage that helps you prepare for retirement.

4. Stability

The costs to buy and sell a home are significant. It is also very stressful and time-consuming. These costs make home ownership a poor choice if you are not planning to live in that home for at least 5 years. Pick any 3-year period from the 10 years of housing data and calculate the costs of owning compared to the costs of renting—renting always wins. You need to be at a point in life that you are ready to put down roots to make the home buying decision.

> ### Summary & Review
>
> 1. What are the three primary financial advantages of home ownership?
> 2. What does history tell us about housing prices in the United States? Using this backdrop as a guide, what can we expect over the next several years?
> 3. What is the rule of thumb as to whether you should rent or buy your housing if you plan on being in the house for 2 years? For 5 years? For 10 years?

The Steps in Buying a Home

If you have concluded that your: (1) life stage, (2) financial capacity, (3) financial advantages, and (4) stability make home ownership desirable, then here are the five steps to a good decision:

1. Know What You Can Afford

A. *Down Payment*: Buying a house starts with knowing how much you have for a down payment. Start with your savings and then dial for dollars to mom, dad, rich Uncle Bob, etc., and determine what you have for a down payment. Check to see if there is any federal or state assistance for which you might qualify. Loans with a down payment of less than 20% of the purchase price require mortgage insurance and have more risk. Try to get a down payment of 20% of the purchase price.

Figure 10:3 Try to get a down payment of 20% of the purchase price.

B. *Closing Costs*: In addition to the down payment, there are other initial costs to buying a home from financing (loan origination fees, loan points, appraisal fee, document fee, etc.) and closing costs (title fees, escrow fees, inspection fees, legal, recording fees, etc.). These fees can vary by location and your real estate agent and loan broker can give you a good estimate of these fees. Initially assume these costs at 3% of the purchase price to the buyer, and 9% of the selling price to the seller.

C. *Mortgage*: Call three or four mortgage lenders/brokers and get a written estimate of their interest rates and fees. Try and talk to two direct lenders and two brokers. Direct mortgage lenders include banks and credit unions—start with where you bank. Mortgage brokers are middlemen who represent several lenders and get paid a commission by those lenders when they originate a mortgage loan. After you have talked to direct lenders and mortgage brokers and have a written estimate of their loan proposals, select the two that seem most qualified and competitive. Meet with these two and get a soft preapproval for a loan and get a clear understanding of the approval process and all fees and terms. Then select the most qualified and competitive lender/broker and get preapproved for a loan. For loan preapproval you will need to show pay stubs, tax returns, and bank statements. During this step, make sure your credit score is accurate. Contact the credit bureau your lender will use (TransUnion, Equifax, or Experian) and pay $8 to $10 and get your credit score and your credit report. Follow their steps to correct any errors. This will qualify you for the lowest interest rate. When you are preapproved for a loan, your offer is much more attractive to a seller and you can save thousands on the final price of your home.

Any loan should allow for a prepayment with no penalty. You do not want your loan assumed by a new buyer and you do not want to assume an existing loan. You want your own loan and any future buyer to get their own loan—do not have any financial entanglements with former owners or future owners. If possible, you want a Nonrecourse Loan. A nonrecourse loan means if you default on the loan the lender can foreclose (take ownership of) your home, but not sue you for additional money. Avoid loans with balloon payments—you want to eventually pay off your home loan. Fixed rate loans are preferable to adjustable rate mortgages in almost all situations, unless interest rates are very high and you are confident they will go lower. If you get a Floating Rate Loan, make sure the rate is fixed for at least 5 years and the loan term is at least 10 years. If you can afford a 15-year fully amortizing loan, you will have a lower interest rate and save thousands in interest over the life of the loan. If you are over 50-years old and are buying or refinancing, you should seriously consider a 15-year fully amortizing loan—it makes it much easier to retire if you have your mortgage paid off. If you are under 62 years old, never have a negative amortization loan where the amount you owe increases over time. A reverse mortgage can help fund your retirement, but get several quotes, understand the terms, and make sure your heirs understand the terms.

D. *Comfort level:* Congratulations! A lender has approved you for a $200,000 loan and you have scrapped together $50,000 (20%) for a down payment. Does that mean you should buy a home for $250,000? Are you comfortable with those payments? Would you be happier in a more modest home and have more money for other things? Sit down and look at your other financial needs and wants and decide how much you are willing to spend on a home.

Figure 10:4 Know what you can afford.

2. Neighborhood Selection

Buying a home is a very emotional decision. Before falling in love with a home, decide which neighborhood or neighborhoods best fit your needs. The neighborhood determines:

A. *Quality of schools* (available through the school districts)
B. *Commute time to work*
C. *Safety and crime issues* (available through police departments)
D. *Friends and neighbors*—for you and your family

E. *Zoning and other Restrictions*—do you want to paint your house pink, rebuild your truck in the front yard over the next 2 years, and raise llamas and roosters? Do you care if your neighbors do? Zoning and home owner associations vary by neighborhood and can significantly affect quality of life and home values.

F. *Other amenities*: shopping, recreation, church, and potentially air quality and temperatures.

Your neighborhood also is the main factor that determines how much your home will go up in value. The neighborhood is more important to your financial and emotional satisfaction of home ownership than the home itself. You can always improve and usually expand a home, but improving a neighborhood is unlikely. They say the three most important factors in real estate are (1) location, (2) location, and (3) location. At this stage, a neighborhood can be a city, a portion of a city, or an area around a school or park.

Get out a map. Plan your strategy. Determine your priorities. Drive around. Talk to people. Use www.Zillow.com to give you an idea of home values in potential neighborhoods. Try to narrow down your search to three or four neighborhoods that best match your priorities.

> ### Summary & Review
> 1. Why should a potential home buyer try to come up with a 20% down payment?
> 2. What loan characteristics are recommended for your mortgage? How is the best way to achieve those desired characteristics? What loan characteristics should be avoided?
> 3. Why is the neighborhood more important to your financial and emotional satisfaction than the home itself?
> 4. What are the three most important factors in real estate?

3. Pick a Real Estate Agent

As you drive around your three or four preferred neighborhoods, notice the "for sale" signs and see if a certain agent or firm tends to be more active. Ideally you want an agent with several years' experience who specializes in your preferred neighborhood. Your mortgage broker might have recommendations. Then select an agent from each neighborhood. Start with at least three agents.

Real estate agents are paid a commission by the seller, typically 6%, when the home is sold. As a buyer, you do not pay any fee to a real estate agent. They are highly motivated to get you to buy. It is probably not a good idea to let a real estate agent know the maximum price you can afford, if you want them to try their best to get a lower offer accepted. Make sure that most of the homes an agent is showing you are listed by another agent, preferable from another brokerage company. It is legal, but a conflict, for an agent to represent both the buyer and the seller.

Do not have any of the agents show you homes at this time, just meet them at their office. Review with them what you want to pay and what neighborhoods you are looking at and why. Go over with them why you like these neighborhoods and ask their opinions. Ask if there is another neighborhood that you should also consider. Find out how familiar they are with these neighborhoods and listen. Keep the focus of this meeting on neighborhoods and their qualifications. Use these meetings to learn more about the neighborhoods and the agents.

Select the two agents you like best. Ask them to each select three homes on the market that they feel would be best for you. Let them know you will have one other agent doing the same thing before you make a final decision on an agent. After you have toured these homes and spent more time with these two agents, decide on a final agent. You want an agent that is knowledgeable and understands what you want. You want an agent that communicates well and does not make you feel pressured.

4. Find Your Home

Now you know what you can afford. You know what neighborhoods are the most desirable for your needs. You have an agent that understands what you want. Now you can tour more homes and make the final home buying decision. Here are factors to consider:

Figure 10:5 Now you can make the final home buying decision.

- **A.** *New versus used*: New homes will typically have added costs of landscaping, window coverings, storage shelves, etc. that often come with existing homes. New homes usually come with some warrantees. Older homes are usually the best value, but have higher maintenance. Older homes have an established neighborhood that is easier to evaluate.
- **B.** *Shack on the block versus castle on the block*: You may feel some prestige owning the nicest home on the street, but your home appreciation will be pulled down by the neighborhood averages. There are more advantages to buying a below average home in an above average neighborhood, than an above average home in a below average neighborhood.
- **C.** *Move in ready versus needs some work*: A fixer-upper is usually the best value if you understand the cost in time, inconvenience, and money it will take to be fixed. Get several quotes and make sure you understand all the costs. Make sure your entire household is comfortable with the hassle of the necessary home improvements.

D. *Just right size versus room to grow*: If you are expecting additions to your household in the next 5 years, allow room to grow into the house. Unfinished basements are a great way to be able to grow a house. Second story additions can be done in most neighborhoods, but are more expensive and disruptive than finishing a basement.

E. *Big yard versus small yard*: Big yards equal big work, but if you love to garden or want more privacy, then they make sense. Having a park nearby is a great way to have many big-yard advantages without the maintenance.

F. *Attached versus detached*: Most people think of a detached single family home, with the requisite white picket fence, when thinking of owning a home. However, more people are choosing attached housing in urban areas to be closer to work, mass transit, and amenities of the urban core. Condominiums (condos) are the typical attached housing, but in some east coast cities they have cooperatives (co-ops). In a Condominium you own the space within your home and have joint ownership, through the condo association, of the exterior walls, land and amenities. A condo where there is no housing above or below you is called a Townhouse. A Co-op is owned by a corporation and you buy stock in the corporation with the rights to live in your home. Some condos were originally rental apartments that were converted in condos. With attached housing you are not responsible for exterior or landscape maintenance, but you do have a homeowner's fee to cover building and grounds maintenance and property taxes.

5. Purchase Negotiation and Inspection Reports

An experienced real estate agent will be helpful, but you need to direct the negotiations. Being preapproved for a loan makes your offer much more attractive. Offering a higher than normal earnest money deposit also makes your offer more attractive. Being able to close the sale sooner is also an advantage.

The best time to buy is when there are few buyers—typically between Thanksgiving and the end of January. A bad winter storm makes your offer more attractive. The worst time to buy is when most people are trying to buy—spring and summer. Interest rates tend to be a little lower and loans get approved a little quicker in the slower months of winter.

Typically there is a good deal of negotiation when you are buying a home. Price is only one thing to negotiate. For example, the furniture and appliances are also open to negotiation. Carpets, drapery/window coverings, shelving attached to the walls and kitchen appliances are included in the sale of an existing home. Other furniture and appliances (washer, dryer, extra refrigerator in garage) are not included unless you ask. Do you see a nice sofa that fits perfectly in the living room? Ask for it. Is there playground equipment, yard equipment, or other items that you will need and the seller is going to have to pay to remove? Ask for it. If the seller is downsizing or moving across the country, they will be very willing to give you a great price on these items.

Your agent will prepare the purchase contract on forms approved by your state. Have your agent walk you through the contract and make sure you understand it. You might want to hire an attorney if you feel it necessary. Keep the response times in the contract as short as possible for the seller and as long as you need for you. Before you give final approval, make sure you have a firm loan commitment and that you have an estimated closing cost statement from the lender showing all the costs to your purchase.

Have an experienced, detailed home inspector ready to do your inspection. Your home needs to be structurally sound and the heating, cooling, plumbing, electrical, and other major components need to be in good condition. A termite or radon inspection should also be considered. Have your lender and real estate agent recommend a few inspectors and select one before you start making offers. Another report to consider having the home seller provide (costs under $20) is the C.L.U.E. Home Sellers Disclosure Report (https://personalreports.lexisnexis.com/homesellers_disclosure_report/landing.jsp). This report provides a 5-year history of insurance claims on a home. When you have an offer accepted, you want the inspection done in the next few days. Any unexpected repairs are a reason to lower the price or walk away.

Buying a home is the largest financial decision most people make. In addition to the financial effects, this decision has significant effects on quality of life issues such as friends, schools, discretionary income, and discretionary time. The home buying process is always emotional. Following the steps in this chapter will also make this decision logical.

Figure 10:6 When you have an offer accepted, you want the inspection done in the next few days.

Summary & Review

1. How is the best way to select the right real estate agent?
2. As you review the considerations under step 4 (Find Your Home), which are the most important to you? Why?
3. What can you do to make your offer more attractive to the seller?
4. Why is a home inspection a good idea? What options do you have if the inspection report reveals a serious defect in the home?

When It's Time to Sell

At some point, you may be on the other side of the transaction—as the seller. When that time comes, your first decision will be whether to try and sell the home yourself, or engage the services of a realtor. As you consider this decision, it might help to note the strength of the real estate market in general, and the strength of the market in your area in particular. A Sellers' Market exists when demand for real estate exceeds supply. This market is usually evidenced by strong pricing, by a relatively short "for sale" time before an offer is received, and sometimes by multiple offers for the same home. Clearly, if such a market exists, the need for a realtor may be less. On the other hand, a Buyers' Market exists when the supply of unsold homes exceeds demand. In this market, there are few buyers and pricing is weak. A home may be up for sale for a relatively long time before an offer is received, and then the offer is likely to be significantly below the asking price. In this kind of market, the seller may need all the assistance they can get, and utilizing the services of a realtor may be helpful. Remember, it is the seller who pays the realtor commissions, which could be approximately 6% of the sales price of the home.

Understand that a realtor's primary role is to help market the home. In this regard, their chief tool is the Multiple List Service or MLS, which is a computerized network of homes for sale, which includes abundant information on each listing. With the MLS at their fingertips, a realtor can sit down with a potential buyer and screen listings for price, for location, for size, or for just about any other characteristics that the buyer deems important. This marketing tool is a huge advantage for the realtor, and it is all free to the buyer. The individual who is looking to sell their home themselves simply doesn't have access to this network.

Other services performed by the realtor include advertising your home, performing some degree of preliminary qualification so that only those potential buyers who are serious and able to buy are coming into your home, and showing your home to potential buyers. The realtor cannot produce a buyer, does not arrange financing for a buyer, and does not handle the closing of the transaction.

If you find yourself in a sellers' market, and you are willing to handle all of the above tasks yourself, your first visit should be to a Title Company. It is the title company who is in the business of handling all of the issues associated with the transfer of ownership in real estate. These include all of the money transfers from buyer to seller, the payment of any associated costs such as appraisals, tax accruals, title insurance, etc., and the recording of ownership on the books of the County. The title company typically has several documents that may help you as you try to sell your home. These include an offer to purchase form that you can then make available to potential buyers. In the end, it will be the title company that facilitates the transfer.

The second decision you will need to make is the price of the home. This is little tricky because a home is not a commodity with a known price and an ongoing market for buying and selling. A lot of time may have passed since the home was last sold, and changes to the structure or simply the changing nature of markets may make the last sales price irrelevant. There are a couple of ways for you to address the price question. The most common is to search out Comparables, which are the prices that similar homes, in the same or similar neighborhood, sold for in the recent past. If you choose a realtor, they will have a listing of comparables that would aid in the price decision. If you choose to sell your home yourself, you will need to do a little research to obtain comparables. Your title company may be able to help with this.

Figure 10:7 Another way to address the pricing issue is to actually have your home appraised.

Another way to address the pricing issue is to actually have your home appraised. This may cost upwards of several hundred dollars, and one of the techniques the appraiser will use is to assess comparables. So, we are essentially back to the same methodology. If you price your home too high, potential buyers may judge that you are not a serious seller, and ignore your listing. Of course, if you price your home too low, you may sell it quicker, but you will leave a lot of money on the table. What you are aiming for is a price just slightly above the market, where you might be able to come down to an offer that is near the market price. What is the fair market price of your home is the real question.

Effective Presentation of Your Home

Don't underestimate the importance of an effective presentation. As any car salesman, waitress, or merchandiser knows, presentation is everything. So, what can you do to make your home look its best? Here are a few suggestions.

Figure 10:8 As any car salesman, waitress, or merchandiser knows, presentation is everything.

Make the Outside Shine. If it needs repainting—repaint. Look particularly at doorways and other areas where traffic and use may have made it look a little dingy. If you have a yard, make sure it is well manicured. Flowers tend to make a positive statement. Clean the windows, get the oil off the driveway, and polish the lamps and doorknobs.

Open up the Inside. Remove any furniture that is tattered or that makes the room look small. Even though you may love that beanbag chair, put it in a friend's garage until your home is sold. To the extent that you can make the rooms look larger, it will help. This is particularly true of closets. Box up half of everything that is in the closets—particularly the entry way closet that is already overflowing—and store it elsewhere for the time being.

Upgrade and Renovate Where Needed. An upgraded bathroom commode or kitchen sink goes a long way toward making the home look well maintained. Remember that the seller is probably going to have an inspection done, so anticipate that dead electrical outlets or leaking plumbing will be identified eventually, and repair them now. Again, a spot of paint and polish will give the buyer a positive impression.

Help the Buyer Identify with the Home. You want the buyer to see themselves living in the house. To help with this, box up any family photographs or personal heirlooms that might make it difficult for them to relate to the home. In addition, little things that give the house a "homey" feel at the time of showing might be helpful. The smell of fresh baking, the soft hum of the dryer running, or similar touches can't go wrong.

Make Sure the Buyer is Accompanied as They Walk through the Home. If you are selling the home yourself, it is expected that you will be in the background ready to answer questions as they view the home. If you have engaged a realtor, they will handle that task for you. The point is the buyer is escorted. This gives the buyer the feeling of being helped, and gives you the peace of mind knowing that the stranger in your home is accompanied.

Summary & Review

1. What is the first decision you will need to make as you approach the task of selling your home? How will you make that decision?
2. What is the role of the title company in the real estate transfer process?
3. As a given parcel of real estate is transferred infrequently, what is the best way to establish a fair market price for that real estate?
4. Name some of the things you can do to enhance the presentation of your home?

Insurance

Chapter 11
Property & Casualty Insurance

Contributed by Robert Eagleston. Copyright © Kendall Hunt Publishing Company.

Chapter Objectives

1. To gain an understanding of the nature of insurance, and of the importance of protecting your assets through proper insurance coverage.
2. Become familiar with the three broad kinds of insurance, and the role that each plays in securing your finances against life's risks.
3. Understand the role of Property & Casualty Insurance, and the two objectives that P&C insurance is designed to meet.
4. Consider the issue of liability, and the threat it may pose to your financial well-being. Note the different sources of liability, and how insurance can help mitigate this risk.
5. Note the applicability of the umbrella insurance policy.
6. Evaluate the basic structure of the automobile insurance policy, and the relevance of each component of this insurance product.
7. Understand the various ways you might reduce the costs of your automobile insurance. Understand the nature of the Deductible, and how it can help keep insurance costs low.
8. Evaluate the basic structure of the homeowners' insurance policy. Be aware of the fundamental components of the homeowner's policy as relating to the building and the contents.
9. Be aware of the two exclusions present in nearly all homeowners' insurance policies. Know how to obtain insurance that might compensate for these exclusions, if necessary, and how to obtain additional insurance on specific high value contents.
10. Identify those actions that you should take following the occurrence of an accident. Know how no-fault insurance affects the claim process.

The Nature of Insurance

As we begin our discussion of insurance, it may be well to define exactly what we are talking about. In broad terms, Insurance is a contract between you and an insurance company, in which they agree to pay up to a certain amount of any financial loss you may sustain as a result of accident, illness, or death. In return, you agree to pay to them a series of Premiums throughout the period that the insurance protection is in force. This arrangement gives you the opportunity to have someone else write the checks if a financial disaster happens in your life. The result is that you become a Policyholder, holding an insurance policy that protects you from a specified amount of loss.

Of course, you want to be sure that the insurance company you select will be around when you need them. A good way to check on the financial strength of an insurance company is to note the rating given them by A.M. Best, the company that rates insurance companies. A.M. Best has been rating insurance companies since 1906, and their rating says a lot about a company's staying power. You can check on A.M. Best's rating for any insurance company by accessing the web. The scale used by A.M. Best is shown in Exhibit 11:1.

Unfortunately the question of whether a financially catastrophic event will ever occur to you is not so much an "if," as a "when." We all hope that we can avoid life's bludgeons, but for most of us, we do get struck from time to time. If you do not have insurance, in which someone else steps up to help with the financial loss, then you are what is called Self-Insured, and you will incur the full brunt of any financial consequence. That can be a major "ouch" in your life.

Exhibit 11:1 A.M. Best Insurance Company Rating Scale

Judged Secure		Judged Vulnerable		Other Indications	
Superior	A++/A+	Fair	B/B-	Under Supervision	E
Excellent	A/A–	Marginal	C++/C+	In Liquidation	F
Good	B++/B+	Weak	C/C-	Suspended	S
		Poor	D		

Figure 11:1 What kind of event can produce a financial hardship, and what kind of insurance do you need to guard against the costs of that event?

What kind of event can produce a financial hardship, and what kind of insurance do you need to guard against the costs of that event? The most common risks we face may be classified as (1) Personal Risks: The loss of income or life due to premature death, illness, and disability; (2) Property Risks: The loss or damage to property due to accident, fire, theft, etc.; and (3) Liability Risks: The loss or damage to someone else's property or person. Exhibit 11:2 summarizes some of those events that may result in financial hardship.

Of course, if you are one of those lucky individuals who manages to go through life without such happenings, then the insurance you bought may never be called on to compensate for the financial loss, and the money you spent on insurance premiums may not be necessary. The question is how can any of us see that clearly into the future. And so, insurance simply guards against what we can't foresee . . . and protects our financial well-being from the worst that may happen. Remember, that insurance does not prevent any of these events from happening. It simply helps mitigate the financial hardships that come when they do.

Exhibit 11:2 The Need for Insurance

If This Where to Happen	This Insurance Would Offset Financial Loss
Automobile Accident	Property and Casualty Insurance
A Fire Burns Your Home	Property and Casualty Insurance
You Injure Someone Who Sues You	Property and Casualty/Umbrella Insurance
You Fall and Break Your Pelvis	Health Insurance
You Find That You Have a Disease	Health Insurance
You Become Disabled in an Accident	Disability Insurance
You Die in an Accident	Life Insurance
Supplement Your Retirement Income	Certain Kinds of Life Insurance

How Much is Enough

Studies have found that most people have either too little insurance—or too much insurance. The problem is insurance is one of those things we buy occasionally without a comprehensive and deliberate game plan. Moreover, we tend to put on our shopping shoes too quickly, without taking the time to ask that fundamental question we introduced in Chapter 8. Do you remember the first step in the Smart Buying protocol: Define the Problem? As pointed out above, the problem is one of protecting ourselves against financial hardship due to certain untoward events. If we start there, we may be able to get a handle on the appropriate level of insurance needed at each juncture.

For example, if you are looking at Automobile Insurance, and you are driving an aging Plymouth, which is not worth more than a few hundred dollars, why would you need to buy insurance on the car itself—especially if that insurance comes with a $500 deductible? Of course you would need insurance to cover possible damage to someone else's car and protection against the medical costs should someone in your car or another car be injured, but you hardly need to arrange reimbursement in the event that old Plymouth is totaled.

Another example; let's say that you are 22 years old, single, have no debts, and no one is counting on you for support. How much life insurance do you really need? Maybe all you need is enough to meet funeral expenses. So, like any other buying decision, let's begin by defining the problem.

We have observed that there are different kinds of insurance for different possible events. The insurance that protects our assets is called Property & Casualty or P&C insurance. Health insurance covers those events that may result in hospitalization or prolonged illness. And of course, life insurance is paid to those who may be relying on us for support should the grim reaper come. This chapter focuses on the first of these; Property & Casualty insurance. Chapter 12 will look at Health Insurance, and Chapter 13 will discuss Life Insurance.

Summary & Review

1. What is insurance? Why would anyone want to buy insurance protection?
2. How can you increase the likelihood that the insurance company you choose will be around when you need them?
3. Define self-insurance. How much financial loss can you sustain through self-insurance?
4. Consider the various events that can result in a significant strain on your finances. Which events do you think you are most vulnerable to at the present time?
5. Name the three broad kinds of insurance. What purposes does each serve?
6. What is the first step in evaluating your insurance needs?

Property & Casualty Coverage

When we purchase an expensive asset such as a car or a home, we are understandably concerned with maintaining that asset, and taking steps to see that this investment is protected against damage or loss. If something happened and we were to lose that asset, we could ill afford to go out and buy another one.

You have just identified the first objective of Property & Casualty (P&C) Insurance—providing the funds to repair or replace a damaged or destroyed asset. A car or a home are typical high cost assets that require insurance protection . . . and we will drill down into each of these in a moment. However, they are not the only assets that you may want insurance coverage on. Your boat or ATV, the camper or RV, in short, any asset that would present you with a financial hardship should it be damaged or destroyed is a candidate for P&C insurance.

There is a second and equally important objective for P&C insurance, and that is protection from the possibility that you or your asset may damage someone else's property or person. This risk is called Liability Risk. If you are found liable, you would then be responsible for the costs to repair or replace the property of another person, or for any medical or other losses they may sustain. Such costs can be considerable, and your insurance coverage would help with those expenses as well.

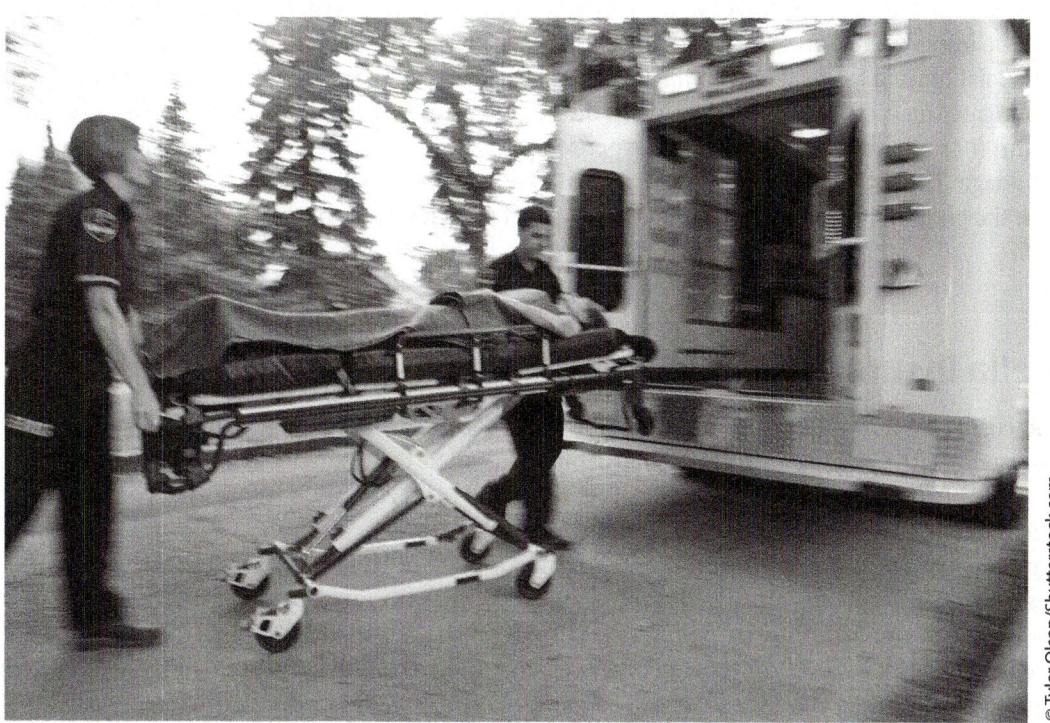

Figure 11:2 If you are found liable, you would then be responsible for the costs to repair or replace the property of another person, or for any medical or other losses they may sustain.

Liability

This issue of liability is so important that we should spend a few minutes discussing some of the aspects of liability risk. First, consider this question. To be liable, do you need to have done something wrong? Do you need to be at fault?

Strict Liability is present when a person is held responsible for their intentional or unintentional actions. If you throw a punch that breaks someone's jaw, you are clearly intending that action, and you would be liable for the consequences. However, if a snow storm leaves your driveway icy and slick, this clearly is not a deliberate action on your part. Nevertheless, you may be held liable if you do not exercise reasonable efforts to mitigate that hazard. Then there is Vicarious Liability in which you are held liable for the actions of someone else. For example, if your child is playing with matches and a fire ensues, you could be held liable even though it was not your fault, and was not even your action.

In our society today, we seem to be absorbed in ongoing efforts to find someone else to blame for much of what happens to us. The notion that "it's not my fault" predominates our thinking. A significant segment of the legal profession makes a living out of finding someone else to be held financially responsible for what happens to us. There is no question that this pursuit of liability has resulted in major changes to society as we make efforts to offset the rising costs of such liability. A predominate reason for the high and rising costs of P&C Insurance is the losses that insurance companies sustain as a result of this liability issue.

There have been repeated calls for reforms to our legal system, which would add a measure of responsibility to the pursuit of liability. Currently, anyone can be sued by anyone over anything . . . there is no restraint on the reach of the liability lottery. You have no doubt seen ads by some lawyers inviting you to hire them to find someone else financially liable for what may have happened to you. One of the proposals suggested by way of reform is the imposition of a financial bond to be required by the plaintiff at the time a suit is filed. The bond would pay the legal costs of the defendant in the event that the suit is found to be frivolous and dismissed, or in the event the plaintiff loses the suit. Actually, this requirement is imposed in Great Britain, and has been found to be effective in reducing the number of liability suits filed. As of this writing, such reforms to the legal system have yet to be implemented in the United States.

The financial burden associated with liability suits is so onerous that many defendants choose to settle out of court to mitigate the costs of the process. Much of the time, such settlements have less to do with the merits of the case, and more to do with the relentless expense of pursuing the issue in the courts. Many lawyers are fond of the old adage: "How much justice can you afford?" Given the costs involved, it is not unusual for a suit to be filed where the plaintiff intends to achieve an out-of-court settlement simply by running up the legal costs for the defendant.

Umbrella Insurance

Given the costs of guarding against liability issues, there is a special type of insurance available which adds protection specific to this kind of financial hardship. It is called Umbrella Insurance. It should be emphasized that Umbrella Insurance is a second line of defense, and is utilized only if the primary insurance protection proves insufficient. Of course, the primary protection is the liability component of your automobile or homeowners' policy—but these policies have limits on the amount of coverage available. Nevertheless, you must have these insurance policies already in force—in the minimum amounts required—before the insurance company will offer you an Umbrella policy.

Umbrella insurance is designed to protect you against the costs of liabilities of all kinds. The premium for such insurance is relatively modest, with costs approximating several hundred dollars per year for $1,000,000 in coverage. The coverage is available to meet both legal expense, and any award that the courts may assess if you are found liable. Should the insurance company decide to settle the suit out of court, the coverage amount would be available to meet the settlement cost as well.

Summary & Review

1. What are the two objectives of Property & Casualty Insurance?
2. What kinds of assets would you want to protect with P&C Insurance?
3. Define Liability. How does the liability issue affect the kind of insurance you wish to have?
4. How does Umbrella Insurance contribute to your financial protection?

Figure 11:3 There is a special type of insurance available which adds protection specific to this kind of financial hardship.

Automobile Insurance

When it comes to protecting ourselves from potential financial loss, our automobile stands near the top of the list. Consider the amount of money tied up in that single asset, as well as the liabilities involved when thousands of pounds of steel and glass are hurtling down the road at speeds that your forbearers thought impossible only a hundred years ago.

Automobile insurance requirements are regulated by each state, but the common protocol is a package of coverage that includes:

- Part A: Liability Coverage: Provides protection for you if you're liable for property damage or bodily injury caused by your automobile.
- Part B: Medical Expense Coverage: Provides coverage for medical bills.
- Part C: Uninsured Motorist's Coverage: Provides protection for property damage or bodily injury caused by another driver who has no liability insurance.
- Part D: Collision and Comprehensive Coverage: Provides coverage for your automobile against collision, and against losses not caused by collision such as theft, a hail storm, or vandalism.

Figure 11:4 When it comes to protecting ourselves from potential financial loss, our automobile stands near the top of the list.

In addition, there are a number of Endorsements, which reference additions to or modifications of the basic policy, which are common in automobile insurance. Such endorsements may include:

- Underinsured Motorists: Coverage of the automobile and of persons for loss or medical expenses sustained from the operation of an underinsured motor vehicle.
- Rental Reimbursement: Coverage to meet rental expense of another car while the insured vehicle is under repair.

Of course, any insurance company will specify the amount of any loss it is willing to cover, and will not pay for losses exceeding the specified amount. You can increase the amount the insurance company will pay by increasing the coverage available, and by paying the higher premiums that such additional coverage requires. The amount of coverage is typically conveyed in a code that may read something like this:

Bodily Injury Liability—100/300

This simply means that when a claim is submitted for Bodily Injury Liability, the insurance company will pay up to $100,000 in medical expenses per person, or up to $300,000 per accident. If, for example, a single person sustained injuries that resulted in a medical bill above $100,000, the insurance company will only pay up to $100,000 of that bill. If a number of people are injured in the same accident, the insurance company will pay up to $100,000 in medical expenses for each person injured, but not more than $300,000 total as a result of that accident.

Often, the insurance company will quote its liability coverage like this:

Liability Coverage—100/300/50

The first two numbers reference bodily injury liability, as discussed earlier. The third number references property damage liability; in this example indicating a $50,000 limit for payment of damages to the property of others.

Keeping Automobile Insurance Premium Low

As already mentioned, one way you have of holding your automobile insurance costs down, is to buy the appropriate amount of coverage. Most states have a minimum level of coverage that is required, generally above 25/50/10, though many states have lower minimums. The 100/300/50 example cited is well above the minimum of most states, but is the recommended coverage level by many insurance companies. You can, of course, get higher coverage levels if you wish. Under the 100/300/50 policy, the insurance company will pay for medical expenses up to $100,000 per person but not to exceed $300,000 per accident, and will pay for property damage up to $50,000.

The size of your premiums also depends on the type of car you are insuring. Newer or more expensive cars and higher performance cars carry higher premiums. Usually, the premium can be reduced if the car has certain safety features such as air bags and antitheft devices, or if you are have multiple insurance policies (multiple vehicles or both car and home insurance) with the same company.

In addition to the type of car you are insuring, the location of that car is a significant factor in the policy premium. If the car is garaged in an urban area, premiums will generally be higher than if it is garaged in a rural location. Sometimes students will have their car insured based on the city where their family lives, and then take that car away with them to a small town when they go to school. It might save a few premium dollars if they notified the insurance company that the car will be garaged in a smaller town versus the city.

Additional premium discounts depend on the nature of the driver. Generally speaking, the female driver is charged a lower premium than the male, and older drivers have lower premiums than younger drivers. If you have demonstrated that you are a careful driver—no tickets and no accidents—the insurance premium will be lower. Moreover, if you are a good student, you may find that those A's result in a reduced insurance premium. Recently, many P&C insurance companies have been looking at your Credit Scores as another part of the formula for calculating your insurance premiums. The higher the Credit Score, the lower the premium—all other things equal. All of these factors have been shown to reveal the likelihood that the insurance company will end up writing a check in response to a claim. If the likelihood of the insurance company paying a claim is higher, then the premium you pay will be higher. If the insurance company believes that the probability of a claim is low, then they adjust the premium you pay accordingly.

Figure 11:5 If the car is garaged in an urban area, premiums will generally be higher than if it is garaged in a rural location.

> ### Get Real
>
> I recently received a letter from my automobile insurance company, which reveals how the ripples from being financially responsible affect other aspects of a person's finances. I quote from this letter.
>
> > "We routinely gather information needed to provide you with quality services at fair prices. We order consumer reports, such as insurance loss history reports from various reporting agencies. These reports may assist in determining your eligibility for insurance and the price you may be charged. Consumer reports may be used for updates, renewals, or extensions of this insurance.
> >
> > "As part of your upcoming renewal, we will be ordering credit information. We may use a credit-based score based on the information contained in the credit report. This credit information may assist in determining the price you are charged for your insurance."
>
> Clearly, the way I manage my debt is evidence of a level of financial responsibility. That level of financial responsibility is seen by the auto insurer as an indication of reduced risk—resulting in a lower premium charge.

Another significant factor in the size of your automobile insurance premium is the size of the Deductible you allow. A deductible is that amount of any insurance claim, which the policyholder pays. Remember our earlier discussion where we began this process with "Define the Problem"? Insurance is not intended to cover every incident and every cost. It is intended to offset the catastrophic expenses that are just too big for us to handle without major damage to our finances. That being said, how much of any incident could you self-insure? Could you come up with the first $100 . . . $500 . . . $1,000 of the costs of an accident? Studies have shown that if you agree to pay the first $500 in costs, as opposed to no deductible at all, you could lower your premium by almost half.

One more avenue to keeping those premium costs low is to simply shop around. It is amazing the difference in costs between different insurance companies. Though you are the same person with the same car looking for the same level of coverage at the same deductible, you will find that one insurance company's quote can be substantially different from another. Here, a note of caution is in order. Don't rely solely on the lowest premium quote as your selection criteria. Make sure that the company you are buying your auto insurance from is available when you need them . . . that they will step up and mitigate the financial hardship should one occur . . . and that they can be relied on to take care of your needs. After all, insurance is not just about writing checks—it is about solving problems. In Appendix II, Application Worksheet 11:1 gives you the opportunity to shop around and compare the auto insurance offered by different companies.

> ### Summary & Review
>
> 1. Name the primary components of the automobile insurance package? What potential losses does each component cover?
> 2. In auto insurance nomenclature, a code such as 25/50/10 may be found to describe the extent of the coverage offered. What does that code mean? In your mind, is 25/50/10 adequate protection?
> 3. Cite some of the ways you might keep your auto insurance premium low, without compromising the protection you are buying.
> 4. What is a deductible? How might it affect your insurance premium?

Homeowners Insurance

Although our home may not have the same liability issues as our car, it is an enormous investment, which should be protected by insurance. Like auto insurance, home insurance is regulated by each state, with various requirements depending on the state. Generally speaking, home insurance is written in different packages, identified by the abbreviation HO. Exhibit 11:3 summarizes the major HO products.

Exhibit 11:3 Major Home Insurance Products

Home Insurance	Form	Coverage
HO-0	Dwelling Fire	Coverage on home only against eight named perils. Does not cover personal property or liability.
HO-1	Basic	Coverage of home and contents against 11 named perils. Not allowed in most states.
HO-2	Broad	Coverage of home and contents against 16 named perils. If a peril isn't specifically named in this policy, it isn't covered.
HO-3	Special	Comprehensive coverage of home and contents for all risks except those specifically excluded. Most common form for single family homes.
HO-4	Contents Broad	Tenants insurance offers personal property and liability protection.
HO-5	Comprehensive	Expanded HO-3 coverage on an open peril basis.
HO-6	Unit-Owners	Condominium insurance covers personal property and interior walls, floors, and ceiling against all Broad form perils.
HO-8	Modified Coverage	Coverage for owner-occupied older home where replacement cost far exceeds the property's market value.

Most states are reluctant to allow home insurance to be sold, which covers only certain perils, arguing that if an event occurs which is not listed as covered, the homeowner finds himself uninsured. This is why a narrow insurance product like HO-1 is not available in most states.

However, there are two perils that are always excluded, even under a comprehensive insurance product like HO-3. Those events are flood and earthquake. If your home is in a flood zone or in a seismically active area, you may wish to obtain flood or earthquake insurance. Although there are private insurance companies that sell flood and earthquake insurance, most of this kind of insurance is bought through a government agency such as FEMA.

Get Real

I live in a desert, and virtually no one in my community has flood insurance. Nobody thought it was necessary . . . until.

It was January—and the surrounding mountains were loaded with snow. We generally get a little rain that time of year, which translates into snow in the higher elevations. However, this year was unusually warm, and when the rains came they melted the snow and both snow and rain swelled the riverbeds to overflowing. One creek, which is bordered by homes and which can normally be stepped across in a single stride, became a raging torrent. Not only were the adjacent homes taken into the flood, but the very ground on which they were built was washed away. Virtually no one had flood insurance, even though their homes were along the edge of a creek bed—because no one thought it was necessary in this dry climate.

Figure 11:6 Although our home may not have the same liability issues as our car, it is an enormous investment, which should be protected by insurance.

Property Coverage

Like automobile insurance, property covered under homeowner's insurance has a maximum payout. If the house is insured for $200,000, the insurance company will pay out claims of up to $200,000 on the structure itself. The structure is referenced in Section I of all HO policies except HO-4, and applies to:

Coverage A: The Dwelling

Coverage B: Other structures on the property

Coverage D: Loss of use

Under Coverage D, the insurance company will pay for your alternative housing in the event that your home is rendered uninhabitable. The length of time the insurance company will make this payment varies, but in most instances is sufficient to allow enough time for the home to be repaired.

Insuring the Contents

As you look through the various HO forms you note that, in most instances, insurance coverage applies to both the structure and the contents. (In the case of renters insurance, HO-4 coverage is primarily for the contents and liability.) This coverage is referenced in Section 1 under:

Coverage C: Personal Property

The protocol is that the contents of a home are insured for an amount up to a given percent of the policy amount. That percentage varies depending on the policy, but in most cases content coverage reaches 50% to 75% of the coverage level. For example, if the homeowner has HO-3 insurance of $200,000, and the contents are covered at a 50% ratio, there is coverage of the contents in amount up to $100,000 as part of the policy. Should a disaster occur, which completely destroys both the home and the contents, the insured would have coverage of $200,000 for the home and an additional $100,000 for the contents, or a total of $300,000 of protection.

Figure 11:7 In most instances, insurance coverage applies to both the structure and the contents.

You might be interested to know that Coverage C: Personal Property, applies regardless of the location of the property. In other words, if you are on vacation and someone steals your camera, it would be covered under the Personal Property provision of your homeowner's insurance.

Having said that, there is a difference in the way some insurance companies value the contents. If the policy values the contents at Actual Cash Value, then the payment you receive will be based on the current replacement cost of the item—less depreciation. That will result in a considerable reduction in reimbursement as each item is valued at its depreciated price. However, if the policy values the contents at Replacement Value, then the payment you receive will be based on repairing or replacing the damaged item—there is no depreciation allowance. When asked which method of content reimbursement they prefer, most students say they would like Replacement Value reimbursement. Which method do you have on your homeowners' insurance policy?

The use of a percent of policy value to meet the costs of the contents of a home is generally adequate, provided that the homeowner does not have any particularly valuable items in the house. If there are antiques or artwork, collectables or jewelry, or other items that increase the value of the contents beyond the ratio that would be used in the policy, it is recommended that the homeowner identify those valuables with a separate Personal Property Floater that would add an additional protection amount for such assets apart from the normal personal property coverage.

This brings us to the importance of identifying the assets that are in the home. When you obtain your homeowners' policy, the insurance company will usually offer a brochure that includes an inventory form that you can fill out—identifying the valued contents of the house. Including receipts for the most costly assets would be a good idea. Another approach would be to walk through the house with a camera, taking pictures of the contents. Should there be a loss, the inventory, receipts, and pictures would verify the existence of the asset.

In addition to the two perils of flood and earthquake, which are excluded from coverage under the typical homeowners' insurance policy, certain personal property is also normally excluded. This includes:

- Pets—including animals, birds, fish, etc.
- Property of roomers, boarders, and other tenants not related to the insured.
- Business property.

Homeowners Liability Coverage

Section II of a homeowner's insurance policy covers personal liability, protecting the policyholder from financial loss if someone is injured on their property or as a result of their actions. The minimum level of liability coverage per accident is $100,000. As discussed above, in today's liability lottery, it is important to have this protection even if the chances of actually filing a claim are slim.

Keeping Home Insurance Premiums Low

Like automobile insurance, there are several ways that you can obtain adequate insurance coverage while keeping your premiums relatively low. The first way is to obtain the appropriate level of coverage. This begins with a question: "What would it cost you to replace this house?" Although this question may have two answers depending on whether you go out and buy another house or rebuild the destroyed house on the same lot, the focus is on replacement. The insurance company can help answer this question, as they understand the relative building costs in your area.

Their focus will be on rebuilding the destroyed house rather than buying another home—for two reasons. First, most of the time the house is not completely destroyed, but only damaged. A fire may be confined to the garage area, or a tree falls on only a portion of the structure. Repairing the existing home is much cheaper than buying a new one. Second, most of the time the damage does not affect the lot itself. The ground is not damaged, only the structure. For this reason, when you answer the question as to what it would cost to replace the home, deduct the cost of the lot from your insurance calculation. Once you and the insurance company have identified the appropriate level of coverage, most homeowners' policies will put that level on a COLA or cost of living adjustment, which increases the coverage automatically each year depending on the change in building costs during the previous year.

Additional premium discounts can be obtained from the following.

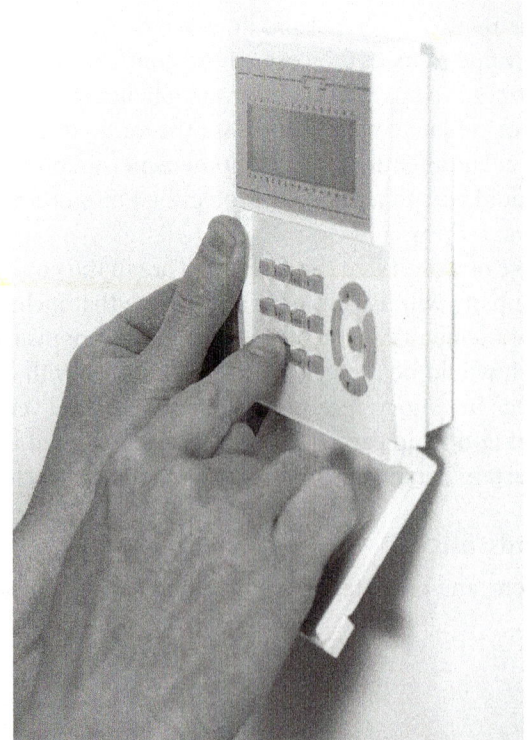

Figure 11:8 Homes that are secured by deadbolt locks, or that have alarm systems, will incur a lower policy premium.

- Homes that are in town and closer to fire protection generally face lower premiums than homes that are in a rural location.
- Homes that are built of brick or stone or other fire resistant materials have lower premiums than homes made of wood.
- Homes that are secured by deadbolt locks, or that have alarm systems, will incur a lower policy premium.
- Like your auto insurance premium, you can reduce your homeowner insurance premium if you elect a higher deductible; effectively self-insuring a somewhat larger amount of any potential loss.
- Again, it pays to shop around. The premium quoted by one insurance company can be substantially different from another provider. If you find a multiline insurer that you are happy with, you will find that insuring both your car and your house with the same company can save you some money. Appendix II, Application Worksheet 11:2, provides a template for shopping your home insurance. You can modify this template and use it to shop for renters insurance (HO-4) if you prefer.

Summary & Review

1. Even the more comprehensive forms of homeowners' insurance exclude two perils. What two perils are excluded from most homeowners' coverage?
2. What is the protocol for insuring the contents of a home? What should the homeowner do if he has contents that are more valuable than the protocol allows, such as antiques or jewelry?
3. What are the two methods of valuing a home's contents for insurance reimbursement purposes?
4. Name some of the ways you might minimize your homeowners' insurance premium. Which of these ways make the most sense to you at this point in your life?

When You Have a Loss

Many times we grimace as we write our premium checks, regretting the fact that we are spending our hard-earned money and not getting anything tangible in return. Question: Which would you regret more, writing a check and not needing to make a claim, or having a huge loss and realizing that there is no one to help you with it. Actually, we would be living a charmed life if we never had a financial catastrophe. Let's hope that you don't need to submit a claim very often. But if you do, it is good to know that you are backstopped by someone with deep pockets and the financial ability to help. Here are a few simple steps you can take to make the process go smoothly.

First, secure the scene of the accident. If it involves automobiles, move the cars to a safe place and warn oncoming drivers of the accident. If anyone is injured, get medical help as soon as possible.

Second, report the accident immediately. Notify the police. Get the names and addresses of any witnesses, together with contact information on any other people involved. In some jurisdictions, the police are slow to respond to any accident that does not involve injury. As a result you may have to do your own investigation. If you have a camera, take pictures of the scene. Write down your recollection of what happened. Don't admit guilt or sign anything. Report the loss to your insurance company as soon as possible, with a formal claim to follow.

Third, do what you can to secure your property. If the accident involves automobiles that are no longer drivable, have them towed to a secure location. If a window has been broken, don't let that damage foster more damage. Board up broken windows or holes in the roof to protect your property from further problems.

Fourth, make a detailed list of everything lost or damaged and submit a formal claim for the losses incurred. Most insurance companies will send an *Adjuster* to inspect the damage. An insurance adjuster is an employee or agent of the insurance company responsible for assessing and mitigating the damage sustained by the policyholder. Cooperate with the adjuster so that your loss can be resolved as soon as possible.

Finally, keep good records of your losses and the insurance company's settlement. This will allow you to determine whether the settlement was fair, what portion of the loss you met as a result of your deductible or other coinsurance, and the possible application of such loss as a deductible expense on your income tax return.

206 Insurance

First, secure the scene of the accident.

Second, report the accident immediately.

Third, do what you can to secure your property.

Fourth, make a detailed list of everything lost or damaged and submit a formal claim.

Finally, keep good records of your losses and the insurance company's settlement.

No-Fault Insurance

Over the years, there has been a lot of haggling over the issue of who is at fault in the event of an accident. This haggling was like sand in the gears, slowing the process of settling the claim and reimbursing the insured. As a result, most states have now implemented No-Fault Insurance, which effectively bypasses the issue—at least initially—of who is to blame.

No-Fault Insurance works like this. When that catastrophe occurs and your property is damaged or medical bills are incurred, it is your insurance company that works with you to assess the loss and pay the claim—regardless of who is at fault. This provides a straightforward and much quicker protocol for resolving the problem and concluding the settlement. The result is that the legal cost associated with establishing blame is not incurred, and those attendant expenses of insurance should be lower.

After your insurance company has taken care of you, they would then go to the other party if they are at fault, and make a written request for reimbursement in a process called Insurance Subrogation. This process is used to recover those amounts that they have compensated you from the liable party—effectively filing a claim against the other person or their insurance company. This process takes place after your claim has been settled, shortening the length of time necessary to resolve your problem.

> ### Summary & Review
> 1. What is the first thing that should be done following an accident?
> 2. Define the role of the Adjustor in the claim process.
> 3. Does your state have a no-fault insurance provision? How does no-fault insurance work?
> 4. Does no-fault insurance mean that there are no liability issues stemming from an accident?

Chapter 12
Health & Disability Insurance

210 Insurance

Contributed by Robert Eagleston. Copyright © Kendall Hunt Publishing Company.

Chapter Objectives

1. Understand how the Affordable Care Act changed health insurance.
2. Know the rules for applying for health insurance.
3. Be aware of those actions that you might take to minimize health problems and improve the quality of life.
4. Become familiar with the different types of health insurance plans and how to distinguish one from another.
5. Consider the concept of disability insurance and the financial consequences of becoming disabled without it.
6. Identify the different types of disability insurance policies.
7. Know what is involved in the disability application process.
8. Evaluate the various features of a disability policy and the meaning of the different definitions of disability.
9. Be aware of the steps involved in filing a disability claim.
10. Become aware of the reasons a Long Term Care policy should be considered as a retirement planning tool.
11. Understand the different options in setting up a Long Term Care policy and how they impact the cost.
12. Consider the political and economic ramifications of the current health-care debate . . . and where we go from here.

Health Insurance

Benjamin Franklin was quoted as saying, "In this world nothing can be said to be certain, except death and taxes." If he were to restate his quote today, he might add a few more items, including "annual changes to our Health insurance policy." Historically, health insurance has been the vehicle most people rely on to protect themselves against the economic hardship that may come from illness or accident. Of course, having insurance does not stop those events from occurring . . . they happen to us from time to time even though we wish they didn't. Health insurance simply helps pay for the soaring medical costs incurred when a prolonged illness or serious accident occurs. Health insurance has been the most rapidly changing and evolving insurance product for some time now, and we have every reason to believe the trend will continue.

January 1, 2014 was the official beginning of many significant changes in the health insurance market with the implementation of the Affordable Care Act. Possibly the most significant change is the fact medical underwriting is no longer a part of the application process, for individuals and groups. Previously, only those with good health could qualify for private health insurance at a reasonable rate, and those who couldn't qualify were forced to pay outrageously high premiums or go without health insurance at all. Now, all U.S. citizens who apply within the appropriate dates are guaranteed to be accepted by all companies. Smoking status, not health, is the only way two individuals who are the same age living within the same zip code can have different rates when applying for a matching plan. Guaranteed acceptance has led to lower rates for those who had trouble qualifying in the past and in many cases higher rates for those who were previously able to qualify. Another change brought about by the Affordable Care Act is that policy features such as certain benefits and policy limits are regulated and mandatory for a plan to be compliant. For example, maternity plans were dwindling to nonexistence, and now all health plans are required to provide maternity coverage, whether it is requested or not.

Those who wish to make changes to their private health plan can do so once every year during Open Enrollment. Open Enrollment is that designated period near the end of each year, in which changes can be made to health insurance subscriptions. Any such changes made will become effective from January 1 of the following year. Outside of Open Enrollment, plan changes can only be made if there is a qualifying event, such as a permanent residence move or the termination of a group plan. We are now compelled to apply for health

Figure 12:1 January 1, 2014 was the official beginning of many significant changes in the health insurance market with the implementation of the Affordable Care Act.

insurance to avoid fines for not being insured. Government subsidies are available to those who cannot afford to pay for health insurance. To qualify, applications need to be completed through the government website and the household income must meet the subsidy criteria. Otherwise, for those who don't qualify for a subsidy, they can go direct to a company's website or through a broker to apply.

Individuals can take out a private health insurance policy or may have an opportunity to procure coverage through a group or association they belong to. The advantage of an employee having coverage through an employer is that at least 50% of the cost, if not more, is subsidized by the employer, which gives them a policy and premium they may not find in the private marketplace. Family members typically are not subsidized and can run more expensive through an employer. It is always a good idea to take a look at the private marketplace and compare available plans to what you can get through your employer or another association, and this should be done on an annual basis. Opting in to a group plan or making plan changes can only be done at renewal unless, similar to individual plans, there is a qualifying event.

More employers have moved from offering one plan to offering sometimes up to 3 different plan options. Whether you are choosing from between 2 or 3 available employer plans or from the private marketplace, the fact that group and individual plans can now only be changed once per year makes having a basic understanding of how plans work extremely important.

Staying Well

Of course, the best way to reduce the cost of health care is to not get sick. You chuckle . . . but it's true. Moreover, we all know what we can do to stay healthy. It is puzzling to note that under current law, the only way a health insurance company can differentiate between those who practice good health-care habits and those who don't, is whether the applicant is a smoker or not. Smoking is clearly a recipe for poor health. Statistics have shown that the smoking male will take an average of 2.5 years off his life, whereas the smoking female will take an average of 1.8 years off her life. This does not count the years when the smoker is sick, struggling to breath. However, weight control is an even bigger issue. The obese male shortens his life by an average of 4.9 years, whereas the obese female lives 4.1 years less than those who are not obese. Like the smoker, most of us can control whether we are overweight or not, and we should develop those habits that will help improve our health.

The following table summarizes those practices that lead to better health. You can get similar information from any doctors' office, together with their suggestions as to how you might achieve better health.

In addition to good health habits, there are things we can do to protect ourselves from accidents. It has been said that the four dumbest words spoken are: "Hey Man . . . Watch This." A little patience and some additional care in our daily activities can help reduce those hurtful "Oops." For example, if you enjoy riding a motorcycle,

Exhibit 12:1 Toward Better Health

- ☐ Eliminate smoking, alcohol, and illegal drugs. Even where a drug might be legal, it can be addictively harmful.
- ☐ Watch your eating habits. Know the food groups, and get plenty of fruits and vegetables. Reduce consumption of sugars, carbonated beverages, and caffeine.
- ☐ Exercise. This means involvement in those activities that will increase your cardiovascular rate. The strong human heart will beat approximately 3.3 billion times in an 80-year life; it is a remarkable machine if cared for properly.
- ☐ Balance your diet with exercise so as to achieve the proper weight for your sex and build. If you find you are getting overweight, take steps to keep it down.
- ☐ Get the proper amount of rest. Doctors will point out that the average adult needs approximately 8 hours of sleep each day and children require even more.
- ☐ See your doctor regularly. A routine annual exam can help identify issues that can be corrected if caught early. If you think there is a health issue, consult your doctor.

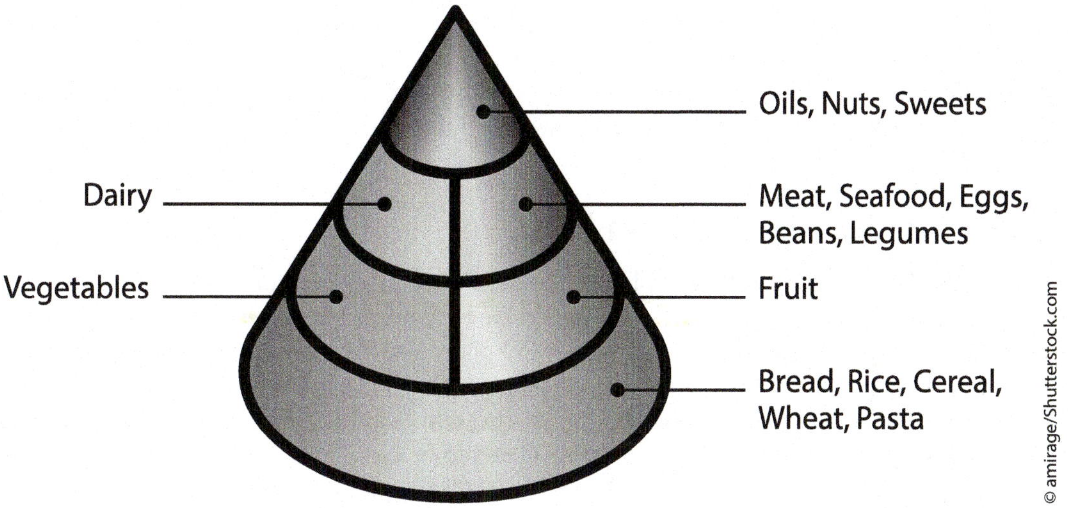

FOOD PYRAMID

Figure 12:2 Know the food groups, and get plenty of fruits and vegetables.

you are probably a better than average driver. You have to be, because you put yourself in harm's way every time you start it up. It is not your driving skills that may lead to an accident, but other drivers who are not as capable as you. And if there is an accident, the motorcycle rider will be hurt far more than the person in the other car. And then there are those activities where a mistake is almost always fatal—such as sky diving or free climbing. We won't get into that.

> **Summary & Review**
>
> 1. How do Affordable Health Care compliant plans compare to older plans?
> 2. Why might a group policy be suitable for a family? What would make it unsuitable?
> 3. What actions can you take to stay well?

Private Sources of Health Insurance and Health Care

Health Maintenance Organization (HMO)

An HMO is a health plan that utilizes primary care physicians as "Gatekeepers" and has patients first go through them to see a specialist. For example, if you are experiencing pain in your foot, you would first go to your primary care physician for an exam. If the problem couldn't be resolved, you would then receive a referral to a reputable foot doctor in the network. Customers enrolled in an HMO also are only covered when they see providers within the plan network. Any services received outside of the network will be their full financial responsibility (outside of emergency situations). HMOs can negotiate lower premiums and co-payments with providers as there is a guarantee their policyholders will only be seeing providers in the network.

The "gatekeeper" system, the out of network restrictions, and the contracted network are all reasons why HMOs are generally less expensive than other plans. They can be ideal for those who do not go to the doctor often and are not opposed to limiting their treatment to providers in network.

Preferred Provider Organization (PPO)

PPOs are more flexible than an HMO, as they allow patients the ability to choose the physicians and specialists they see without having to go through a "gatekeeper" first. Although there is greater freedom to see providers, patients do have incentive to stay within the network. Out of network providers will have a higher out-of-pocket cost, and patients will need to pay the provider directly and file the claim with the health insurance company to get reimbursed. Some PPO plans have co-pays, but many do not and require the deductible to be satisfied before the coinsurance kicks in.

PPO plans usually have higher premiums than HMO plans, and they are best suited for those who want the flexibility to see providers of their choice while knowing all visits will provide coverage to some degree.

Exclusive Provider Organization (EPO)

EPOs are a mixture of an HMO and PPO plan, with more of an HMO resemblance. Like a PPO, there isn't a need to go through a "gatekeeper" and any provider in the network is fair game. However, like an HMO, there isn't any coverage available outside of the network. EPO plans also have lower co-pays and premiums like the HMOs due also to the fact the plans can negotiate lower rates with providers.

EPOs work well for individuals who don't want to deal with waiting to see a specialist and are looking to spend the least amount on a monthly basis. They also need to be committed to staying within the network.

High Deductible/Catastrophic (HSA)

Health Savings Account (HSA) plans are ones that meet the criteria and allow for the establishment of a Health Savings Account. These plans are designed to control health costs by offering lower plan premiums with the opportunity to establish a Health Savings Account, which can accept optional contributions up to an annual limit that are tax-deductible. The actual savings account can be set up through the health company or any large bank. Money contributed can be used for qualifying medical, dental, and vision expenses, and the IRS sets forth individual and family contribution limits each year. A key feature of HSAs is that the money not used in a year carries over to the next, as opposed to the "use it or lose it" flex plans many have through an employer. This allows account holders to build their balance to help offset the cost of future medical, dental, or visions needs they'll encounter, including in retirement. Most HSA-qualified plans have the same characteristics of a

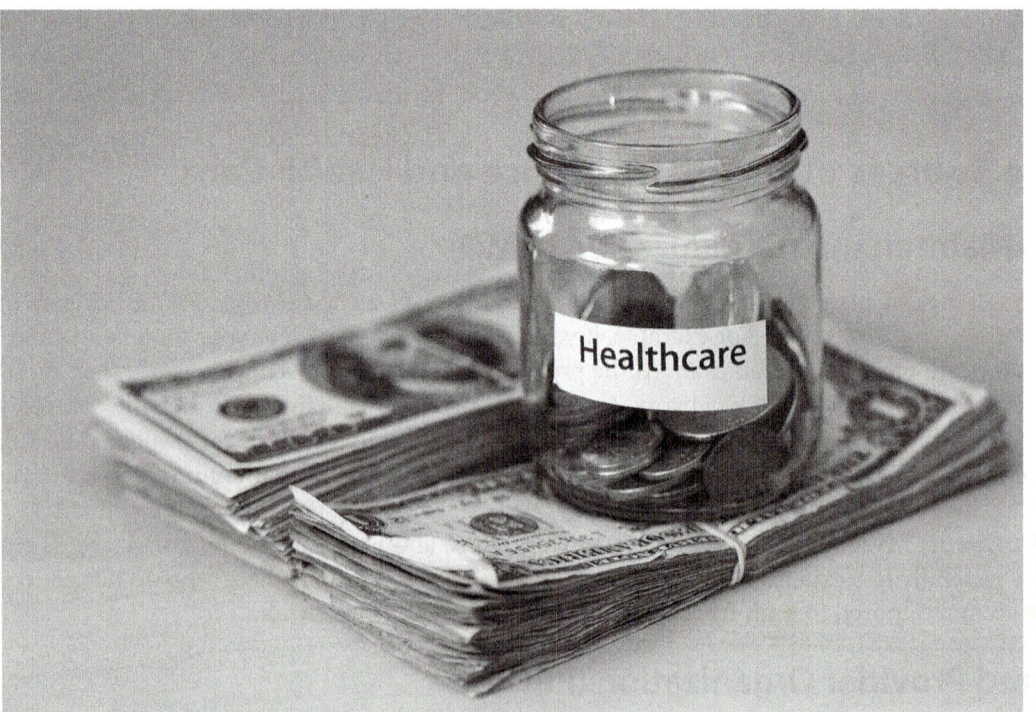

Figure 12:3 Money contributed to a Health Savings Account (HSA) can be used for qualifying medical, dental, and vision expenses.

PPO plan (although this shouldn't be assumed in all cases) and provide coverage for visits in and outside the network. Like PPO plans, there is a financial incentive to stay inside the network to avoid lower coinsurance and higher out of pocket costs. Also, HSA plans don't have co-pays and charge the discounted network rate up until the deductible is met.

HSA plans may not be appropriate for someone who likes predictable medical expenses or who has knowledge of significant future medical needs. They do work well for individuals who want to gain more control over how their health dollars are spent by minimizing their monthly premium and allowing for the tax deductible funding of an HSA account.

Government Health-Care Programs

Medicare

Medicare is a Federal government health insurance program for people 65 and older, and for people of any age with certain permanent medical or disabling conditions. It is administered by the Health-Care Financing Administration, and funded in part from a Medicare tax imposed on earnings.

Medicare has four parts.

Part A provides hospital insurance benefits, helping to pay for inpatient hospital care, inpatient care in a skilled nursing facility, home health care, and hospice care.

Part B provides physician insurance benefits, helping to pay for doctor's services, outpatient care, and a variety of other medical services and equipment.

Part C—sometimes called Medicare Advantage—includes all benefits and services covered under Part A and Part B, and typically includes Medicare prescription drug coverage (Part D). Part C is run by Medicare-approved private insurance companies, and usually includes extra benefits and services for an extra cost.

Part D helps cover the cost of prescription drugs. It is similarly run by Medicare-approved private insurance companies and is designed to help lower prescription drug costs.

Increasingly, many individuals find that the proportion of health-care costs paid by Medicare is declining to the point where their co-payment responsibility poses an economic hardship. Accordingly, many people have purchased a supplemental insurance policy popularly called Medigap Insurance. Medigap insurance may be purchased from a private insurance company, or may be available through the Medicare Advantage (Medicare Part C) program that provides additional benefits for an additional cost. This is supplemental health-care insurance designed to help meet those medical costs not covered by Medicare. Medigap is not sold by the Federal government, but is available from many private insurance companies. As the bulk of the medical expense is still covered by Medicare, the cost of this supplemental insurance is relatively nominal. This could change if the coverage provided by Medicare continues to decline, thrusting more of the burden on supplemental health-care plans.

Medicaid

Medicaid is a government health insurance program, which is designed to provide medical assistance to low income individuals. Unlike Medicare, Medicaid is administered by each state, within certain broad requirements as outlined by the Federal government. In qualifying individuals to receive Medicaid, the law looks at income levels, bank and savings account balances, and assets.

Summary & Review

1. Name the four private sources of health insurance and health care. What makes each different?
2. Discuss the biggest drawback of an HMO plan. Are there advantages of an HMO plan?
3. What are the benefits of a Health Savings Account?
4. What government health-care programs are available? What are the qualifications to enroll in government health-care programs?

Disability Insurance

Figure 12:4 The ability to generate an income by doing what we do and know is our most valuable asset.

One of the keys to understanding the importance of disability insurance is to first understand the concept of it. We acquire many assets in our lifetime. Some, such as a home, automobile, or jewelry, can carry significant value. Whether by choice or to satisfy the terms of a bank loan, insuring these valuable assets tends to be second nature to us. We wouldn't think of purchasing a dream home and then leaving it open to the many possible exposures without an insurance policy in place. Some of us wouldn't think twice about insuring a new cell phone against potential damages and defects. The ability to generate an income by doing what we do and know is our most valuable asset. Not only is this our most valuable asset, but it is what makes the purchase and maintenance of all other assets possible. Think about how a sudden work and income stoppage would affect you financially. How would you maintain your current lifestyle? Do you have enough savings to carry you for a significant period? The implementation of a disability insurance policy is how we insure our most valuable asset and can provide the financial solutions to the problems that arise when we lose our ability to do what we do and know.

The most common form of disability insurance is disability income, which is designed to replace your paycheck if disabled. Some of the other types are:

1. **Business Overhead Expense:** Designed specifically to reimburse business owners for overhead expenses incurred while they are disabled. Expenses covered under the policy can include rent, utilities, employees' salaries, taxes, expenses, depreciation, and scheduled payments of debt principal. Benefit periods are typically 12 months and can be up to 24 months.
2. **Loan-Disability:** Disability coverage that matches the loan terms and provide for the continuation of payments for the life of the loan in a disability. These policies are especially useful when a disability policy is a requirement to secure a loan and to free up the monthly benefit on a personal Disability or Overhead policy.

3. **Disability Buyout**: Many buy–sell agreements address disability and the scenario under which a non-disabled partner would buyout a disabled partner. A disability buyout policy helps to fund the buy–sell agreement by providing the nondisabled partner or the business with the funds necessary to purchase the disabled partner's interest.
4. **Retirement Plan Contribution Disability**: Provides for the continuation of contributions made to a retirement plan. Benefits are paid to a trust and the assets are then invested by a trustee, but at the insured's direction.

Not all disability policies are created equal, and a common mistake individuals make is assuming a policy will work how they think it should instead of taking the time to understand the details before it is purchased.

Disability insurance can be purchased on an individual or group basis. A group policy may be available through an association or an employer, and its relatively low cost is what makes it most attractive. Some of the reasons for group policies being less expensive are that they can be canceled by the insurance company or the association, rates increase (scheduled increases based on certain ages or periods), premiums can be adjusted based on the claims experience of the group and they often contain more restrictive definitions of disability and contract provisions when compared to a properly structured individual policy. Group policies require you to meet qualification requirements on a regular basis to maintain eligibility. A couple of the standard qualifiers are that you have to be an active member or employee of a specific association or company, and that you have to be working a certain number of hours. Again, group policies are less expensive than most individual policies, and understanding the differences between an available group and individual policy will make determining if the savings a group policy offers is justified.

The following benefits and features should all be clearly understood when considering the purchase of a Disability policy:

Renewability: The renewability provision determines whether or not the company can alter your policy in the future. Policies can be guaranteed renewable only or both noncancelable and guaranteed renewable. Policies that are guaranteed renewable only cannot be canceled or changed by the insurance company as long as the insured continues to pay premiums. However, insurance companies can legally increase premiums in

Figure 12:5 Policies that are guaranteed renewable cannot be canceled or changed by the insurance company as long as the insured continues to pay premiums.

the future, provided the rate increase is approved by the state insurance department and applied to the entire class of policyholders. Noncancelable and guaranteed renewable policies cannot experience increases in premium, provision changes, or cancellations as long as the policy is in force. The noncancelable and guaranteed renewable policies do cost more, but they offer the greatest level of protection against undesirable changes in your policy.

Definition of Disability: A company's definition of disability is a key feature, if not the most important feature, to consider and thoroughly understand before purchasing a policy. The "Own Occupation" definition of disability considers you disabled if you can't perform the duties of your current occupation, but you are working and being compensated in another occupation. For example, if you were working as a dentist and injured your hand to the degree you couldn't treat patients, you would suffer a loss of your income source to go along with the physical pain. If physically able, you may decide to stay within the field of dentistry and get a job teaching at a dental school close by, or you may decide to enter into another field and get a job as a realtor. In either case, you would be able to receive compensation from your new job while collecting your full disability benefit, provided you could show proof you were unable to perform the duties of your job as a dentist. The "Transitional Occupation" definition is similar to the "Own Occupation" definition, in that you are considered to be disabled if you can't perform the duties of your occupation, but the definition will not allow you to exceed your pre-disability income. If you were making $100,000/year as a dentist and had a $5,000/month benefit (or $60,000/year) and a teaching salary of $70,000/year, your disability benefit would be reduced to keep your combined compensation (disability benefits + new job income) at $100,000. The third definition is the "Any Occupation" definition. This is the most restrictive, as one would be considered totally disabled if they were both unable to perform the duties of their occupation and were not working in another occupation. The dentist who became a teacher or a realtor in the previous example could not be considered totally disabled under this definition. All three definitions can be found in group and individual policies. What makes the interpretation difficult is that many group and individual policies advertise their policy as having the "Own Occupation" definition, when the language clearly suggests it is not. Remember, if stipulations are added to the definition, such as your inability to make more money than your pre-disability income or your inability to work in another occupation to qualify, the policy is not an "Own Occupation" policy.

Residual Disability: A very good possibility for someone who is injured or sick is that they would be able to work in the same occupation, but with some limitations that would affect their ability to maintain their same income. The Residual Disability, or Partial Disability rider, allows you to collect a percentage of your monthly benefit equal to your income percentage loss if you are still working in your occupation but experience a loss of income due to a sickness or disability. Most companies require you to have an income loss of at least 20%, and some require it to be 15%. To be considered totally disabled, most companies set the income percentage loss at 80%. As an example, if you were making $100,000 in your current job and experienced an accident or sickness that forced you to work less or at a slower pace, resulting in an income loss of $30,000 (or 30%), you would be able to collect on 30% of your benefit. An important detail to check for is whether or not total disability is required before a residual or partial benefit can be paid. The total disability requirement is unfavorable, as you may have an injury that slows you down, but does not first take you out of working. A policy that doesn't require you to be totally disabled can pay a percentage of your benefit even if you never stopped working.

Cost of Living Adjustment: We can look years into the past and find several examples of how the cost of what we buy has increased. Food items and other goods that once could be purchased for a nickel can now cost over $10, and the new car that used to cost $500 can cost as much as or even more than $50,000. Inflation has caused our buying power to decrease over time, and we can be reasonably sure it will continue to do so. Most disability policies offer a Cost of Living Adjustment, or COLA rider, which helps to offset the effect of inflation by increasing the monthly benefit at the end of each year in a claim. Policies with the COLA rider will either increase by a set percentage or will increase up to a maximum percentage, with the increase being tied to the Consumer Price Index. Three questions to ask regarding the COLA rider are (1) Is the interest credited to the benefit compound or simple? (2) Does the policy have a cap the COLA rider can take the benefit to? (3) If I return to work, do I get to keep the increased benefit at the same price I was paying previously, or do I have to purchase the increased benefit?

Figure 12:6 We can look years into the past and find several examples of how the cost of what we buy has increased.

Future Increase Option: A common concern individuals have with disability insurance is that they qualify for a certain amount today, but they worry their health may not be as favorable a year or two later when it is time to increase their monthly benefit. The Future Increase or Future Purchase Option is a feature that allows you to secure the ability to apply for a certain amount in the future without having to go through medical underwriting (financials would have to justify any increase). Considering how likely it is to have an accident, injury, receive a diagnosis, or take a medication, which will make qualifying for a disability policy difficult or impossible, having the option to increase is a valuable option, when available.

Catastrophic Disability: This rider is used to supplement the base disability benefit if the insured is unable to perform two or more activities of daily living (ADLs) without some assistance, experiences an irrevocable disability, or suffers from a cognitive impairment. The six activities of daily living are bathing, eating, dressing, transferring, toileting, and continence, and Alzheimer's and Dementia are two examples of a cognitive impairment. Somebody who had a $10,000/month policy with a $5,000 catastrophic rider would receive $10,000 only if unable to perform the duties of their occupation but able to perform all six ADLs. The same individual would receive $15,000/month if they couldn't perform the duties of their occupation and needed help with at least two of the ADLs.

Your net income helps determine how much monthly benefit you qualify for. Groups will typically insure a percentage of your income to a maximum monthly benefit, and individual policies will give a maximum monthly benefit based on what your income is. The income companies look at is your net income (after expenses) and before taxes. For business owners, any W2 income is combined with business profit to make up your total income. Unearned income, such as capital gains and rental income, may reduce the amount of income considered for coverage.

Health plays a major role in disability insurance. Along with income, it is the determining factor whether or not you'll be approved for coverage, if any specific conditions or body parts will be excluded and what your health classification will be. There are many who see and have the need to secure a disability policy, but they lack the good health to qualify. Group policies through an employer or an association will at times offer a certain amount of monthly benefit without medical underwriting, which is extremely valuable and generous for those who wouldn't otherwise qualify. There is certain medical history that will be dealt with similarly by all companies, such as a recent cancer diagnosis or a heart attack, but several other sicknesses or injuries can receive different responses from two or three different companies. Always know that the disability market consists of several companies, and it is important to be willing to explore alternate companies if your first choice doesn't give you desirable results

Disability Income policies can be paid either before-tax as a business expense (for business owners) or after-tax from a personal account. The consequence of paying for a disability policy before-tax is the benefit will be taxed. Policies are typically paid for personally after-tax for this reason. Business Overhead premiums, on the other hand, are paid for through the business and deductible as a business expense.

Those who experience the misfortune of becoming disabled and have a disability policy in place will need to know what to do in relation to their policy and when they can expect their first check. A disability claim starts on the date of diagnosis or when the accident/injury occurred. To receive benefits, an elimination period of 30, 60, 90, or 180 days first has to be satisfied and then another 30 days needs to pass to earn the first month's check. For example, someone who has a policy with a 90-day elimination period will have to satisfy the 90-day period, go one more month and then receive their check, which ends up being 120 days after their disability started. Policies decrease in cost as you increase your elimination period, but you must make sure there are savings to support you during the elimination period if you choose to extend it. Along with the elimination period needing to be satisfied, claim paperwork has to be completed by the insured and any doctors being seen for the disability. Follow-up requests for financial and medical information are made throughout a claim. Those who return to work have the option to reinstate their policy payments and can collect benefits in the future if they become disabled again. By default, agents are left out dealing with a claim after they make the initial phone call to the company to report the claim. They can play a key role in helping to facilitate the properly completed paperwork in a timely manner and can help to ensure checks are received the day they're supposed to, and so their involvement should be insisted on.

Get Real

I will never forget my visit to a client's home who had previously been diagnosed with multiple sclerosis. He had owned his successful dental practice for a number of years but was forced to sell it and retire soon after the diagnosis. Fortunately for him and his family, he had purchased the maximum amount of disability he could, and his family was able to maintain a comfortable lifestyle. I felt a high level of sadness for this client, as I tried to imagine what he had gone through in a short time and the path he still had ahead of him. While sad, I was also very thankful and relieved he saw the importance of protecting his most valuable asset and implementing disability insurance while he could.

Summary & Review

1. What is a Disability Income policy insuring?
2. Identify the different types of Disability insurance. Under which scenarios would each by utilized.
3. Discuss the differences between individual and group disability. What is the feature that makes a group policy the most attractive?
4. Explain the difference between the three definitions of disability. Which is the most favorable?
5. How many days would it take for someone with a 90-day elimination period to receive their first check?

Long Term Care

Many retirees who worked and saved for years to live a comfortable retirement are encountering economic challenges when faced with long term care needs (nursing home, assisted living, and home health care). The cost of long term care can be expensive and can drain retirement funds at a rapid pace, especially when it wasn't adequately planned for. One solution to make sure retirement doesn't get cut short due to the cost of care is to save more money in the working years and hope it's enough, and another is to go ahead and pay for future care today by purchasing a Long Term Care insurance policy.

Long Term Care insurance provides a daily, weekly, or monthly benefit in the event you and/or your spouse ever require nursing home, home health, or assisted living care. A common misconception is that the purchase of the insurance is reserved for those in their later years or for those who are already receiving care. Age is a factor in the rates charged, but health plays the most significant role in applying for coverage. Someone in poor health will not qualify for a policy, which is why the ideal time to apply is when you are younger and typically in better health. To qualify to receive benefits, one must be unable to perform at least two of the activities of daily living (bathing, eating, dressing, transferring, toileting, and continence) or have a severe cognitive impairment, such as dementia or Alzheimer's disease.

When looking to purchase a Long Term Care policy, the following items should be considered:

1. Contract Type: Policies can either be "reimbursement" or "indemnity (cash)" policies. A Reimbursement Policy will pay the lesser of the cost of care or the maximum benefit and an Indemnity Policy will pay the full daily benefit, regardless of the cost of care. For example, if the policy was for $200/day and the cost of care was $170, the reimbursement policy would pay $170 and the indemnity policy would pay out the full $200.

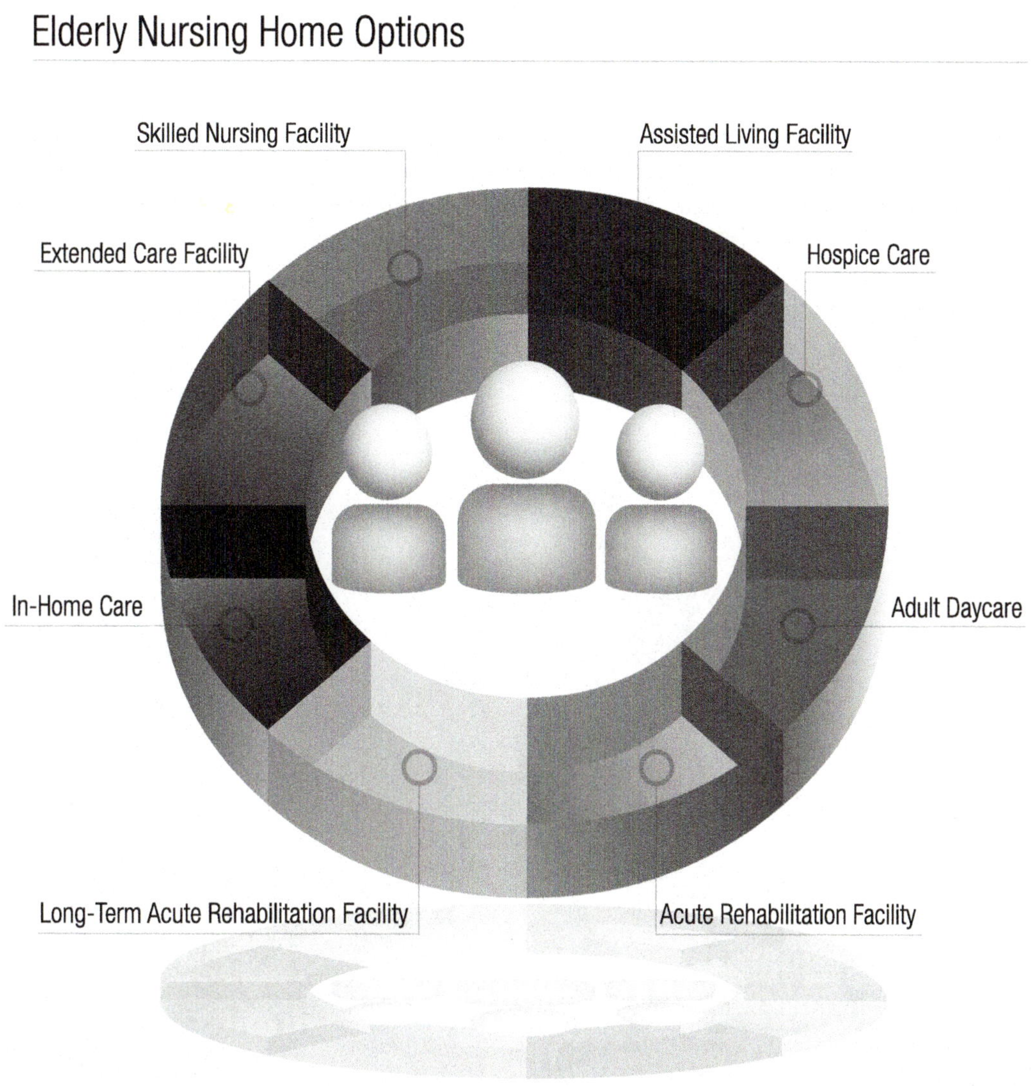

Elderly Nursing Home Options

- Skilled Nursing Facility
- Assisted Living Facility
- Extended Care Facility
- Hospice Care
- In-Home Care
- Adult Daycare
- Long-Term Acute Rehabilitation Facility
- Acute Rehabilitation Facility

© John T Takai/Shutterstock.com

Figure 12:7 Long Term Care insurance provides a daily, weekly, or monthly benefit in the event you and/or your spouse ever require nursing home, home health, or assisted living care.

2. Daily Benefit: The Daily Benefit is the maximum amount a policy will pay for care. There is a wide range of amounts to choose from, and researching the current costs in the area you plan to live in is advised. Also, be aware that some policies pay up to 100% coverage for nursing home care and a lesser percentage for home health care.

3. Elimination Period: The Elimination Period, or waiting period, represents the number of days you need to have been eligible for care before a policy will begin paying benefits. As with Disability insurance, policy premiums increase as the length of the elimination period decreases.

4. Benefit Period: The Benefit Period is the minimum length of time you will receive benefits, but it also provides the multiplier to determine the maximum benefit dollar amount, which could extend the benefit period. If you were to buy a policy with a $200/day benefit and a 3-year benefit period, your total pool to draw from would be $219,000 ($200/day × 1,095 days). You couldn't receive more than $200/day, but you could extend the 3-year benefit period if you were to take less on a daily basis.

5. Inflation Protection: This can account for over half of the policy premium and is a critical benefit for someone who purchases a policy in their younger years and doesn't use it until later in life. The inflation rider increases the daily benefit to keep up with the increasing cost of care, according to the terms of the rider annually, starting at the first policy anniversary and continuing throughout the claim. Increases can be based on simple or compound interest and have a set percentage attached (i.e., 5%).

There are discounts available and tax advantages with Long Term Care. A significant discount of between 25% and 40% is given by companies to those who purchase a Long Term Care policy with their spouse or partner. Some companies will give a lesser discount if only one of you purchase a policy. Along with discounted rates for those purchasing a policy jointly, there are tax benefits available to individuals and business owners. Long Term Care is one of the few benefits that can be partly or fully deductible and pay out the benefits tax-free. The entity type for business owners, the percentage of medical expenses to overall income, and age of each policyholder helps to determine the deductible amount. A policy shouldn't be purchased for the tax benefits alone, but they should be taken advantage of.

Figure 12:8 Long Term Care is one of the few benefits that can be partly or fully deductible and pay out the benefits tax-free.

> **Summary & Review**
>
> 1. Define Long Term Care? What three scenarios does it provide a benefit for?
> 2. Why isn't it a good idea to wait until an older age or until you are in a home to purchase a policy?
> 3. What are the triggers to receive benefits?
> 4. Identify the feature that helps increase the benefit each year. Why is it important?
> 5. Explain why it makes sense for spouses to purchase a policy together. Can partners get a discount as well?

What We Want When We Get Sick

Most of us take our health for granted; we just expect to always have it. So when we find ourselves sick or injured—and hurting—we become impatient and want the health-care system to make us better . . . Now. Because so much of the cost of paying hospital and doctor bills comes from various health insurance or government programs, we typically lack the incentive to make the most economical decisions when it comes to our health care.

For example, let's say that you had a serious abdominal pain that literally doubles you over, leaving you gasping for breath. You went to the hospital, where the doctor began an examination to determine the source of the problem. He told you that there were several tests that could be given, including one that costs $1,500, one that costs $2,300, and one that costs $1,000. As you lay there hurting, you are probably less concerned with the costs than with the results—unless you had to pay for them yourself. If the doctor said that they could do any or all of these tests once they have your check to pay for them, what would be your response now? I expect you would be a little more interested in some kind of cost/benefit ratio, especially if you had to pay the attendant costs up front.

At the same time, your doctor is looking over his shoulder at our current legal system, which is always on the prowl for opportunities to sue. It is unlikely that he is willing to leave an opening for someone to say that he didn't do everything he could to diagnose the problem as quickly as possible—even if he feels that one or two of the tests are redundant or less reliable. To protect himself from legal claims, he may well be motivated to order all of the tests. After all, he isn't paying for them.

So, where is the incentive to hold costs down? The person demanding health-care services is not the one paying the bill. If he were, his demands might be a bit more considered. The person providing the health-care services wants to help identify the problem and correct it as soon as possible, but he is concerned that anything he might not do could become grounds for a legal action. As a result, he is not likely to economize. The net result is that at least two and maybe all three tests are ordered. And this is before we even come to the topic of treatment.

Politics and the Economy of Health Care

Over the years, health care has become more and more of a political issue . . . with overtones of entitlement. Of course, the Constitution does not declare that each citizen has the right to affordable health care, but that seems to be the conclusion that the political debate has come too. So in an effort to provide this growing entitlement, government expenditures for health care have been exploding.

Look at this problem from a political perspective. Would you be more likely to vote for an individual who says he will expand the health-care program and/or lower its costs, or would you be more likely to vote for an individual who campaigns that the government can't afford to pay everyone's health-care bill and we should reduce health-care benefits and/or increase costs. Do you see the problem? In a democracy, we typically vote our own interests.

Both Benjamin Franklin and Thomas Jefferson worried about the conduct of the voter. Benjamin Franklin remarked that: "We have given you a Republic . . . if you can keep it." And Thomas Jefferson said: "I fear for my Republic most, when the electorate discovers that they can vote themselves a largess from the Federal Treasury."

So, where do we go from here? If we socialize medicine and put doctors and hospitals on a government payroll so that we can provide medical care to everyone, we will end up with fewer doctors and hospitals and more people wanting their services. Socialism always works that way—it reduces supplies while increasing demand. If we turn toward having the consumer pay for whatever level of care he chooses (and can afford) we may hear those horror stories where one person can't get the same level or access to the health-care system that another person might receive. The economics of consumer pay would dictate different grades of health care. Is there another course that would help rein in skyrocketing costs while allowing each of us access to an adequate level of health care?

Summary & Review

1. Why is it that patients and doctors so often lack the incentive to use health-care services economically?
2. In your opinion, has the entrance of politics into the health-care debate helped or hurt the current health-care environment?
3. What do you think should be done to maintain the quality of health care while controlling its costs?

Chapter 13
Life Insurance

Contributed by Robert Eagleston. Copyright © Kendall Hunt Publishing Company.

Chapter Objectives

1. Consider the several different personal and business uses for life insurance.
2. Identify the individuals who are candidates for life insurance.
3. Understand the steps of applying for life insurance and how to determine the correct amount.
4. Note the differences between Term and Permanent Life Insurance and the situations for which each is appropriate.
5. Understand how the different types of Term policies work and how to best utilize them.
6. Be aware of the three different types of Permanent insurance: Whole Life, Universal Life, and Variable Life.
7. Understand the dynamics of the cash value offered on Permanent life insurance, and how this feature can turn your life insurance policy into an important retirement product.
8. Identify the three common settlement options associated with the life insurance product.

Chapter Objectives

9. Understand the purpose of an Annuity and when they are used.
10. Gain an awareness of the difference between Fixed and Variable Annuities.
11. Note how adding guarantees affect the Annuity payout.

Life Insurance

Life Insurance is designed to provide a specified sum or Death Benefit to a named Beneficiary in the event of an insured's death. Policy proceeds can be used to take care of an immediate need and can be used to replace the income of the insured. The financial loss created when a wage earner dies can be devastating and makes the purchase of a life insurance policy vital to providing financial security to a deceased's beneficiaries.

Life insurance is purchased for specific reasons, which include:

1. Lifestyle Maintenance—to replace an insured's income and allow for an individual or family to continue to maintain a similar or even the same lifestyle.
2. Debt Elimination—obligations such as a mortgage or a car loan can be paid off using policy proceeds.
3. Childcare—coverage on a nonworking parent is key in helping to provide for the cost of childcare.
4. Business Continuation—policies purchased on a key employee in a business help offset the loss of revenue the employee's death would cause.
5. Retirement—policies that build cash value can provide retirement funds.
6. Estate Planning—estate taxes can be paid for by a life policy.

Figure 13:1 Policies that build cash value can provide retirement funds.

There is a common misconception that life insurance is only for those who have families or for somebody who is worth a great deal of money. It is applicable to several individuals, including:

1. **Wage Earners**: This is the most obvious case, as a wage earner typically has dependents that rely on their income.
2. **Nonworking Parents**: The cost of raising children is expensive. Some surviving parents may choose to work less and help take care of the children, which could cause a loss of income.
3. **Children**: Although children aren't typically a source of income, a life insurance policy on them is useful in case there is a death with its attendant funeral expenses and medical bills. Possibly an even more worthwhile reason to insure a child is to lock in the low rate that their age would produce. Most child policies allow for the addition of a future purchase option, which allows for the purchase of additional coverage at future dates without having to qualify medically.
4. **Business Partnerships**: Having a buy–sell agreement funded with life insurance provides for the purchase of the deceased business owner's interest and eliminates the problems any unintended partner could cause.
5. **High Net worth Individuals:** An estate tax liability can force the undesired liquidation of assets within an estate to pay the tax. Life insurance can be purchased to help cover the estate tax and preserve assets.
6. **Those Wishing to Leave a Legacy:** A relatively small premium payment can translate into a sizable gift left to a preferred school, church, or other organization.

Someone looking to apply for life insurance needs to first establish an Insurable Interest between the owner and the beneficiary. An example of an insurable interest would be a husband naming his wife as beneficiary, as she depends on his income to provide for her living expenses. A friend naming an unrelated friend or acquaintance without any financial interest or business connection is not a permissible situation.

Health plays a key role in the qualification process. Life insurance companies have a number of different health categories, and final rates are determined by the category you are approved in. A health exam conducted by a third party examiner—along with medical questions, your medical records ordered by the insurance company, and a phone interview containing follow-up medical questions, are all put together to determine your health category. Not all companies use the same guidelines regarding health issues, and so it is important to at least explore other companies if your first choice gives you a lower health rating due to your health.

Your income is the main factor in determining the total amount of death benefit available to you. The maximum amount of coverage available represents your "Human Life Value," or the present value of the total amount of income you will earn in your working career. Your "Human Life Value" is usually the maximum amount of death benefit an insurance company will issue, although estate size, family size, and other factors will be considered if a higher amount is desired.

Determining the Proper Amount of Life Insurance

If you ask a life insurance agent whether you need additional life insurance, the answer will always be yes. It is important that you feel comfortable with the amount of life insurance you have, knowing that it is sufficient to meet the purposes for which it is intended. When we talk about the life insurance needed to provide a source of income for loved ones, there are four standard methods for determining the proper amount.

1. The Easy Method. This simplified method applies a rule of thumb to a wage-earners life insurance requirement. The rule of thumb says that the average family will need approximately 70% of the wage-earner's salary, for a period of roughly 7 years, before it can adjust to the loss of income stemming from the death of the provider. If the family income was $50,000 per annum, 70% of $50,000 is $35,000 per year. If this amount is paid for 7 years, then according to this method, the proper amount of life insurance would be approximately ($50,000 × 70%) × 7 = $245,000. Of course, both the 70% of income and the 7-years duration are somewhat arbitrary, and you may wish to modify those numbers if you think some adjustment is appropriate.

2. The DINK Method. If you are single, or married to a spouse who earns more than you do, and have no other dependents, your life insurance requirements are minimal. According to this method, you should have enough insurance to pay off your debts, including funeral expenses, so that your spouse will not be burdened by these costs should you die.

3. Nonworking Spouse Method. If your spouse stays at home to look after the children or other dependents, we sometimes overlook how valuable that contribution is from a financial standpoint. What would it cost to have someone else look after your dependents should your spouse die? If the dependents are young, this cost could mount up significantly over the years until the child comes of age. Accordingly, it may be a good idea to have life insurance on your nonworking spouse so that the means are available to pay for dependent care if necessary. Again using a rough rule of thumb; multiply the number of years until the youngest child reaches 18 by $12,000 to determine the amount of insurance the nonworking spouse should have. If the youngest child is 5 years old, this method would suggest a suitable life insurance requirement of $156,000. ($12,000 × 13 Years = $156,000).

Figure 13:2 What would it cost to have someone else look after your dependents should your spouse die?

4. The Family Need Method. Each of the above calculations assumes an average family. As none of us comes from an average family, you may need to make some adjustments to compensate for your particular circumstances. Such circumstances as the size of your family, any special needs dependents, the size and nature of other family assets, and alternative sources of income, should be weighed to derive the most suitable number.

> ### Summary & Review
> 1. Although most of us think of life insurance as a means of providing for our loved ones in the event of our death, there are a number of other purposes for life insurance. What other reasons are there for buying life insurance?
> 2. What does Insurable Interest mean? Why is it important?
> 3. How might you calculate the amount of life insurance you should have to provide for your dependents?

Types of Life Insurance

Life insurance can be broken down into two types: Term and Permanent. Buying versus renting a house is a good analogy to use when comparing the two. Renting a home and purchasing Term insurance are similar. Both provide benefits (shelter and coverage) for a set period, neither builds cash value or equity, and they both come to an end, with no obligations on the part of either party, once the contract is fulfilled. Purchasing a home and Permanent insurance are similar in that they can both provide benefits for as long as they are needed, which could be until death—and they both can build cash value or equity. Owning a home can be advantageous for some and not for others. Likewise, Permanent insurance is a perfect fit for some, with Term insurance being more appropriate for others.

Term Life

An advantage and appeal to Term insurance is its low cost. The main reason term insurance is offered at such a relatively low price is that the odds are high you will be alive when the Term period is over. Very few term policies result in a death claim, which makes it feasible for an insurance company to offer a high face amount at a low cost. Limited cash flow, a short-term need, or having the desire to spend the least amount possible on life insurance, are all reasons why Term insurance is chosen by some. The four main types of Term insurance are annual renewable, level, decreasing, and return of premium.

An annual renewable Term policy maintains the same death benefit every year and has an annually increasing premium to a specified age. Premiums rise significantly as the policy gets closer to maturity. Annual renewable term policies are ideal when the need for coverage is very short term or if conversion to a whole life policy in the early years is a goal.

Level Term has a defined coverage period (i.e., 10, 15, 20, and 30 years), with a set payment throughout the period. Many companies will let policyholders extend coverage past the defined period for a significant price increase.

Decreasing Term offers a level premium with a death benefit that decreases annually until it reaches zero. Decreasing Term is also referred to as "mortgage life insurance."

There are some companies that offer a return of premium Term policy. These policies have an added charge and return all or a portion of premiums paid, provided there was not a death, at the end of the term period.

Term insurance can provide:

1. The highest level of death benefit at the lowest cost.
2. Coverage for a business loan or a home mortgage.
3. A supplement for whole life insurance or a work policy.
4. An affordable amount needed now with the ability to convert to Permanent insurance later.

Figure 13:3 Term insurance can provide the highest level of death benefit at the lowest cost.

Although inexpensive in the short term, those who renew each time a fixed period ends, or who keep an annual renewable Term policy while they get older, find that Term insurance can be expensive and even cost prohibitive in your later years. It is important to remember that Term life insurance is most useful to fulfill a short-term need. For this reason, Term insurance is not an appropriate tool for estate planning, charitable giving, or to fund any other type of long-term planning strategy.

Permanent Insurance

Permanent insurance provides protection that can be lifelong, and the policy can accumulate money on a tax-deferred basis. When comparing Term and Permanent rates, these two considerations reveal why Permanent insurance is more expensive than Term. There are scenarios where Permanent insurance is really the only option, such as:

1. You desire to have a policy that you cannot outlive.
2. You would like the opportunity to build and utilize its cash value feature.
3. You have a need to buy life insurance for estate planning purposes.

Just as you wouldn't purchase Term insurance for a long-term need, Permanent insurance shouldn't be considered for short-term needs. Policies are structured to collect a large portion of fees or expenses up front, leaving the policy with little value for the first number of years. Some purchase Permanent insurance strictly to use it as an investment or retirement planning tool, and typically see positive growth after 10 or 15 years. If they are able to contribute additional premiums into the policy in the early years, the owner could see positive cash flow even sooner.

From the standpoint of your retirement, a major advantage of Permanent insurance is its Cash Value. Cash Value is tantamount to a savings account, which builds with the payment of each premium. The cash value always belongs to the owner of the policy (or to their beneficiary in the event of their death) and can be borrowed or withdrawn at any time. The cash value is in addition to the Death Benefit, which is the contracted amount the beneficiary receives on the death of the insured.

Let's assume that an individual bought a $100,000 whole life insurance policy with annual premium requirements of $2,723. Note that the amount of the death benefit is guaranteed, and cannot be reduced as long as the premium payments are made. Note also that the premium payments are fixed, and cannot be raised even though the insured grows older and perhaps suffers from ill health down the road. The accumulated premiums paid, the amount of the guaranteed death benefits, and the growth of the insurance policy's cash value—for this particular example—are illustrated in the following graph.

Exhibit 13:1 Whole Life Insurance Cumulative Premiums, Cash Value, and Death Benefit

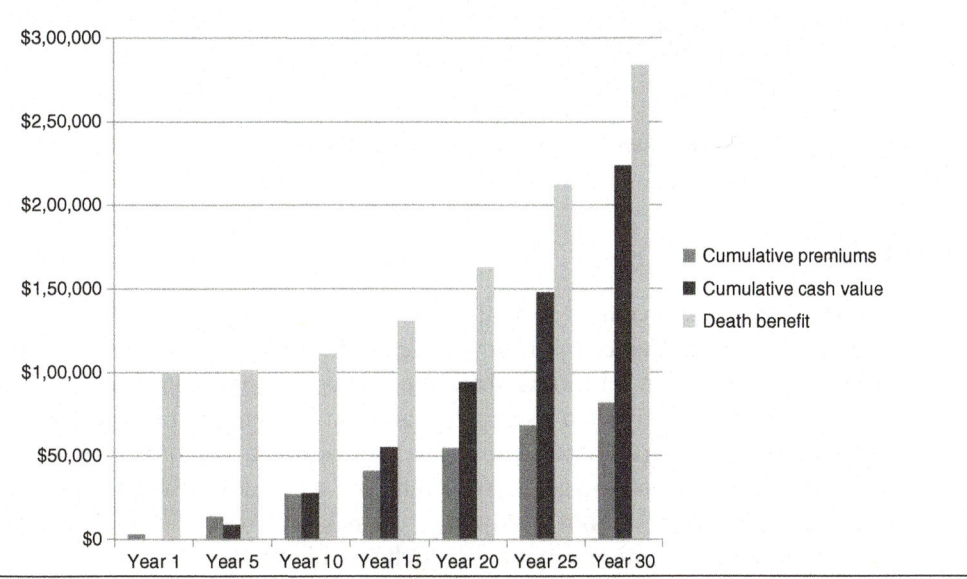

Although a whole life insurance policy typically has a base guaranteed cash value growth rate, many insurance companies pay sums that exceed the base guarantee. Moreover, the amount of the death benefit is increased over time as dividends may be used to purchase additional paid-up insurance. In our example, the accumulated cash value equals the total accumulated premiums paid in year 10. Following year 10, the cash value added each year exceeds the premium expense.

Consider what this means. From an investment standpoint, the premiums paid through year 10 have not resulted in any significant gains. It's as if each premium dollar was placed in a bucket, and at year 10 those premium dollars are returned to you in the form of the accumulated cash value. Some are critical of this feature, pointing out that the owner of the policy experiences no return on his investment for 10 years. What you have gained is a level of insurance protection throughout that period, which, as you reach the point where the cash value catches up with the premiums paid—is essentially free. As cash value grows and premium payments don't, the later years experience hefty gains in the return on your premium dollar—all the while enjoying the protection of the death benefit should the policyholder die. Clearly Permanent life insurance can become an important estate planning vehicle, in addition to mitigating the risks to your dependents of your death.

Once you establish an interest in or need for Permanent insurance, the challenge may be choosing the type that is most appropriate. The three basic types of Permanent insurance are Whole Life, Variable Life, and Universal Life.

Whole Life

Whole Life is attractive for those who want a safe and predictable policy whose growth is tied to the performance and guarantees of the company they purchased it from. The death benefit, cash value, and premium payment can all be guaranteed on a whole life policy. The guaranteed values associated with whole life policies mean that the death benefit cannot decline, the cash value will grow at a minimum rate, and the premiums you pay cannot be raised. In this world of market fluctuations and financial uncertainty, the guarantees of a strong insurance company cannot be overestimated.

Figure 13:4 Whole life is attractive for those who want a safe and predictable policy whose growth is tied to the performance and guarantees of the company.

Universal Life

The appeal of Universal Life policies centers around the fact that premium payments can be flexible. There is incentive to pay more than is needed early on in the life of the policy to cover the increased charges and expenses you will face as you get older. It is not realistic to count on a Universal Life policy to remain in force into your late ages without having contributed a significant amount of premium in early years to help offset the high cost of insurance fees in later years. There are Universal Life products that offer a set premium to guarantee coverage to a specific age. With this, you get a fixed premium, a guaranteed death benefit to a certain age, but also the realistic expectation there will not be any cash to speak of in the policy. This scenario works if you are committed to never missing a premium payment (which would eliminate the guarantees if you did) and were looking to secure a long-term death benefit for the least amount of premium.

Variable Universal Life

Variable Life builds cash value, but its performance and growth is tied to separate accounts linked to stocks, bonds, or mutual funds. These policies are considered a securities product and have the possibility of higher returns and cash value than a whole life policy; but they also carry the risk of losing some or all of the cash value due to poor investment performance. The "Universal" part of it also allows for flexible premium payments. Like the Universal Life policy, you run the same risk of having future problems paying the higher cost of insurance if you hadn't contributed enough and experienced an adequate return with the separate accounts to maintain the policy. There are also Indexed Universal Life policies that are not a securities product and tie the growth of cash value to a stock index, such as the S&P 500. These policies provide a downside guarantee, but also cap the upside at a certain percentage return and participation rate.

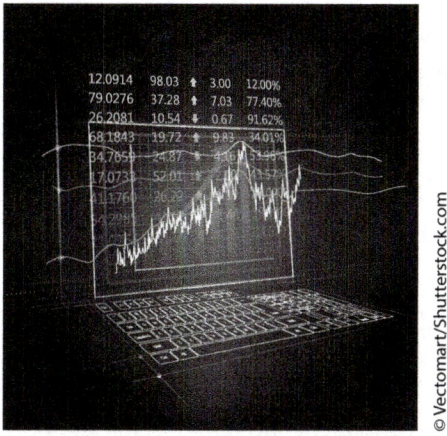

Figure 13:5 Variable Universal Life insurance builds cash value, but the performance and growth is tied to stocks, bonds, or mutual funds.

Mutual versus Stock Company

The type of life insurance company you choose does have an impact on your Permanent policy. A mutual company is owned by policyholders and operates for the benefit of the policyholders. Profits realized by a mutual company can be shared with policyholders in the form of a dividend. Dividends are never guaranteed, but they typically are paid and can be used to increase cash value, reduce a policy loan, purchase additional insurance, or pay part or all of the policy premium.

A Stock Company is owned by shareholders who are typically not policyholders, and operates for their benefit. Profits realized by a stock company are similarly shared with its stockholders in the form of dividend payments.

There has been a long and inconclusive debate as to whether the Mutual life insurance company, or the Stock life insurance company, offers the better product. Most research done on this subject shows that their rates are fairly comparable.

Buy Term and Invest the Difference

A common strategy that is discussed and debated is whether it's best to buy a Permanent life policy such as whole life, and have a steadily increasing cash value, or to buy a less expensive Term policy and invest the difference in premiums to potentially get a higher overall return. Because the variable in this case is the investment you choose and its return, there is really no way of knowing if it will end up being the best option or not. The following three questions should be considered if you are looking to implement this strategy:

1. Will you really invest the difference?
2. What will you invest the difference in?
3. Will you have an insurance need that extends beyond the term period?

Knowing you will be disciplined enough to invest the difference, having an idea of where and how your money is going to be invested, and understanding that you truly would be ok to have the term policy expire when it is set to, will put you in a better position to make this strategy work. However, the risk of the investment not performing well and/or the death benefit need extending beyond the term period should be strongly considered.

Get Real

I attended a college football game a number of years ago with a friend who had been diagnosed with stage four lung cancer the year before. He had worked in the insurance industry for several years, yet he sadly found himself to be heavily underinsured based on the lifestyle his family had become accustomed to living. He knew his death was imminent, and he said to me: "I would do anything I could right now to put more life insurance in place for my family. Please use my story to help others avoid the same mistake." I think of this conversation often, particularly when I evaluate my own life insurance and how it relates to my family's needs.

Summary & Review

1. Explain the difference between Permanent and Term insurance. Under what scenario does the purchase of Permanent insurance make sense?
2. How might Permanent insurance be used to accumulate resources that may be utilized in retirement?
3. What are the three different types of Permanent Insurance? Which carries the most risk?
4. How can buying Term and investing the difference work out to your disadvantage?

Buying Life Insurance

There are two important questions that should be answered when considering buying life insurance. First: "Who are you trying to protect—who are you buying life insurance for?" Second: "Who are you buying life insurance from?"

As noted previously, there is a difference if we are looking for long-term protection for our loved ones, versus a Credit Life policy that is used to repay a personal debt should the borrower die before doing so. Short-term protection can be best accomplished through Term Insurance, whereas long-term protection and estate planning issues are best met through Permanent Insurance. A review of who the beneficiary is, why you are providing for that beneficiary, and the length of time you wish to provide, will lead you in the direction of the more appropriate policy.

The price of life insurance varies considerably among life insurance companies. But price should not be your only consideration. Consider the strength of the company you are buying life insurance from. After all, it would not do to have made premium payments for a period of years, only to find that the company you have been investing in is going out of business. Consult the A.M. Best Ratings (remember we introduced the A.M. Best rating scale in Chapter 11), to satisfy yourself that your life insurance company will be able to meet its insurance obligations.

As to the relative value of the life insurance policy under consideration, you may wish to ask the agent to provide you with the Interest Adjusted Index. The Interest Adjusted Index uses time value of money calculations to show the cost of life insurance as a return on the premium dollars paid. Remember our discussion of debt management, where we pointed out the two numbers that would allow you to compare the relative cost of one lender over another; those numbers were the Finance Charge and the Annual Percentage Rate or APR. Well, the Interest Adjusted Index is like the APR—it enables you to compare the products of different companies.

Figure 13:6 Consider the strength of the company you are buying life insurance from.

Settlement Options

On the death of the policyholder, there are a number of settlement options which, depending on the circumstances of the beneficiary, may be considered.

Once the claim (and attending death certificate) has been filed, there is always the option of receiving a lump sum check from the insurance company. This check would be in the amount of the death benefit and, if the insurance policy is a Permanent insurance policy, for the amount of the cash value as well. Although there may be circumstances where this option is desirable, if the beneficiary is a dependent who is relying on those funds to provide a source of income for a period, this option may not be the best one.

When we talked about the different methods of calculating the proper amount of life insurance a person should have, we noted that one rule of thumb was that the dependents should have enough money to provide approximately 70% of their former income level for a period of roughly 7 years (The Easy Method). If a methodology similar to this is used to determine the amount of life insurance to be provided, wouldn't it make sense to arrange benefit payments in that amount as well? This option is referred to as the Limited Installment Payment option, and it provides that the life insurance benefits will be paid in equal periodic installments over a specified number of years. Bingo—you have provided exactly what you wanted to provide.

A third settlement option is called the Life Income option. Under this option, the life insurance benefits are paid in equal periodic installments over the remaining lifetime of the beneficiary. If the beneficiary should pass away before the remaining benefits are fully paid, the balance is paid into the beneficiaries' estate.

It is important to remember that, although the premiums paid on a life insurance policy are not deductible for income tax purposes, the death benefit proceeds paid by the insurer on the death of the insured are not included in gross income for federal and state income tax purposes. Similarly, the cash value of a Permanent life insurance policy increases on a tax deferred basis—not subject to current income taxes. Like an Independent Retirement Account, the cash value is not taxed until the owner withdraws the money from the policy. As a result, life insurance proceeds are an extremely important component of any retirement and estate planning effort. We will spend more time discussing retirement and legacy planning in Chapters 19 and 20.

> ### Summary & Review
>
> 1. What are the two important questions that should be answered in the course of buying life insurance?
> 2. What is the Interest Adjusted Index? How is it useful in comparing life insurance products?
> 3. Name the three most common settlement options in a life insurance policy. Which one makes the most sense for you?

Annuities

Figure 13:7 An annuity is a product that provides a stream of payments.

Individuals look to life insurance to provide a specified payment to a named beneficiary in the event of their death. The thought of leaving loved ones without adequate resources to live comfortably can cause concern and discomfort. At some point, the concern on the part of an individual who lives long enough may shift from the fear of a premature death to outliving the retirement savings they worked their entire career to build. An annuity is a product that provides a stream of payments that cannot be outlived. In other words, it offers financial protection against living too long. Annuities also provide for tax-deferred growth on your money while in the accumulation phase, and a death benefit in the form of payments to beneficiaries in the event you die before all payments are received.

If the implementation of an annuity is appropriate, the first decision you will need to make is whether you want to start receiving payments now or wait until a later date. The two basic annuity types are immediate and deferred. An Immediate Annuity starts to pay, or annuitize, just after a lump sum is given to the insurance company. With a Deferred Annuity, the payments will start at some point in the future. In a Deferred Annuity, you have the option of contributing a lump sum now and watching it grow, or making a series of payments to the insurance company over time. Whether you contribute a lump sum or make payments, funds in a deferred annuity grow tax deferred until you are ready to start taking a stream of income.

The second decision to make is whether you want a fixed or variable annuity. A Fixed Annuity offers a guaranteed interest rate for a set period. They are primarily invested in high-grade corporate bonds and government securities, which is why companies can safely offer the guaranteed returns they do. A Variable Annuity allows you to take on risk to potentially receive higher returns. Money can be invested in sub-accounts tied to various investment options, which include conservative choices as well as more aggressive ones. Make sure to inquire about the fees and expenses associated with any variable annuity you consider, especially the surrender penalty.

The third decision involves the guarantees that can be built into an annuity. Without any guarantees, you run the risk of dying early and losing some or a good portion of the money paid into the annuity. To protect against losing money, the insurance company can guarantee the annuity payment for a certain number of years or even guarantee the refund of the contract value in the event of your death. For example, a 10-year certain annuity guarantees the annuity payment for at least 10 years. A refund annuity guarantees that you or a named beneficiary will receive the full amount that was originally contributed into the annuity. Remember that the annuity payment you receive is affected by the guarantees offered, and goes down with each guarantee added.

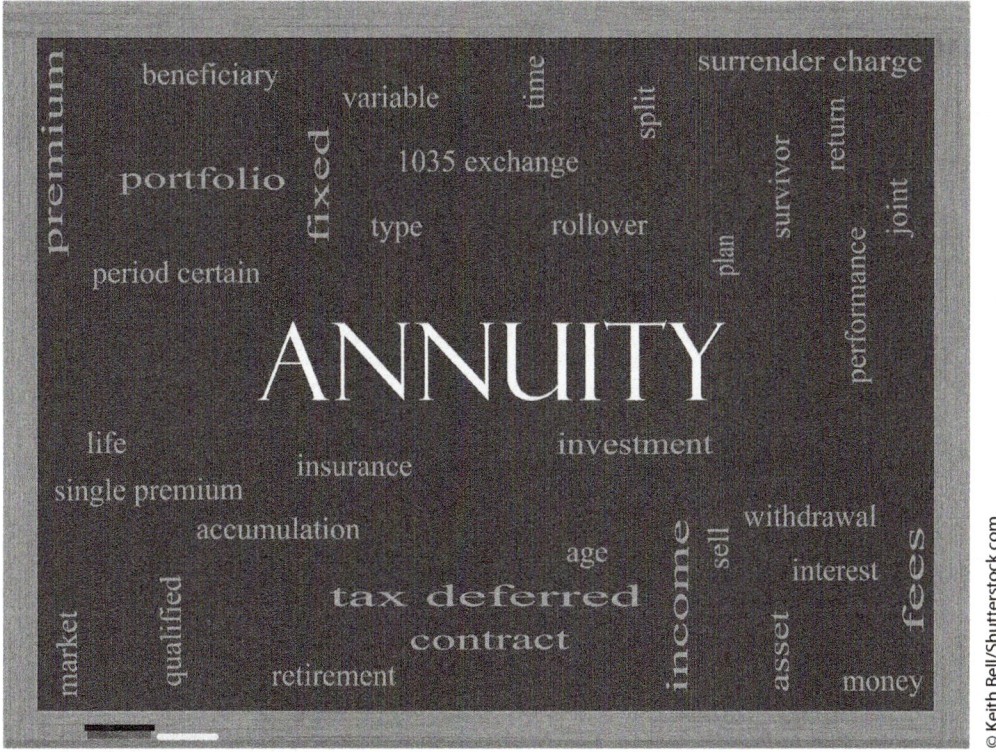

Figure 13:8 In what ways is an annuity different from life insurance?

Summary & Review

1. In what ways is an Annuity different than Life insurance?
2. Why might it be advantageous to delay annuity payments?
3. What should be considered when choosing between a fixed and a variable Annuity?
4. How would adding guarantees affect an Annuity?

Investments

Chapter 14
Fundamentals Of Investment

Chapter Objectives

1. Be aware of the four alternative means by which wealth is accumulated, and the role of savings and investments in wealth management.
2. Understand the nature of the Investor Profile... and especially your own Investor Profile.
3. Consider the advantages and disadvantages of the traditional full service brokerage account versus a discount brokerage account.
4. Become familiar with various investment alternatives, together with some of the advantages and disadvantages of each.
5. There are several concepts that apply to all investment categories. Understand the nature of income versus appreciation, safety versus risk, and liquidity, as important considerations in your investment selection process.
6. Evaluate the different kinds of risk, and their impact on investment potential.
7. Be aware of the classic investment con, and how it is perpetrated.
8. Understand the nature of diversification, and how it can be achieved. Know the usefulness of the Investment Opportunity Set in identifying the most efficient trade-off between risk and return.
9. Be aware of the mechanics of the asset allocation process as a means of implementing diversification.
10. Note the potential sources of investment information, and how such information can aid in the investment process.

Earned Income

Perhaps a good place to begin, as we examine the fundamentals of investment, is with a schematic. The following exhibit helps put into perspective the four different avenues that create income and potentially wealth.

Exhibit 14:1 The Four Paths to Income

Hourly Earnings	Salaried Earnings
Income received based on hours worked, including wages, tips, etc. May include incentive formulas.	Income based on annual compensation agreement, including salary, bonus, etc. May include performance formulas.
Earnings from Securities Investments	Earnings from Business and Real Estate
Dividend, interest, and capital gains received from holdings in stocks, bonds, and other securities.	Income, rent, and capital gains received from ownership in businesses, real estate, and commodities.

Most of us begin life in the top left quadrant, earning a wage as we cut lawns or serve burgers. However, there are many professions where hourly billing is the chief generator of revenues, including lawyers and consultants. The point is you earn revenue for the time that you work.

Figure 14:1 The point is you earn revenue for the time that you work.

For those who receive a salary—the top right quadrant—time spent on the job is assumed, and earnings usually flow on a semimonthly payout based on an annual compensation agreement. (We touched on this in Chapter 3.) Many times, salaried employees work more hours than might be expected, and they are typically not compensated for the additional hours worked.

As you study the top two quadrants, what do you see? In both cases, the income received is based on personal efforts. You need to be actively employed to receive earnings. This is as it should be. Few of us expect to be paid simply because we are here.

The bottom left quadrant identifies those earnings that are derived from securities investment. If you bought a share of stock or a bond with your savings, you would expect to realize dividends or interest, and possible a capital gain, as a result of that investment. We would not buy securities if we did not expect some kind of return from that holding.

The bottom right quadrant similarly identifies those earnings that are derived from a business that you have invested in, or from real estate property you may own. These earnings may come in the form of profits or rent, and possibly capital gains, which are paid to the owner. Again, you have taken your savings and invested in a business or a property in the expectation that there will be a return earned.

As you study the bottom two quadrants, what do you see? In both cases, the income received is a return on investment. It is based on the time value of money concepts we discussed in Chapter 1, and flows from the fact that you have accumulated savings that you invest in various ways. If you did not have such savings, there would be no investments, and the bottom two quadrants would not exist.

There are certain types of income that do not fit neatly into one quadrant, but may overlap into another. If you own a business, for example, you may give yourself a salary, in addition to a share of the profits earned. Or, you might invest in a security such as a Real Estate Investment Trust (REIT), which evidences ownership in real estate, and therefore, your earnings come ultimately from the property owned.

The Internal Revenue Service draws a distinction between the top two quadrants and the bottom two quadrants, which is misleading. It uses the term "earned income" when referring to the top quadrants, because the earnings come as a result of your personal efforts. It uses the term "unearned income" when referring to the bottom quadrants, because those earnings do not come from your personal efforts, but from the investments your savings acquired. Can you see the misnomer? If you had not worked and skimped and saved, there would be no savings to invest. To infer that the income from such savings is not earned is inaccurate—but that is the label conferred. The only income that may properly be labeled "unearned income" might be your lottery winnings—if you ever receive them. Nevertheless, income taxes are assessed on both earned income and unearned income, with a number of provisos as discussed in Chapter 4.

Over the next four chapters, we will be examining investment alternatives in the bottom left quadrant—Investment Securities (Chapter 15) and Mutual Funds (Chapter 16), and in the bottom right quadrant—Real Estate and Commodities (Chapter 17) and Entrepreneurial Investment Opportunities (Chapter 18).

The Goal of Savings

Wouldn't it be nice to reach a point in life where your savings can get up, get dressed, and go to work for you? Your savings produce a number of benefits; helping you to reach your goals, providing financial security, and accumulating resources to be drawn on in retirement. To the extent that those savings grow over time, the end result can be dramatic.

Lets' go back to the time value of money tables introduced in Chapter 1. If you were able to save a portion of your income each year beginning at age 20, and if that invested savings earned an average of 5% per annum over the next 40 years, the factor from Table B (Future Amount of an Annuity) would be 120.8. Multiply that by the number of dollars you are able to save, and you have the future amount at age 60. Say you were able to save $100 per month or $1,200 per year. That means, at age 60, you would have approximately $145,000 (120.8 × $1,200) accumulated in your account.

Wait a minute. If you are saving $1,200 per year, times 40 years, you have managed to set aside only $48,000. Where did the other $97,000 come from? That is the compounded earnings from your savings at the assumed 5% per annum rate. In other words, you would have $2 in earnings for every $1 in savings at the end of the 40-year period. You would have tripled your money. This provides both financial security, and a respectable addition to your retirement income goal.

Sometimes we delay starting our savings program because our budget is tight and we don't have big dollars to set aside. It is true that your budget needs to be in balance before you can consistently set aside money in savings, but you don't need big bucks to begin. Even if you can regularly set aside just a few dollars a month, two things happen as you begin to save. First, you start to develop a habit. Putting some money into savings each payday can be a very constructive habit. Second, you are now in a position to ask the question: "What do I do with this money?" As you ask that question, you start to push yourself up the learning curve in terms of your investment options. If you don't put money aside, there will not be any reason for you to ask that question. Importantly, it doesn't matter how much money you put into savings. The benefits of developing a good habit and pushing yourself up the investment learning curve will happen even with a small amount of money.

Moreover, if you really want to grow that nest egg, add to your regular savings effort those occasions when you have some extra money come your way. And that happens more often than you think. Consider the following opportunities to boost your savings.

- Gifts at birthdays, graduation, or other occasions. When you get an unexpected check, drop it into savings.
- Occasions when you underspend your budget. For example, in the spring and fall when your utility bill is lower than budgeted—drop the unexpected windfall into your savings.

Figure 14:2 Wouldn't it be nice to reach a point in life where your savings can get up, get dressed, and go to work for you?

- Other events where you find a check coming your way. This might include a tax refund or a rebate from a purchase.
- Avoid using open lines of credit that might encourage you to spend. Such spending must be repaid with tomorrows dollars, which may crowd out your savings capability.

As you direct these additional funds into your investment program, you will find that the relatively modest regular contribution you began with can be doubled and tripled over the course of a year. When is the best time to begin your savings effort? Why not now, and where you stand.

Summary & Review

1. What are the four avenues to income? How are they different?
2. The source of the earnings in the bottom two quadrants is your savings. Do you have a component for savings in your budget?
3. How does the time value of money contribute to the growth in savings?
4. What means might you employ to accelerate your regular savings program?

Figure 14:3 If you really want to grow that nest egg, take advantage of those occasions when you have some extra money come your way.

Your Investor Profile

Each investor is different. Each has their own unique personality—their own unique savings goals. Some are risk takers, and the notion of putting their savings at risk for a potentially large return, is appealing. Others would not be able to sleep at night if they thought they might lose a portion of their savings. Some have detailed savings goals that are near term. Others have only general savings goals that are a long way off. Some need current earnings from their savings. Others are looking for long-term gains. Like your resume, there is no one-size-fits-all.

> ### Get Real
>
> I am often asked by students, what they should invest in. I always give the same answer: "I don't have any idea." This is because the student asking the question has not provided enough information about himself or his investment goals, to allow for a satisfactory answer. There are a number of factors that should be considered before asking that question. For example, if the student is saving money for a down payment on a condo, and he hopes to be able to buy that condo within the next year, placing that savings in the stock market would not be wise. The fact is, there are different investments for different circumstances—and those circumstances should be evaluated before a suitable investment can be recommended.

For this reason, it is important that you understand your Investor Profile. The investor profile describes your unique circumstances, investment goals, and attitude toward your investments. It takes into account a host of considerations, including your appetite for risk, the amount and source of your income, your tax bracket, your age, the expected timing of your savings goals, and so forth. If you have contacted an investment advisor to help you with your investment selections, this is probably the first thing they will ask you. Following are the kinds of questions that should be considered in defining ones' investor profile. For a more comprehensive Risk Profile Questionnaire, see Article 14:1 in Appendix I.

Many of you will choose to be your own investment manager, and look forward to selecting your own investments. Although this may save you commission dollars, it also means that you will be the one to determine your own investor profile. Take some time in doing so. It is important to understand the game plan before you run out onto the field.

Exhibit 14:2 Investor Profile – Sample Questions

What is your current age?	48
What is your main objective for your investments?	retirement
Please indicate the approximate number of years until you anticipate beginning withdrawals.	20 yrs
How many months of cash reserves do you have?	7 mo
How predictable (or stable) and sufficient is your source of income?	50%
Please indicate your approximate family gross annual income.	36,000
Please indicate your approximate grow family net worth.	
Rank your understanding and comfort level with investing and capital markets.	little
How do you feel about fluctuations in the value of your portfolio?	"

A case study titled "Suitability—A Retail Responsibility" is included in Appendix I, Article 14:2. This is a fictional story about one person's struggle trying to get a handle on her own investor profile. This case also introduces a number of important investment concepts.

The Broker

Whether you are buying a real estate investment or stocks and bonds, you will be enlisting the support of a broker to help effect the transaction. Though you may find that you can get much of the information you need on the web, the web will not get you onto the floor of the exchange. To actually buy or sell securities, you need a brokerage account.

There are many brokers to choose from, and a healthy competition currently exists between what are called full service brokers that provide a range of research and investment services, and the discount brokers that provide primarily trading services.

Perhaps the greatest benefit from a full service brokerage account is the full-time professional who is at your side. These individuals are licensed, generally have considerable experience, and are backed by significant research capabilities. They work to provide you with satisfactory investments. As noted, they generally begin with an evaluation of your investment profile. Only then, do they make those recommendations that are consistent with your circumstances and goals. Of course, all of this support costs money, and they will charge a fee or a commission for their efforts. Real estate brokers generally charge up to 10% commission when they sell commercial property (this fee is typically paid by the seller). Securities brokers general charge roughly $100 to buy or sell a block of stock.

At the other end of the brokerage spectrum are the discount brokers, which typically operate through a web-based account platform. With these accounts, there is no one looking over your shoulder to make sure you get it right—to make sure that your investment selections are appropriate for your circumstances. So you need to work out your own investor profile, and then determine those investment selections that are suitable. Once you have done so, you access your account on the web, and do your own buying and selling through that account. The commission for trading securities with a discount brokerage account will be roughly $7–$10 per trade.

Figure 14:4 You will be enlisting the support of a broker to help effect the transaction.

Which Club Should I Choose

Once you have worked out your investor profile and identified your investment goals, you will need to decide where to open your brokerage account. When you have done that, you are in a position to begin identifying those investments that make the most sense. May we go back to an analogy first introduced in Chapter 1? Recalling our discussion of goals, we pointed out that not having goals was like going onto a golf course with no idea where the cup is. If we are going to be successful at the game, we need to know where we are heading . . . we need to know where the cup is.

When we are talking about investments, there is a wide variety of alternative possibilities. Choosing which investment you should pursue is like choosing which club from your golf bag is the best one to use for your next shot. Each club is intended to serve a specific purpose. You would probably not choose a driver to putt the ball a few feet. Similarly, there are investments designed to reach longer-term goals, and others designed to reach shorter-term goals. There are those investment clubs that pay a relatively high level of current income, and those that depend more on appreciation to produce a return. Reminder—It is important that your goals be specific and measurable. This is especially true of your investment goals. Knowing how much money you will need, and when, are important ingredients in achieving your investment objective. Knowing where you are going will help you select the right club for the job.

Let's take a minute and look at some of the clubs that are available in your investment bag. Exhibit 14:3 points out some of the advantages and disadvantages of each.

Savings Account is a cash deposit at a bank, credit union, or other depository institution. It pays regular interest, is typically insured, and can be withdrawn at any time. Goals that are less than 12 months away are usually better met with savings than with other kinds of investments.

Certificate of Deposit is also a cash deposit at a depository institution, represented by a certificate that pays a fixed rate of interest for a fixed period. Both the rate of interest and the period vary.

Common Stock is a certificate of ownership of a corporation. Each share of common stock is an equity interest in a corporation, and each holder is a voting owner of that corporation.

Preferred Stock is a class of equity, which has preference in terms of dividend payment and liquidation value. The preferred stock has a specified dividend payment, has a specified maturity date, and is nonvoting.

Figure 14:5 Knowing where you are going will help you select the right club for the job.

Bond is a certificate of debt. Bonds have a specified interest requirement and a specified repayment or maturity date. Bonds may be issued by corporations, municipalities, or other government entities.

Small Business is an investment in an enterprise. Whether it is a retail establishment like a restaurant or a dry cleaning store, a service entity like a plumbing business or accounting firm, or a production operation like a mining claim or a farm, the investment represents direct ownership in a business operation. The context of that investment varies given the nature of the business and the structure of the organization.

Real Estate is title to property—including land and structure. A real estate holding entitles the owner to the income and appreciation from the property, and to the opportunity to develop that property subject to zoning and other government regulations. Real Estate ownership has no maturity date, and title may be held indefinitely.

Commodities include the ownership of tangible goods. Commodities may be divided into two classes based on whether they are Fungible—that is the degree to which the good is generic and comparable to all other like goods. Fully fungible goods include agricultural products, metals (including precious metals), energy commodities, etc. The second class includes those goods that are not fungible—that are unique. These include gemstones, art, collectables, and similar tangible assets.

Of course, the table 14:3 serves only as a summary. Within each of these categories is a broad range of advantages and disadvantages . . . of potential and pitfalls. We cannot say that all common stocks have the same level of appreciation potential, any more than we can say that all real estate is costly to maintain. Yet, on average, these advantages and disadvantages are typical of the respective investment category.

As you look through these alternatives, it may be that you have some familiarity with one or two categories. Perhaps you have used these investment clubs before, and you are comfortable with them. The next several

Exhibit 14:3 Investment Alternatives

	Advantage	Disadvantages
Savings Account	Relative Safety	Lower Return
	High Liquidity	No Appreciation
Certificate Deposit	Relative Safety	Limited Liquidity
	Higher Return	No Appreciation
Common Stock	Appreciation Potential	Volatility in Price
	Easily Traded	Lower Current Income
Preferred Stock	Priority of Payment	Limited Appreciation Potential
	Higher Current Income	Dividends Not Mandatory
Bonds	Regular Income	Limited Appreciation Potential
	Repayment at Maturity	Decline in Price if Rates Rise
Small Business	Potential Upside if Successful	Marketing and Financial Risks
	Direct Control and Management	Limited Liquidity
Real Estate	Tangible Asset	Difficult and Costly To Sell
	Income and Appreciation Potential	Costly To Maintain
Commodities	Tangible Asset	Volatility in Price
	Significant Growth Potential	No Current Income

chapters will give you the opportunity to gain a working knowledge of each investment category, so that you will have the knowledge to select that club that will work best for you.

Summary & Review

1. What is an Investor Profile? Why is it important?
2. What are the differences between a full service broker and a discount broker?
3. Given your own Investor Profile, which investment category makes the most sense? Why?

Income versus Appreciation

Regardless of which investment category you may select, there are several considerations that apply to all of them. One of those considerations is the nature of the return you can expect. As pointed out previously, few of us would make an investment if we did not anticipate some kind of gain from that investment. The question is, what kind of return can you expect from each category?

Perhaps the best way to view this is to plot a line . . . a continuum. At one end of the line are those investments that offer regular income. Whether the income is called interest or dividends or rent, it is an ongoing payment that you can rely on. At the other end of the line are those investments that pay no regular income at all, but where the return is in the form of appreciation. It may be that the potential appreciation is significant,

Figure 14:6 The question is, what kind of return can you expect from each category?

but it does not come in the form of a steady cash flow. Capital appreciation comes only as the value of the investment increases. Such a continuum would look like this:

```
/-----------------------------------------------------------------/
Regular                                                    Capital
Income                                                Appreciation
```

Now, you can hold any potential investment up to that line, and identify its place on the continuum. Your passbook savings account would place all the way to the left, as the only return you will receive will be periodic interest payments. On the other hand, that gold coin you bought, and tucked away in your safety deposit box, would place all the way to the right, as there is no income coming from that investment, but only the potential for appreciation should the price of gold go up.

The primary question is, where on this line should you be. If you are young and you are looking for an investment to help build your retirement fund, perhaps you are less concerned with current income than you are with capital appreciation. If that is so, you may want to look at investment categories where capital appreciation is the focus. Alternatively, if you are providing a trust fund where the recipient is in need of regular support from the investment you have made, you may be more interested in a category that pays regular income. You see, it depends on your investor profile, and the nature of your investment goals.

Safety versus Risk

Another consideration that applies to all investment categories is the issue of safety versus risk. Again, it may help if you look at that trade-off as a continuum, with very safe investments at one end and risky investments at the other.

Safe   Risky

When we talk about risk, there are many different kinds of risks that may affect your investments. Let's look at a few of them.

Interest Rate Risk stems from a rise in interest rates. If your investment pays a fixed rate of return—such as a bond—the value of that investment declines when general market rates move higher. Also, positive borrowing leverage is more difficult to achieve as interest rates increase, and market activity is slowed by higher borrowing costs. Note that an increase in interest rates affects longer-term securities more than shorter-term securities, and affects smaller-coupon securities more than higher-coupon securities.

Credit Risk is the risk inherent in the decline or failure of the business. When this occurs, dividends, interest, or rent is not paid, and the value of the principal itself is compromised.

Market Risk is the uncertainties surrounding the market as a whole. Economic upheavals, political challenges, changes in market sentiment toward an industry or investment type, or other broad issues, may cause the market some concern. Although Market Risk may not directly affect the operation of the enterprise itself, it does affect how investors value that operation.

Regulatory Risk is the risk that a change in government, regulations, taxes, or other political issues will adversely affect an investment.

Inflation Risk is the risk that a rise in inflation, due to a decline in the value of the currency or an increase in the price of goods and services, will reduce profitability and the concurrent value of the investment.

Again, look at your passbook savings account as an example, and place it on the line where you think it should be. If you placed it all the way to the left, you are right. Most passbook savings accounts are with savings institutions that are relatively strong financially. In addition, most such accounts are insured. You might say that your passbook savings account has both a belt and suspenders. Alternatively, a share of common stock in a small and struggling mining concern might be regarded as fairly risky, especially if the ore they are mining is running out.

Here it is helpful to regard your Investor Profile, and your temperament for risk. It is a fairly easy matter for any investment professional to increase the return you are getting from your investments. There are always alternatives that pay more. However, with that higher return often comes a higher level of risk. Can you accept the possibility that you will lose a significant portion of your investment if you pursue that higher level of risk?

The Classic Investment Con

This brings us to a very important point. Most investment professionals are honestly trying to produce the best investment results for their clients. However, there are always a few who try to take advantage of the unwary to line their own pockets. Let's describe the modus operandi that is often used.

They approach you with a compliment—such as how astute you are and how you are able to grasp the unique opportunity they are about to offer. They then talk about a special investment with a very high return and relatively low level of risk. We all know that risk and return are positively correlated—with a higher return typically corresponding to a higher level of risk. The relationship between risk and return might be illustrated in the following graph.

Exhibit 14:4 Risk versus Return

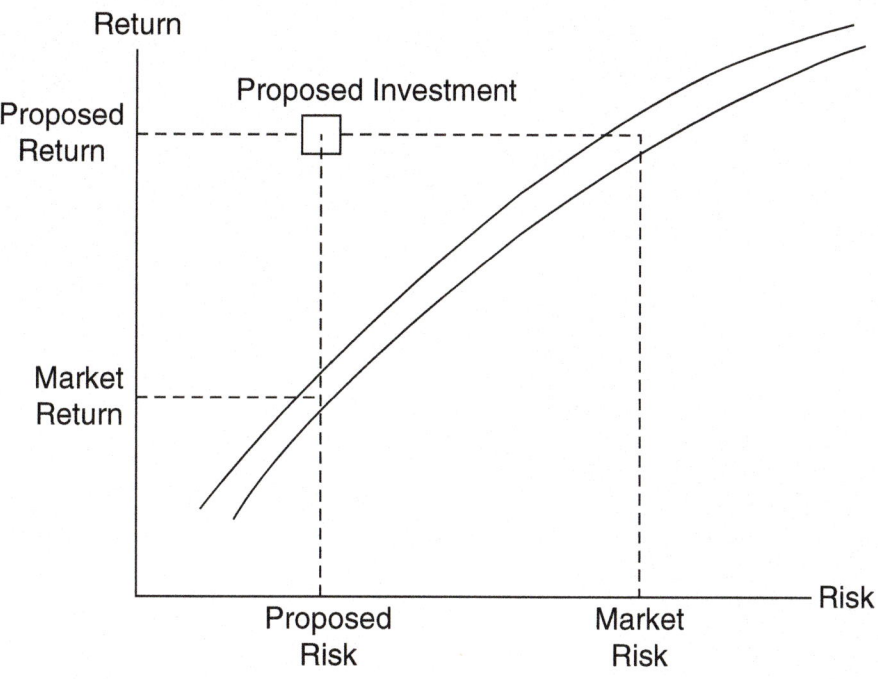

Risk

Of course, if investments with a high level of risk always paid a high return, there would be little risk. The uncertainty comes with the fact that high risk investments don't always come through, and many fail to return the principal invested, let alone any gain. And so, investors who pursue higher risk opportunities do so with the understanding that many of their investments won't pan out, but those that do will be especially profitable.

But the person offering you this unique investment plays down the risk, and plays up the return, suggesting that this particular opportunity enjoys a relatively good return with a comparatively low level of risk. How can you tell that this is a fraud in the making? Look at the graph. The lines on the graph represent market returns available at given levels of risk. Although the risk/reward trade-off is not precise, and is most often a range rather than a single point, it nevertheless represents where the market would fund an investment of a given level of risk. If the risk is truly low, as asserted, the entity offering the investment could get all the money they needed at a much lower rate. They could borrow from banks, sell stock or bonds, or get funding from a dozen other sources at much lower cost than what they are offering to pay you. So why are they offering this sweet opportunity to you?

In reality, the risk of this investment is much higher than asserted—if it is an investment at all and not smoke and mirrors. Paying a return that high is consistent with a much higher level of risk. It is not our purpose here to disparage any high risk investment. But it is important that the investor understands that it is a high risk investment, and that if you choose to make such an investment it should be consistent with your investor profile and goals.

Liquidity

One more consideration that applies to all investment types is the issue of liquidity. We talked about liquidity in Chapter 2, as we discussed the proper listing of assets on a balance sheet. Remember that liquidity asks the

Figure 14:7 With that higher return often comes a higher level of risk.

question: "How easy is this asset to spend?" Or, in the case of investments, how easy would it be to convert this investment into easily spendable cash. Once more, this concept might be more understandable if we viewed it as a continuum, with those investments that are very liquid at one end and those that are less liquid at the other end.

        Liquid   Ill-Liquid

Your passbook savings account is as close to cash as you can get, and can be turned into cash in a moment. However, if you are holding a real estate duplex, it may be much harder to turn that investment into cash. Common stock is, for the most part, quite liquid in terms of the time it takes to sell it, though there may be a few days delay from the time of sale until you actually get your money. A piece of art may be much less liquid, as it generally takes time to sell and time to realize the money from the sale.

The Right Club

There are many considerations in choosing the investment club that is best for each situation. Your selection process might begin with the three aspects discussed above. Let's take an example, and see how it works. Say

Figure 14:8 How easy would it be to convert this investment into easily spendable cash.

that you wanted to buy your first home; possibly a condominium you have been saving for. You have a little money put away, and you would like to invest that money so that it will grow into an adequate down payment. Let's say that you would like to be able to make this purchase in 4 years, giving you time to graduate and get started in your career. You have concluded that it will take that long for you to build up the credit profile necessary to qualify for the loan you will be seeking.

Looking at the first consideration—Income versus Appreciation, you conclude that this goal does not require any current income. You would be happy with appreciation, given your 4-year time frame. On the other hand, you sure don't want to start over again trying to accumulate the down payment necessary, so you conclude that you want an investment that is safe and one where the amount available in year four is predictable. In terms of liquidity, you don't need to access this money before year four, but you will need it on that date. Which of the alternative investment clubs has a focus on appreciation, is relatively safe and predictable, and can be converted to cash easily in year four?

As you look through your clubs, perhaps a Certificate of Deposit is a possibility. A 4-year CD would be perfect in terms of safety and predictability, and your timetable. Perhaps you could get a little better appreciation if you considered a low coupon bond, selling at a discount and maturing in 4 years. (We will be discussing these and other aspects of bonds in the next chapter.) Can you see how the process works? As you become more familiar with each of the investment categories and what they represent, you will be better able to match up the club with the goal, and manage your investments in a way that will bring you success.

Summary & Review

1. What are the three considerations that are common to all kinds of investments?
2. How would you relate these considerations to your various investment goals?
3. Given considerations of return and risk, and the trade-offs inherent in these two issues, how would you know when you are being conned in an investment opportunity?

Diversification

As you examine some of your goals—financial security, for example—you conclude that you want to get started now . . . that a longer time frame can be a major advantage relative to your time value of money. You may be looking closely at longer-term investments such as bonds, common stocks, or possibly real estate. Perhaps you don't have a lot of time to manage your investments yourself, so you may be thinking of investing all of your money in a mutual fund, possibly one that has the investment objective of investing in discounted long-term bonds primarily for capital appreciation. Moreover, the particular mutual fund you are looking may have had an average annual return of 6.8% over the past 10 years, and a standard deviation (a measure of investment volatility or risk) of 10%. Those numbers may seem pretty attractive, and their investment objective would certainly be consistent with your goal of building financial security. But before you put all of your money into a single investment, consider the merits of diversification.

Diversification is the process of spreading investment assets across a number of different categories to reduce the risks inherent in a single category. Although bonds have historically been a conservative and sound investment, they are subject to their own risks. Don't misunderstand; having bonds in your conservative financial security portfolio is a good idea. But having all of your funds in a single investment category is pretty risky.

Look at the following chart. The plot on Exhibit 14:5 examines the trade-off between risk and return from a combination of bonds and stocks. Although a portfolio with 100% bonds has a relatively low level of risk, look what happens when we add a few stocks to your holdings. By diversifying into another investment category, we have mitigated some of the risks of bonds, and actually reduced the overall risk of the portfolio. At the same time, we have boosted your return. Adding a few more stocks reduces risk further and boosts return further. This continues until we have approximately 70% bonds and 30% stocks in the portfolio, at which point the addition of still more stocks begins to increase the overall risk.

Exhibit 14:5 Investment Opportunity Set of Stocks versus Bonds

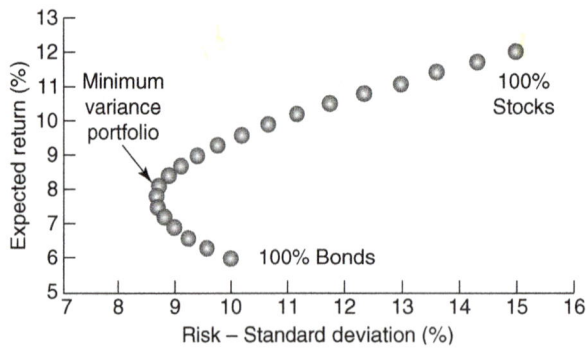

This trade-off is called the Efficient Frontier, (also commonly referred to as the Investment Opportunity Set) and indicates the allocation of various investment alternatives that produces the best level of return for a given level of risk. The point where we have the lowest risk or the minimum variance would be the point where safety is maximized. From this point, any other combination of stocks and bonds will increase risk. Understand that the risks inherent in bonds don't go away. We simply reduce the concentration of investments subject to those particular risks. On the other hand, we are adding alternative investments with a different set of risks. If the market should tumble in one direction, those investments with one set of risks might be affected, but those with a different set of risks would be less affected. The result is that we have reduced the concentration of investments subject to a particular set of risks. Of course, we can always increase return, but note how the concentration of risk rises as we increase the proportion of stocks.

The Allocation Process

This introduces another concept into the process of selecting the right investment club for the right goal. Goals that can be met with a relatively small investment don't usually need to be diversified into several investment categories. Let's face it, if your goal is to raise $1,000 by next year so you can take that road trip, trying to diversify that money into two or three different types of investment would take more time and effort than it might be worth. However, if your goal entails a larger or longer effort, requiring a significant portion of your savings, diversification of your holdings would help reduce overall risk.

The process of identifying alternative investment categories, and allocating your savings over a number of such categories, is called Asset Allocation. Simply put, it means spreading your eggs into a number of different baskets, so that the risks of one kind of investment do not apply to your entire portfolio.

Figure 14:9 Simply put, it means spreading your eggs into a number of different baskets.

The principal ingredient in effective asset allocation is to make sure that the investments made are different enough so that they do not share the same risks. For example, buying two shares of stock may not constitute diversification, especially if both stocks are of oil-producing corporations. They are too similar . . . and share the same kinds of risks.

Investment alternatives that are positively correlated do not make for good diversification. Look for investments that have a zero correlation or a negative correlation, so that the risks faced by one are not shared by the other. Of course, any investment you choose needs to be consistent with your Investor Profile and Goals. The following pie chart illustrates the kind of asset allocation that would result in a fairly well diversified portfolio.

Exhibit 14:6 Asset Allocation

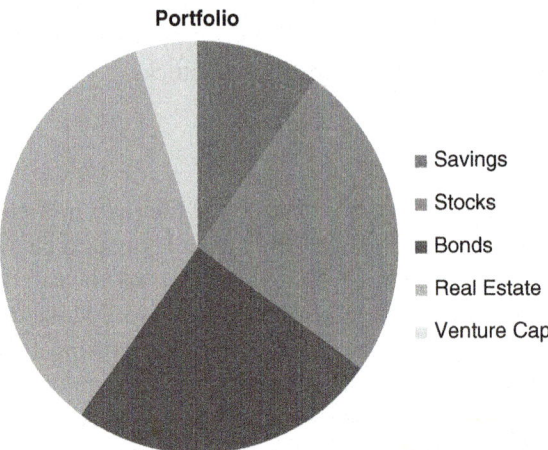

> ## Summary & Review
>
> 1. What is Diversification? How is it achieved?
> 2. How does an understanding of the Investment Opportunity Set aid in the diversification process?
> 3. In the course of diversification, do we actually make a risk go away? How does the addition of alternative investments with different risk profiles reduce risk?
> 4. What is the goal of the Asset Allocation process?

Investment Information

Where can you go to get the information you need to make good investment decisions? Well, the problem today is not finding a source, but wading through a host of alternative sources trying to find the one that works best.

The most extensive and most timely source of investment information is the web. Here you have a dizzying array of sites pertaining to virtually every possible investment. If you know the particular investment option you would like to pursue, you might try going to the home page of the company, broker, or dealer you wish to research. For example, if you wish to investigate the preferred stock of a public utility or bank, the home page of that company will provide news releases, income statements, balance sheets, and other information on the company and on the preferred stock you are considering. In addition, there are a number of independent research sites that could provide you with ideas and answers. Yahoo has a finance site: Finance.Yahoo.com, which is a virtual library of research information. And it's free! Google is another site that will allow you to do a word search for the investment alternative you wish to explore. Other independent research sites that focus on securities include Morningstar, Lipper, Standard & Poor's, and Value Line.

Printed material available in newspapers, magazines, and reports from brokers and dealers may not be quite as timely as the web, but do provide a thoughtful source of information. This medium is especially valuable if you are trying to get an education on a particular topic, or in the process of trying to sort out a strategic game plan. As we have tried to emphasize throughout this book, it is important to lay the foundations for your decisions and actions through careful analysis and a deliberate approach.

Fundamentals of Investment 259

Figure 14:10 Here you have a dizzying array of sites pertaining to virtually every possible investment.

Chapter 15
Investment Securities

Chapter Objectives

1. Understand what a registered security is, and what it means to the security holder.
2. Become familiar with the major types of orders that are used to transact investment securities. Examine Dollar Cost Averaging and Dividend Reinvestment as strategies in a long-term investment program.
3. Consider some of the important characteristics of common stock, including the rights of ownership, the potential for dividend payments, and those factors that would contribute to the success of a corporation and appreciation in the value of their stock.
4. Be aware of the three dates that mark a dividend payment. Understand the nature of a stock dividend or stock split.
5. Understand the nature of indexes in tracking common stock averages.
6. Examine some of the means by which common stocks might be evaluated. This would include the different ways by which stocks might be viewed, and some of those analytical considerations that offer insight into the nature and potential of stocks.
7. Be able to calculate the return on both stocks and bonds, including the current yield and the total return or yield to maturity.
8. Be familiar with those characteristics that distinguish one bond from another. Note the document that describes those characteristics, and how bonds are identified.

Chapter Objectives

9. Differentiate between the three major issuers of bonds, and the types of bonds they issue.
10. Understand the two ways in which bonds might be redeemed prior to maturity, together with the ramifications of each.
11. Cite the nomenclature used by the rating agencies in judging the creditworthiness of bonds.

Investment Securities

When we talk about Investment Securities, we typically talk about stocks and bonds. In the end, these are only pieces of paper, but they can be quite valuable. Securities are typically registered documents (registered either in the name of the owner or in "Street Name" on behalf of the owner), evidencing the ownership by the buyer. Once registered, the buyer will receive all of the information and distributions pertaining to that security. For example, in the United States the buyer will receive quarterly and annual reports from the corporation who issued the security, if he owns common stock he will receive the notice of the annual meeting and the voting materials, he will receive the dividend or interest payments on his stock or bond holdings, and, if he holds bonds, he will receive the principal payment at the maturity date.

Trading Investment Securities

To transact an Investment Security, a buyer or a seller must have a brokerage account. As good as the web is, it will not take you to the floor of a securities exchange or allow you to buy and sell securities directly. When it comes to buying and selling securities, there are a number of approaches that might be taken. Let's examine the more common types of orders you might consider.

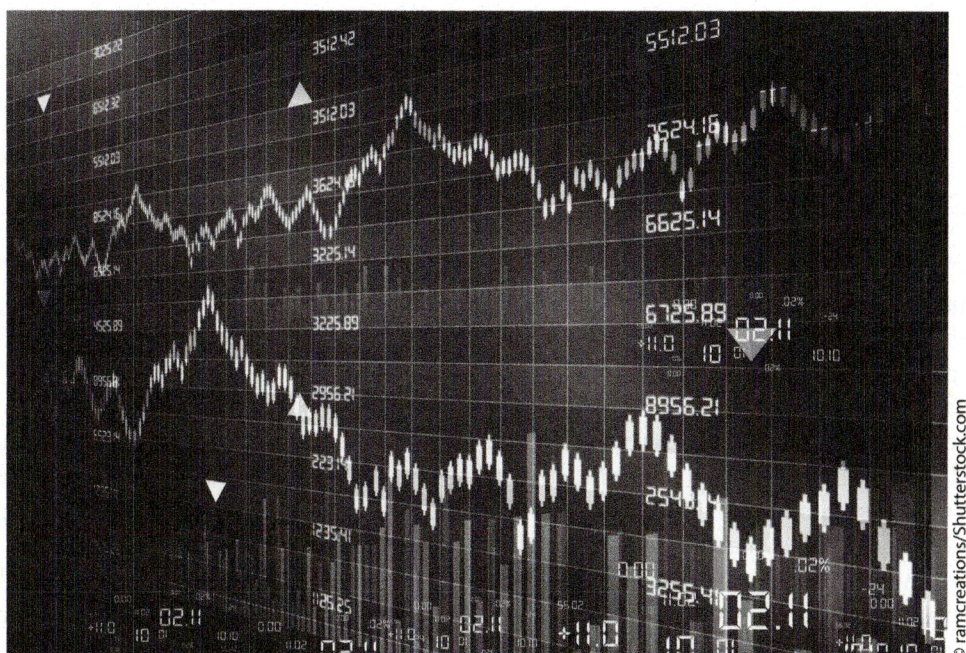

Figure 15:1 When you place a market order, you are telling the broker to buy or sell that security right now at whatever price the market is quoting.

Market Order. When you place a Market Order for an investment security, you are telling the broker to buy or sell that security right now at whatever price the market is quoting. For large and liquid stocks, this order is executed very quickly—almost before you hang up the phone or take your finger off the computer key. For the majority of stocks or bonds, this type of order is satisfactory. However, there are two instances when you might wish to consider a different type of order.

The first instance is when the stock or bond you would like to trade is showing a very large spread between the bid price and the ask price. Like many things that are bought and sold, there is a difference between the price the buyer would like to pay—the Bid, and the price the seller would like to receive—the Ask. The Bid price is almost always lower than the Ask price. In real estate transactions, this can amount to thousands of dollars. In investment securities, the difference could be mere pennies. However, on occasion, that spread increases to the point where it becomes an issue. A market order to buy a security will go to the marketplace and pay the Ask price, as that is the price the buy order can be accomplished right now. Similarly, a market order to sell a security will go to the marketplace and receive the Bid price, as that is the price the sell order can be accomplished right now. If you think that the spread is too large, and you don't want to pay the ask or receive the bid, you may wish to consider a different type of order.

The other instance when a market order may not be desirable is when the price of a security is experiencing considerable volatility. We all know that stock prices go up and down all the time. Even bond prices bounce around on occasion, though their level of price volatility is not nearly as great. However, if you owned a stock where the price varied in a single day like the one portrayed below, at what price would you like to sell the security? At what price would you like to buy this security?

Exhibit 15:1 Price Volatility of Company X Common Stock

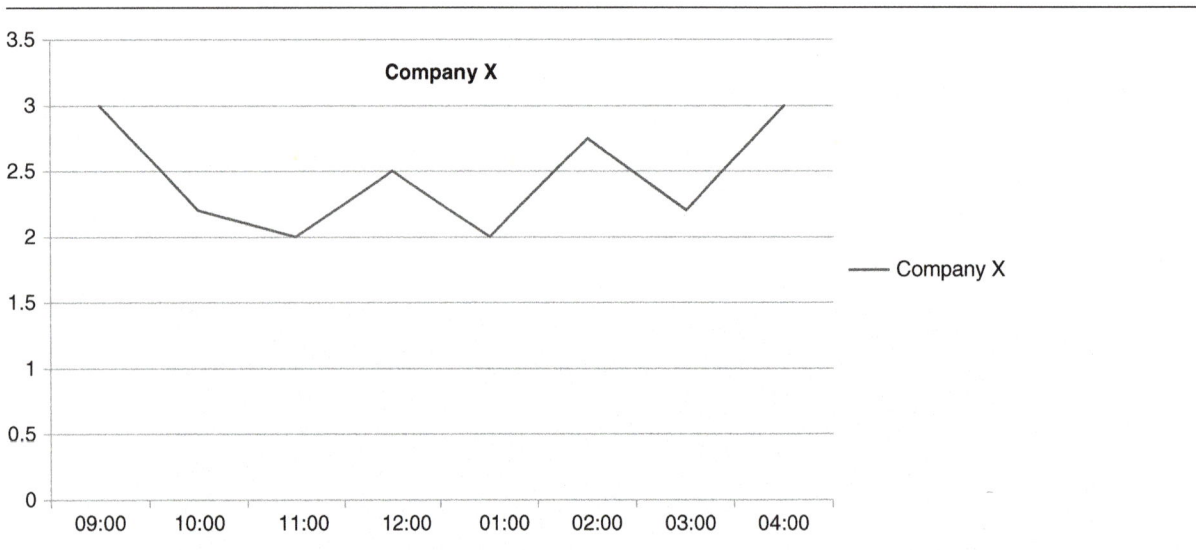

Clearly, you might be a disappointed seller if you put in a market order to sell at around noon. However, recognizing the price volatility, you might wish to consider a different type of order—one that allows you to set a designated price that you would be willing to accept.

Limit Order. Designating a particular price that you are willing to pay if you're a buyer, or that you are be willing to receive if you're a seller, is possible in a Limit Order. With a limit order, you specify the price. If the stock or bond reaches that price, then the transaction will occur. If the stock or bond does not reach that price, then there is no transaction. Most limit orders expire at the end of the day, however you might place a limit order "Good Till Canceled" which will extend the life of that order until you cancel it. Looking at the price trading pattern in Exhibit 15:1, a buyer may wish to place a limit order below $2.50 per share, where a seller may wish to place a limit order above $2.50 per share. Although this would relieve the market participant of the uncertainty of buying or selling at whatever price the stock happens to be trading at the moment, it also adds uncertainty to the transaction—the uncertainty that the stock does not reach the limit price and therefore, does not trade.

Stop Loss. Let's point out one more type of order that is seen relatively often among common stock buyers. Once you buy a stock, you may wish to place a safety net underneath your position in case unforeseen

Figure 15:2 Once you buy a stock, you may wish to place a safety net underneath your position in case unforeseen circumstances cause it to take a free fall in price.

circumstances cause it to take a free fall in price. This safety net is called a Stop Loss order, and technically, it's not an order at all. Rather, you ask your broker to monitor your stocks price. If that price falls to a point, which you have designated in advance, then the Stop Loss turns into a sell at market order. There is no charge for placing a Stop Loss on your position, unless the stop loss is reached and the ensuing market order is executed. Although it may seem comforting to have such a safety net in place, be careful that you don't set the stop loss price to close against the normal trading range of the stock. In our example above, if you had bought the stock at $2.50 per share, you might be tempted to put your safety net at $2.00, so that you would not lose more than about $0.50 per share if the price declined. However, had you done so, you would have sold your stock within hours, given normal trading volatility. If you choose to use Stop Loss orders, make sure that you allow room for such volatility, or you may find that you are selling a stock you really didn't want to sell.

A slight derivation of the stop loss order is called a trailing stop loss order. Here, the safety net is set as a percent of the purchase price. In the days and weeks that follow your purchase, should the price of the stock increase, the level of the stop loss would increase right along with it, maintaining your safety net at the percent of market price you have designated. Of course, if the price of the stock declines, the safety net does not decline. As a result, any trailing stop loss you put on your stock should be monitored to determine if it needs to be adjusted.

Investment Strategies

Your investment in securities is tangent to a goal . . . there is a purpose in mind when you buy stocks or bonds. As such, you have selected a particular golf club because it is the right one to use to reach your goal. In the pages that follow, we will describe some of the characteristics of investment security clubs, and how they might be utilized. If your goal is a long one, such as your retirement, and you will be making regular contributions toward that goal, there are several investment strategies you may wish to consider.

First, recognize that it takes time for securities to appreciate. Their growth in price occurs hand in hand with the growth of the corporation that issued them. Recognizing that fact, a Buy-and-Hold strategy may make sense. When you follow this approach, you are not concerned with the ups and downs of the market; you are buying for the long term. This minimizes brokerage commissions that might occur from short-term trading, and maximizes long-term gains.

One method of implementing a buy-and-hold strategy successfully is by investing the same dollar amount in each period, regardless of the level of the market in that period. This is called Dollar Cost Averaging. Applied to a common stock, it works like this:

Exhibit 15:2 Dollar Cost Averaging

Period	Amount Invested	Share Price	# Shares Purchased	Total Shares Owned
1	$1,000	$50.00	20	20
2	1,000	62.50	16	36
3	1,000	43.48	23	59
4	1,000	52.63	19	78
5	1,000	58.82	17	95

Over the five periods (they could be monthly, quarterly, semiannual, or annual periods) you have invested a total of $5,000, and have bought 95 shares of common stock. That is an average cost of $52.63 per share, well below the current price of $58.82. If you look closely at the table, you will see that you are buying more shares when the price is down and fewer shares when the price is up. This is as it should be. You should be buying more when the price is low, and buying less when the price is high. The discipline imposed by dollar cost averaging generally results in a profit over time.

Many times, corporations will offer shareholders the opportunity to reinvest their dividends, using the cash dividend to buy more stock. If you want to add to your common stock holding, such Dividend Reinvestment Plans give you the opportunity to compound your results, while sparing yourself the brokerage commission. Over time, the additional stock accumulated through the dividend reinvestment plan can be significant.

Summary & Review

1. What is an Investment Security? How is the ownership of an investment security evidenced?
2. What are the advantages and disadvantages of a Market Order? When might you feel comfortable using a market order?
3. Describe a Limit Order. What is the principle disadvantage of limit orders?
4. One of the drawbacks of a stop loss safety net is the possibility that market volatility triggers a sell you really didn't mean to happen. How can you defend against this drawback?
5. Explain how dollar cost averaging works. How would this kind of discipline help an investor avoid getting caught up in the mood of the market?

A Certificate of Ownership

In legal terms, a corporation is an individual—entitled to all of the rights of an individual and able to function in society as an individual. The laws that establish this unique entity allow that the corporation may be owned by individuals or institutions. This ownership in a corporation is evidenced by Common Stock. Corporations sell common stock to raise funds to meet expenses, to finance growth, or other uses.

Because the common stockholder is the owner, all of the other suppliers, employees, and bondholders, which the corporation engages, must be paid first, before the common stockholder receives anything. However, as the owner, the common stock is able to benefit from any growth in revenues and earnings, which the corporation achieves, and is entitled to all of the net earnings of the corporation after all other expenses—including taxes—have been paid. Let's look at a few of the characteristics of common stock.

First, as the owner, each share of common stock is entitled to vote in the overall management of the corporation. Voting typically occurs once each year, on the event of the annual meeting. It is here that the stockholder casts his ballot to elect the board of directors (the ultimate authority of the corporation), to appoint auditors who would be responsible for validating the correctness of the financial records, and to approve any other matters that might come before the owners. It is not unusual for the stockholder to give his vote to management, appointing management to be his proxy and voting his common shares in his place.

Second, once common stock has been issued, it exists indefinitely. Those who purchase common stock do not expect to sell those shares back to the corporation. If an owner no longer wishes to hold his stock, he may offer it for sale in the stock market. At times, the corporation itself may buy its own shares. If it does, those shares would be placed as Treasury Stock, to be used in employee compensation programs, for the purchase of other business, or for other transactions where such stock may be used instead of cash.

One more characteristic we should note. In the event that the corporation fails, all of its indebtedness, including bills and debts and taxes, will be paid before the stockholder receives anything. Most often in this case, there is not enough money to meet all expenses, and the common stockholder receives nothing. Clearly, an investor who wants to buy common stock is looking to purchase only those corporations whose revenues and earnings are growing, and whose common stock is increasing in value.

Figure 15:3 This ownership of a corporation is evidenced by common stock.

Dividends

As noted, the stockholder is entitled to the net income of the corporation after all other expenses have been paid. However, as the corporation usually wants to retain that money for use in its business, the common stockholder most often receives only a fraction of the income in the form of Dividends. The dividend is a cash distribution given to the stockholder from the net earnings of the corporation. Dividends are not required, and many corporations do not pay a dividend but retain all of the income for use in the business. Any dividends paid are declared at such times and in such amounts as the board of directors may determine. In the United States, if a dividend is declared, it is typically paid quarterly. As noted in the previous chapter, common stock dividends are typically relatively modest, and most investors buy common stocks for their appreciation potential rather than their current income.

Three dates to keep in mind when viewing a dividend. First, is the Declaration Date; the date when the board of directors declare the dividend. The board will, at the declaration date, announce both the amount of the dividend and the record date. The Record Date is the most important date to keep in mind. To be entitled to a dividend, the stockholder must be a holder of the stock on the record date. If an investor sells his stock a day earlier, he will not be entitled to the dividend, even though he may have held his stock for years. Similarly, if he buys his shares a day after the record date, he will not be entitled to the dividend. For this reason, the record date is often referred to as the ex-dividend date, or simply the ex-date. The third date is simply the Payment Date, or the date when payment is actually made. These three dates occur in fairly rapid order, with the record date being a week or two after the declaration date, and the payment date being a week or two after the record date.

Occasionally, a board of directors will declare a stock dividend, also called a Stock Split. In this declaration, the board is simply slicing up the pie into smaller pieces. If, for example, the board declares a 2-for-1 stock split, they are issuing an additional share of stock for each share that you own—giving you two shares instead of one. This does not enlarge the pie, but simply cuts it in two. In this event, the market price of a single common stock will drop by half, as you now have two shares where before you had only one. The purpose of a stock split is to increase the number of common shares outstanding, though it also has the effect of reducing the market price of each share.

Figure 15:4 The dividend is a cash distribution given to the stockholder.

> ### Get Real
>
> One day my brother's wife returned from the hairdresser, excited to share news of a wonderful investment opportunity. At the hairdresser, she had learned that a local company was about to issue a stock dividend in the amount of one share for every five shares held by the owner. That means, she confided, that there is an opportunity to get 20% more stock if we buy before the dividend occurs.
>
> Her husband acknowledged that they would, indeed, end up with six shares of stock for every five shares they had before the stock dividend. Then he asked if she had also learned whether revenues and income would rise by 20%—whether they were selling 20% more product or realizing 20% more profits. If not, he assured her, then the underlying business that is represented by the common stock has not changed. Creating more shares does not mean a bigger business; it simply divides the existing business into slightly smaller pieces. As a result, the value of each of the five existing shares will decline by 4%, to accommodate the inclusion of a sixth share. If you reduce the value of five shares by 4% each, you will not end up 20% richer after the stock dividend ... you will end up with one more share of stock—that's all.

Preferred Stock

On the heels of our discussion of dividends, might be a good place to talk about Preferred Stock. This is because Preferred Stock is so named, because it enjoys preferred standing with respect to the dividend paid. Most preferred stock carries a specified dividend amount, which is usually designated as a percent of the par value of the preferred stock. For example, it is common today for preferred stock to have a par value of $25.00 per share. If a preferred issue has a 5% dividend, that means that it would be expected to pay $1.25 per year ($25.00 × 5%), usually in quarterly installments. However, like any stock, the preferred dividend is not legally required, and a board may choose not to declare the preferred dividend. (Of course, any corporation that fails to pay the required preferred dividend would probably be in financial trouble, and the value of their preferred shares would drop significantly.)

There are several characteristics of preferred stock, which make it look more like a bond than a stock. Two of those characteristics have already been mentioned ... a par value and a specified rate of return. In addition, preferred stock has a maturity date, on which the corporation is obligated to redeem the preferred shares at par. Taken together, these characteristics suggest fixed income rather than stock. However, preferred stock does not enjoy the level of seniority that bonds have in the event the corporation fails. In such an event, preferred shares would rank just one step ahead of common shares in the food chain, and well below the claims of bondholders and other creditors.

> ### Summary & Review
>
> 1. What does it mean when we say that the common stockholder is the owner of the corporation? What rights does that ownership provide to the stockholder?
> 2. While not all corporations pay a dividend on their common stock, those that do follow a sequence of steps, each marked by a date. What is that sequence?
> 3. What is a stock dividend—sometimes referred to as a stock split? If you are aware of a pending stock split in time to buy the stock before it occurs, will this information make you rich?
> 4. In what ways is preferred stock different from common stock? Is it likely that preferred stock will appreciate in value to the same extent as common stock?

Dissecting Stocks

Common stocks are not all alike. Each is as different as the corporation they represent. There are several ways that an investor might view stocks, and each approach presents a very different collection of stocks.

Perhaps one of the more common divisions is between Value Stocks and Growth Stocks. Value Stocks are those issued by corporations that are relatively mature, where increases in revenues and earnings are modest ... if at all. These stocks usually pay a better than average dividend, can be purchased a bit cheaper than most other stocks, and are usually more stable in price. Growth Stocks, on the other hand, are issued by corporations that are younger, where revenues and earnings are growing faster, and where prospects for continued expansion are good. These stocks typically pay a modest dividend ... if at all, are more expensive than most other stocks, and experience greater volatility in the price of the shares. For additional discussion on this theme, see the article "Growth Versus Value—A Stock Pickers Conundrum" found in Appendix I.

Another way that one might view stocks is by considering the size of the corporation. The term Capitalization describes the total market value of the common stock of a corporation. It is determined by taking the price per common share, and multiplying it by the number of shares outstanding. The biggest corporations are called "Large Cap," and are typically over $10 billion in capitalization. Medium-sized corporations are called "Mid Cap," when the total value of their capitalization is between $1 billion and $10 billion. "Small Cap" would be those corporations that are less than $1 billion in capitalization. An investor would be focused on large cap stocks if he wants to own the largest corporations. He would be focused on small cap stocks if he wants smaller corporations, which are often younger.

A third way that an investor might dissect the market is by looking at the kind or type of stock he is buying. There are five popular types of stocks. Of course, there is no magic in limiting our division to five kinds of stocks. Perhaps you can think of another grouping of similar stocks that would make sense.

Blue Chip: The largest and most prominent corporations. Blue Chip stocks are usually older companies, dominant in their industry, and financially strong in terms of capitalization and profitability.

Income Stocks: Those stocks that pay a steady and above average dividend. We have noted previously that stocks may not pay any dividend, and those that do often pay a relatively modest dividend. This type is an exception—and their dividend yield often compares favorably with bonds and other income securities.

Cyclical Stocks: Stocks that mirror the business cycle. They go up when the business cycle is on the upswing, and down when the business cycle is declining. Recognizing that the stock market is a leading indicator, these stocks usually begin rising or falling in price ahead of when the actual business cycle occurs.

Defensive Stocks: These stocks are the opposite of cyclical stocks. This type does not perform quite as well when the business cycle is rising, but does not go down as much when the business cycle is falling. They are relatively more stable in price than the average stock, which gives them their defensive characteristics.

Speculative Stocks: This kind of stock represents corporations that are new, which are involved in pioneering technology, or which offer a product or service that is relatively untested or of unknown quality. The potential of speculative stocks could be significant, if the uncertainties can be resolved.

Figure 15:5 Perhaps you have heard the phrase Bull Market or Bear Market.

Stock Market Indexes

Sometimes, it is useful for us to look at the stock market in terms of averages. Perhaps you have heard the phrase Bull Market or Bear Market. A bull market means that average stock prices have been rising over an extended period of time. A bear market means that average stock prices have been falling over an extended period of time.

There are a great many indexes that represent the average of a given market segment. There are indexes for United States' stocks and foreign stocks, indexes for industries, for size of company, for type of stock, and for type of market. Remember that an index is only an index. The number does not represent dollars or any other commodity. All indexes began at some point in the past with an arbitrary number, and that number has changed since inception as the market segment it represents has changed. Therefore, the value of an index is only in representing the change of a given segment. Some of the more popular indexes are detailed in Exhibit 15:3.

Exhibit 15:3 Stock Market Indexes

Dow Jones Industrial Average:	An index of 30 of the largest U.S. industrial corporations. Began in 1896, the names represented by the DJIA have changed over time, but continue to represent the largest Blue Chip stocks in America.
S&P 500 Index:	An index of 500 of the most dominant stocks in the United States initially established in 1957, the prominence of this index has grown to the point where it is a recognized leading indicator of the business cycle.
NASDAQ Composite:	This index goes back to 1971, when the NASDAQ first began trading. The NASDAQ is the second largest stock market in the world, constituting an electronic quotation system, as opposed to an exchange. (The largest stock market in the world is the New York Stock Exchange.)

Summary & Review

1. There are a number of approaches used in understanding the similarities and differences in common stocks. One of those approaches attaches the label Value Stock and Growth Stock to different kinds of common stock. What does that label mean?
2. Another approach in dissecting common stocks would be to divide the market into the kind or type of stocks that are available. Name the six commonly recognized stock divisions? What does each represent?
3. Indexes are used to mark averages and changes in those averages over time. Which of the three indexes discussed above do you think best represents the U.S. stock market as a whole?

A Few Analytical Considerations

If we are to select those stocks that represent sound investments, with better than average prospects of going up in market price, it is going to take a little more effort than simply throwing darts at a list of names. Bearing in mind that we generally make an investment in common stocks in the hope that the price of that stock will rise over time, let's look at some of the considerations that might be employed in evaluating a potential common stock investment.

Revenue per Share: The success of a corporation will depend largely on whether or not they are able to sell their product. If they are able to sell more product this year than they did last year, the growth in revenues will attest to their success. If we look at the total revenues produced, divided by the number of common shares outstanding, we have a number called revenue per share. Ideally, this number should be rising over time.

Earnings per Share (EPS): We have noted that the net earnings of a corporation belong to the stockholder. It is always best if we look at net earnings in terms of the earnings per share of common stock. This calculation—Earnings per Share or EPS—is reached by taking the total net earnings, subtracting out any preferred dividends, and dividing the remainder by the number of common shares outstanding. Again, this number should be rising over time. If the corporation is subject to seasonal influences, it is best to look at EPS changes for the same quarter year after year. If seasonal influences are not material, you could simply look at EPS quarter after quarter, to see if the number is growing.

Price Earnings Ratio (P/E Ratio): This is the single most prominent measure in common stock analysis. It judges the relative expensiveness of a share of common stock. It is calculated by dividing the market price of a share of stock by the earnings per share for the most recent 12 months. The result is a factor that reflects how many times the current year's earnings you are paying to own a share of stock. For example, if you are looking at a stock selling for $15.00 per share, and the earnings per share for the last 12 months totaled $1.00, the price earnings ratio is $15.00/$1.00 = 15.0x. It is not unusual for a Growth stock to have a P/E ratio above the averages, or for a Value stock to have a P/E ratio below the averages.

Current Yield: The current yield measures the return from the dividend paid. It is calculated by dividing the annual dividend by the price of the stock. If the stock is paying a dividend of 10 cents per quarter or 40 cents per year, and given our example of a $15 share price, the current yield is $0.40/$15.00 = 2.67%. This dividend rate is better than average. Of course, the shareholder would be interested in the question of whether the dividend is rising over time. If it is, then your dividend yield would actually be increasing as a percentage of the price you paid for the stock.

Total Return: Investors want to know how their investment has fared over time. Part of this answer lies in the dividend that is being paid, and the current yield that the shareholder is receiving. However, most investors buy common stock not for the dividend, but for the potential appreciation. If you paid $15.00 when you bought the stock 2 years ago, and now the shares are selling for $25.00, you have unrealized appreciation of $10.00 or nearly 67%. Good for you. However, as a percentage return should always be quoted on an annual basis, this works out to roughly 33% appreciation per year over your 2-year holding period. But wait. To get the total return, we need to add both the annual dividend and the appreciation. This gives us a total annual return of just under 36% per annum. Of course, as long as you are holding that stock, any appreciation will increase and decrease with fluctuations in the share price. It is only after you have sold your holdings that the unrealized return becomes a realized return . . . and any capital gain you realized becomes taxable.

Beta: We all know how volatile the stock market can be at times. Perhaps you would want to know if the stock you own is as volatile as the market. Beta is the measure of how volatile an individual stock is when compared to the market. The market is always 1.00, no matter how high it has risen or how far it has declined. If you find that one stock has a beta of 0.75, it indicates that this stock is less volatile than the market—whether the market is going up or going down. If another stock's beta is 1.5, this stock is expected to be more volatile than the market—again, in both directions. Therefore, if the market goes up by 10%, the first stock will rise by only 7.5% on its beta of 0.75. However, if the market goes down by 10%, the second stock will decline by 15% on its beta of 1.5x.

Figure 15:6 Perhaps you would want to know if the stock you own is as volatile as the market.

Alpha: Although beta suggests a level of price volatility when compared with the market as a whole, there are always a host of considerations that have little to do with the market, but a lot to do with the individual characteristics of the company. Those considerations that are unique to each corporation are called Alpha. A technological innovation, a research breakthrough, a change in management, or a means of improving operating efficiency and reducing costs, all represent alpha factors that will have a profound effect on the success of the corporation, and on the price of the common stock, regardless of what the market as a whole is doing. An article titled "In Search of Alpha—Understanding Changes in Security Prices" can shed additional light on this topic. It is available in Appendix I.

> ### Summary & Review
>
> 1. If you are looking to buy common stock, why is it important to look for corporations that are experiencing growth in revenues and net income?
> 2. As you look over some of the considerations that might be employed in evaluating the investment potential of a common stock, which ones do you think are most useful? Why?
> 3. How do you calculate the total return from a stock investment?

A Certificate of Indebtedness

There are times when an entity may wish to borrow funds to finance growth, seasonal needs, or other uses. Many times, they will obtain loans from banks or other lenders. However, if the entity has established itself financially, it may also have the option to raise money by selling bonds in the financial markets. Selling bonds is simply another path to funding, which they may choose to go down if the terms are attractive.

A Bond is basically a certificate of indebtedness. It evidences a borrowing by the issuing entity. All of the features, conditions, covenants, and other information relative to the bond are contained in an issuing document called the Indenture. The indenture must be complete, as it is the principle authenticating device. Among the features present in each and every indenture are:

Figure 15:7 A Bond is basically a certificate of indebtedness.

Size of Offering: The number of bonds to be sold and the amount of money to be raised by the sale of the bonds. Typically, bonds have a Face or Par Value equal to $1,000 per bond.

Date of Offering: The date when interest begins to accrue on the bonds.

Coupon: The annual interest rate that will be paid on the bonds. For most bonds, the coupon is fixed at the Date of Offering, and remains fixed throughout the life of the bonds. A 0% Coupon Bond is a bond that pays no periodic interest. Such bonds are issued at a discount price below par value, producing a return when the bond is repaid at par value. Occasionally, bonds are issued with a variable coupon, which adjusts from time to time with changes in interest rates. When this happens, they are called variable coupon bonds.

Coupon Payment Dates: The dates when interest is paid. Typically, the first Coupon Payment Date is 6 months from the Date of Offering, with subsequent interest payments every 6 months. For example, if the Coupon is 5%, and given a Face value of $1,000, that bond would pay interest of $25 every 6 months, or $50 per year. Occasionally, interest is paid more often than twice a year, but these are exceptions.

Maturity Date: The final date when the indebtedness is repaid. At Maturity, the Bonds are redeemed at Face value, usually $1,000 per bond.

Discount: A price per bond below Face value, or less than $1,000. Note that bond prices are typically quoted as a percent of Face value. For example, a price quote of 99.5 means 99.5% of Face value, or $1,000 × 0.995 = $995.00. This price is a discount.

Premium: A price per bond above Face value, or above $1,000. Again, note that a bond price quote of 101.5 is 101.5% of Face value, or $1,000 × 1.015 = $1,015.00. This price is a premium.

Default and Acceleration Clause: This provision in the indenture explains the events that would constitute a default in the promises made by the borrowing entity. As bonds represent indebtedness, the borrower makes certain promises, including a pledge to pay interest and principal when due. If those promises are broken, the bonds can be declared in default, and the bondholders can demand that all interest, together with all principal, be repaid immediately. There are usually certain other promises that are supported by the default and acceleration clause, including promises to maintain a specified level of financial solvency, to maintain earnings at a level that will exceed the interest requirement by a given ratio, and not to issue additional bonds above a stipulated amount.

Of course, there is other information conveyed in the indenture as well. As every bond offering has an indenture detailing the terms of that bond, can you visualize how many indentures that may involve? Although a corporation may have only one class of common stock outstanding, it may have dozens of bond issues that have been sold over the years. For this reason, most bonds are not identified by a letter symbol, as stocks are, but by a Cusip Number. A cusip number is typically nine digits, such as 123456AB7. Each cusip number is unique to a specific bond, with its own Date of Offering, Coupon, and Maturity Date.

Summary & Review

1. Why might a borrower choose to sell bonds to raise needed funds?
2. What is the Indenture? Why is it necessary?
3. If I were to suggest that you should buy a Philadelphia Airport 5% due 2/15/2025, what kind of bond have I just recommended?
4. What is the Default and Acceleration Clause of the Indenture? What does this do to strengthen a bonds place in the food chain?
5. What is a Cusip number?

Who Issues Bonds

When we talked about stocks earlier in this chapter, we were talking about corporations, as they are the only entity to issue stocks. Bonds, however, are issued by corporations, by state and local governments, and by national governments. As a result, bond markets are many times larger than stock markets, and the aggregate dollar amount of bonds outstanding is enormous.

Corporate Bonds

When a corporation issues bonds, it does so to raise money to finance its ongoing activities or to finance expansion. There are different kinds of bonds that may be issued by corporations.

One of the more common types of corporate bonds is called a Debenture. Don't confuse this with the Indenture—which is the document detailing the terms of a bond offering. A Debenture is a senior, unsecured bond, supported by the full faith and credit of the corporation. Financially strong corporations, which have evidenced the ability to pay their debt on time, often issue debentures.

If the corporation is not quite as strong, they may find that the market is not exactly knocking over chairs to buy their unsecured debt. In this instance, they may be obliged to offer some kind of collateral in support of their borrowing. The most common type of collateral offered is real estate, and a Mortgage Bond might be offered with a pledge of real estate to guaranty the corporations' repayment of interest and principal. Another kind of collateral might be the equipment that the corporation operates. Equipment Trust Certificates are often issued by airlines or railroads, with a lien on their aircraft or railroad cars in support of their borrowing.

Occasionally, a corporation will issue a Convertible Bond, which the bondholder may convert into a specified number of shares of common stock at some point down the road. There are several reasons why a corporation might want to issue a convertible bond. First, because of the conversion feature, this bond attracts an investor who might be interested in owning the stock of the corporation eventually, but would rather have the strength of a coupon paying bond for the present. He knows he can convert his bond into shares of stock if the price of the stock rises to the point where the conversion is desirable. But if the stock price fails to increase, he can always get his money back from the bond at maturity. Second, because of the attraction of the conversion feature, convertible bonds typically pay a lower coupon than comparable debentures. Finally, if the investor does decide to covert his bond into common stock, the corporation does not have to repay that bond at maturity.

If the corporation is up against indenture limits as to the amount of senior debt it can issue, it may issue Subordinated Bonds. These bonds rank junior to debentures or to mortgage bonds, and would be permitted as long as their issuance does not exceed any limitations as to total debt imposed by the indenture.

If you are looking to buy corporate bonds, look at the financial strength of the corporation—the level of earnings available to meet the interest requirement, and the amount of debt outstanding.

Municipal Bonds

When a state or local government entity needs to raise funds, it may turn to bonds as a means of financing. Bonds issued by state or local government are called Municipal Bonds, and they are of two basic types.

A General Obligation (GO) bond is similar to a corporate Debenture, in that it is an unsecured, full faith and credit obligations of the issuer. However, there is a big difference between the municipal GO and the corporate debenture. The municipal GO is backed by the taxing power of the state or local government. In the indenture describing the GO, there is a promise to the effect that the governmental entity will raise taxes to whatever level it needs to, to raise enough money to meet the interest and principal requirements on its bond. For this reason, municipal GOs are often called unlimited tax bonds, as the source of payment is tax revenues, and taxes can be raised if necessary to produce money to pay the bonds. If you are going to buy a GO, look at the state or local government that is offering the bonds—their tax base, collection rate, and the cost of their aggregate indebtedness versus the funds available to pay their debt.

The other type of municipal debt is called Revenue bonds. These bonds are not generally supported by taxes, but rely on the revenues from a particular project to provide the money needed for payment of interest and principal. For example, a municipality that needs to expand its water and sewer services may issue revenue bonds to raise the necessary funding, with the bonds to be repaid from water and sewer assessments. If you are looking to buy a revenue bond, focus on the organization or project—on the revenues expected from that project, and their ability to meet the costs of the bonds.

Whether the municipality issues GO bonds or revenue bonds, a big advantage to investors is the fact that the interest received on most municipal bonds is exempt from Federal income taxes. To the investor holding such municipal bonds, the interest is an exclusion from his Adjusted Gross Income. This means that, depending on

Figure 15:8 A municipality that needs to expand its water and sewer services, may issue revenue bonds to raise the necessary funding.

the investors tax bracket, a municipal bond paying 5%, for example, could actually be more profitable than a corporate bond paying 6%. Here's how it works.

Let's say that you are in the 20% tax bracket, which means that the Federal Government is taking 20% of your income for taxes. If you choose to buy a tax-exempt municipal bond, you would not have to share the income from that bond with Uncle Sam. As a result, the interest from the municipal bond is worth more. To find out how much more, divide the coupon of that municipal bond by 1 – your tax rate. In our example, we have 5%/(1 - 0.20) or 5/0.80 = 6.25%. This is called the Taxable Equivalent Yield, as it shows how much you would have to earn on a taxable basis, to equal the 5% you will earn on a tax-free basis. Clearly, the 6.25% is higher than the 6% you would be making from the corporate bond, making the municipal option more profitable after taxes.

Of course, you could look at it from the taxable standpoint. Multiply the taxable yield, in our example 6%, by 1 – your tax rate. That is 6% × (1 - 0.20) or 6 × 0.80 = 4.80%. The conclusion is the same. At the 20% tax rate, the 5% municipal bond is more profitable after taxes than the 6% corporate bond.

Treasury Bonds

The largest issuer of debt in the world is the U.S. Federal government, which issues bonds to finance its ongoing operational needs. The department that handles the sale of bonds for the Federal government is the U.S. Treasury. The Treasury issues primarily three types of bonds.

Treasury Bills are short-term indebtedness. They have a face value of $1,000, are 0% coupon that are sold at a discount, and mature in 1 year or less.

Treasury Notes are intermediate-term indebtedness. They also have a face value of $1,000, carry a coupon that is established at the Date of Offering and paid semiannually, and mature in 1 to 10 years.

Treasury Bonds (which include savings bonds) are long-term indebtedness. They have a face value of $1,000, carry a coupon that is established at the Date of Offering and paid semiannually, and mature in more than 10 years.

The interest earned on Treasury borrowings are subject to Federal income taxes, but are not subject to state income taxes. There is growing concern by many investors as to the amount of debt being issued by the Federal government, and the governments' ability to meet the repayment requirements on its indebtedness. This concern is underlined by the fact that most of the proceeds from the issuance of Treasury debt are used to meet ongoing operational needs, not to build productive capacity. It is like borrowing to buy food. The money is not used to build infrastructure and expand revenues, which could be used to repay the debt, but is simply given up to meet the day's expenses. This leaves more debt to repay at the end of the day with no commensurate increase in the ability to pay that debt.

> ### Summary & Review
>
> 1. Who are the three issuers of bonds?
> 2. What is a Debenture? What are the advantages of this type of bond over other types of corporate debt?
> 3. How does a municipal General Obligation bond compare to a corporate Debenture?
> 4. A significant advantage of most Municipal bonds is the fact that the interest paid is exempt from Federal Income Tax. If you were looking at a corporate bond paying 5%, and a municipal bond paying 4%, and assuming you are in the 10% Federal tax bracket, which bond is the most profitable for you after taxes?
> 5. Why are people increasingly concerned with the ongoing issuance of Treasury debt?

Early Redemption Provisions

A significant proportion of both corporate bonds and municipal bonds carry provisions in their indentures, which allow them to be repaid prior to maturity. There are two ways that a bond might be redeemed before its maturity date. These early repayment terms are referred to as Call Provisions and Sinking Fund Provisions.

Figure 15:9 A significant proportion of both corporate bonds and municipal bonds carry provisions in their indentures, which allow them to be repaid prior to maturity.

If the bonds have a Call Provision (and many bonds are noncallable, which means that they do not have this characteristic), the issuer of the bonds has the option to prepay their bonds at any time on or after a given date. Typically, the call date begins a number of years after the bonds are first issued. Most of the time, the terms of the Call Provision require the issuer to pay a premium price if they decide to repay the bonds early, but that premium price usually declines over time to where they only have to pay face value to redeem the bonds near the maturity date. Remember, this is an option, not a requirement. The issuer may choose not to repay their bonds early—especially if interest rates have gone up and the borrower is paying a relatively low rate of interest on the bonds.

If the bonds have a Sinking Fund Provision (and again many bonds do not have this characteristic) the issuer of the bonds is obligated to redeem a given number of bonds at each sinking fund date. This early redemption requirement is intended to spread out the repayment burden over a longer period, as opposed to having the entire repayment occur at once on the maturity date. The first sinking fund repayment date usually occurs 5 or 10 years before the final maturity. From that date until maturity, a given number of bonds would be redeemed each year. Redemptions for the sinking fund occur at face value.

If a given bond has a call provision or a sinking fund provision, there exists the possibility that your bonds will be redeemed at or near face value prior to the maturity date. Here is a potential problem. If you pay a premium price for your bonds, you may be setting yourself up for a loss. Let's say that you paid 102 ($1,020.00) for a bond with a higher than average coupon. You were willing to pay that premium price because the bonds don't mature for 10 years and you would be able to earn a good current yield over the next decade. However, if these bonds have a sinking fund requirement that begins 10 years prior to maturity, it is possible that your bonds could be redeemed in any of the next 10 years—at face value. If that happens, you would have a loss of $20 per bond in the year your bonds were redeemed. Be careful about paying a premium price for bonds that are callable or that have a sinking fund.

Current Yield and Yield to Maturity

This brings us to an important point. Remember the calculation of current yield introduced in our discussion of stocks. It is simply the annual dividend divided by the price paid. If you bought a bond with a 3% coupon at a price of 96 ($960.00), your current yield would be 3.1% ($30/$960). However, with a bond there is a feature that does not exist in a stock, and that feature is the maturity date. There is the promise of the issuer to pay face value at maturity . . . a promise that does not exist in a stock. This feature means that you will have a built-in capital gain if you paid a discount for the bond, or a capital loss if you paid a premium price. In our example, you paid a discount price of $960, so when you are paid face value of $1,000, you will have a $40 capital gain. That event will occur on the maturity date—or on the call date of sinking fund date if the bonds have these early redemption provisions.

As a result, you have a built-in gain or loss that should be added or subtracted from your current yield to show the total return from this investment. This total return is called Yield to Maturity. Continuing our example; if this bond has a maturity date 4 years from now, and assuming there are no call provisions or sinking fund requirements, your capital gain would average about $10 per year, or roughly 1% each year. So your Yield to Maturity would be equal to the current yield (3.1%) plus the additional capital gain per year (1%) for a total return of approximately 4.1% per annum. (There are yield to maturity calculation programs on most financial calculators, which would give you the exact number.)

> ### Summary & Review
>
> 1. Name the two ways that a bond might be redeemed prior to its maturity date.
> 2. What is the danger inherent if you pay a premium price for a bond and either of these early redemption provisions exists?
> 3. In calculating the return from a bond investment, what additional feature is included in the Yield to Maturity calculation?

Ratings

As you consider a bond investment, you will want to assure yourself that the issuer of the bond has the financial capability to pay interest and principal when due—even if that due date is years from now. In researching the bond issuer, you have an ally. There are several research organizations that are in the business of rating the financial fitness of bond issuers. The largest of these ratings organizations, together with a summary of their ratings, are listed in Exhibit 15:4.

Exhibit 15:4 Bond Rating Organizations

	Fitch	Standard & Poor's	Moody's
Long-Term Ratings	----------	----------------------	------------
Excellent Quality	AAA	AAA	Aaa
High Quality	AA (+/−)	AA (+/−)	Aa (1, 2, 3)
Good Quality	A (+/−)	A (+/−)	A (1, 2, 3)
Satisfactory Quality	BBB (+/−)	BBB (+/−)	Baa (1, 2, 3)
Non-Investment Grade	BB (+/−)	BB (+/−)	Ba (1, 2, 3)
Variable Quality	B (+/−)	B (+/−)	B (1, 2, 3)
Vulnerable	CCC (+/−)	CCC (+/−)	Caa (1, 2, 3)
Highly Speculative	CC (+/−)	CC (+/−)	Ca
In Arrears	C (+/−)	C (+/−)	C (Default)
Defaulted	D	D	—
Short-Term Ratings			
Best Quality	F-1 (+)	A-1	P-1
Adequate Quality	F-2	A-2	P-2
Fair Quality	F-3	A-3	P-3

Both Fitch and Standard & Poor's mark gradations between the letter grades with a + or a -. For example, an A+ would be just a small step below AA-. Moody's uses numbers to mark gradations, with 1 being the best, 2 being medium quality, and 3 being the lowest quality. As such, their A1, would be a small step below their Aa3.

Not only do these rating agencies offer a rating evaluation when the bonds are first introduced, but they maintain ongoing surveillance of the issuer and will change the rating if the prospects of the borrower change—either up or down. Therefore, by consulting the rating on a given bond, you can get some idea of the financial capability of the borrower at any point in time.

Figure 15:10 Not only do these rating agencies offer a rating evaluation when the bonds are first introduced, but they maintain ongoing surveillance of the issuer and will change the rating if the prospects of the borrower change.

Summary & Review

1. Name the three largest bond rating organizations. What is the nomenclature that they use in conveying their opinion as to the financial strength of the borrower?
2. If you are looking to invest in a bond, how might you utilize the efforts of a bond rating organization?
3. While there are many who offer their research and opinion as to the prospects of a stock investment, stocks do not enjoy the same kind of rating protocol that bonds have. Why?

Chapter 16
Mutual Funds

The Fund Snapshot Webpage of the T. Rowe Price Capital Appreciation Fund is reprinted with permission from T. Rowe Price. Copyright © 2014.

Chapter Objectives

1. Understand the nature and structure of a Mutual Fund, including the role of the Prospectus as an informational source for investors.
2. Be aware of the four major advantages for investing in a mutual fund. Consider the Family of Funds concept, and its role in the marketing of mutual funds.
3. Know the calculation of Net Asset Value, and its importance in the pricing of a mutual fund share.
4. Describe the difference between an Open-End and a Closed-End mutual fund. Know how each is priced and traded.
5. Understand the various costs associated with a mutual fund, including the Management or Expense ratio, the 12b-1 fee, the Contingent Deferred Sales Charge, and the Load.

Chapter Objectives

6. Be familiar with the different kinds of mutual funds, including some of the specialty funds that serve particular purposes.

7. Identify organizations that offer evaluations of mutual funds and mutual fund performance. Understand their grading nomenclature. Know how to perform research on the composition, operation, and performance of a mutual fund.

8. Understand the nature of the returns possible from investing in mutual funds, and how to calculate the return on this investment.

What is a Mutual Fund

A Mutual Fund is a bucket. It may hold stocks or bonds or real estate, or a combination of these investments. There are literally thousands of mutual funds totaling trillions of dollars, each with a defined Investment Objective specifying what the fund is trying to accomplish, and what investments it is using to reach its goals. Mutual funds are offered by subsidiaries of banks, insurance companies, and by investment management companies.

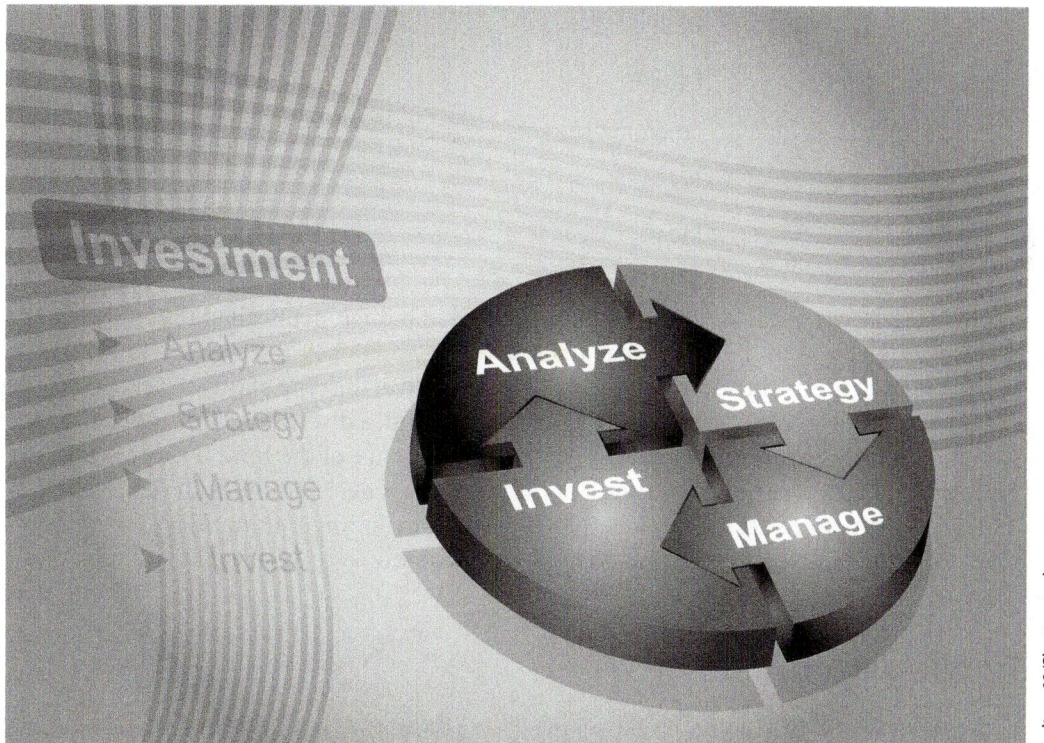

Figure 16:1 The Investment Objective specifies what the fund is trying to accomplish, and what investments it is using to reach its goals.

A Mutual Fund is a security. Like stocks or bonds, ownership resides in a piece of paper, evidencing your account in a mutual fund. You and I and millions of other investors thereby own a piece of that bucket. We are participants in a pool which, together, provide the money that is invested by the portfolio manager.

Our ownership in that bucket entitles us to our share of the earnings produced by the holdings of that mutual fund, and to our share of any appreciation experienced by those holdings.

A Mutual Fund is an organization, with its own board of directors. Each mutual fund is managed by a portfolio manager, backed by a team of analysts and traders and support staff. Most mutual funds are part of a mutual fund family, which have dozens of mutual funds of all types. Once an account is opened with a mutual fund family, the investor may move his account from one mutual fund bucket to another . . . to another . . . or to several others if he chooses.

Exhibit 16:1 Types of Mutual Funds

Stock Funds	**Bond Funds**	**Other Mutual Fund Types**
Growth	Corporate	Real Estate (REIT)
Value	Municipal	Life Cycle
Income	Treasury	Balanced
Appreciation	Long Term	Money Market Fund: Taxable
Large Cap	Intermediate Term	Money Market Fund: Municipal
Mid Cap	Short Term	Money Market Fund: Treasury
Small Cap	High Quality	
Foreign	High Yield	
Regional	Foreign	
Sector	Emerging Markets	
Industry	Regional	
Index	Index	

The complete description of the mutual fund is contained in a document called the Prospectus. You might say that the prospectus is to a mutual fund, what an indenture is to a bond. The prospectus contains everything pertaining to that mutual fund—including the investment objective, the type of investments employed to reach that investment objective, a listing of the larger holdings in the fund, a discussion of the portfolio manager—his credentials and tenure with the fund, a discussion of the performance of the fund for recent periods and since the fund was formed, a comparison of the fund's performance to a declared index or benchmark, a summary of the fees charged, instructions on how to buy into the fund—including minimum amounts, instructions on how to sell the fund, and contact information, to mention just a few.

Why Choose a Mutual Fund

As there are costs associated with a mutual fund (we will discuss those costs in a moment), you may ask the question: "Why would I want to put my money in a pool—and pay someone else to manage it—rather than buy my own securities directly?" Good question. There are four reasons why mutual funds have become so popular with investors.

The first reason you have already touched on: "and pay someone else to manage it." Most of us are involved in activities all day every day which have little to do with managing our investments. Perhaps you work in health care, or in the hospitality industry. The point is you may need someone else who has the time and ability to watch that bucket and take care of it. Professional Management is one reason why investors like mutual funds. There is a team dedicated to making that bucket perform as well as possible. That doesn't mean that all mutual funds perform well all of the time. If the investments placed in that bucket don't do well, the mutual

fund doesn't do well. But the portfolio manager is working to realize the defined Investment Objective of his fund, and he is focused on that goal every day—all day long.

Let's say that you have $3,000 to invest. How many bonds can you buy for $3,000? How many different kinds of stocks can you buy for that amount? It is hard to diversify your portfolio with a limited amount of money, isn't it? Another reason people like mutual funds is because they can pool their $3,000 with the money of many other investors and buy a diversified portfolio. When you buy a mutual fund, you buy an interest in hundreds of different stocks or bonds or real estate properties. Diversification is achieved instantly—within the bounds of the type of mutual fund selected and its investment objective. Most mutual funds do have a minimum investment required to set up an account. The minimum investment required may range from $1,500 to $25,000 or more, with $2,500 being a rough average. Many mutual fund families will waive this minimum if you agree to a regular schedule of deposits into the mutual fund. This is particularly useful if you are setting up an Independent Retirement Account (IRA), and agreeing to make regular contributions into the account.

Although diversification is a fundamental risk mitigating device, it does not mean that all of the risks of the mutual fund have gone away. For example, if you have chosen a long-term taxable bond fund as one of your holdings, it is likely that this fund has invested in thousands of different bonds from hundreds of different corporations. Although the risks of a single corporation defaulting on its payments have definitely been minimized, the interest rate risk that would follow from a rise in interest rates has not. For this particular fund, that risk remains very real. Diversification through a mutual fund does offer a reduction in those risks associated with one or just a few holdings; by spreading its investments across hundreds or even thousands of positions.

We pointed out earlier how many mutual funds are part of a mutual fund family. The mutual fund family offers a variety of different kinds of funds. If you wish to sell out of the particular mutual fund you own, and perhaps reinvest that money in a different mutual fund ... or in several alternative funds, you can do so with a phone call. Alternatively, if you wish to receive the proceeds from the sell, those proceeds can be in your hands within 3 days. This high level of liquidity is another reason why people like mutual funds. Exhibit 16:2 summarizes what a Family of Mutual Funds may look like. At the same time, it offers an assessment of the risk and return potential of each mutual fund in that family.

The fourth reason people like mutual funds stems from the fact that, along with managing your assets, the mutual fund will keep an accounting of securities bought and sold, capital gains and losses realized, and dividends and interest received. These accounting services are reflected in your account statement, which shows

Exhibit 16:2 A Family of Mutual Funds

	Risk and Return Potential				
	Very Low	Low	Moderate	High	Very High
Money Markets					
Taxable Money Market Fund	X				
Municipal Money Market Fund	X				
Bonds					
Short Term Bond Fund	X				
Intermediate Bond Fund		X			
Long Term Bond Fund			X		
High Yield Bond Fund					X
Short Term Municipal Bond Fund		X			
Intermediate Municipal Bond Fund			X		

Continued

	Risk and Return Potential				
	Very Low	Low	Moderate	High	Very High
Long Term Municipal Bond Fund				X	
High Yield Municipal Bond Fund					X
International Bond Fund					X
<u>Stocks</u>					
Blue Chip Stocks				X	
Defensive Stock Fund			X		
Equity Income Fund				X	
Value Fund				X	
Growth Fund					X
Small Cap Fund				X	
Mid Cap Fund				X	
Large Cap Fund				X	
International Stock Fund					X

the value of your account and the flow of funds into and out of your position. At tax time, the mutual fund company will even show you where this data should be posted on your tax return. Most mutual funds offer checkbook convenience or a direct link with your checking account.

> ### Summary & Review
> 1. What is a mutual fund? How is a mutual fund organized?
> 2. What is a prospectus? What information does the Investment Objective convey?
> 3. As you review the list of alternative mutual funds, what type of fund do you think makes the most sense for you now, given your investor profile and portfolio goals?
> 4. While all mutual funds have a minimum account size, some waive this restriction under certain conditions. Under what conditions might a mutual fund waive its minimum account size requirement?
> 5. What are the four reasons investors like mutual funds?

Net Asset Value

Visualize hundreds, or even thousands, of individual holdings in your mutual fund, all moving up and down in price throughout the course of the day. How would you possibly be able to calculate the total value of your fund, given all that volatility? It sounds a bit like herding cats, doesn't it. Well, it is virtually impossible to get an accurate total, unless you wait until all of those prices hold still . . . at the end of the day. When the market closes, each security posts a closing price. It is then, that a mutual fund is able to total up the value of all of its holdings.

Most mutual funds have very few liabilities—but there may be some. If you take the total of all the holdings in the fund—including the cash that is not invested, and subtract any liabilities, you have the net assets of the fund. Does this formula sound familiar? When we talked about common stocks, we introduced a term called Book Value, which was the total of all the assets of the corporation less all the liabilities. In effect, it was the net worth of the corporation. All we then had to do was to divide the net worth by the number of shares outstanding, and we had book value per share. Well, the same formula applies to mutual funds. At the end of the day when the net assets have been calculated, divide that total by the number of shares outstanding, and you have the Net Asset Value, or NAV.

The NAV reflects the value of an individual share or piece of the mutual fund bucket. If the underlying assets in the fund rise in price over time, the NAV will rise as well. If the value of the holdings in the fund decline, the NAV will decline as well. As it is necessary to wait until the end of the day to do this calculation, NAV is produced only once a day, after the close of the markets.

Open-End versus Closed-End

Most mutual funds are Open-End funds. That means, there is no fixed number of shares that may be bought, or that may be outstanding. If you wish to buy in to an open-end fund, the fund will simply create additional shares and sell them to you. If you wish to sell your position, the fund will take your shares back and retire them. As a result, the number of shares outstanding at any one time may vary.

Open-end funds are usually bought and sold at their Net Asset Value. There is a scenario where an investor may pay more than NAV to own a share, which we will talk about later. However, for the majority of open-end

Figure 16:2 Open-end fund means there is no fixed number of shares that may be bought, or that may be outstanding

fund purchases, you are essentially paying book value for a share of the fund.

This is another reason why the NAV cannot be calculated until the end of the day. With people calling in to buy shares or to sell shares all day long, there is no way to know how many shares are outstanding until the end of the day. As the calculation of the NAV requires the number of shares outstanding as its denominator, that can only be determined with the close of markets.

One caveat that needs to be pointed out as we discuss open-end mutual funds. It is possible that a portfolio manager may decide to close an open-end fund to new investors. He may do this, for example, if the fund invests in smaller companies that have limited share trading volume. A large amount of money in his fund could not all be invested in the best of these smaller companies, leaving significant sums idle or, even worse, invested in less than desirable companies. Even if the manager decides to close the fund to new investors, existing investors can sell their shares if they wish, and can usually buy additional shares to add to their positions.

Approximately 10% of all mutual funds are Closed-End funds. This means that a specified number of shares were issued—at a specified price—at the time the fund was established. Once those shares were sold, the fund was closed, and no additional shares will be sold. Obviously, to buy a closed-end fund, it is necessary for you to purchase shares from someone who already owns them. This is not as hard as it sounds. The shares of closed-end funds have their own unique letter symbol—much like common stocks, are easily traded, and you can place an order for them through your broker in much the same way as you would place an order for a stock or bond.

Because there are a limited number of shares available for any closed-end fund, there is typically a premium price associated with those shares. It is not unusual for a closed-end fund to be priced 5% to 8% above its net asset value, reflecting the scarcity value of those shares.

> ### Summary & Review
> 1. What is Net Asset Value (NAV)? How is it calculated?
> 2. What is the difference between an Open-End mutual fund, and a Closed-End fund?
> 3. Is it possible for an open-end fund to be closed? Explain.
> 4. Why is it that Closed-End funds usually sell at a premium to net asset value and Open-End funds do not?

The Costs of a Mutual Fund

Let's come back to the issue of the costs of a mutual fund. Clearly, if the mutual fund is to perform well, it will need to hire those individuals who have the ability to research and buy appropriate investments. It will need to have personnel to help answer your questions and guide you in the selection of the fund that is suitable to your needs, and accountants to help in the preparation of your reports. Yet, with all that they do, you may be surprised at how modest the charges are.

All mutual funds charge what is called a Management or Expense Ratio. The management ratio varies depending on the type of fund, but is always a percentage of the assets under management. A money market fund may charge as little as 0.25% of assets under management—that is one quarter of one percent per year. On the other hand, an international stock fund may charge something like 1.5% per annum to keep up with its worldwide holdings. Given the wide variety of mutual funds, there is no average management ratio, but generally speaking, stock funds charge more than bond funds, and bond funds charge more than money market funds.

A second fee that may be charged on a mutual fund is called a 12b-1 fee, named after the provision in the law that allows it. This fee can be charged to offset the costs of documentation, including printing and distribution. Obviously, preparation of a prospectus, quarterly reports, and annual reports can be costly. However, most mutual funds waive their right to charge a 12b-1 fee. If it is charged, such fees may average around 1%.

Another fee that a mutual fund may charge is called a Contingent Deferred Sales Charge or CDSC. As it is so easy to buy into and sell out of a mutual fund, some investors take advantage of that liquidity to flip a fund after holding it for only a day or two. The net result is that the portfolio manager does not have time to invest their money into securities, before it is withdrawn again. To discourage this practice, the fund may assess this sales charge if the investor has been in the fund less than 30 or 60 days. If this sales charge is assessed, it may be as much as 5% of assets.

It was mentioned above that an open-end fund typically trades at net asset value, but there may be a scenario where the investor pays more than NAV to own a share. Let's assume that you have engaged an investment advisor to help you with your investments. That advisor may be an independent counselor, or may be a broker. When you do a trade with that advisor, they collect a commission to compensate them for the time they spend with you. But if you agree that a particular open-end mutual fund is a suitable investment, and you can buy that fund at NAV—how does your investment advisor get paid? There is no commission for buying an open-end fund at NAV.

The answer lies in another kind of charge called a Load. A load is a sales commission paid to an investment advisor when they transact shares in a mutual fund on your behalf. Many mutual funds have a defined load ranging from 3% to 5% or more. Other mutual funds, called no-load funds, do not offer a sales commission. Then there is a third category of fund, which offers multiple classes of shares, some of which are no-load and some of which carry a load. This third category is the very same mutual fund, with the same portfolio manager, and the same assets, but with different marketing channels. The marketing channel that is no-load is sold directly to investors. The marketing channel that carries a load is sold through investment advisors, which are not inclined to recommend a fund if there is no prospect of their getting paid.

Figure 16:3 A Load is a sales commission paid to an investment advisor when they transact shares in a mutual fund on your behalf.

Although most load funds assess the sales commission when you buy, there are a few who assess what is called a back-end load – paying the sales commission when you sell. The prospectus will detail whether there is a load, and if so, what the load fee is and when it is assessed.

Specialty Mutual Funds

Exhibit 16:1 listed many of the types of mutual funds available. Given our discussion of investment securities in the last chapter, many of these titles were probably familiar to you. However, a few of the types of mutual funds mentioned may be unfamiliar.

One type that has grown in popularity over the last decade is called Index Funds. You remember that an index is simply a number that represents the average performance of a given market segment. It is the midpoint between the securities that do well, and those that do poorly. Many mutual fund portfolios attempt to outperform their respective market through careful research and active buying and selling of securities—this is called Active Management. Active managers can outperform their index if they are successful in identifying and buying those securities that are the better performers, and avoiding those that perform poorly. Some portfolios try only to mimic the performance of their respective market by buying a representative sample of the shares, which constitute the index for that market—this is called Passive Management. Those portfolios that mimic their respective market segment are called index funds. For example, one of the more prominent U.S. stock market indexes is called the S&P 500 Stock Market Index. A mutual fund that would invest in each of those 500 companies—trying to perform the same as the index itself would perform—would be an S&P 500 Index Fund.

There are a growing number of what are called Exchange Traded Funds, which behave much like an index fund, trying to perform exactly as their respective market segments. These funds may invest in stocks, bonds, or commodities, and are similar in many respects to closed-end funds. They trade very near their net asset value, and are available through an exchange on in the over-the-counter markets. There are some important differences, however, between the traditional mutual fund and an exchange traded fund. Exchange traded funds may trade at any time during the business day based on Bid and Ask pricing, and do not need to wait for the calculation of NAV at day's end. In addition, there is no minimum account size when purchasing exchange traded funds. The investor may buy as little as one share if he chooses. Finally, an investor pursuing exchange traded funds may use limit orders, stop loss orders, and other more speculative trading techniques, just as he can when buying and selling common stock.

Another specialty mutual fund is actually a series of funds called Life Cycle funds. These funds own a combination of stocks and bonds. When you are young, with many years of potential appreciation in front of you, the appropriate life cycle fund would be heavily weighted in common stocks. As you grow older, with a growing need for current income and a more defensive investment posture, the appropriate life cycle fund would be more heavily weighted in bonds. Rather than trying to buy multiple mutual funds to achieve the right proportion of stocks and bonds as you advance in years, this single fund concept would allow you to migrate to accepted proportions as you grow older.

A Real Estate Investment Trust (REIT) is a mutual fund that invests in real estate properties. This fund will have a portfolio of shopping centers, office buildings, warehouses, and the like, instead of securities. Net Asset Value is calculated in much the same way, and their prospectus will detail the various characteristics and operating features of the fund. We will spend time talking about REIT's in Chapter 18.

Money Market Funds grew in popularity in the 1970s, when banks were regulated in terms of the interest rates they could pay on their savings accounts. Though banks tried to compensate for such regulations by offering small gifts with the opening of a savings account, they could not compete in an environment where interest rates were high and rising. The first money market fund was offered in 1971, and this type of open-end mutual fund has experienced phenomenal growth ever sense.

Though a money market fund is not insured, the shares have always traded at $1.00 (two known exceptions were quickly remedied by the money market fund). As such, they behave like a savings account in terms of their limited volatility. Yet the yield available on a money market fund is much higher than the yield available on a traditional savings account. This is because the pool of funds provided by investors is placed in high quality, short-term debt, including bonds, commercial paper, and other short-term securities. The

Figure 16:4 Money Market Funds grew in popularity in the 1970s, when banks were regulated in terms of the interest rates they could pay on their savings accounts.

interest earned on these investments is passed through to the mutual fund holder on a monthly basis.

All major mutual fund families offer money market funds, and many offer multiple money market funds, that invest in taxable bonds, or municipal bonds, or treasury debt. As all money market funds are bought at $1.00 per share and sold at $1.00 per share, the only differentiation is in the yield that is paid.

> ### Summary & Review
> 1. The fee that is commonly charged on all mutual funds is called a Management or Expense Ratio. How is this fee assessed?
> 2. What is a 12b-1 fee? Do all funds charge this fee?
> 3. What is the difference between a Load fund and a No-Load fund? Why do some funds assess a load?
> 4. An Index fund is a type of passively managed fund. Explain?
> 5. Why is it that money market funds have grown so rapidly in such a short period?

Grading of Mutual Funds

Once you have considered your investor profile, and established your goals, you may find that there are literally dozens of mutual funds that are consistent with your profile and goals. How do you choose among them? There are two prominent organizations that are in the business of grading mutual funds.

One is Lipper Analytical Services. Lipper evaluates mutual funds based on their investment objective and the respective type of mutual fund. They then calculate the average performance of that group. The mutual fund you may be looking at will either be above the Lipper average or below the Lipper average, for its respective group. In addition, Lipper offers what is called the Lipper Award, which is the gold medal of mutual fund performance. The single mutual fund that outperforms all others in its group for a 1-year period is given the Lipper Award. Lipper does not offer silver or bronze medals—only the gold.

Figure 16:5 There are two prominent organizations that are in the business of grading mutual funds.

Another organization that evaluates mutual funds is called Morningstar. Morningstar grades mutual funds on the basis of a five-star approach. The grading is awarded for different time periods, including overall, 3-year, 5-year, and 10-year time spans. The best mutual funds are awarded 5-Stars, better than average performers receive 4-Stars, average funds rate 3-Stars, below average receive 2-Stars, and the worst performers receive

1-Star. One way you might approach your mutual fund quest is to look for those funds rated four or five stars from Morningstar.

Both of these organizations offer comprehensive research services, and are well regarded in the investment industry.

Researching a Mutual Fund

As we have pointed out, a good place to start your hunt for the right mutual fund is with mutual fund evaluators

Get Real

For several years, I managed a Precious Metals Mutual Fund for a nationally known mutual fund family. One day the phone rang, and it was the marketing department asking if I would speak to a particular shareholder. Usually, the marketing department did not ask the portfolio manager to visit with shareholders; it was their job to answer queries and help the investor with their transactions. But in this instance, they needed to involve the portfolio manager. I took the call, and began visiting with the investor. It did not take me long to determine why the account representative was so alarmed. This individual had invested her entire life savings into the Precious Metals Fund . . . all of it. When I asked her why she had not diversified her investments a bit more, she answered that the performance of this fund had been so remarkable in the prior year (this fund had earned the Lipper Award in the prior year), and she was hopeful that it would perform as well this year.

Figure 16:6 This fund had earned the Lipper Award in the prior year and she was hopeful that it would perform as well this year.

I thanked her for her confidence, but pointed out that a mutual fund that can go up 87% in a year, can also drop 87% in a year . . . and precious metals funds were often quite volatile. I asked how she would feel if the fund dropped 87%. We then spoke about diversification, and the importance of spreading her eggs among a number of different baskets. When I transferred her call back to the marketing department, she was ready to spread her savings among a number of different funds—though she insisted that a portion remain with the Precious Metals Fund. We were able to produce a good return the next year, though not as good as the year before.

such as Lipper or Morningstar. Both of these services are available online. One way to begin is to set up a screen that will evaluate all mutual funds according to the specific criteria you establish. For example, if you are using the Morningstar site, you can screen all mutual funds for those that are of a particular type, and simultaneously for those of that kind that are rated four or five stars. This gives you a list of the better rated funds of the type you desire.

With that information, you may wish to dig further into the specifics of the more promising candidates. You can do this best by going directly to the mutual fund home page. For example, let's say that your screen produced a couple of fund candidates from the mutual fund family T. Rowe Price. One of those candidates was their Capital Appreciation Fund. If you go to the home page for this fund, you find the following:

Exhibit 16:3 Capital Appreciation Fund

Note that we have combined several information tabs—Fund Snapshot, Fund Objective, and Fund Expenses/Minimums, in our exhibit. Additional information may be obtained under the tabs Fund Performance, Fund Composition, and Management Commentary.

Spend a minute digesting the information in this exhibit. Note that this is a 5-Star fund, with performance returns compared with a couple of benchmarks—the Lipper Mixed-Asset Growth category, and the S&P 500 Index. Performance comparisons are made for a number of time periods . . . 1 year, 3 years, 5 years, 10 years, and since the fund began in 1986. At the top, the net asset value is reported, together with the change from the prior day and the range for the past 12 months. Look at the size of this bucket! That's a lot of assets to manage.

Under the Fund Objective is the Investment Objective, together with the strategy the portfolio manager is undertaking to reach that objective. There is then a discussion of the type of investor profile, which may find this fund suitable, including a discussion of the risks inherent in this fund.

We learn in the Fund Expenses/Minimums information what the management or expense ratio is, and whether there is a contingent deferred sales charge (redemption fee), a 12b-1 fee, or a load. We also find the minimum account size, which in this case is $2,500. Similar information is available at any mutual fund home page.

> ### Summary & Review
>
> 1. Name the two organizations that are in the business of grading mutual funds. How do they differ?
> 2. If you were considering investing in a mutual fund, how would you conduct your research? What characteristics would you look for?
> 3. Why is it important for a mutual fund to compare its performance to an index or benchmark?

Gains and Taxes

You make money in a mutual fund the same way you make money in any security, by the payment of regular income via dividends and interest, and by appreciation. The dividends and interest paid by the underlying holdings of the fund are passed along to the fund holder after deducting the management fee and any other expenses that may be charged. Because the fund distributes virtually all of its earnings to the shareholder, the fund itself is not taxed. It is the shareholder who is taxed on the income received (unless the income is from Municipal Bonds, which, as you remember, are not subject to Federal income taxes).

The second source of return is appreciation, and here we have two levels of potential gains to consider. First, is the level of capital gains and losses that stem from your purchase of the fund. For example, if you were to buy an open-end mutual fund at a net asset value of $22.22, and a couple of years later sell that position at a price of $23.33, you would have a long-term capital gain of $1.11. You control when you buy and you control when you sell . . . the decision is yours. You expect to pay taxes on the capital gain, and duly report the transactions on your tax return for the year in which you sold your shares.

But during the time you held the fund, the portfolio manager is also doing some buying and selling. He is trading in the holdings of the fund, and his decisions are quite independent of yours. You have no control over when he trades, or how much appreciation he has earned in the process. If he has made money on the holdings in the fund, that appreciation goes into the net value calculation, and is reflected in the NAV price that is tabulated every day. When he sells a holding that appreciation becomes a capital gain; short term if he sells in less than 365 days, or long term if he owned that position for longer than 365 days. Though you did not have control over this level of buying and selling, guess who gets to pay the taxes on those capital gains? That's right—it's your gain or loss . . . you get to pay the taxes.

Though the capital gains and losses accrued throughout the course of the year when the portfolio manager buys and sells, most mutual funds report and pay any such gains near the end of the year—typically in December. You can take the capital gain payment in cash, or reinvest it back into more shares of the mutual fund. As part of the accounting services the mutual fund company provides, they will detail the amount of gains, and whether it is short term or long term.

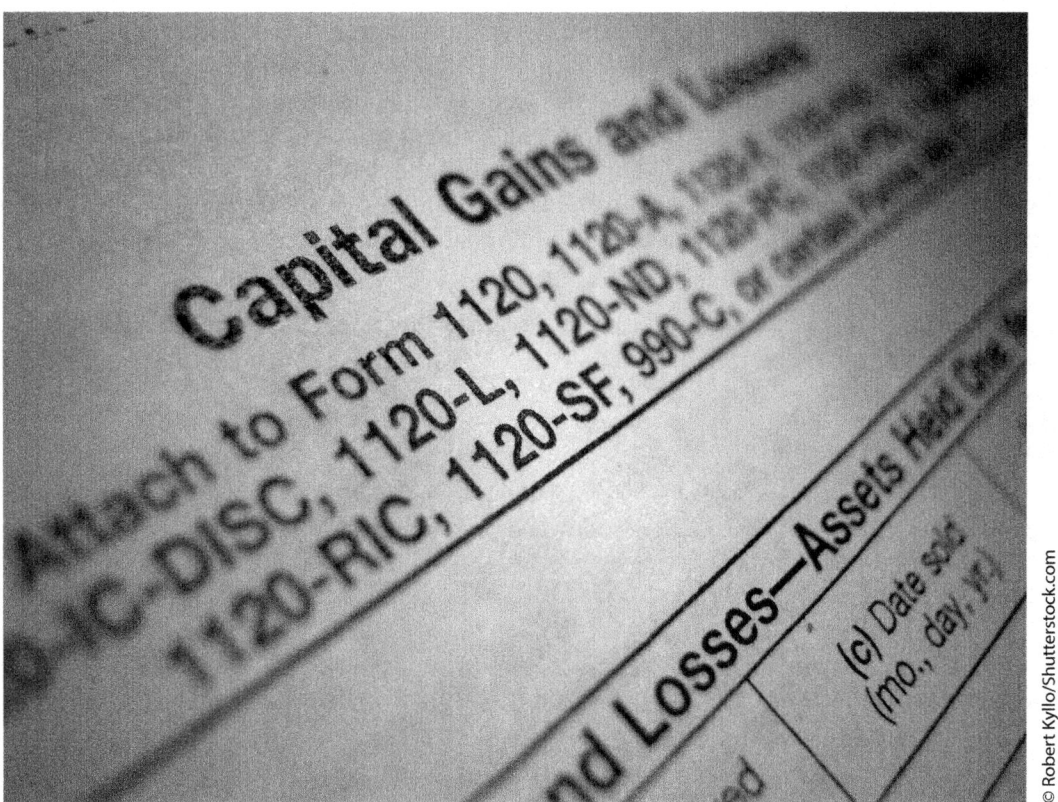

Figure 16:7 Though you did not have control over this level of buying and selling, guess who gets to pay the taxes on those capital gains.

Total Return

Given the extra layer of ownership—you own the fund and the fund owns the securities—calculating the total return is a little bit more involved than if you owned the security directly. As always, the return should be reported as an annual number, and it is composed of three ingredients.

- Income Distributions
- Capital Gains Realized by the Fund
- Change in the Market Value of Your Shares When Sold

Let's say that you bought an open-end, no-load Value Fund, which invests in a portfolio of common and preferred stocks with above average dividends and below average Price/Earnings Ratios. At the time of purchase, you paid $22.22 per share for 100 shares of this fund for a total investment of $2,222.00. At the end of 2 years, you find that this fund has produced the following:

- Income Distributions: $11.11 per Month × 24 Months = $266.64. This is a 6% annual return.
- Capital Gains of $44.44 in the first year, and $55.55 in the second year. This is an additional 2% return in the first year, and a 2.5% return in the second year.
- You sold your shares at the end of year 2 for $23.33 per share or $2,333.00. This is a long-term capital gain of $1.11 per share or $111.00 for all 100 shares, a 5% gain.

So, the total return over the 2-year period in which you held this mutual fund is:

Income of $266.64 + Capital Gains of $99.99 + Change in Market Value of Shares of $111.00 = total of $477.63. Of course, this is over a 2-year period, so to get the average annual gain we divide by two, giving us $238.81 per year. Now if we divide that total return number into the initial investment amount: $238.81/$2,222.00, giving us an average annual total return on our investment of about 10.7%. Not bad. Of course, this presumes that we withdrew the income and the capital gains as they were paid. Had we reinvested that cash flow, there would have been additional shares purchased, and additional earnings and capital gains stemming from those purchases—the magic of compounding!

Summary & Review

1. What are the three potential sources of return from a mutual fund?
2. When we say that capital gains can occur at two levels, what do we mean?
3. Given your current investor profile and goals, would you be more inclined to receive any income and capital gain distributions, or to reinvest them?

Chapter 17
Real Estate And Commodities

300 Investments

Chapter Objectives

1. Develop an increased understanding of real estate investing, and of those concepts which will improve your investment acumen.
2. Understand the three broad ways in which investments in real estate might be made. Be aware of the pros and cons of each avenue to real estate investing.
3. One of the avenues to real estate investing—using the stock market—is recommended for passive real estate investing. Consider the various securities which constitute such indirect real estate investing.
4. Another avenue to real estate investing—joining a group—typically comes with some qualifications and contingencies. Understand the nature of such groups and the requirements for participation.
5. The third avenue to real estate investing—owning your own properties—generally requires a more active commitment by the investor. Know the implications of such a commitment.

Chapter Objectives

6. Consider various types of direct real estate investment, and how you might prepare yourself to invest in real estate.
7. Understand the nature of commodity investing, and the different types of commodities that are available.
8. Note the nature of the commodity spot market and the futures commodity market, and be aware of the important differences between these two markets.
9. Be aware of the characteristics of the commodity futures market, which enable the investor to leverage his money, and of the attendant risks.

Real Estate Investing

Real estate has always been a popular investment because it is familiar, tangible and real. Everyone needs a place to live. People frequent shopping centers, office building, and hotels. You can grow food and play golf on real estate. We are experienced and comfortable with real estate. You can also see, touch and explore real estate—it is more tangible than a stock or bond investment.

To better understand real estate investing, there are some truths about investing, any type of investing, that need to be understood. There are thousands of ways you can earn money to fund a comfortable lifestyle and prepare for retirement. Each career requires different skills. However, if you ever hope to be financially secure, you must become a competent investor.

Figure 17:1 Real estate has always been a popular investment because it is familiar and real.

Nine Truths of Investing

Investing Truth 1: Saving. The first step to investing is to have money to invest. That means you must first become a saver before you can become an investor. If you are not saving at least 10% of your income, you are spending too much. We have referenced earlier a great book on saving and investing. It is titled *The Richest Man in Babylon*, and written by George Clason. This classic book, published over 90 years ago, is less than 140 pages and teaches timeless truths about saving and investing.

Investing Truth 2: Financial Foundation. Before you make your first investment, there are three things you need to do first to provide a solid foundation for your financial future:

1. Pay off all your credit card debt. Interest rates on your credit card debt (15%–30%) are much higher than the returns you can reasonably expect (5%–12%) to earn investing. Going forward, pay credit cards off each month.
2. Buy medical insurance. Half of personal bankruptcies are caused by unexpected medical bills.
3. Buy disability insurance. Your risks of a disability from an accident or medical problem are much higher than the risk of death. If you die, the costs to take care of you are very small—burial costs can be very cheap. If you are disabled, the costs to take care of you can be very high for a very long time. Life insurance is to help provide for your dependents after you die. If you are single and have no dependents, do you really need life insurance? If you are married with no children and both work, you probably need little or no life insurance. However, if you have moved out of your parent's basement, you need medical and disability insurance.

Investing Truth 3: First Two Rules of Investing. Warren Buffett is considered the most successful investor of our time. Reading his letters to investors in the Berkshire-Hathaway annual stockholders report are a treasure trove of great investment insight. Attending his annual Berkshire-Hathaway shareholders annual meeting is considered the "Woodstock of Capitalism." Here are his first two rules of investing:

1. Rule Number 1: Never lose money
2. Rule Number 2: Don't forget Rule Number 1

Most investors focus initially on the upside potential. Buffet initially focuses on the downside, before he looks at the upside. All investments have risks; so identify and measure the risks. Always understand the risks of your investments and make sure they are managed so they cannot sink your financial ship.

Investing Truth 4: No Shortcuts. To learn any complex skill, like investing, it takes study and practice. In his bestselling book *Outliers: The Story of Success*, Malcolm Gladwell gives several examples of his theory: that it takes 10,000 hours (5–10 years) of focused study and practice to learn a complex skill. This is true for investing. The best investors alive today are all over 40 years old, most are over 60 years old (Warren Buffett is over 80 years old). You will make mistakes investing, all investors do. Learn from your mistakes. It will take years to become competent, but if you start in your 20s, you can become competent by age 40. It used to be the norm for young people to serve an apprenticeship for several years to learn their job skills. These apprenticeship periods provided the 10,000 hours and a mentor to help train the next generation. If you can find a mentor to help you in your first 5–10 years of investing, you will learn more and make fewer mistakes. There are always articulate, personable people, often fairly young, promising unbelievable returns. Be skeptical.

Investing Truth 5: Be an "Intelligent Investor." Who does Warren Buffett consider his greatest teacher and mentor? Benjamin Graham. Benjamin Graham wrote the book, *The Intelligent Investor*. Warren Buffett calls this book, published over 60 years ago, "By far the best book on investing ever written." Graham defined "intelligent" as nothing to do with a high IQ, but being patient, disciplined, and eager to learn. According to Graham, the "Intelligent Investor" does three things:

1. Thoroughly analyzes the investment
2. Protects themselves against serious losses
3. Aspires to adequate, not extra ordinary, performance

Figure 17:2 The challenge for every investor is to try and understand the facts before emotion takes over.

Graham believed that investment opportunities swing on a pendulum between unsustainable optimism and unjustified pessimism. The intelligent investor is a realist who buys from the pessimists and sells to optimists. Warren Buffett expressed this concept as, "Be fearful when others are greedy and be greedy when others are fearful."

Investing Truth 6: Emotion is Your Biggest Enemy. Most people make decisions guided by emotion and then attempt to justify their decisions with logic. The challenge for every investor is to try and understand the facts before emotion takes over. If you accept this premise that most investors, including yourself, are emotional, then you have big advantage in the market. Benjamin Graham defines the "Intelligent Investor" as unemotional, patient, and disciplined.

Investing Truth 7: Diversification is Your Best Friend. A good friend has your back and keeps you from making big mistakes. Diversification does that for your investments. However, there is a paradox about diversification: Nearly all the very wealthy people made their money in a single company or single industry (Rockefellers, Bill Gates, Mark Zuckerman). In your career, you will make most of your money in a single industry or even a single company—that is the norm and to be expected. You need focus for a successful career, but you need diversification for successful investing. For the typical investor, trying to build their net worth year-by year, diversification is critical. Try and have no more than 20% of your investments in any single investment. A limit of 10% is even safer. For the purposes of this chapter, your business or the home you live in are not considered investments. Your home may increase in value over time, but typically non-investment reasons such as having more control of your living space and settling down are driving forces in buying a home.

Investing Truth 8: Investment Timing Paradox. The investment pendulum swings from overvalued to undervalued for all investments over time; however, no long-term successful investors, such as Warren Buffett, Peter Lynch, or Benjamin Graham, tried to jump in and out by timing the market. They bought when values were fair and held as long as they felt future values would increase. As we learned as a child from the tortoise and the hare, slow and steady wins the race. Market timers are speculators. They do not take the time to understand the investment, but rather try to anticipate market fluctuations. Don't speculate; be an "Intelligent Investor."

Investing Truth 9: Lynch's Rule, Have a Competitive Advantage. Peter Lynch (age 70), the investment guru of Fidelity Magellan Fund from 1977 through 1990, had the best performance of any large mutual fund over a 10+ year period. Lynch believed in the power of common knowledge. Lynch's rule is, "You can outperform the experts if you use your edge by investing in companies or industries you already understand."

Figure 17:3 The more you trade, the lower your returns.

Understanding a company means more than buying its products, it means you understand why it is better than the competition and if that comparative advantage is sustainable. You understand its financial condition and whether the investment is fairly valued. This doesn't mean you buy your company's stock or your neighbor's house when it is for sale. Remember Investing Truth 7: Diversification. Lynch's Rule helps explain the attraction to real estate investing—we live and work with real estate. Real estate gives us a sense of security in our investing—a false sense of security if we have not taken the time to be an "Intelligent Investor" (Investing Truth 5). Always try to have an edge or "Competitive Advantage" in your investments.

Summary and Review

1. Why is real estate such a popular investment option?
2. As you review the "nine truths of investing," which ones do you think are particularly relevant to you and your investment style?
3. The first two "truths of investing" pertain to building your financial foundation before you start investing. Why do you think this is important?

Three Investment Lessons from the Stock Market

The stock market is the most analyzed investment market in the world, and lessons learned from the stock market can be applied to real estate investing. Here are three lessons that apply to real estate:

1. **Individual investors underperform the market.** The typical individual investor underperforms the stock market by a wide margin. Not doing the homework on the investment, being too emotional, making too many

trades, not being diversified, and the transaction costs of the trades all combine for sub-par performance. According to Dalbar Inc., the stock market average annual return from 1984 to 2003 was 12.98%—very good results. However, the average stock market investor averaged only 3.51%. According to Benjamin Graham, the "Intelligent Investor" should analyze several years of financial statements to understand what makes the company grow and what the profits should be. This analysis takes a lot of time and effort—more than most investors are willing to do. This explains why the average investor is not well suited to becoming a successful investor.

2. Mutual funds underperform the market. The typical mutual fund underperforms the stock market, but by a much smaller margin. In any year there are many mutual funds that outperform the overall stock market. These high-performing funds are heavily advertised by their sponsors, but there are always more mutual funds that underperform the market each year. The fund sponsors do not advertise these underperforming funds as much. According to Lipper Inc., looking back from 2002, only 31% of mutual funds outperformed the overall stock market for 10 years and 15% outperformed the stock market for 20 years. Mutual funds charge higher fees than index funds, which hurt performance.

3. The more you trade, the lower your returns. Day traders and market timers do not take the time to study and understand the companies they are buying and selling. Their brokers make money from all their trades, but they don't. According to Dalbar Inc., unlike the stock market that averaged 12.98% between 1984 and 2003, or even the typical stock market investor who averaged 3.51%, the average market timing equity investor lost 3.29%.

What Kind of Investor Are You

If you go to the store to buy a pair of shoes, there are two critical questions you need to know before you buy:

1. What size feet do you have?
2. What is the purpose for the shoes? (basketball, beach, work, church, etc).

Most of us know the answers to these questions before we walk in the store. To walk out with the right shoes, you need to know these two facts. Knowing your friend's shoe size will not help you buy the right shoes. Knowing the average shoe size of the members of your favorite basketball team will not help you buy your basketball shoes. The shoes need to fit your feet. The purpose of the shoes needs to match your purpose.

Investing is similar. There are some key facts you need to understand about yourself before you invest:

Active versus Passive Investor. There are two types of investors and both can be very successful. To be an Active Investor takes much more time. Most investors attempt to be an active investor, but do not have the time or interest to be an active investor. So far in this chapter, I have left a trail of clues for you to determine if you are an active or Passive Investor. You are an active investor if you can say yes to all of the following questions:

1. Did you make a list of books to read as you read this chapter? Bonus points if you have already read investment books and articles.
2. Would you prefer to listen to an interview of Warren Buffett or an interview of a favorite sports star? Bonus points if you already knew and followed Warren Buffett, Peter Lynch, or Benjamin Graham—investment super stars.
3. Are you thinking about who could be your investment mentor and how soon you can start on your 10,000-hour apprenticeship? Bonus points if you are already investing and learning from your successes and mistakes.

If you answered yes to these three questions and are willing to put in the time to read books, listen to the experts and have the patience to put in the hours of practice, then you can become a successful active investor. If not, you are a passive investor and you will save yourself a lot of grief by accepting the fact that you are not destined to be an active investor. Being a passive investor is like being a passive accountant, plumber, or dentist—you chose to hire an expert and spend your time doing other things. Most people have the passive

Figure 17:4 Being a passive investor is like being a passive accountant, plumber, or dentist—you chose to hire an expert and spend your time doing other things.

investor mentality and their investment portfolio will grow more by using a professional advisor. They will also have more time for family, career, and hobbies.

Risk Tolerance. All investments have risks. All investment markets have weak cycles when values drop. Most investors are more comfortable with a slower and steadier pace of a tortoise, than the boom and bust pace of a hare. Hiding your money under your mattress or earning 0.2% on a bank certificate of deposit may seem safe, but after taxes and inflation you are certain to lose. You need to take some risks to be successful, but as Benjamin Graham said, "Aspire to adequate, not extra ordinary, performance." Understanding the investment and being diversified are your best risk protections. The average performance of the stock market, including dividends, over the last 100 years is about 8% a year. After taxes and inflation, an 8% annual return should be "adequate, not extra ordinary." If you can find several investments that can reasonably be expected to achieve 8% returns, then chose the investments with the least risk (Buffet Rules 1 and 2).

Time Frame to Invest. If you are 2 years from retirement or are saving to buy a house, then you do not have time to recover from an investment loss—you need to be more conservative. If you have 20 years before you need to tap your investment portfolio, then you can take more risks—provided you are being compensated by higher potential returns.

If you understand

A. The Nine Investing Truths
B. Three lessons from the stock market
C. Have a better idea of what kind of investor you are

Then you are prepared to make good real estate investment decisions.

> **Summary and Review**
>
> 1. If I asked a classroom how many were above-average drivers, about three quarters of the students would likely raise their hands. Yet, by definition, only half of the students would actually be above average—that is what average means. Why do you think so many individuals and mutual funds fail to outperform market averages?
> 2. We have introduced the topic of your Investor Profile in Chapter 14, and have touched on it again here to underscore its importance. What does your investment profile reveal in the categories of active versus passive, risk tolerance, and your time frame to invest?
> 3. Why do you think we spend so much time emphasizing the importance of understanding what kind of investor you are?

There are Three Broad Ways To Invest in Real Estate

1. **Do it Yourself.** You own 100% of the real estate and make all decisions on buying, managing, financing, and selling. This is a direct investment—you hold legal title.
    a. **Advantages.** You are in control. You make the decisions, and your work and knowledge significantly affect how the investment performs. Tax benefits may be available to you to offset other income (check with your accountant).
    b. **Disadvantages.** You now have a second job that will require a lot of time. Even if you hire a competent manager, you will have issues you will need to handle. Financing the investment will limit your ability to get other personal financing. The size of your investment could be so limited that it makes diversification difficult. For example, the management fee for a very mediocre manager of a house can easily be 10%, but the management fee for a very experienced, profession management company on a large apartment project can be 3%. Size does matter.
2. **Join a Group.** This could include a limited partnership (LP), limited liability company (LLC), tenant-in-common (TIC), or private corporation where you rely on the expertise of a general partner, managing member, or other person to make most of the buying, managing, financing, and selling decisions. This is an indirect investment—the LP, LLC, TIC, and so on hold legal title.
    a. **Advantages.** You have some control in key decisions and someone else has all the day-to-day responsibilities for the investment. You are able to buy larger properties and achieve some economies of scale and diversification.
    b. **Disadvantages.** Most of the defaults and foreclosures of investment real estate in the last recession were these types of ownership structures. These ownership structures are typically higher leveraged (70%+) and there is not much in cash reserves held for problems. The general partner or managing member (sponsor) does not typically have the financial reserves to cover significant cash shortfalls. Understand the fees being charged by the sponsor. Often the sponsor makes a nice profit regardless of how the investment performs. Ideally, you want the sponsor to only earn enough in fees to keep their doors open and then their profit comes only after the investors are making their profits. Any tax benefits accrue until you sell.
3. **Use the Stock Market.** Most publicly traded real estate companies operate as Real Estate Investment Trusts (REITs). REIT stocks trade daily on the stock exchanges. They have the tax advantage that profits are not taxed at the company level like most corporations, but are passed through to the individual owners similar to an LP or LLC. There are apartment REITs, retail REITs, office REITS, industrial/warehouse REITs, hotel REITS, health care REITs, timber or farm REITS, storage REITs and recreation REITS (golf

Figure 17:5 Most publicly traded real estate companies operate as Real Estate Investment Trusts (REITs).

and skiing). Some REITs specialize in certain parts of the United States. This is an indirect investment—the REIT or public corporation holds title.

a. **Advantages.** Valuation—you know what your investment is worth at the end of every business day. Liquidity—you can buy or sell on any business day. Safety—REITs typically are leveraged between 30% and 50%; so they can withstand soft markets without defaults, plus the financial statements are audited by independent accountants. Diversification—REITs own hundreds of properties in many markets. You can buy REITs for most property types.

b. **Disadvantages.** Control—you have no control over the day-to-day operations or the land-term strategies. Less real—you might not be able to see or touch any of your investments. Any tax benefits stay at the trust or corporate level.

Who Should Use the Stock Market to Invest in Real Estate

If you are a passive investor (be honest, 90% of you are) and have an investment portfolio of under $500,000; then you are better off using the stock market to invest in real estate. You do not want more than 10%–20% of your investment portfolio in real estate (Investing Truth 7: Diversification), so that leaves a maximum of $50,000–$100,000 for real estate. To join a group (LP, LLC, or TIC), investments usually start at $100,000, so you need an investment portfolio of at least $500,000.

Choosing a good real estate stock investment advisor is not simple. Ideally you want an advisor who specializes in real estate stocks and has the 10,000 hours and a track record to prove their competence in real estate stocks. The problem is that real estate stocks represent a small percentage of the overall stock market and the more established advisors cover all the market and rely on stock analysts to tell them which stocks, including real estate stocks, to buy. The second problem is because real estate stocks represent a small percentage of the stock market, the more experienced advisors focus on the more typical stocks.

In picking an investment advisor, you are looking more at personality and experience than stock picking intelligence. Following are some guidelines:

1. They have been in the business through at least one full economic cycle (10 years); hopefully two or three cycles (Investing Truth 4: No Shortcuts).
2. Their focus is not to push stocks, but to help you.
   a. Save your money and stick with your plan.
   b. Define your investment goals and risk tolerances.
   c. Come up with a comprehensive investment plan, including real estate stocks if you want, that get you to your financial goals (a Benjamin Graham type of approach—thoroughly analyzes your situation).
3. They are not emotional (a Benjamin Graham type person—patient and disciplined).
4. Has a great smile and a golf handicap under 10 (just kidding!).
5. They are backed by a firm with the analysts, reports, and tools to help your advisor succeed. Bonus points if they have access to Green Street Advisors' reports. Additional bonus points if they encourage index fund, (ETF), and REIT investing.
6. You feel comfortable they understand you, they communicate well and you trust them.

Ask several friends for recommendations and interview at least three advisors at their offices, not your home. Narrow your choice down to two and ask them to come up with a beginning portfolio for you. Meet with them and go over their choices that they feel are best for you. You are looking for the slow and steady tortoise plan with maybe 10%–20% in higher risk/higher return investments. If one broker/advisor has several "hot stocks" and chances to get rich quick with thinly traded, small capitalized, or "Initial Public Offering" (IPO) stocks, then run away!

A stock analyst's intelligence is very critical and you do not care about their personality. If your potential advisor has one or two analysts that they really like to follow, get their last 5 years of recommendations, upgrades, and downgrades. Did they beat the market? Most don't beat the market, which is why you are typically better off buying the market in an index fund, EFT (Exchange Traded Fund), or REIT (they have these for real estate stocks). An EFT is an "Exchange Traded Fund," which is a basket of stocks from a country or industry. There is only one real estate analyst group that I know who have consistently beat the real estate market for 10+ years, and they only analyze real estate stocks—Green Street Advisors. If your investment advisor can provide you access to their very expensive and detailed analysis, then you have a competitive advantage. If not, your safest and most profitable passive approach to real estate investing success is to invest in an REIT EFT.

> ### Summary and Review
> 1. Name the three broad avenues leading to real estate investment.
> 2. What features of your Investor Profile would lead you to choose the stock market as a means of investing in real estate? Why?
> 3. What kind of stock market investments would constitute indirect real estate holdings?

When Should You Join a Group (LP, LLC, TI"C, etc.) to Invest in Real Estate

If you can say yes to the following five conditions, then joining a private group to invest in real estate makes sense:

1. To join most groups, you need to be an Accredited Investor. An Accredited Investor, per the Securities and Exchange Commission, is

Figure 17:6 To join most groups, you need to be an Accredited Investor.

    a. A natural person who has individual net worth, or joint net worth with the person's spouse, that exceeds $1 million at the time of the purchase, excluding the value of the primary residence of such person.

    b. A natural person with income exceeding $200,000 in each of the two most recent years or joint income with a spouse exceeding $300,000 for those years and a reasonable expectation of the same income level in the current year.

2. Your total investment portfolio is at least $500,000. If you want to diversify and have no more than 20% of your investment portfolio in real estate, then you need $100,000 for real estate so you can invest in at one real estate group (LP, LLC, TIC, etc.), which typically require a minimum investment of $100,000. Even better if you have $1,000,000 so you can invest with two real estate groups and get more diversification.

3. You have a basic understanding of real estate cycles, markets, valuation, and management.

4. You have read and understand the investment prospectus and can answer the following questions: What decisions can the manager make without your approval? What decisions require the majority approval? If you have a bad manager, how can you replace them? How is the manager compensated? How much of your investment gets to the investment after all fees and commissions? Can the manager earn a profit before you earn a profit? How are the risks in this investment managed and minimized? Are the assumptions of rents, vacancy, operating expenses, and other key factors reasonable? Is the return attractive relative to the risks?—they should be higher than the 8% average rate you can earn in the stock market.

5. Does the manager have at least 10 years of experience? Does the manager have a successful track record of prior investments? Does the manager have the financial capacity to handle a reasonable shortfall?

Figure 17:7 You need a competitive advantage to beat the average investor.

When Should You Go it Alone and Directly Invest in Real Estate

If you have come this far in the chapter and realize that I have attempted to discourage 90% of you from directly buying individual properties, then you would be correct. If you are among the remaining 10%, who consider themselves active investors and are not turned off, but attracted to the time demands of buying, managing, and maintaining real estate; then let me put up two more hurdles for you to clear before I will help you on this quest.

1—Competitive Advantage (Lynch's Rule)

You need a competitive advantage to beat the average investor or you should buy a REIT, ETF, or index fund (or buy into a LP, LLC, or other group investment). Here are a few examples of competitive advantages:

1. You are a real estate broker or appraiser and know the market better than most and see the good opportunities before most.
2. You have carpenter, plumber, painter, and other maintenance skills. You and can fix almost anything and enjoy fixing things. If you cannot fix it, you have a buddy that can fix it fast and cheap.

3. You have a rich uncle or foreign investor who is willing to provide equity capital for a very low cost and help you with financing so your interest costs are low. He is very patient and will allow you to make mistakes and learn the business.

You need a competitive advantage in finding the investment, managing/maintaining the investment, or obtaining funds for the investment. If you do not have a competitive advantage, you are at a disadvantage and cannot expect competitive returns.

2—Real Estate Skills

Review again the nine Investing Truths and make sure you understand real estate valuation, management, maintenance, and financing enough to be competent. It might be wise to start small with buying a house or condo to rent. Then move up to additional houses or a duplex or 4-plex. Then grow your portfolio as your skill level increases.

Types of Direct Real Estate Investment

Your home or your vacation home (unless you rent it out most of the year) is not considered real estate investment. The following are some examples of real estate investment:

1. Undeveloped land—this is one of the most risky types of properties. You are relying on good things to happen that you cannot control (business expansion, population growth, new jobs, availability of utilities, entitlement risk, etc) to have the land value increase. In the meantime, you have to continue to spend more money on this investment every year for taxes, insurance, and so on. If things work out, you can achieve spectacular returns. Owning undeveloped land is highly speculative, even when you own it debt free.
2. Farm and Timberland—this is less risky than undeveloped land, but the annual all-cash returns are typically very low—below 3%. The upside potential is you hope to find a buyer who will accept an even lower return of about 2%. Some people buy this type of property for the same reason they buy gold—as insurance against economic collapse. Some people buy this type of property for sentimental reasons, that is, grandpa used to have a farm like this. People who are buying for emotional reasons will typically pay more than a disciplined investor. Sell to these emotional people, but do not try and compete with them in buying.
3. Office, Retail and Industrial—These types of investments typically require much more money that is available to the typical investor. Owning a single property with one or two tenants is very risky, even if you own it debt free. The costs of replacing a tenant in lost rent, broker commissions, and tenant improvement costs can be 20%–50% of what you originally paid for the property and the new rent might not be any higher. Unless your business will occupy a big portion of the property and you are confident that your business has long-term viability (you have a competitive advantage), then these real estate investments are best left to the big boys who can own enough to achieve economies of scale and diversification.
4. Home Rentals—this is by far the most popular real estate investment for the direct investor. Investors typically have been home owners and have an understanding of the buying, maintaining, and selling of homes (Lynch Rule). It is also easier to afford to invest in homes. It is easier to increase your investment portfolio as your funds available to invest increase. Finally, attractive financing is available for homes. (Try getting a 75% non-recourse loan to value loan on land or a small office, retail, or industrial building—not possible.) The advantages of home rental investing also create its biggest disadvantage—too many investors have driven the returns very low. If you are realistic on operating costs like management fees (do you expect to work for free or have your family work for free?), maintenance costs, taxes, insurance, and capital replacement (appliances, water heater, furnace,

roof, etc.), then even if the tenant pays all utilities (gas, electric, cable, water, sewer, and trash) these expenses will average 35%–50% of the income you collect (see Table 17:1). If you buy all-cash your first year return, with realistic expenses, will probably be under 4% —better than farmland or timberland and better than most will do in office, retail, or industrial, but about the same as you could do buying a REIT.

5. Apartments—most direct real estate investors will buy duplexes or 4-plexes for two reasons: 1) they do not have the funds to buy larger apartment properties; and 2) the Non-Recourse Financing availability for housing from 1 to 4 units is excellent. Because it is relatively easy to buy these small apartments, there are many buyers and the yields are very low. The returns get better as you get to 20 unit apartments. The economies of scale further increase (returns increase) when you get apartment projects with over 100 units. Few investors have the capital and experience to start with apartments, most start with buying homes.

Figure 17:8 Most direct real estate investors will buy homes, duplexes or 4-plexes.

How To Begin

If you decide to pursue direct investing in home rentals, study Chapter 10 "The Housing Decision." A good book to read before you get started is, *How to Buy & Manage Rental Properties* by Irene Milin and Mike Milin. Large investment firms have recently bought up thousands of homes and have entered this niche. A good article on what they are doing and what they look for when they invest is http://www.multifamilyexecutive.com/rent-trends/homing-in-single-family-rental-firms-ponder-end-game_o.aspx?dfpzone=general.

In this chapter, I have provided many reasons not to be a direct investor because it requires a bigger commitment than most people are willing to make. Those who do make the commitment and stick with it almost always end up with success. Cash flow increases with inflation, other income can be sheltered from taxes and your mortgage loans get paid down each month. You can achieve long-term all-cash returns of about 6%–8%

and leveraged returns of 10%+ if you are an "Intelligent Investor." Buy additional property as your savings allows. Over time you can become financially secure.

When Is Real Estate Right for You

Real estate should be a part of a diversified investment portfolio. It is a good hedge against inflation and rising interest rates; plus it can provide competitive returns. For most people the best way to invest in real estate is through the stock market with a REIT ETF (Exchange Traded Fund—index fund for real estate stocks). For the few brave souls who are convinced they have the time, energy, and skills to be a direct real estate investor, rental homes are the best starting point for the following reasons:

1. The initial investment is doable for a disciplined saver.
2. Non-recourse financing is readily available.
3. They are less management intensive, the residents tend to take care of themselves more than apartment residents (especially if you follow the Milin book).
4. Diversification is more achievable.
5. Your exit from the investment is easier than other types of real estate (homes are relatively easy to sell).

> **Summary and Review**
>
> 1. What kinds of qualifications would you need to participate in a real estate group?
> 2. What investor characteristics are important when you choose to invest directly in real estate?
> 3. What type of real estate would you chose to make a direct investment in? Why?

What Is a Commodity?

While it might be argued that real estate is a type of Commodity, given its importance as a tangible and tradable source of value, most of the time this term is reserved for those products which come from real estate—that is from agriculture or mining. A quick look at the cash price commodity table from the *Wall Street Journal* provides a listing of those products which are commonly regarded as commodity investments.

The cash price of a commodity is the price quoted for current delivery. This is usually referred to as the Spot Price or the spot market.

It is important to note that the commodity you might be investing in is undifferentiated from other like commodities being purchased and sold. By that we mean that an ounce of gold is an ounce of gold, and it doesn't matter whether it comes from Canada or Brazil or New Guinea—it is identical to any other ounce of equal gold content. An investor who deals in oats or cheddar cheese or hams is dealing with a homogeneous product just like the next order of oats or cheddar cheese or hams.

There is an enormous market that deals in these same commodities, but for future settlement; referred to as the Futures Market. In the futures market, we typically speak in terms of a very large quantity of a given product for each contract entered into. Here, commodities don't trade in bushels or pounds, but rather in 5,000 bushel lots (corn or oats), 25,000 pound units (copper), or 42,000 gallon contracts (gasoline). The larger contract size makes trading of the related commodity for future settlement more economical. Futures contracts may settle anywhere from a month to several years down the road, with most futures commodity contracts settling within a matter of months.

Exhibit 17:1 Cash prices: Spot market commodities

These prices reflect buying and selling of a variety of actual or "physical" commodities in the marketplace-separate from the futures price on an exchange, which reflects what the commodity might be worth in future months...

	Bid	Ask	Tue Price	Previous	Year Ago
Energy					
Propane, tet, Mont Belvieu, Texas, gal.-G	...	...	**0.4512**	0.4688	1.0252
Butane, normal, Mont Belvieu, Texas, gal.-G	...	...	**0.5522**	0.5946	1.2179
Natural Gas, Henry Hub-I	...	...	**3.070**	3.010	4.520
Natural Gas, Transco Zone 6 NY, $ per MMBtu-I	...	...	**3.110**	3.100	3.240
Coal, Central Appalachia, 12,500 Btu, 1.2 SO2-R,W	...	...	**52.850**	52.850	62.170
Precious metals					
Gold, per troy oz					
Engelhard industrial bullion	...	...	**1217.82**	1230.74	1291.64
Krugerrand, wholesale-E	...	1255.70	**1255.70**	1277.33	1346.49
Maple Leaf, troy oz.-E	...	1267.77	**1267.77**	1289.61	1359.44
Silver, troy oz.					
Engelhard industrial bullion	...	...	**17.4000**	17.6900	19.2700
Coins, wholesale $1,000 face val-A	...	13400	**13400**	13808	15422
Other metals					
Aluminum, LME, $ per metric ton.	...	...	**n.a.**	1795.5	1724.5
Copper, high grade: Comex spot price $ per lb.	...	...	**2.8615**	2.9300	3.1560
Iron Ore, 62% Fe CFR China-S	...	...	**58.4**	59.0	97.5

Continued

	Bid	Ask	Tue Price	Previous	Year Ago
Zinc, Ryan's Notes N. Am, cents/lb-D	...	...	**110.285**	112.077	102.483
Fibers and textiles					
Burlap, 10-oz, 40-inch NY yard-N,W	...	...	**0.4400**	0.4350	0.4300
Cotton, 1 1/16 strand lw-md Mmphs, per lb-U	...	...	**0.6285**	0.6342	0.8400
Wool, 64s, staple, Terr. delivery lb.-U,W	...	...	**3.95**	3.95	4.37
Grains and feeds					
Barley, top-quality Mnpls; $ per bu.-U	...	...	**n.a.**	n.a.	6.35
Corn, No. 2 yellow. Cent. Ill. bu-BP,U	...	...	**3.4950**	3.5750	4.5750
Oats, No. 2 milling, Mnpls; $ per bu.-U	2.6300	3.0300	**2.8300**	2.8850	3.8425
Rice, 5% Broken White, Thailand-L,W	...	...	**369.00**	369.00	370.00
Wheat, Spring 14%-pro Mnpls; $/bu.-U	7.2425	7.7425	**7.4925**	7.8200	8.8075
Foods					
Beef, carcass equiv. index value,					
Broilers, dressed 'A'; per lb.-U	...	...	**1.1446**	1.1446	1.0982
Butter, AA Chicago, lb	...	...	**1.9050**	1.9300	2.1675
Cheddar cheese, blocks, Chicago lb.	...	...	**163.00**	163.00	196.00
Milk, Nonfat dry, Chicago lb.	...	...	**90**	90	179
Coffee, Colombian, NY lb.	...	...	**1.5988**	1.5540	2.0700
Hams, 17-20 lbs, Mid-US lb fob-U	...	...	**n.a.**	n.a.	n.a.

	Bid	Ask	Tue Price	Previous	Year Ago
Hogs, Iowa-South Minnesota avg. cwt-U	...	...	77.84	80.52	106.68
Raw sugar FOB, $/ metric ton-K	...	...	283.25	283.75	384.00

Source: WSJ Market Data Group.
Historical data for Wheat, hard, KC are unavailable from 4/19/2011 through 5/4/2015

Key to sources and other codes: A, ask; B, bid; BP, country elevator bids to producers; C, corrected; D, RyansNotes; E, Manfra,Tordella & Brooks; G, ICE; I, Natural Gas Intelligence; K, Kingsman; L, livericeindex.com; M, midday; R, SNL Energy; W, weekly; N, nominal; S, The Steel Index; T, Cotlook Limited; U, USDA; Z, not quoted.

The Commodity Futures Contract

To understand the origins of commodity futures investing, let's take a step back and view the larger picture. Let's say that you are a farmer in South Dakota, and you are getting ready to plant wheat seed over several thousand acres of land. Given the costs of the seed, and the labor required to plant it and harvest it, you wonder what the price of wheat will be when it comes time to sell your harvest in the late summer or early fall. Wouldn't it be nice to know right now… before you put a seed in the ground… what price you will receive.

Put the shoe on the other foot. Let's say you are a buyer for Kellogg's, and you are lining up supplies of grain for the breakfast cereals you will be producing over the next year. Wouldn't it be nice to know in advance, the price you will be paying for your wheat or corn or other ingredients, well before you begin processing it. Enter the commodity futures contract.

The farmer in South Dakota can go into the marketplace right now and sell his wheat in today's market, for delivery at a date of his choosing in the future, and know immediately what price he will be receiving on that date. He doesn't have to contend with the ups and downs of a fickle market; he can lock in his price today. Similarly, the buyer for Kellogg can enter into a commodity futures contract, to buy a given quantity of wheat or corn to be delivered at a date in the future, and know exactly what he will be paying when that delivery date arrives. It takes a great deal of uncertainty out of the equation for both the grower and the user. It doesn't matter if prices go up or down between now and the delivery date… their agreement is firm at a price agreed upon today.

Over time, others have entered into the commodity futures trading business. These other participants may not be producers or users, but simply investors who are buying and selling commodities in anticipation that future prices, as they actually unfold closer to the delivery date, will be higher or lower than the prices entered into today. If you are an investor who believes that a freeze in Florida will cause the price of orange juice to rise over the next several months, you might consider buying the orange juice commodity at today's price, and then selling it closer to the delivery date at a higher price. Of course, if you are wrong and the price of orange juice declines, your sell at some date in the future might well result in a loss. But that is in the nature of the price fluctuations for any commodity.

An illustration into Commodities Trading

Let's take a commodity that most people understand, and many investors have actually bought—gold. There is nothing mysterious about gold. It is a mineral that is in relatively short supply, which has a multitude of uses, and which is accepted by many as a store of value. To unmask the mystique of gold—simply consider it as another currency. Like the dollar or the euro or the yen, it is a medium of exchange.

Figure 17:9 Wouldn't it be nice to know, before you put a seed in the ground, what price you will receive.

Now, certain conditions might occur which would strengthen or weaken the currency you subscribe too. Among the conditions which might cause your currency to decline in value are

1. Interest Rates in your economy are low relative to other economies.
2. Your economy is experiencing a high or rising rate of inflation.
3. Your government is spending more money than it is taking in—resulting in significant deficit spending.
4. The balance of trade is in deficit. That is, you are buying more from others then they are buying from you, resulting in more of your currency going out and less of their currency coming in.
5. Your government is printing too much of your currency, driving down its value.

As these conditions drive the value of your currency down, you may wish to find another currency, which will hold its value better. Gold may be one of those options. As an alternative currency, it is often purchased by investors who believe that their currency will decline. This results in a rise in the price of gold—at least in their currency. Someone holding a stronger currency may find that the price of gold in their currency has remained relatively stable, and as a result they would be less interested in the gold alternative.

How to Invest in Commodities

Commodities, whether in the spot market for cash or in the futures market, can be bought and sold through your securities broker. There are a great many strategies that are used by commodities investors, but the bottom line for most of them is the ability to anticipate commodity price movements over time. While it is not our intent to elaborate on commodities strategies here, there are several significant differences between dealing in the cash market and trading through the futures exchange that need to be pointed out.

First, all commodity futures contracts are made with the exchange, not with another buyer or seller. This protocol is designed to insure performance under each contract, whether any other party performs or not.

Second, most investments in the commodities futures market do not anticipate actual delivery of product. While in the cash market the investor pays the spot price and receives the corresponding product, in the futures market the investor may net out his position by selling what he has bought, (or buying back what he has sold), prior to any actual delivery. Of course, in the example of our farmer from South Dakota and the buyer from Kellogg, their contracts anticipate that actual delivery will take place.

Third, remember that a commodity futures contract specifies a given quantity of a certain product be exchanged at a specified date in the future, for a price which is determined today. Since the actual exchange takes place at a later date, the only investment required today is a down payment—called Initial Margin. The amount of the initial margin varies according to contract type and size, but typically ranges between 5% and 15% of the total contract value. This means that you can invest in a substantial quantity of a commodity for a relatively small up-front investment. It is the classic instance of the tail wagging the dog. Because your initial investment is relatively small, the return on your investment could be substantial if you are successful in anticipating future prices. On the other hand, if prices move against you, you could lose all of your investment.

Figure 17:10 It is the classic instance of the tail wagging the dog.

Summary and Review

1. What is the definition of commodities? Name some of the products which routinely trade in commodities markets.
2. When speaking of commodities, what is the spot market? How is trading conducted in the spot market?
3. How is futures commodity trading different from the spot market?
4. Why might an investor be willing to participate in the commodities market?

Chapter 18
Entrepreneurial Investment Opportunities

Chapter Objectives

1. Understand the possible risks and rewards of investing in entrepreneurial ventures.
2. Be aware of the value of investments in entrepreneurial ventures to free enterprise, the economy, and technology and innovation.
3. Explore the life cycle of entrepreneurial ventures and the funding or investing options at each stage.
4. Understand the uniqueness of "start-up" or development stage investing.
5. Contrast early-stage investing with rapid-growth-stage investing.
6. Understand the return on investing in entrepreneurial ventures and the nature of monetizing events related to such investments.
7. Determine who should be an investor in entrepreneurial opportunities.
8. Understand the process and requirements of attracting entrepreneurial investors.

Risk and Reward

The Small Business Administration (SBA) tells us that "About half of all new (business) establishments survive five years or more and about one-third survive 10 years or more. As one would expect, the probability of survival increases with a firm's age. Survival rates have changed little over time."* That simply means that of all the businesses started this year, only about half of them will still be operating 5 years from now. Historically, over an extended period, these survival rates pertaining to small businesses have remained a business reality.

Such are the risks of small business and entrepreneurial pursuits. The bubbles of many ideas burst. The dreams of many Entrepreneurs can become nightmares. In the "cold, cruel world" of business, "survival of the fittest" is the governing principle, and therefore, for many varied reasons, small businesses falter and fail.

However, some small business dreams do come true. When you consider the incredible stories behind the successes of companies such as Apple, Microsoft, Dell, Google, Facebook, EBay, Nike, Starbucks, The Lego Group, etc., it's obvious that innovation and creative thinking can result in very positive outcomes. The right idea, with the right market, the right team, and proper financial backing, can be wildly successful, and provide great returns for both founders and investors.

So which will it be—risk or reward? Wouldn't we all like to have the crystal ball that would give us the answer to that question for each new business idea or concept? Starting or investing in an entrepreneurial enterprise can be very rewarding, but being realistic, and clearly understanding both the upside (potential rewards) and downside (potential risks) outcomes, is a critical requirement, if investing in entrepreneurship is what you are going to do.

The Value of Investments in Entrepreneurship

Referencing the SBA once again, in the U.S. economy small businesses make up

- 99.7 Percent of U.S. employer firms
- 64 Percent of new, private-sector jobs
- 49.2 Percent of private-sector employment
- 98 Percent of firms exporting goods
- 16 Times more patents per employee than larger patenting firms[†]

Small companies are clearly the underpinning of a strong U.S. economy—the life blood of a healthy economy. They are also the source of innovation and growth. Since the time of the Industrial Revolution, technological change and innovation has been the driving force for economic growth and expansion in the United States. Technology and innovation create a very important means to the development of new markets, market expansion, and economic efficiencies not otherwise available.

Investments in small business, and particularly high-technology-based businesses, are fundamental to the culture of industry and industrial advancement we live in. Historically, they are the catalyst to each of the following:

- Job creation
- Contributions to Gross Domestic Product (GDP) growth
- Emergence of new services and industries
- Workforce support and transformation
- General business innovation

In today's economy, businesses have to be quick on their feet and decisive concerning adapting to and implementing technological advancement. It's obvious that there is a direct correlation between a robust and expanding economy and the adoption of innovation and technology. Many, very successful companies have been the beneficiaries of exploited technological change and development.

---

* www.sba.gov/advocacy, "Frequently Asked Questions," page 3.

† www.sba.gov/advocacy, "Frequently Asked Questions," pages 1 & 3.

Figure 18:1 Small companies are clearly the underpinning of a strong U.S. economy: The life blood of a healthy economy.

Summary and Review

1. As noted, about half of all new businesses are gone in 5 years, and two-thirds of them fail to reach their tenth birthday. Why do you suppose so many businesses fail?
2. Reviewing the importance of small business in terms of jobs, productivity, and innovation, what factors do you suspect are most likely to undermine the survival of entrepreneurial ventures.
3. Many small businesses have taken advantage of today's revolution in technology, while others find niches in everyday products and services. If you were to pursue an entrepreneurial venture, what would it be?

The Life Cycle of Entrepreneurial Ventures

All companies, including entrepreneurial companies, have a definable life cycle. The typical life cycle is illustrated by the Exhibit 18:1.

As illustrated, there is no volume of business activity in the **Pre Start-Up Phase**. This is the very earliest stage of a business' life, when the business is an idea developing into a concept, that can ultimately become an actual functioning or operating business. During this conceptual phase, feasibility of the idea is being evaluated, and a business model is being contemplated and explored. The need for various resources (people, facilities, capital, etc.) is being considered and plans for marshaling such resources are being created. At this stage, all of the costs and risks of proceeding are generally being borne by the entrepreneur.

During the **Launch/Start-Up Phase** an actual business begins to take shape. Ideas turn into product designs, prototypes, and test markets. A team of people begins to take shape. Sources of capital, beyond those available to the founder entrepreneur, are being sought. Formally or informally a vison, mission, and plan are being developed. It is during this phase that critical decisions are made about who the target customers are and whether or not there is an actual need for the products or services that the company will offer. The rest of the life cycle doesn't matter if there are not sufficient customers, with the requisite financial resources, for whom the company's product or service fills a need or solves a problem. At this critical point, either feasibility can be proven sufficiently to justify proceeding with the venture, or the company can "pivot" in a different, more feasible direction, or the "plug can be pulled," so to speak, to stop, and contain losses.

Exhibit 18:1 Life Cycle of an Entrepreneurial Business

Time	Volume
Pre Start Up	0
Launch/Start Up	10
	20
Market Establishment/Penetration	30
	50
Rapid Market Growth/Shakeout	80
	110
	130
Mature Markets	140
	135
Decline	125

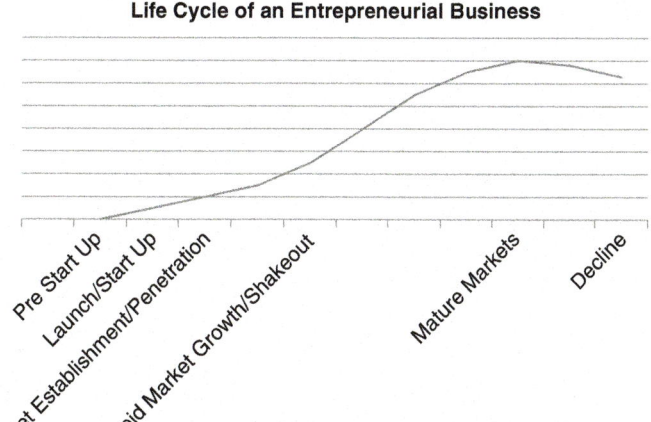

Life Cycle of an Entrepreneurial Business

Assuming all goes well during the launch phase, then the real fun begins! The **Market Establishment/Penetration Phase** presents a unique set of issues and problems to the entrepreneur. It is at this stage that critical decisions are made with respect to the following: 1) what markets will be targeted and how fast they will be penetrated, 2) which and how many key people will be hired to accommodate the growth, 3) how the "ramp up" will be financed (i.e., where needed capital will come from), as well as other things, including but not limited to distribution channel development, intellectual property protection, machinery, equipment, facilities and operations & processes management, inventory and supply chain management, and accounting and financial structure development. At this stage of a company's development, there are varied and significant challenges. How those challenges are tackled will make or break the enterprise, and will be the basis for either continued, rapid growth or failure and termination of operations. This phase of development is key to a company taking its place and establishing its turf in the market place.

Once a market has been established and the need and demand for a product confirmed, the inevitable entry of competitors occurs. A growing market always attracts the attention of others. So the **Rapid Market Growth & Shakeout Phase** creates a defining time for any company. It's a time when various competing companies are jockeying for position and are trying to differentiate themselves from the crowd. The well-positioned and well-managed companies survive and even thrive. Those that are weaker fall by the wayside and are sifted out. Because of the volumes of business at this stage of a company's life, capital needs are ever increasing, but the careful, strategic deployment of capital is more important than the amount of capital per se. Which marketing campaign will provide the best returns and market penetration? How much inventory needs to be in the pipeline and when does it need to be there to fulfill customer demand? Does the company have enough human resources to deal with the levels of business being achieved?

Figure 18:2 A growing market always attracts the attention of others.

When the **Mature Markets Phase** is reached, some critical decisions need to be made. Competition doesn't go away, but the number and nature of competitors is more clear. Also, the size of the market and who the targeted customers are clear. Competition for market share is fierce and predictable. The market continues to expand to include even late adopters of the product. Product differentiation is more important than ever. Product manufacturing and delivery processes are being refined, and related costs contained. All of this takes additional resources, including investments of capital from various sources. This is also a very critical phase for innovation and new product introduction. Without something new or product revitalization, decline is what's on the horizon.

Finally, the **Decline Phase** inevitably comes to those companies that don't properly anticipate product life cycles and market changes affecting them. Well-timed new product launches or product upgrades and enhancements can postpone or even eliminate this phase. The truly successful companies are attuned to market trends and innovation to such a degree that they can overcome the decline phase.

Summary and Review

1. Name the six phases in the life cycle of a company.
2. What tasks are associated with the Start-Up/Launch Phase of an entrepreneurial venture?
3. What can a business do to lengthen its life cycle and delay the onset of the Decline Phase?

Investment and Funding Sources at Various Life Cycle Phases

With the typical life cycle of an entrepreneurial business in mind, we can now look at the various sources for funding such ventures at various times in their life cycle. We must first consider the risks of funding an entrepreneurial business at each stage of its life.

During the life cycle of an entrepreneurial business the risk of failure or loss varies, as illustrated in the following graph:

Exhibit 18:2 Risk Throughout Entrepreneurial Business Life Cycle

Time	Volume
Pre Start Up	150
Launch/Start Up	100
	70
Market Establishment/Penetration	50
	40
Rapid Market Growth/Shakeout	30
	25
	35
Mature Markets	50
	70
Decline	90

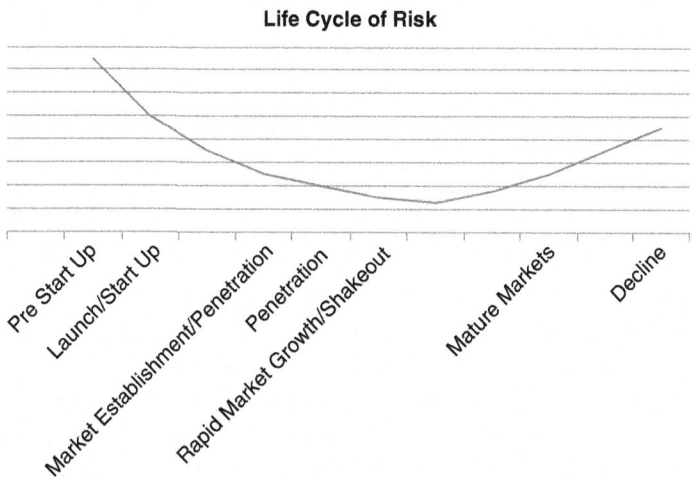

As illustrated, the more established in the market place a company is, the less the risk of its failure to make good on its operations and create value for its investors or lenders. No company is completely risk free. There is no such thing as a sure thing. But consistent revenue growth and profitability do a lot to mitigate potential risk. The risk curve shown might be significantly different for certain industries. The risk curve for a software development company would be very different than the curve for a company specializing in food production and delivery systems. Investing in a new iron mine might be less risky to an investor than an investment in an electric car battery technology company.

An investor, in any company, seeks a return that properly compensates them for the risk they undertake by investing in the company, rather than investing in something else. In other words, the reward needs to be commensurate with the risk taken. So an investor in an early stage company, like a start-up company or one in the early stages of market penetration, will expect a much higher return than an investor in later stage companies.

The following table (Exhibit 18:3) summarizes the appetite that various investors have for investing in companies at various stages of their life cycle:

Exhibit 18:3 Investors at Various Stages of a Life Cycle

	Pre Start Up	Launch Start Up	Market Establishment/ Penetration	Rapid Growth/ Shakeout	Mature	Decline
Bootstrapping	X	X				
Family & Friends	X	X				
Crowd Funding		X	X			
Government Programs	X	X				
Angel Investors		X	X			
Venture Capitalists			X	X		
Initial Public Offerings			X	X		
Secondary Offerings			X	X	X	
Mergers & Acquisitions			X	X	X	X
Debt			X	X	X	
	Early Growth		**High Growth**		**Stable Growth**	**Decline**

There may be exceptions to what is shown in Exhibit 18:3, but they would be just that—exceptions, not the rule. The concept is similar to what drives the use of Prime Interest Rates. The so-called "prime" borrowers, those with years of proven success and ability to repay loans, borrow at the prime rate. All other companies borrow at prime plus an additional interest rate, because lending to them presents a greater risk than lending to a prime borrower. Likewise, a fledgling company faces a significant amount of unknowns and related risk—many more than an established company. Therefore, investors in nascent or early-stage companies seek to be compensated for the risk they bear with a greater return or higher cost of capital.

Let's explore each of the available funding options at various stages of a company's life. In doing so, we will also be exploring the nature of the investors at each stage and the applicability of investment opportunities in various circumstances.

Self-Funding

Almost all entrepreneurial ventures begin with some sort of self-funding. That simply means that those starting a company are going to invest some of their own money during the start-up. Such investments may be in the form of using savings accounts, credit cards or money provided by family and friends. The risk of this is of course that if things don't turn out as planned, some of these investors may become "former" friends and family! For that reason alone, be sure that all important stakeholders are fully aware of the potential risks and rewards of their investment.

Throughout the early stages of a company's development, entrepreneurs use a method of financing referred to as "bootstrapping." Early on, the entrepreneur is managing every nickel and dime, to get as much out of a little as possible. Stated another way, the entrepreneur is pulling him or herself up by the bootstraps, and making it work with what is available.

"I just sold enough blood to keep my website afloat for another month. Now, if you excuse me, I need to go pass out."

Figure 18:3 Throughout the early stages of a company's development, entrepreneurs use a method of financing referred to as "bootstrapping."

It doesn't take a million dollars to start a company. In the September 2014 edition of *The Inc. 500*, listed entrepreneurs were asked how much they used to start up their business. Of the 500 asked, 59% used less than $10,000 to start their business, and a total of 74% used less than $50,000. With proper planning and "penny pinching" the dreams of a company can be pursued for much less than one might think. The Inc. 500 entrepreneurs referred to above succeeded with family savings, "sweat equity" (capital created by hard work and dedication) and learning how to "get blood from a stone"[*].

Crowdfunding

A fairly new phenomenon in funding early stage companies is that of Crowdfunding. There are companies such as Kickstarter and Indiegogo that assist fledgling companies in raising the capital critical to the early stages of development. They help make dreams a reality by providing a forum for promoting entrepreneurial ideas, and gathering like-minded people to invest in and help with the development of such ideas.

A company may have a new technology or gadget, a new food concept, a movie idea, or even a philanthropic pursuit that needs money to develop and grow. Such are the prime candidates for a crowdfunding campaign. The companies using this method of funding publicize their ideas through a host website, offer something in return for those who discover and decide to invest in the projects presented (such as the products being developed or recognition with the project), and get pledges or investments from interested parties to fill capital needs.

Crowdfunding is generally not for the investment in stock ownership of a company. Such investments are regulated by the U.S. Securities and Exchange Commission and State. Crowdfunding raises capital that might otherwise be raised in a stock offering, but without all of the regulatory and reporting burden of a stock offering.

Government Programs

Some people believe that there are government grants available for business investment. That is generally "urban legend" and not reality. By observation we see that the government is not in the business of helping people finance a for-profit enterprise. Instead government's role tends to help level the playing field in certain circumstances, such as when someone is disadvantaged or pursuing something for the common good that is not a for-profit enterprise. In such cases, there may be grants for community and arts development, historical and resource preservation, and those discriminated against.

An exception to this comes in the form of SBIR (Small Business Innovation Research) /STTR (Small Business Technology Transfer) programs. In 1982, Congress passed the Small Business Innovation Development Act in an effort to stimulate innovation, meet federal research needs, and give small businesses a better chance of competing with very large government contractors. The Act, as extended through 2017, requires government agencies with budgets in excess of $100 million to set aside 2.8% of their budgets to be used in the SBIR/STTR Programs. Qualifying companies can receive up to $150,000 to be used over 6 months in a Phase I award, up to $1 million to be used over 2 years in a Phase II award, and a Phase III award (with private company matching investments) for commercialization of a product. The government "red tape" to secure these grants is substantial, and the innovations being developed must be of interest to specific government agencies, but because of the amounts involved, pursuing these grants can be worth the effort.

Angel Investors

There are some entrepreneurs that so enjoy starting and growing new businesses that they do it over and over again. These we call "serial entrepreneurs." These are the people who tend to invest early in what is called the "seed funding" stage of a new enterprise. They are "well-healed"/affluent people. They not only invest but also help guide and manage new companies through the critical early stages of a new venture's life. These investors are more than a source of capital. They are mentors and networking facilitators for entrepreneurs. They have "been there, done that," and as such, are a valuable experience resource to a nascent company and entrepreneur. They know the risks and potential pitfalls facing a start-up company.

---

[*] *Inc. 500*, September, 2014, page 59.

Angel Investors generally invest their own funds in a company. They buy stock (common or preferred) for a non-controlling (less than 50%) ownership interest and a place on the governing board of the company. They provide capital that helps bridge the gap between family and friends investors and the more formal venture capital investors. They can invest a few thousand to a few million, depending on the opportunity. While angel funding is more readily available than venture capital funding, it is capital that is quite difficult and time consuming to raise.

Figure 18:4 Angel investors are more than a source of capital. They are mentors and networking facilitators for entrepreneurs.

Venture Capital

Venture Capital is financing that is available to early-stage, high-potential companies. Companies that have a very large market potential, and prospects for rapid growth are called "gazelles," and are good candidates for this type of funding. Typically, venture capital funding is used after self-financing and angel investor rounds of financing. Reflective of the risk undertaken by venture capitalists, their investment usually results in a controlling interest and/or a significant ownership percentage of the company. Venture capitalists are very selective of the companies they invest in. Of the millions of companies that start operations every year, a relative few (less than a thousand) get funded with venture capital.

Venture capital firms raise funds for investment from various private and public investors (such as public and corporate pension funds, insurance companies, foundations, and high net-worth individuals). Venture capital firms are typically set up as partnerships, with the general partners doing the investing and managing of the funds and funded companies, and limited partners providing the funds to be invested. Some venture capital funds specialize in certain industries, and most are seeking to invest in new ideas, innovation, and inventions.

Venture capital found its genesis in Silicon Valley. In fact, the vast majority of venture capital invested each year still emanates from the many venture capital firms residing on Sand Hill Road, in Menlo Park, California. Because of the demand for venture capital, venture capitalists see numerous business plans each year. A funded plan must have the kind of sizzle and attractiveness that catches the eye of a potential investor. As we will discuss in a moment, a well-presented business plan, with a compelling story is a must to attract venture capital.

Initial Public Offering

After a couple of rounds of venture capital investment, if a company is on a fast and sustainable growth ramp, an Initial Public Offering or IPO may be a very good source of the large amounts of capital needed. Selling stock to the public is very different from the private rounds of financing utilized to this point in a company's life cycle. An IPO requires registration with the Security & Exchange Commission (SEC) and compliance with individual state laws governing the sale of equity securities. The company's operations and financial results must be reported/disclosed in a registration statement filed with the SEC, and the offering needs to be underwritten sold and distributed by a large underwriting or investment banking company.

An IPO is a great way for early investors in a company to get a return of and on their investment. It also opens up opportunities for large amounts of capital to finance continued growth and expansion of operations. Once a company has gone public, it is subject to all of the rules, regulations, and disclosures required of public companies. That comes with a cost of maintaining compliance with a significant number of rules and regulations, as well as the cost of privacy traded for full public disclosure of operations.

Figure 18:5 After a couple of rounds of venture capital investment, if a company is on a fast and sustainable growth ramp, an IPO may be a good source of capital.

Mergers and Acquisitions

At various times in the life cycle of a company, there are opportunities for mergers and/or acquisitions that can provide needed capital, expansion prospects, or transactions that will "monetize" or provide a return on owner investments tied up in the company. Mergers and acquisitions (M&A) theory and applications are complex and a specialty discipline in the financial world. They encompass such transactions as friendly or hostile takeovers, leveraged buyouts, strategic acquisitions, etc. Full volumes have been dedicated to the study and analysis of M&A activity. Suffice it to say, your investment in an entrepreneurial company may at some point be subject to an M&A transaction, and it may be a beneficial way to enhance your investment or cash out your investment, to varying degrees.

Debt versus Equity

Raising the capital needed for any venture can be done either by selling stock (an equity transaction) or by incurring debt. Selling stock often dilutes the ownership of founding or early stockholders. In fact, dilution is the key driver as to how many early stock sales are made and for what percentage of the company. Debt is the alternative to equity financing, but it obligates the company to pay interest and generally make a long-term commitment requiring use of cash generated from operations to pay back the loans. The trade-off of debt versus equity is one of locked-in debt service obligations versus reduced controlling interest in a company.

So where is the line of demarcation between the right amount of debt and the right amount of equity? Too much debt unnecessarily encumbers the company's operations and can affect liquidity to the point of actually hindering or jeopardizing healthy, ongoing business activities. Too little debt dilutes ownership control because of the equity sold. The answer lies in industry norms for the comparison of debt to equity. A company's debt to equity ratio indicates how much risk its creditors are taking—that is how much more debt the company has compared to every dollar of equity invested in the company. Airlines, for example, have a debt to equity ratio of three or four to one (three to four dollars of debt for every dollar of equity invested). By contrast, a software development company would have a 2-to-1 debt to equity ratio. Grocery stores historically have a debt to equity ratio of around 2.5–1, whereas web retailers tend toward 1.5 to 1.

> ### Summary and Review
> 1. At what point(s) is the risks associated with a business most acute?
> 2. Of the various funding sources discussed above, which one(s) are most likely to be utilized at the Launch/Start-Up Phase of a company's life cycle?
> 3. The U.S. government does have certain programs available to help fund small business. What are these programs, and how would a venture qualify for their assistance?
> 4. What does the acronym IPO mean? At what point would this be a viable funding option?

Uniqueness of "Start-up" or Development Stage Investing

Because there are so many issues and unanswered questions as well as so many potential pitfalls for a start-up or development stage company, investing at this stage of a company's life cycle presents unique risks. Investors in companies in the start-up/development phase need to be fully aware of the high risk of losing their entire investment.

Think about how many different ways the operations of a start-up company can come apart! The market for the company's products may not live up to expectations and sales volumes may not materialize as anticipated. Required capital for the venture may be inadequate or delayed in coming. Having the right people for the job, the right complement of skills and abilities, is critical to new venture success. Without the right people on board, a new venture may be doomed. The meeting of regulatory requirements, accessing raw materials, and distribution methods are also critical to a start-up's success. Failure to properly plan for and marshal key resources can quickly unravel a new company's operations. For a start-up there are generally more "unknowns" than "knowns," and thus the dangers of failure are more prevalent than in other stages of a company's development. Think also of the pressures of putting your life savings and money provided by friends and family into a venture, as well as putting other career aspirations on hold.

For start-up companies, the newness is both a blessing and a curse. The brightness of hope that comes with a new location, fresh paint, new equipment, and all of the great expectations is real. The thrill of following one's dreams is real too. But equally real are all of the possibilities of failure from missed guesses, hidden problems and unanticipated hurdles, and the pressures of very hard work, relationship neglect, and little to show for all the effort initially.

Figure 18:6 For start-up companies the newness is both a blessing and a curse.

To be fair to those who invest in a start-up/entrepreneurial venture, the risk of loss needs to be carefully and clearly spelled out. Unbridled optimism has been known to overshadow common sense and a realistic view of the world. Investors need to be aware of the inherent risks in new venture investing. The term "qualified investor" probably best describes those best fit to invest in start-up ventures.

Rapid-Growth-Stage Investors

Investors in growth stage companies, like angel investors, venture capitalists, and those investing in IPO's, face a different type of risk exposure than those investing earlier in start-up/development stage companies. Generally, any feasibility issues related to the earlier stages of development of a company have been resolved. These investors are making a bet on expected continuing market expansion for the company's products and management skills of a team of people critical to working through an ever-increasing number of complex issues. At this stage, large amounts of capital are normally needed to fuel and sustain the growth. Therefore, very sophisticated investment banking and underwriting firms, with very sophisticated deal analysis capabilities, are key to the process of raising capital at this stage of a company's growth.

Return on Investment (ROI): Liquidity and Monetizing Events

Any investor is always looking for a return on their investment. All investors have choices as to how to deploy their cash investments—they have various alternatives in which to invest. They can keep their money hidden in a mattress for fear or risk of losing it! Such non investments actually yield a negative ROI, as inflation eats away at the basic value of uninvested cash assets, and idle cash actually loses buying power.

Most investors are also looking to maximize their ROI. They are walking the fine line between investment gains and losses. All would prefer gains, and the bigger the better, but some of the investments that are the biggest gainers also come with the greatest risk of loss. For instance, we might invest in a promising company such as Apple, Facebook, or Tesla. Depending on when we cash out such investments, we would probably have a wonderful ROI. But for every company that turns out to be a winner, there are tens of thousands that don't make it, and investors left holding an empty bag.

The matter is summarized simply. We can invest in more sure things, like Fortune 500 companies' stocks and bonds. If we do, based on historical data, our ROI will be fairly predictable overall. The same can be said of investments in things like mutual funds. These are fairly conservative investments—meaning that they are investments with less risk and fairly consistent rewards.

But we may also invest in entrepreneurial ventures, which present a very different risk and reward structure. As an example, venture capitalists expect returns of 5–20 times their investment in 5–7 years. They expect to monetize their investment through an IPO or M&A transaction in the fairly short term. Some of their investments flame out, while the chosen few are "gazelles" that experience incredible growth in operations and value. But the overall venture capital portfolio needs to show a reasonable ROI. The winners have to offset the losers so that a reasonable ROI can be achieved.

Figure 18:7 Most investors are looking to maximize their ROI. They are walking the fine line between investment gains and losses.

Who Should Be an Investor in Entrepreneurial Ventures?

So who should be an investor in entrepreneurial ventures? Certainly not the more cautious or conservative investor.

Investing in entrepreneurship is not for the "faint of heart." It is also generally not for passive investors, but instead for those who are "hands on" and participative in their investments. Such investors essentially need to be entrepreneurs themselves, so that they are philosophically aligned with the entrepreneurial world—its great rewards and possible failures—and are energized by the journey a new venture takes.

A well-suited investor in an entrepreneurial venture is one that has their own business background and experience. They may have owned and developed their own business (like many angel investors), or they have sufficient business experience of their own to know the potential pitfalls and critical issues of starting and running a company (like many venture capitalists).

We often speak of the "fire in the belly" of an entrepreneur. That term refers to the characteristics common to successful entrepreneurs. Such attributes as total commitment, drive, determination, perseverance and persistence. Fire in the belly is characterized by the goal-oriented, initiative, and personal responsibility taking of entrepreneurs. If one is to invest in entrepreneurial ventures, they need to have similar attributes.

Other possible investors in entrepreneurial ventures include the founders and early employees. Such investing helps insure a proprietary interest of the team in all that the company aspires to and does.

In a sense, investing in entrepreneurial ventures is also done by suppliers and customers. Suppliers are extending credit to a new company with the hope and expectation of growth or expansion. They are also making a bet that the bills for supplies, raw materials, and so on will be paid from successful and profitable operations. Customers make a bet on the company with their buying dollars. They vote by buying products or services, and thereby help with funding that allows the business to grow and go!

Summary and Review

1. At which phase in a company's life cycle is funding likely to be the most expensive? Why?
2. An investor who invests in the early stages of an entrepreneurial venture is typically expecting a relatively high Return on Investment (ROI). Why? How will such a return likely be achieved?
3. Who should be an investor in entrepreneurial ventures? Who should not invest in such projects?

How to Attract Capital to Entrepreneurial Ventures

So you want to be an entrepreneur? Do you have the desire to pursue your dream and make something new, innovative, and game-changing? Do you want to not only start something but grow it and diversify and expand it into something significant? Then maybe, just maybe, you're truly an entrepreneur.

If you want to fund an entrepreneurial venture, there is a fairly standard path to follow. You will need the following things:

Business Plan

The old adage in business is "Fail to Plan; Plan to Fail." Such is very true of entrepreneurial ventures.

A well-written and well thought out business plan is fundamental to business success. It provides a way to systematically look at every aspect of a business, identify the timing and needs of various things, and plan accordingly. It formalizes thinking and memorializes vision and mission.

Figure 18:8 A well-written and well thought out business plan is fundamental to business success.

A business plan serves three important purposes, summarized in order of importance:

1. Testing feasibility—a business plan represents a virtual tour of a company, and answers the "what if" questions surrounding a company. It provides its authors with insights into possible paths to follow and stumbling blocks that may be encountered. It ultimately will give confidence to its users about the direction and prospects of the company. It is a document that says, "We can do this because we've thought it out and planned appropriately."
2. Management document—once a business plan is written, it can be a useful tool for managing a company. It can be the source of work plans, budgets, and so on. It will provide the basis for measuring the progress of the company, and provide the basis for pivoting to correct or improve outcomes.
3. Selling document—the business plan might just be the way to sell your idea to an investor. If the only reason you write the plan is to attract investors, it won't be a meaningful and effective plan. Be genuine in writing your plan. If your story is compelling, that will be the message of your business plan.

The following things will be key parts of a good business plan. They are things key to the success of any business.

Markets and Marketing

No business will succeed without customers. Markets define a collection or group of customers. For a company to succeed, markets have to be properly identified and researched, to determine that there are sufficient customers, willing to pay an acceptable price to make a market.

Customers are those who have a need or want a problem solved. If your product or service fills a need or solves a problem, then you probably have a market.

A business plan needs to analyze and research a market, and determine how best to reach customers and get them to buy. This is done with a specific marketing plan, that outlines methods and tactics to be used, and when.

Team

Ultimately what makes a company successful is the people who make it go. Founders of companies can only do so much on their own. The most successful companies are those with the right team/people to run them. A successful venture capitalist once told me, "I bet on the jokey, not the horse". In other words, it was who was in the saddle, guiding the company and urging it on, that was more important than the company itself. Those that have been successful jockeys in the past tend to be successful in the future.

Resources

Marshaling the proper resources to help a company grow and go is a significant and important job in an entrepreneurial venture. If you don't have enough money at the right time, you are doomed to failure. Likewise, being without proper physical facilities, equipment, inventory, and the like will hinder or even stop operations. Planning to meet resources' needs and consumption is critical and a very important part of any business plan.

Myth has it that entrepreneurs are born, not made. Anyone can be taught to be an entrepreneur. It just takes learning, networking, planning, and dedication to get there. It also takes the right kind of investors and financing to help entrepreneurs succeed.

Summary and Review

1. What is the first step an entrepreneur needs to take if he is to find funding for his venture?
2. What three important purposes are served by a carefully prepared Business Plan?
3. What is the key ingredient…the defining feature…that will determine a ventures success?

Retirement

Chapter 19
Retirement

"We can afford to retire in 20 years, but only if our credit cards retire in 10 years."

© Contributed by John Packer. Copyright © Kendall Hunt Publishing Company.

Chapter Objectives

1. Given today's demographics, a person reaching age 65 can expect to live another 15 years—on average. Consider the implications of this number.
2. Understand the important prerequisites to a successful retirement.
3. Be aware of those factors that should be considered in your retirement plan, so that the transition into retirement will be easier.
4. Note the alternative sources of funding, which you will rely on for your support in retirement.
5. Understand the nature of Social Security as a retirement funding vehicle.
6. Be aware of other sources of retirement funding, including Pension Plans, IRAs, savings and investments, and life insurance and annuities.
7. Learn the difference between a Defined Benefit Plan and a Defined Contribution Plan, together with the advantages and disadvantages of each.
8. Know the advantages which Independent Retirement Accounts have in building a reservoir of funding for retirement.
9. Understand the potential contribution which certain life insurance policies and annuities may have on your retirement income.
10. Consider the implications which inflation holds for your retirement funding efforts.

What Are the Demographics?

Most young people give little thought to retirement. It's just too far out there .... I've got enough to worry about now ... I probably won't live long enough to retire anyway. Actually, most of us will live to retirement. Then, once you reach the ripe old age of 65, the typical American will live another 15 years in retirement. That's right. The average life expectancy today in America is 79.8 years. Of course, that means that half of us will live even longer than that. What does this mean?

It means that we are under the necessity of providing a standard of living for ourselves for a considerable period of time beyond the point where we stop working and earning. It means that we need to put enough resources into the barn to take care of our needs when we are no longer active in the field gathering our food. It means that, for an average of 15 years following retirement, we must live off the fat we have set aside.

Actually, the younger you are, the better able you are to accomplish this task. This is because time is on your side. The sooner you start putting funds toward a goal of retirement and allow the time value of money to work in your favor, the better stocked your barn will be when it comes time to draw on your resources. Consider—if you begin saving for retirement at age 25 and put just $3,000 per year ($250 per month) toward that goal, and if you are able to earn an average of 5% per annum on those funds, you will have accumulated $362,400 by the time you reach 65. The following table summarizes the effect that the time value of money has on savings.

So, if you are young ... time is your ally. We spent some time talking about the time value of money in Chapter 1, so if there are other assumptions you would like to use, whether it is the amount to be saved, the length of time your savings is compounding, or the rate earned, please feel free to do your own calculations. Application Worksheet 19:2 in Appendix II can help you do this.

Exhibit 19:1 Saving For Retirement—Accumulation to Age 65 @ 5% Per Annum

Age Begun	Years Saving	Amount Saved	Earnings	Total Available	Earnings % Total
25	40	$120,000	$242,400	$362,400	67
35	30	$ 90,000	$109,314	$199,314	55
45	20	$ 60,000	$ 39,198	$ 99,198	40
55	10	$ 30,000	$ 7,734	$ 37,734	21

Figure 19:1 The sooner you start putting funds toward a goal of retirement and allow the time value of money to work in your favor, the better stocked your barn will be when it comes time to draw on your resources.

Prerequisites to a Successful Retirement

When we speak of retirement, most of us think of that time in life when we don't have to set the alarm clock; when we can plan our day without the necessity of going to work; when we can enjoy hobby's or grandchildren or whatever interests us. Sounds good doesn't it. Retirement can be a rewarding phase of life, but it can also be a difficult time of life if we have not made those preparations necessary for its success. Remember, retirement means letting go of that job, which has provided you with income, which has given you a reason to get up and get going each day, which has filled your life with purpose and a measure of belonging and participation. To walk away from all that can be traumatic if you are not prepared.

There are three prerequisites to your retirement, which are important if you are to successfully navigate that stage in your life.

Prerequisite No. 1: Be Debt Free

There are many times throughout life when you might need to borrow for one reason or another. When you did, the lender would look at your income level—do a few calculations such as Debt-To-Income Ratio—and determine whether you qualified for that loan. At retirement, that income is no longer there. Facing a reduction in income is a whole lot easier if all of your debts have been paid and there are no borrowings left to repay. Set a goal to be free of all debt by the time you retire, including any mortgage on your home. There will be plenty of other uses for your income without channeling a portion of it toward debt repayment.

The following table summarizes those expenses, which are likely to decline with retirement, and reminds us of those expenses, which may possibly increase during those years. Clearing the decks of as many expenses as possible means that you have more flexibility to direct your more limited resources in the paths you choose.

Exhibit 19:2 Expense Patterns in Retirement

Expenses Likely To Decrease	Expenses Likely To Increase
Work Expenses and Equipment	Health Care
Clothing	Insurance
Transportation Costs	Food Away From Home
Debt Service Payments	Leisure and Entertainment
Income Taxes (Lower Tax Bracket)	

Prerequisite No. 2: Have a Plan

As indicated above, retirement means stepping away from the job. But it also means stepping away from the structure – the associations – and the purpose which has filled so much of your life for so many years. That is not as easy as it sounds. Ask most teachers how they felt the semester after they retired, and you will hear something like: "When school started up again I felt left out . . . like everyone was moving forward except for me." And so it is with retirement.

Studies have shown that individuals who step into retirement without making any adjustments to their life plan to compensate for the absence of regular work are more likely to age quicker and die sooner than those who have a plan for their retirement years. What elements are important in your retirement? Consider the following:

- Have a plan as to where you will live. For many retired people, a smaller home in a warmer climate sounds good. For others, a location near the children is more desirable. Still others cannot imagine leaving the home they have lived in for so many years. Whatever your choice, examine the pros and cons and consider carefully important factors such as climate, costs, availability of medical care, and presence of those associations and activities you enjoy.

- Have a plan to replace the social support system you enjoyed at work. It is especially important to nurture associations to interact regularly with other people so that a sense of belonging and participation are present. New associations can be derived from your community, from your church or club, from those places where you pursue a hobby or participate in activities. The point is, you are active in your contact with others.

- Have a plan to invest your time in those activities you find rewarding. Whether you volunteer to serve or join an organization, which sponsors regular activities, or simply travel—it is important that you know what you are going to do with your time. It is hard on the human spirit to lie in bed (unless we are sick or injured), without any reason to get up and without any purpose to animate our energies. What will you do today … is an important question that needs answering in advance.

- Have a plan to engage in some kind of **fitness or exercise regimen.** Whether it is walking or riding a bike or bowling or pickle ball, it is important to stay physically active. The hormones that are produced during such activity not only serve to strengthen us physically but also serve to strengthen us emotionally—and put a brighter color to our day.

Figure 19:2 Studies have shown that individuals who step into retirement without making any adjustments to their life plan to compensate for the absence of regular work are more likely to age quicker and die sooner than those who have a plan for their retirement years.

The anxiety that comes when we move into retirement thinking "now what do I do" can be dispelled if you know exactly what you want to do, and prepare a retirement plan accordingly.

Summary & Review

1. How do the demographics of today's longer life spans affect retirement planning?
2. If you are young, you have an ally in your retirement planning—time. How are younger people better positioned to prepare for retirement than those who are older?
3. What is the first prerequisite to retirement planning? Why is that important?
4. Waking up the morning after retirement without a plan can be traumatic. What kinds of planning can help the transition into retirement?

Prerequisite No. 3: Prepare Financially

For most people, stepping away from the job means that those workday checks stop coming. There are exceptions, of course, but most of us need to prepare for the loss of that source of income. You have a lifetime to put away reserves against the day when the checks stop, and the sooner you begin putting some resources into the goal of retirement independence, the better.

It is vitally important that you have multiple sources of income available to you at retirement. This is essential for two reasons. First, any one source is likely to be relatively nominal and usually does not—by itself—compensate for the loss of income at retirement. Second, should one source of income dry up for some reason, you would have alternative sources of income to rely on.

Experts are divided over how much income is necessary to sustain your lifestyle at retirement. A generally accepted rule of thumb would be somewhere in the 60%–80% of your former income level. Let's examine some of the more likely sources of income which could—if you prepare—be available to you at retirement.

Social Security

In the United States, the Social Security program begins with a tax, which is levied on the income of most individuals. Currently, the Social Security tax is 12.4% of all income earned up to a given amount, with half of that or 6.2% paid by the employee in the form of payroll withholding, and the other half or 6.2% paid by the employer. Self-employed individuals pay both halves. The amount of the base wage on which Social Security taxes are collected increases each year and was $117,000 in 2014. (There are some wage earners who are not taxed by the Social Security system, most notably Federal Government employees—who have their own retirement program.)

The purpose of this tax is to fund a program in which benefits can then be paid to retired individuals and certain disabled people. Social Security pays disability benefits if you have worked long enough and have a medical condition that prevents you from working and is expected to prevent you from working, for at least 12 months. Even if you are eligible, Social Security benefits are not paid automatically. You need to apply for benefits. Today, Social Security is the principle source of retirement income for most Americans.

Figure 19:3 Social Security benefits are not paid automatically. You need to apply for benefits.

A person who has worked long enough and who is credited with Social Security retirement benefits based on the amount of Social Security taxes he has paid will receive those benefits on a monthly basis according to a formula, which includes their birth date and the age they select for retirement. For many years, the formula allowed full benefits beginning at age 65. However, today, if the person applying for benefits was born between 1943 and 1954, he must wait until he is 66 to receive 100% of Social Security benefits. A person born after 1960 must wait until he is 67 to receive full benefits. Under current law, a person may apply for Social Security benefits as early as age 62. Looking at the formula for a person born after 1960, the proportion of benefits paid at each age beginning at age 62 is as follows:

Exhibit 19:3 Social Security Benefits by Age for a Person Born after 1960

Age at Which Social Security Benefits Begin	Percentage of Full Benefits Received
62	70
63	75
64	80
65	86.7
66	93.3
67	100

If a person begins receiving Social Security benefits as a spouse, they will receive 50% of the benefit their spouse would receive. Once a person begins receiving Social Security, his benefits are adjusted each year based on a cost-of-living index. Your Social Security benefits may be reduced if you continue to work after retirement and earn above a certain amount per year—depending on your age and the amount you earn. Up to 85% of your Social Security benefits may be subject to federal income tax.

There is a notion among many that their Social Security taxes are placed in a trust fund, which is then managed by the Federal Government until such time as they are ready to withdraw those funds. Actually, no such trust fund exists. The Federal Government simply gives you an IOU, which we hope they will be able to pay when the time comes for you to begin drawing Social Security benefits. If you are concerned about the viability of Uncle Sam's IOUs, then you can appreciate the wisdom of identifying additional avenues of retirement income—and not putting all of your eggs into Uncle Sam's promises. According to the Social Security actuaries, by 2033, payroll taxes collected will be enough to pay only about 77 cents for each dollar of benefits. As a result, it is very likely that additional changes to the Social Security System will result in higher taxes and/or lower benefits in the future.

Summary & Review

1. Explain why it is important to have a number of income sources available at retirement?
2. Most Americans today rely on Social Security as their primary source of income at retirement. Discuss some of the features of the Social Security program.
3. Do you think it is wise to make Social Security the primary source of income in retirement?

Employer Retirement Programs

The Employee Retirement Income Security Act (ERISA) does not require an employer to offer a retirement program, and many firms do not have a company sponsored Pension Plan. For those who do offer some kind of retirement benefit, ERISA requires certain minimum standards as to eligibility and funding. The rules under which the employee becomes Vested—establishes ownership of Pension Plan assets as a permanent right—varies according to the type of Pension Plan offered.

Most pension plans can be categorized as either a Defined Benefit Plan or a Defined Contribution Plan.

A Defined Benefit Plan is a retirement program where the financial benefits paid at retirement are specified according to a formula. Most Defined Benefit formulas consist of some percentage of the income earned in the final years of employment, weighted by the number of years of total employment with the company. Employees may become Vested after a given number of years' employment. For example, a formula may offer a retirement benefit equal to 40% of the average income earned in the final 5 years of employment, with 100% of that benefit paid if the employee has been with the firm for 10 years or more, 50% of that benefit paid if the employee has been with the firm for 5–10 years, and 0% if the employee has been with the firm less than 5 years.

As you can see, the liability to adequately fund and regularly pay benefits under a Defined Benefit Plan rests solely with the company. It is up to the company to fund their plan. Too often, when earnings sag, the money necessary to meet this liability is simply not available. This resulted in what accountants call an "unfunded pension liability." Most of the older industrial companies in America offered a Defined Benefit Plan, and you can often find an entry on their Balance Sheet called "unfunded pension liability". This has created problems for many companies, and you will occasionally read news reports about a large firm offering their employees some incentive—usually a lump sum payment—to opt out of the pension obligation.

Figure 19:4 A Defined Benefit Plan is a retirement program, where the financial benefits paid at retirement are specified according to a formula.

As a result, most firms who offer a pension plan have begun using a Defined Contribution Plan. There are several types of Defined Contribution Plans, including a Money Purchase Pension Plan—where your employer sets aside a certain amount each year; a Stock Bonus Plan—where your employer's contribution is used to buy stock in your company for you, which stock is held in trust until you retire; a Profit Sharing Plan—where your employer's contribution depends on the company's profits, and a Salary Reduction or 401k plan.

The Salary Reduction or 401k plan is by far the most popular, so let's spend a few moments drilling down into that plan. In a 401k plan, the employer obligates himself to make regular contributions to a pension plan trustee based on a formula, which typically consists of some percentage of the contributions the employee makes, up to a specified maximum. For example, if the employee agrees to have 10% of his salary withheld and placed in the pension plan, the employer may match his contribution up to 7% of his salary. This means that the employee's 10% goes into the 401k fund, plus the employers 7%, bringing the total contribution to 17% of the employees' salary. Typically, there is also some caveat in the formula by which the employee becomes Vested in the company's contribution based on the number of years the employee has worked for the firm. For instance, the employee may be entitled to 100% of the employers contribution if he has worked there for 7 years or more, 80% if he has worked there for 6 years, 60% for 5 years, 40% for 4 years, 20% for 3 years, and 0% of the company's contribution if he has worked at the firm for less than 3 years. Of course, the amount which the employee contributes always belongs to him ... it is the company's contribution where Vesting interest is concerned and that his longevity earns.

The funds contributed under the 401k Plan are than managed by a trustee, usually according to a number of different investment options, which the employee selects. The employee may select to have his money invested in aggressive securities or more conservative savings—or he may divide his pension plan assets among several investment options. This kind of Defined Contribution Plan is a type of Independent Retirement Account or IRA and is governed by the regulations pertaining to IRAs. As a result, the employees' contributions are exempt from current income taxes and the assets of the fund are effectively restricted to be used only at retirement.

Note that the liability for setting aside pension assets under the 401k Plan rests not only with the company but also with the employee. If you decide that you can't spare a portion of your income to be diverted into the pension fund, the company is under no obligation to add a dime. On the other hand, if you put a percentage of your salary into the fund that is at least equal to the minimum amount the company has agreed to match, you can double the amount going into the plan with the help of the company's matching contribution. Also note that under any Defined Contribution Plan, the company is required to fund its matching obligation each year, so there is no "unfunded pension liability" to worry about.

A word of advice: If you ever work for a company, which offers a Defined Contribution Plan, find room in your budget to set aside at least as much as the company will match. This will serve to help fund your goal of a successful retirement by maximizing the amount of your pension proceeds. There is an opportunity in Appendix II under Application Worksheet 19:1 for you to work through an example of using a Defined Contribution 401k versus your own savings account to fund retirement plan assets. After you've had a chance to work through it, step back and note the differences.

Figure 19:5 The funds contributed under a 401k plan are managed by a trustee, usually according to a number of different investment options, which the employee selects.

350 Retirement

The following table summarizes some of the important features of the Defined Benefit and Defined Contribution Plans.

Exhibit 19:4 Features of Defined Benefit and Defined Contribution Plans

	Defined Benefit Plan	**Defined Contribution Plan**
Funding	Funded entirely by employer. ERISA sets minimum funding standards.	Employer contribution dependent on Employee contribution—typically a matching formula.
Managing Funds	Employer typically manages funds.	Trustee typically manages funds after employee chooses among investment options.
Benefits Paid	Benefits paid at retirement based on formula.	Benefits paid at retirement based on contributions made & investment performance.
Guarantee of Benefits	Pension Benefit Guarantee Corp (PBGC) guarantees a portion of benefits.	No guarantee of benefits.
Leaving Before Retirement Age	Vested benefits remains with plan until retirement.	Employee may transfer Vested benefits under rollover IRA.

Summary & Review

1. Name the two types of Pension Plans. Describe the differences between them.
2. What does the term Vested mean? How is that important to you?
3. Under a Defined Benefit Plan, where does the responsibility for funding and meeting regular benefit payments lie?
4. Under a Defined Contribution Plan, where does the responsibility for funding and meeting regular benefit payments lie?

Savings and Investments

A third source of income at retirement is your own savings and investments. This would include other IRSs which you may have opened and funded at various points in your life, as well as other savings and investments, which you have set aside along the way.

Independent Retirement Accounts or IRAs were first introduced in 1974 with passage of the Employee Retirement Income and Security Act (ERISA). The specifics regarding this retirement funding option have been modified a number of times since, with the result that IRA's are an important and viable vehicle to help you fund your retirement savings. One type of IRA—the 401k—is used by employers as a pension product, as we have discussed previously. Another type of IRA—the Keogh Plan—is used primarily by self-employed individuals to accomplish basically the same result as the 401k does for employers.

A third type of IRA—the Traditional IRA—is a common retirement program used by individuals. Remember, that the IRA is only the program … it is not the investment. Any funds placed in an IRA must still be invested and most types of securities are eligible for inclusion in an IRA. Also, all IRAs must have a custodian—a trustee who maintains the program, invests the funds, and reports to you. Today, most any kind of financial institutions can be your IRA custodian, including brokers, mutual fund companies, banks, and credit unions. They will invest the funds according to your instructions. Money placed in a Traditional IRA is excluded from your current income taxes, which is a substantial benefit. However, once you begin withdrawing those funds at retirement, the amount withdrawn then becomes ordinary income for income tax purposes.

Another type of IRA—Roth IRA—has become very popular recently. Like the Traditional IRA, funds in a Roth IRA are invested by a custodian in a range of securities under an investment plan you have chosen. But unlike the Traditional IRA, money placed in a Roth IRA is included in your taxable income for current income taxes. Why, you might ask, would I choose a Roth IRA if I must pay taxes on the amount invested? Good question? You might choose this product because, when you retire and begin withdrawing those funds, not only is the amount you deposited free from income taxes (you have already paid taxes on the principle when you placed it in the fund) but all of the income accrued over the years—dividends, interest, capital gains—is free from income taxes. That means that the investment returns in a Roth IRA are not just tax deferred as they are in a Traditional IRA—they are tax exempt. A brief look back at Exhibit 19:1 will show that, given the number of years of investment gains, the prospect of having those gains flow to the retiree free from income taxes, is a major benefit. Over longer periods of time, the accumulated investment income can be much larger than the amount contributed to the fund.

Figure 19:6 It is vitally important that you have multiple sources of income available to you at retirement.

The maximum amount you may deposit in an IRA has been increasing over time. As of 2013, an individual under the age of 50 can place up to $5,500 in an IRA, whereas an individual over 50 can place up to $6,500 in an IRA. Although IRA funds may be withdrawn at any time, there are only a few limited circumstances when money can be withdrawn without a substantial tax penalty. Money can be withdrawn penalty free beginning at age 59½, and you must begin taking distributions by age 70½. So you see IRAs are intended to fund your retirement goal and nothing else. At retirement, you may withdraw your IRA in a lump sum, in installments, or place it in an annuity, which may guarantee payments over your lifetime. Remember, unless it is a Roth IRA, all IRA withdraws are taxable in the year withdrawn.

Your other goals, and another potential source of earnings at retirement, would be met with savings and investments outside of an IRA. Although these do not enjoy the tax benefits that an IRA offers, use of these funds is not restricted as it is with an IRA. Such non-IRA savings and investments would include any securities, real estate, or other investments you have made, which could provide you with dividends, interest, and rents in your retirement.

> ### Summary & Review
>
> 1. What advantages does an Independent Retirement Account (IRA) offer in helping to meet your goal of retirement funding?
> 2. Explain the difference between a Traditional IRA and a Roth IRA. Which makes the most sense for you?
> 3. An IRA does have certain limitations. What are they?
> 4. Why is it important to have savings and investments outside of the IRA program?

Insurance and Annuities

You recall from our discussion of life insurance found in Chapter 13, that one of the purposes of life insurance is to provide a source of income in retirement. Of course, this is available only from Permanent Insurance, where a Cash Value has accumulated over time. Like any other time value of money calculation, the growth in cash value is small in the early years, but the curve steepens over time and eventually becomes substantial.

> ### Get Real
>
> A number of years ago, I purchased a whole life policy from a major life insurance company. My goal was twofold. First, to provide a death benefit for those I wished to support. Second, to produce a growth in cash value to aid in funding my retirement. The annual premium on this policy is $27,235, unchanged from the day I bought it. This year's contribution to cash value was $46,117, up from $42,141 the year before. As you can see, the annual contribution to cash value now exceeds the annual premium by a substantial amount. Although I can continue to pay the premium and realize substantial growth in cash value, I now have the option to let the cash value additions pay the premium and still add growth to the total cash value each year.
>
> Alternatively, I can convert the cash value to an immediate annuity and begin realizing regular income. At this juncture, I am content to continue paying the premium so as to maximize the growth in cash value.

You recall that an Annuity is simply a stream of payments. Many individuals who are approaching retirement will take a lump sum of money and buy an Annuity from a major life insurance company, thereby insuring themselves of a steady flow of funds—together with a competitive rate of return—for the life of the annuity or the balance of their life. The source of the lump sum that is used to buy the annuity varies, sometimes coming from the sale of other assets, a buyout from a business enterprise, or the sale of their home in the event they wish to downsize at retirement. An individual who holds a Permanent Life Insurance policy, which has accumulated a cash value can use that cash value to purchase an Annuity.

We spent some time discussing Annuities in Chapter 13, but it may be well to touch on that subject again here. One of the features of Annuities, which appeals to many is the ability to choose how the payout is to be structured. The three most common types of payouts are the following:

- Lifetime Payout: The annuity provider agrees to make regular payments for the rest of your life. This, of course, is an uncertain time frame and so the size of each annuity payment will be lower. But if you live a long time, the overall payment received could be higher.

- Period Certain: This annuity provides regular payments for a defined period of time. If you die before you receive the specified number of payments, your beneficiary will receive the balance of the payments due.
- Joint & Survivor: Payments are made for as long as either of the two people identified are alive. This is often chosen by couples as a means of insuring continued income to the surviving spouse.

Figure 19:7 An individual who holds a Permanent Life Insurance policy, which has accumulated a cash value, can use that cash value to purchase an Annuity.

Reverse Annuity Mortgage

If your house is your largest single asset as you approach retirement, you have a problem. This is because your house does not pay you anything... there is no rent that you can collect from yourself. Rather, your house is a significant cost, always requiring repairs and maintenance. This observation has traditionally been true... until now.

A new product was introduced a few years ago called a Reverse Annuity Mortgage. A Reverse Annuity Mortgage is an arrangement that provides cash payments at retirement based on the value of your home. On the death of the homeowners, their heirs either give up ownership to the home or purchase it from the reverse mortgage company. Of course, this works best if the home is not encumbered by any other loans—so the mortgage and any home improvement loans or other liens should be paid prior to pursuing a Reverse Annuity Mortgage.

It works this way. You effectively sell your home to a reverse mortgage company, who uses it as collateral to buy an annuity for you from a life insurance company. The amount which is paid to you is called the Principal Limit, and it is based on a formula, which includes the homes appraised value, the age of the borrower, and the expected interest rate. For example, given a home appraised at $250,000 and a borrower who is 65 years old, and given an expected interest rate of 5.5%, the Principal Limit would be $119,000. The annuity which is purchased with this money would then pay a regular sum to the homeowner until his death.

Reviews of this financial arrangement are mixed. Although it is certainly a potential source of income for a person in retirement, this arrangement effectively takes the home off the table as far as estate planning is concerned. You may wish to discuss this with your heirs, who may or may not have an emotional tie to the family home. Also, you can see from our discussion of the Principal Limit that the amount actually obtained in the sale of the home is considerably below its appraised value. This is a result of the fact that you don't actually give up your home for use by the new buyer, but continue to live in it until your death. It is only after your death that the reverse mortgage company is able to take possession and realize a return from their investment. Clearly, this avenue of retirement funding is not for everyone.

The Inflation Monster

We have touched on the topic of inflation several times in the course of these chapters, but it is nowhere more critical to our planning than in retirement. Remember the Rule of 72 …. Divide the current inflation rate into 72 to determine how long it will take for prices to double. Well, if inflation is running at just 1.8% per annum (we are currently higher than that as you know), then prices will double in 72/1.8 = 39 years. That means, by the time you finally do retire, the price of everything from gas to milk, from airline tickets to cell phones, will have doubled on average.

Retirees who are on a fixed retirement income are literally devastated by inflation. It is not just the inflation that occurs between now and when they retire, but the inflation that occurs while they are in retirement that makes life uncertain. Perhaps they planned on having an income of $5000 per month throughout their retirement years. Perhaps they met that goal and found, with social security and their pension, that they could scrape together $5000 monthly. Yeh—they made it! What is that $5000 worth 5 or 10 years later if inflation is running at say 3% per annum? In 5 years their fixed monthly stipend of $5000 will have an effective buying power of less than $4300, and in 10 years it will be worth less than $3700. They will have lost a quarter of their resources, not to bad investments or overspending, but to the insidious erosion of inflation.

During their working years, this may not have seemed as onerous, since they typically received a raise from time to time, which allowed them to keep up with inflation. But if they retire on a fixed income, they worry that they will outlive their resources … and then what! The bottom line is that inflation is an important challenge in our retirement planning and should be taken into account as we prepare financially for our retired years.

Figure 19:8 Retirees who are on a fixed income are literally devastated by inflation.

The Bottom Line

So, how much will you need at retirement? As you have probably concluded from the above discussion, there are a variety of answers to that question. The amount needed is a function of your current age and when you plan to retire, your income level and standard of living, the various sources of income available to you, and inflation. Application Worksheet 19:2 provides you with a form that might be helpful as you try to get a handle on the bottom line. You can use it to refine your retirement goal and define the amount you should be saving now to reach that goal.

Summary & Review

1. What kind of life insurance do you need if you are going to rely on it to help fund your retirement?
2. Describe what an Annuity is. What role can an Annuity play in your retirement funding? What are the various payout options from an Annuity?
3. How can inflation play havoc with your retirement planning?

Chapter 20
Your Legacy

Contributed by Denton Whitney. Copyright © Kendall Hunt Publishing Company

"*I am the master of my fate: I am the captain of my soul.*" (William Ernest Henley)

Chapter Objectives

1. Understand what legacy planning and estate planning are and why they are important.
2. Plan to avoid three common estate planning pitfalls by recognizing the warning signs.
3. Recognize how to avoid three common myths threatening your legacy.
4. Identify three values to help you foster peace and unity with your loved ones.
5. Decide when you will plan your estate.

Legacy Planning & Estate Planning

Our ultimate fate is the legacy we leave our loved ones. Unfortunately, we often fail to master our legacies—to deliberately shape what we leave behind. We strive to build our careers and fortunes and maximize our free time, all of which are important in building our legacies. Yet we miss opportunities to define what and how we will leave our personal and financial legacies to our loved ones to help them build successful, happy lives. Your **legacy** is what you give others. While the property and money you leave behind when you pass away is part of your legacy, your legacy is much more than this—it includes the values and memories and feelings you leave with others.

Most of this chapter will focus on **estate planning**—documenting decisions about who will receive your assets when you pass away (your **beneficiaries**), how and when your beneficiaries will receive your assets, and who will manage the process to give your assets to your beneficiaries. (Note: the terms *estate* and *legacy* are

Figure 20:1 Your legacy is what you give others.

used interchangeably throughout this chapter.) Successful estate planning also includes documenting decisions about who will care for any minor children of yours after you pass away, and who will manage your assets and make health-care decisions for you, if you become unable to do so yourself.

But despite the focus on many detailed estate planning decisions, it is important to remember *why* they matter and that they are just a means to an end, which is to pass on your legacy of love and provide one last financial gift to help your loved ones find happiness and build their own legacies. This is *legacy* planning, and it makes the process more inspired, more effective, more motivational, more enjoyable, and more bonding. Legacy planning prepares you, your children, and your grandchildren for futures together. It involves understanding your goals, your family, and your situation and personalizing your plan to really meet your goals and connect with and uplift your loved ones and pass on not only your assets, but more importantly, your values, insights, and experiences.

The goal of estate planning is to minimize the costs and risks and to maximize the benefits and opportunities your loved ones will have with the assets you leave behind when you pass away or become unable to manage your financial and medical decisions while you are alive. Planning your estate involves more than just preparing a few estate plan documents. It requires thoughtfully deciding how your *unique* situation and goals can best be fulfilled through your *personalized* estate plan. When you *master* your legacy, you minimize significant costs, delays, contention, and stress in your loved ones' lives. More importantly, you foster love and unity with those you care about most.

Figure 20:2 Legacy planning prepares you, your children, and your grandchildren for futures together.

Creating your estate plan is an investment that will be a boon to those you love most, especially the person you select to take care of your estate distributions when you are gone. It is a selfless gift that serves your loved ones and the individual who will administer your estate. In a way, estate planning is like "legacy insurance" that helps protect your family when you pass away.

> ### Summary & Review
> 1. While legacy planning and estate planning are terms often used interchangeably, how would you distinguish between them?
> 2. Why is legacy planning an important part of life's preparation?
> 3. An important part of legacy planning involves situations while you are still alive. Can you elaborate on what those situations might be, and how you might prepare for them?

Three Important Legacy Planning Warnings

Warning #1: The cost of not having a legacy plan far exceeds the value of an investment in a legacy plan

Take a minute to review the list of common reasons people don't do their estate planning in Exhibit 20:1, and select the top two reasons for you.

Exhibit 20:1 Reasons I Have Not Planned My Legacy

Select the top two reasons that you have not planned your legacy or updated it within the past 7 years:

- ☐ I don't think I have enough assets worth planning for.
- ☐ I am uncomfortable thinking about and planning for my death or incapacity.
- ☐ I don't know where to begin
- ☐ I am unsure how to plan well enough to not waste my time or get bamboozled.
- ☐ I am worried it will cost too much.
- ☐ It's not really necessary—in the end it all works out anyway.
- ☐ I feel invincible—the likelihood of my death or incapacity right now is low.
- ☐ I am too busy with more important things, including family, work, and life in general.

Let's consider each of these reasons for not planning.

1. **I don't think I have enough assets worth planning for**

   Bob is on his deathbed. He is with his nurse, his wife, his daughter, and two sons, and knows the end is near. So he says: "Chad, I want you to take the Gahanna houses. Sue, take the apartments in Columbus Plaza. Jan, take the offices over in Dublin. Sarah, my dear wife, please take all of the buildings downtown. The nurse is blown away, and as Bob slips away, she says, "Mrs. Jones, your husband must have been such a hard worker to have all this property. Sarah replies, "Property! What property?! . . . Bob has a paper route."

   Most people do not realize how much of a legacy and how many assets they have to plan to share with loved ones *and* how much more time, expense, and stress their loved ones will face when they do not plan their estate. This is especially true for anyone who owns a home or has life insurance.

Figure 20:3 What happens if you do not plan your estate is exponentially more uncomfortable than thinking about and planning your estate.

2. **I am uncomfortable thinking about and planning for my death or incapacity**

   What happens if you do not plan your estate is exponentially more *uncomfortable* than thinking about and planning your estate. If you do not prepare, the government, a judge and an attorney will make decisions for you and your loved ones. But they do not know you or your children and do not mind receiving more of your money for your failure to think about and plan for your eventual passing and possible incapacity.

3. **I don't know where to begin or how to make sure I do my estate planning right without wasting my time or getting bamboozled**

   You are in the right book and even the right chapter to begin learning what you need to know to plan your estate efficiently and find the help you need.

4. **I am concerned it will cost too much**

   A wise man once said, "A fool can earn money; but it takes a wise man to save and dispose of it to his own advantage." Estate planning is a wise investment in a gift to the loved ones you leave behind. It requires real unselfishness and generosity to spend the time, money, and effort required to plan this gift correctly and completely for your loved ones. People are often penny-wise and pound-foolish and fail to understand and appropriately weigh the costs and benefits involved in planning this gift.

   For example, several family members of a client came to me to administer their mother's estate after their mother had passed away. She had a very old Will that was stored in her safety deposit box. One son had access to the safety deposit box as her power of attorney. But when their mother died the power of attorney ended, so the bank holding the safety deposit box refused to allow access to the Will without an order from the **probate court** (probate court is a special court that oversees the distribution of assets and appoints executors and guardians for individuals and family members when people pass away or become unable to manage their assets or care for themselves). But because the court required the Will to open her probate case

Figure 20:4 People are often penny-wise and pound-foolish and fail to understand and appropriately weigh the costs and benefits involved in planning.

(a standard requirement), the children were in a catch-22 that required thousands of dollars of legal work to get the bank to release the Will and open the case, which was just the beginning of a long, expensive probate case that could have been *one-tenth* of the total cost if they and their mother had worked with an effective estate planning attorney to help them make informed decisions about her estate before she had passed away.

5. **It's not really necessary—in the end it all works out anyway**

    While it is true that in the end life goes on for our loved ones and expenses and decisions about guardians and fiduciaries eventually work themselves out, the unnecessary costs, delays, stress, and conflict created when we fail to plan far outweigh the cost and effort of planning. So why make your loved ones deal with greater costs, delays, stress, and conflict and also risk having decisions made for them that you could have avoided with some essential planning?

6. **I feel invincible. I don't need to plan my legacy until I'm old or in bad health**

    Although you may know you are not invincible, you may rationalize that you are healthy and relatively young and the likelihood of death or incapacity at this point in your life is too low to worry about yet. But this rationale fails when accidents and sudden illnesses occur. It also fails when you get too old to fully manage your affairs independently, so your children end up making many of your financial and estate plan decisions for you.

7. **I have been too busy with more important things, including family, work, and life in general**

    A brain surgeon once spoke about performing an operation on a wealthy man who soon passed away. Someone asked him, "How much wealth did he leave?" The answer, of course, was, "All of it!" We can't take any of our things with us when we go. However, our memories and love go with us and remain with our loved ones when we pass away. So prioritizing time with and for family and loved ones is essential. Planning is one of the biggest financial gifts your loved ones may ever receive from you, as you carefully select your guardians and key agents. Legacy planning done right is actually one important way to prioritize time *for* your loved ones and builds bonds with them now and in the future.

Why Plan Your Legacy Now?

What are your plans for today? … For next week? … Next month? Many of us plan for the immediate future, but we often fail to plan for the time when we can no longer make decisions about how we want to build and share our legacy to best serve our loved ones. We prepare for trivial events, such as watching our favorite team or TV show, and for events that may never happen, such as house fires and hurricanes, but we do not prepare for our potential incapacity or for the one event that we know we will all face for sure: *our death*. There are so many possible risks and opportunities to plan for that last-minute planning does not end well. And the costs

Figure 20:5 Prepare for the one event that we know we will all face for sure: *our death*.

of procrastinating your legacy planning are often just as high as the costs of not having a legacy plan at all, and both of these costs far exceed any perceived potential benefit from failing to plan now.

> ### Summary & Review
> 1. What reasons do you have for delaying your legacy planning so far?
> 2. When do you think this essential part of your Personal Financial Plan should be put in place?
> 3. What will be the first step that you take in preparing your legacy plan?

Warning #2: We never know when an emergency will hit, where we will be when it happens, and what the actual result will be

Our inability to foresee tornados in our lives suggests that the sooner we prepare for any situation and our inevitable passing or disability, the better off we are. This is especially true if you have young children. And it only becomes more urgent as we age. And because life changes quickly, effective legacy planning involves preparing robust plans with contingency options to respond appropriately to best meet your specific goals in different circumstances. Two options that generally fail to help people to prepare plans that achieve the results they really want and need are (1) do-it-yourself approaches and (2) hiring a generalist to help you.

1. **Do-It-Yourself Approaches**

   There are various online services that have you complete estate planning information in forms and then spit out your documents with instructions on what to do with them, including how to sign them correctly. These services generally charge a few hundred dollars to prepare your estate plan documents. They provide a few benefits. The initial cost for the documents may be one-tenth of the cost of a plan by an expert estate planning attorney. They are also often faster for *you* to complete because they don't require you to meet with an expert to discuss what all of the terms mean, the various options that may work best to accomplish your goals, and the costs and benefits of various decisions.

Figure 20:6 There are various online services that have you complete estate planning information in forms.

But when an offer seems too good to be true, it is often a sign that the offer is in fact not true. You often get what you pay for, especially when planning your legacy. The time and effort saved by using online estate planning tools generally removes most of the value of really *planning* your legacy (versus just having some documents that allow you to check estate planning off of your to-do list). It is akin to paying a nominal fee to obtain a bachelor's degree in just a couple months of reading a few books—although the fee is nominal, the cost still outweighs the worthless value of such a "degree."

Beyond the understanding required to plan effectively, the simplistic clauses in online documents fail to cover many circumstances and contingencies that should be addressed in any legacy plan. And there is a risk of wording your wishes incorrectly, possibly changing the meaning and eventual application of the wishes written in your documents. For example, often clients bring me their old docs that they think says one thing, but would actually lead to a very different result. These documents also usually do not list backup agents, so after one spouse passes away, no one will be listed to serve as an agent and your beneficiaries could waste time and money determining in court who the agent should be.

Figure 20:7 The real value of effective legacy planning is achieved when your planning process involves educating and coaching you on decisions that will save your loved ones money, unnecessary delays, stress, conflict, and work.

In theory, these online services are great. In practice, they do not provide much value even when the documents are completed correctly, which in my experience is rare. In fact, clients sometimes show me their estate documents that they created online, only to realize that they failed to sign them correctly; whatever time and money they spent creating them was worthless.

To plan your legacy correctly and completely, time and effort is actually required to understand and evaluate what *you* really need and how to accomplish it for your loved ones. So, if you decide to take the low cost route, you can actually plan your estate for free by going to your local library and checking out and reading at least two books on estate planning. There are many good books on estate planning that your local library will have available to you. To me, someone who has a do-it-yourselfer mindset, this is potentially a great option for very self-motivated, organized, and interested individuals to plan their legacy. The biggest potential downfall to this approach is that it may be easy to procrastinate getting it done. One benefit that expert estate planning attorneys provide, beyond really educating you on your options, is coaching you through the process (like an exercise coach) and helping you follow through the process until your plan is in place and then follow up every few years afterward to help you keep it up-to-date.

2. Generalist Attorneys

The results of estate document preparation using a generalist attorney are similar to those of online document preparation. This is the case with any attorney who just gets your information and does not spend *significant* time with you finding out about your specific situation, goals, values, and family, and advising on your options according to that info. You might save time and money (though you may not), because your attorney will not spend much time discussing your values and goals and will use short and simple templates for your documents. But if they charge hourly, you may avoid talking to them or the fees will quickly rise. Estate documents drafted by nonexperts generally do not address issues of probate avoidance, tax savings, and contingency plans. And children may get assets as soon as they turn eighteen and waste whatever they receive. The real value of effective legacy planning is achieved when your planning process involves educating and coaching you on decisions that will save your loved ones money, unnecessary delay, stress, conflict, and work. So, it is important to find someone who provides this kind of process for you, generally at a flat fee, to help you achieve your goals.

Summary & Review

1. Name two approaches for preparing your legacy plan that are sometimes used, but often fail to achieve the desired goals.
2. What would the Do-It-Yourself approach require of you to produce satisfactory results?
3. What are some common service differences between generalist attorneys and attorneys who focus their practice primarily on legacy planning?
4. What two main types of different billing methods do attorneys use in estate planning?

Warning #3: A Will isn't the only tool that will protect your assets and your family in case of death or incapacity

Legacy planning deals with much more than just preparing a Will. **A Will** is a document that directs where your assets will go when you pass away and who will carry out their distribution and care for any children of yours who are under the age of eighteen. The person who carries out the distribution of your assets is called your **executor**. He or she works with an attorney in probate court.

Incapacitation is the inability to make financial and medical decisions due to mental or physical health conditions, such as undergoing an operation, a short- or long-term coma, Alzheimer's disease or dementia. If you become incapacitated, How will your bills be paid, health-care decisions be made, assets protected, and children provided for? When you create your legacy plan correctly and completely, in addition to preparing a

---

Get Real

Case: Due to heart attack, 27-year-old Terri Schiavo suffered severe brain damage and ended up in a vegetative state. Her husband wanted to remove her from life support, but her parents wanted her to remain on life support. She did not have a living will indicating her wishes as to whether she wanted to remain on life support or be removed from life support in this instance. After 15 years on life support and 7 years of legal battles and millions of dollars in medical and legal costs, Schiavo was removed from life support.

Case Question: Look up "health-care power of attorney," "living will," and "Terri Schiavo" online and read about them on Wikipedia. Who would you want to serve as your initial and backup powers of attorney? What medical decisions will you authorize your health-care power of attorney to make for you? What directions will you include in your living will regarding your care in a vegetative state?

Will, you also complete (1) a **durable power of attorney** to authorize someone to act on your behalf for financial decisions and sign legal and financial documents for you, (2) a **health-care power of attorney** to authorize someone to make medical decisions for you if you cannot do so at some point yourself, (3) a **living will** to direct that you be removed from life support if you end up in a permanently vegetative state, and (4) a **HIPAA waiver** to authorize your loved ones to obtain your medical information from your medical providers.

Many states provide free standardized health-care power of attorney and living will forms with directions for completing them. They tend to be detailed and well-written. But, if you use them, it is *absolutely essential* to (1) read them carefully to really understand the terms and the decisions you are making, (2) ensure you have backups for your primary agent listed, and (3) sign them correctly and completely (usually in front of a notary).

Exhibit 20:2 Five Essential Estate Planning Documents

- ☐ Will
- ☐ Financial Durable Power of Attorney
- ☐ Living Will
- ☐ Health-Care Power of Attorney
- ☐ HIPAA Waiver

Summary & Review

1. While a Will is the first document people think of when they do estate planning, what other documents are important? Why is each document important?
2. If some of these attendant documents are provided by the State in which you live, what should you do to ensure that they help you to achieve your goals?
3. Even if your assets are modest at this time, why is it important for you to implement some of these documents now?

Three Legacy Planning Myths

Many myths exist that may prevent you from successfully planning your legacy.

Myth #1: I have a Will, so my estate won't go through probate.
Fact: A will does not avoid probate.

Depending on the state in which you live, when the probate court oversees the distribution of your assets, the process generally takes from 6 to 18 months. This process creates work, stress, and conflict for your executor and loved ones, it publicizes the amount and details of your assets and the names of your beneficiaries; and it generally costs 3%–7% of your estate (the lower the value of your estate, the higher the percentage of the costs, because the probate paper chase will take time and paperwork regardless of the value of your estate.)

One client of mine came to me after his mother passed away thinking everything was in order. Unfortunately, the estate had to go through probate and one of the adult children who was struggling financially thought he should have a larger share of the assets for caring for his mother. This cost the estate thousands of dollars more than it should have, especially since the assets were minimal to begin with, and drug the case on well over a year and caused caustic contention among the siblings. Most, if not all, of these issues could have been avoided if their mother had ensured her assets would avoid probate.

There are two main ways to avoid probate:

1. **Beneficiary designations** are contracts that indicate who will receive a specified asset when you pass away. Beneficiary designations are available for life insurance, most investment accounts, and payable

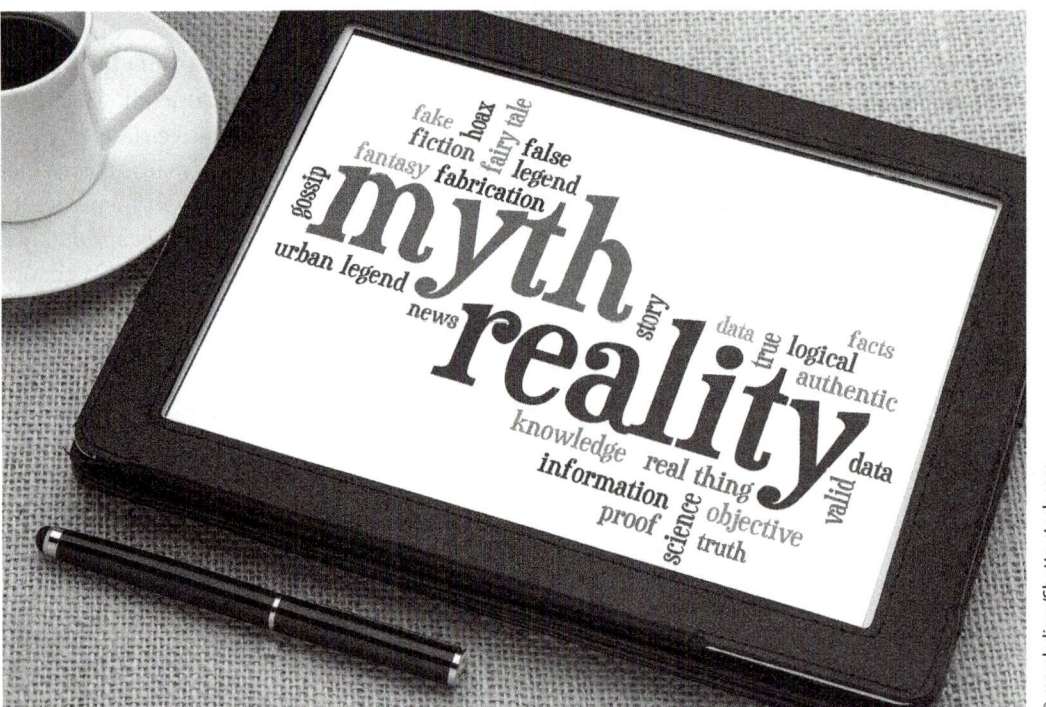

Figure 20:8 Many myths exist that may prevent you from successfully planning your legacy.

on death bank accounts, among other specific assets. *If* they are drafted correctly and you have simple assets, they can be one simple way to avoid probate. However, they are not all written the same which may cause a few unintended consequences. For example, one of my clients had a small insurance policy that no one discovered until he passed away. Unfortunately, the listed beneficiary was "the estate of . . .," which in many states means that it had to go through probate, costing the estate more time and money. This client also had a son who had predeceased my client, leaving behind several children. Although my client wanted his assets for any deceased children to be split among the deceased child's own children (my client's grandchildren), his retirement beneficiary designation did not state this, so the assets had to go to the deceased son's siblings instead of to his children.

2. **Trusts** are agreements for assets to be held under specified terms that outline who is to manage the assets, who is to benefit from the assets, and how the assets may be managed and used. In all trusts, there are three roles: a ***grantor*** is the person who creates the trust and gives responsibility for the assets to a ***trustee*** to manage the trust assets for the benefit of the ***beneficiary*** who gets to benefit from the assets in the trust. Trusts are robust tools that avoid probate and provide broad flexibility to grantors. There are many types of trusts depending on the purpose of the trust. For our purposes, unless indicated otherwise I will refer mainly to revocable living trusts (also called "living trusts" and "revocable trusts") in this chapter. A revocable living trust is a trust that enables assets to avoid probate and minimize potential taxes. Trusts allow you to avoid probate because the assets held in trust are not owned in your name, but are owned in the name of the trust. With living trusts, grantors manage their assets in their trust while they are living, and they generally choose to be both the trustees and the beneficiaries. In other words, grantors create their trust, manage the assets in it as the trustees, and use the assets for their personal benefit as the beneficiaries with complete flexibility and control of the assets just as they would if the assets were directly owned in the name of the grantors.

Costs of a Trust: A trust generally is more expensive to have created for you than a Will. However, the initial expense of a trust is usually very nominal compared with the total value of your assets and also compared with other financial fees you will pay throughout your life. These expenses will generally easily be recouped through significantly reduced estate administration costs after you pass away. The bigger "cost" of a trust is the time and organization required to **"fund" your trust**, which means to put your assets in the name of your trust, so they are owned by the trust. This process generally just requires going to the institution that holds the information about ownership of your asset (e.g., bank, brokerage, county recorder [for your home]), and giving them a summary document of your trust, called a **Certification of Trust**, and asking them to change the ownership of your asset to be in the name of your trust. For a trust to provide *any* value at all, you must have assets actually named in your trust, which is simple to do, but takes time and commitment to get it done. Any assets not owned by the trust and that do not have beneficiary designations will generally have to go through probate, so it is important to be thorough when funding your trust.

Benefits of a Trust: The main benefits of a living trust stem from the fact that your assets avoid probate when they are in your trust. Your assets can be transferred to your beneficiaries in just a couple of months. The cost to administer the process of transferring your assets are generally less than half of what they would be when transferred through probate (1%–3% vs. 3%–7%). Your assets can be passed to your loved ones privately, without any public record of your assets and who is receiving them. Stress and conflict among beneficiaries decrease with trusts because they are generally harder to challenge than Wills and they do not requires as much time to give beneficiaries their share of the assets. Trusts also greatly reduce the burden to oversee the transfer process on the **successor trustee**, the person named who serves as the trustee after the original trustees are no longer serving (often a family member), so the benefit to the successor trustee can be significant.

The benefit of using a trust to just using nontrust beneficiary designations is that a trust is much more robust and flexible. A trust can be used to transfer all of your assets in a single unified manner, without differing terms. Additionally, for property such as your home, a trust allows the property to be managed and sold under a single trustee's discretion, which can avoid many of the costs, conflicts, and additional time required when multiple beneficiaries inherit a home and have to work together to sell a home that they all own jointly. If you do not own your own home or you have minimal assets or just one beneficiary (or two beneficiaries who get along extremely well), then beneficiary designations on your assets are often sufficient to avoid probate all of its various costs without having to create a trust. The steps to either fund your trust or add beneficiary designations are similar and require approximately the same amount of time and effort. Either way, it will be well worth your effort to allow your beneficiaries to avoid the probate process.

Figure 20:9 For property such as your home, a trust allows the property to be managed and sold under a single trustee's direction.

> **Summary & Review**
>
> 1. What is probate? What are two main ways to avoid probate?
> 2. What are the three principal roles fulfilled by parties in a trust agreement?
> 3. While there are many types of trusts, revocable living trusts are the most common and the foundation for any trust based legacy plan. What are some advantages of using a living trust in your legacy plan?

Myth #2: I have a trust, health-care directives and power of attorney, so my legacy plan is set.
Fact: Legacy plans fail for many reasons.

An elderly man was losing his hearing. His doctor gave him hearing aids. The man went back to the doctor a month later for a checkup and the doctor said, "Your hearing is perfect. Your family must be really pleased that you can hear again." The man replied, "Oh, I haven't told my family yet. I just sit around and listen to their conversations. I've changed my Will three times!"

Although this is just a humorous story, I cringe for this man's family as I imagine them finding multiple drafts of Wills and trying to determine which one is correct and what he really wanted. Here are two common reasons plan fail:(1) failing to communicate your wishes and instructions clearly to your loved ones and (2) failing to ensure your plan is completed correctly.

To ensure you legacy plan is communicated clearly, it is essential that you plan how your documents will be stored safely and retrieved easily when needed and that you communicate as much of your plan as you can to your loved ones and your key agents, including your successor trustees, executors, powers of attorney, health-care powers of attorney, and living will notification contacts. Legacy plans should be reviewed regularly—at least every 3 years and after major life events, such as marriage, divorce, deaths, out-of-state moves, and major changes in assets. Finding an attorney who will review your plan with you without pressuring you to update items or up-sell you on more options with more fees is crucial to the success of your plan. Make sure that outdated documents are destroyed and that you communicate with your loved ones and key agents on updates. It is also important to record your passwords and the location of critical documents, keys, and each of your accounts, and assets (see worksheets).

To ensure your plan is completed correctly, make sure your documents are signed correctly and drafted to actually accomplish what you want them to do and remain up-to-date with any changes in the law. If you create a trust, the number one mistake with trusts is failing to actually fund them. It pains me when new clients bring in a trust that they or their deceased parent paid for and worked to create only to discover that it was not funded. This happens with trusts I have seen drafted by small, medium, and large firms. It is critical to screen for trust funding when you select an attorney—find out how she helps ensure that clients fund their trusts, including re-titling your home into your trust. Even if you do not end up creating a trust, if the attorney has a system to ensure clients fund their trust, they will be more likely to have other systems in place to ensure your plan will actually work for you.

Myth #3: My family and beneficiaries will never fight over my (piddly) assets.
Fact: Money tempts people to do crazy things, even for minimal amounts.

Conflicts among beneficiaries is easily the quickest and most destructive force to any estate. So failing to plan for and minimize current and potential conflicts among beneficiaries can be a major mistake. Take time to think through potential conflicts that currently exist or could exist among beneficiaries, agents, and loved ones, and plan ways to minimize those conflicts through your legacy planning. Here are a few key ways to help manage and minimize potential conflicts among beneficiaries:

- Enjoy using or giving away as many of your assets as you can while you are still alive and well.
- Use a **no-contest clause**, which states that if any beneficiary challenges your Will or trust, they will not receive any inheritance that you have otherwise designated in your Will or trust.

- Consider including requirements for any conflicts to be resolved through mediation and/or arbitration.
- Label or record specific assets to be given to certain children when you pass way. Do not tell family members that they can have specific items when you pass away, without also documenting it, otherwise you may tell multiple beneficiaries that they can have the same item or a beneficiary may fight your executor or trustee to receive an item you "promised" them.
- Create a trust to allow for more efficient transfer of assets outside of the probate forum.

It is worth noting that most of us are blessed with much more than we realize. This is especially apparent when we consider the high standard of living we enjoy in America and when we factor in all of the resources we may be giving our beneficiaries, including life insurance, home equity and retirement assets. So it really is worth taking time to plan how we will share whatever wealth we enjoy with others in ways that deter conflict and unwise use of our financial gifts and that truly help increase the happiness of our beneficiaries. Therefore, it is not only important to decide *who* will receive your assets, it is also important to define when they will be able to use and/or control them and how they will be able to use or be restricted from using those assets to lead to their happiness and foster unity with us and with other loved ones.

Summary & Review

1. What are some of the reasons legacy plans fail?
2. What are some of the key ways to minimize conflicts among potential beneficiaries?
3. What is a no-contest clause?

Figure 20:10 My family and beneficiaries will never fight over my (piddly) assets.

Three key values needed to foster peace and unity with loved ones through your legacy planning
Here are a few final tips on legacy planning.

Figure 20:11 Most of us are blessed with much more than we realize.

1. **Value #1: Courage**

   It takes courage to prioritize tackling the tough issues addressed in legacy planning. For example, courage is required to recognize and address potential conflicts over your estate. This is especially true, even though it may be harder, if you are in a second marriage; are nearing retirement; own a business; are worried about long-term care costs; or have a child with a disability, addiction, high risk of lawsuit, unstable marriage or problematic spouse, or financial problems. Another example of the need for courage is determining who will care for your minor children if you cannot do so yourself. Courage is also required to address the potential need for long-term care and determining how you will pay for it, who will care for you if you cannot care for yourself. Legacy planning requires facing our eventual death or incapacity and tackling decisions about those sensitive topics with courage.

2. **Value #2: Learning**

   Legacy planning requires that you study reliable resources to help you plan your legacy and find an attorney who will educate you (not sell you) about the best options available to and the costs and benefits of each option and help coach you through the sometimes complex legacy planning process.

   We have already addressed do-it-yourself options. Reading at least two good books on estate planning and preparing your own documents is a good "C" plan, *if* you really implement it correctly and completely. And a good "C" plan is better than no plan at all. But when you find a trustworthy estate planning attorney to help you with your legacy planning, you can obtain an "A plan." But there are risks to hiring an expert to help you plan your legacy: you may find the wrong attorney, it will cost more than a DIY plan, and it may still not be right or complete. So here are three keys to finding a good legacy planning attorney:

   - He should charge a flat fee and have a systematic approach to serve you long-term and ensure your plan is correct and complete, including ensuring that trusts are fully funded.
   - Her personality should fit with yours.

Exhibit 20:3 Reasons for Planning Your Legacy/Estate

Review the following list of "Reasons for Planning Your Legacy" and put a check by the column most applicable to you for each item, then add them up. . . .What is a vital item for you?
Place a check under the most applicable column for each reason, then add up each column:

#	Reason to Plan Your Legacy	N/A	Want	Vital
1	Avoid probate			
2	Ensure your estate is administered cost-effectively and efficiently			
3	Minimize stress and conflict among loved ones when you pass away			
4	Select who will manage your assets if you are unable to or you pass			
5	Select guardians for your minor dependents if you can't care for them			
6	Maximize estate for spouse			
7	Preserve estate for children or grandchildren			
8	Leave something to charities or individuals other than your family			
9	Minimize taxes			
10	Protect assets for loved ones who have disabilities or addictions			
11	Protect assets for children from divorce, predators, creditors, lawsuits			
12	Protect assets from long-term care costs for Medicaid eligibility			
13	Determine who will make health-care decisions for you if you can't			
14	Ensure no extreme measures are taken to keep you alive			
15	Plan how to share your values and life story with your loved ones			
16	Other:			
	TOTAL COUNT IN EACH COLUMN			

- He should ask many questions and share several options with you to plan for your situation, coaching you through dozens of decisions to create a personalized plan for you.
- Legacy planning is complicated enough without trying to do it alone or with the help of someone you do not trust or is just not a good fit for you. To select a legacy planner whom you trust, start by creating clear criteria to evaluate candidates. Prepare specific questions to determine how well they meet your criteria, then contact a few legacy planners to see how well they meet your criteria. Here are five questions you may consider asking for starters:

1. *Why* do they practice legacy planning?
2. How much experience do they have *specifically in legacy planning*?
3. How much of their work is *focused solely on legacy planning*?
4. How do they *follow up* to ensure your plan will really work for you?
5. Do they believe they can provide you with the *best service possible*? Why?

3. **Value #3: Love**

As noted throughout this chapter, legacy planning is about helping your loved ones be happy and successful. It requires love to invest the time, money, and effort required to plan your legacy successfully. Beyond sharing your assets with your loved ones, legacy planning can help you share your values and memories to truly connect with loved ones while you are living and after you pass away.

You can start doing this by asking yourself "how can I share my love, values, and appreciation with my loved ones now and when I am gone?" For me, I have found that having a voice recorder (or phone voice recording app) available when I return home for family reunions to record special conversations with my mom, grandma, and other family members has been a great blessing to me and my family. When I did this last, I had a list of about 100 questions to ask loved ones and recorded them as they answered them. I then burned the recordings to CDs and sent them to my family the following Christmas. We felt more unified as we each listened to the recordings we had made the prior summer when were together. You can record your own messages in letters, journals, and audio and video recordings about your values, insights, and experiences and share them with your loved ones on special birthdays and milestones, such as graduations, marriage, and the birth of children. This really captures the real purpose of legacy planning and fills sometimes challenging planning process with meaning and heart.

Application Question: How will you ensure you remain a positive presence in your family's life now and after you pass away?

Summary & Review

1. What are the three key values needed for successful legacy planning?
2. What criteria do you regard as most important in choosing a professional to help you to complete your legacy plan?
3. Beyond preparing the key documents prepared in common legacy plans, how will you pass on your legacy to your loved ones?

APPENDIX I
ADDITIONAL READINGS & CASE STUDIES

Chapter 8:   Article 8:1 – How a Family of Four Manages To Live Well On Just $14,000 Per Year

Chapter 9:   Article 9:1 – Car Buyers Burned by Negative Equity

Chapter 14:   Article 14:1 – Risk Profile Questionnaire

                 Article 14:2 – Suitability

                 Article 14:3 – A State of Mind

Chapter 15:   Article 15:1 – Growth Versus Value

                 Article 15:2 – In Search of Alpha

Copyrighted 2015. Business Insider, Inc. 117301:0515DS
From Risk Profile Questionnaire by Soltis Investment Advisors. Copyright © Soltis Investment Advisors. Reprinted by permission.
Copyright © 2003 USA Today, a division of Gannett Co. Inc. Reprinted by permission.

How a Family of Four Manages to Live Well on Just $14,000 Per Year

By Mandi Woodruff | Business Insider—Tue, Feb 26, 2013 1:33 PM EST

In the years since the recession, the median household income in the U.S. has dropped to just over $50,000, while fixed costs like health care, higher education, and housing have only soared. Now imagine trying to support a family of four on a fraction of that income.

It's a reality that stay-at-home wife and mother of two Danielle Wagasky has lived for the last four years. And, perhaps a little surprisingly, she wouldn't have it any other way.

Wagasky, 28, lives with her her husband, Jason, 31, and their two young children in a three-bedroom family home in Las Vegas, Nevada. While Jason, a member of the U.S. Army, completes his undergraduate studies, the family's only source of income is the $14,000 annual cost of living allowance he receives under the G.I. Bill. Despite all odds, the family has barely any credit card debt, no car payment, and no mortgage to speak of.

Wagasky has been sharing her journey to living meaningfully and frugally on her blog, Blissful and Domestic, since 2009.

She was kind enough to chat with BI and tell us how she makes it work.

"My husband told me he'd heard about this book, [America's Cheapest Family Gets You Right on the Money]," she said. "We talked about it over the phone and I read it and thought how it could apply to us."

The couple had a single savings goal in mind—scraping together $30,000 for a downpayment on their home in their native Henderson, Nevada.

The mindless spending was out, and Wagasky came up with a budget she could make work. "I changed the way I was grocery shopping and started working my way up," she said.

She stopped eating out and learned how to cook

Wagasky barely knew her way around a kitchen when she started her money makeover.

Now she's an avid cookbook collector (she checks them out from libraries or asks for them as gifts to save), and it's one of the simplest ways she's managed to cutback on spending.

With a $7 bread-maker she scored at a local thrift shop, she never spends on store bought slices. She's not shy about professing her love for wholesale stores like Costco, which is her go-to source for baking ingredients.

Everything in the home is either hand-sewn and or made from scratch

"Everything must be budgeted," Wagasky wrote in a June entry on her blog. "From family outings, to toiletries to clothes purchases. It must be budgeted."

And she takes Do-It-Yourself to the extreme. Everything from laundry soap and clothing to the kitchen her husband installed in their new home was either crafted by hand or thrifted.

She swears by this home-made laundry detergent recipe.

The family swapped cable for Netflix and Hulu

When it come to cutting costs, cable was as easy luxury to part ways with.

With two children aged 6 and 8 to entertain, Wagasky invests $14.99 in a Netflix plan and recently added Hulu to the mix.

The family also uses a simple antennae to pick up basic cable channels.

She goes to the grocery store once per month, pays cash, and never goes over budget

With a single source of fixed income, there's no room for impulse purchases in the Wagasky household.

They budget $400 for groceries each month and that's it.

"Once that $400 is gone, it is gone," she writes. "There are no extra shopping trips made because there is no more money."

They are a cash-only household but keep a credit card for emergencies

Wagasky said they have no credit debt, but they do charge emergency expenses on plastic when absolutely necessary.

"We recently had some medical bills we had to pay, and we were able to take our savings and pay those down as fast as we could," she said.

They fill up their tanks once per month and combine errands as much as possible

With gas prices creeping higher each all the time, the Wagaskys watch their mileage like hawks.

That means combining errands together and doing all they can to make one tank of gas last a month.

"We know we don't get to drive and visit family often, so when we do we cherish it," she wrote in a blog entry.

"We don't go just for an hour, we stay and visit and even run errands that may be close to where we have family. We try to remember that when the gas is gone. . .it is gone."

They paid for both of their cars in cash and have no car payments

After Wagasky's husband left active duty and started school, the couple knew they would only have $14,000 per year to live on.

So they paid off the $8,000 he owed on his truck while he was earning more and they could afford the expense.

They also bought a van, which they saved $10,000 for initially and were able to pay the remaining $12,000 owed within a year.

Having zero car payments is a nice relief.

She skips all kiddie snacks in favor of healthier, cheaper DIY options

Like anyone with simple math skills, Wagasky was quick to realize how much cash she was wasting on prepackaged snacks for her children.

She cut them out completely and whips up homemade granola bars and trail mix instead.

If she can freeze food, she will

If you're on a tight food budget, your freezer will become your best friend.

Wagasky chops vegetables and fruits and freezes them for a month. She actually does the same for dairy products like cheese, butter and yogurt.

"I am able to freeze about 8 gallons of milk each month," she writes. "They sit at the bottom of my freezer and we thaw them out when we need them." Baked goods get the same chilly treatment.

She uses a food co-op to save on fresh produce

Wagasky was dubious about joining a food co-op, but after three months, she realized she would never beat the savings or quality she found.

Food co-ops pool membership fees together in order to fund a monthly harvest that's distributed at designated pick-up points.

A couple of times per month, Wagasky gets a basketful of in-season produce for $15—way better bargain than she'd ever find in stores.

They took advantage of Nevada's declining housing market to score a cheap foreclosure.

By the time Wagasky's husband came home from Iraq, they had managed to scrape together the $30,000 they needed for a downpayment on a home.

"But we decided the best option would be not to have a mortgage payment at all," she said. "We found a fixer-upper that didn't have a kitchen . . . and we paid cash."

Price tag: $28,000. With the leftover cash, they were able to finish the kitchen and install wood flooring throughout the house.

Car Buyers Burned By Negative Equity

By David Kiley, USA TODAY

DETROIT—A large number of auto buyers owe more on their trade-ins than the vehicles are worth, making it tough for dealers, and expensive for buyers, to finance new purchases.

Edmunds.com, an auto shopping service, reports that 40% of new car buyers are "upside down" with an average negative equity of $2,200. J.D. Power and Associates says negative equity for an average buyer has nearly doubled since 2000 to $1,200.

It is a growing phenomenon because big discounts on new cars have the effect of depressing the value of used cars, and 5- and 6-year loans means it takes longer for car owners to achieve positive equity in a new vehicle.

"Every extra dollar (of discounts) we put on a Dodge Durango comes off the trade-in value of a used Durango," says Chrysler Financial spokesman James Ryan.

Mark Eddins of Friendly Chevrolet in Dallas estimates that 90% of his customers are upside down, often owing $10,000 to $15,000 more than the trade-in is worth. "It's an awful thing for our business," says Eddins. It is a bigger problem for customers of automakers who do the most discounting and attract the longest term loans—General Motors, Ford, Chrysler, Mitsubishi, Hyundai, Suzuki. Many Toyota and Honda dealers report only about 15% of their customers are upside down.

In the hole, buyers usually add the amount they owe on their trade-in onto the loan for the new car. And they often stretch out the loan to keep monthly payments low. The longer the loan, the longer it takes to owe less than the vehicle's depreciating value.

The Consumer Banker's Association reports that 82% of new vehicle loans last year were longer than 4 years; 31% were longer than 5 years. In California, some dealers are writing 7-year loans.

The problem has spawned a new profit center for some dealers, who are promoting gap insurance. Gap pays the difference between what is owed and what regular insurance will cover if a vehicle is totaled in a wreck or stolen—usually up to 130% of the vehicle's value.

Dealers typically charge $500–$700 for gap coverage that can be bought online for $300 or so.

"We are selling a ton of gap insurance to individual vehicle buyers, where it used to be most of our business was with leased cars" to protect the leasing company, says Dave Hurt, president of Drivers Select Gap Insurance.

Risk Profile Questionnaire

What Type of Investor Are You?

Your risk tolerance is a critical component in assisting Soltis to determine which asset allocation strategy to recommend to you. The following questionnaire will help you evaluate your attitude towards risk and determine what type of investor you are. After you answer the questions below, Soltis will use your answers as a tool to recommend a suitable portfolio.

1. Please indicate your current age range:
   1) 70 and over
   2) 60 to 69
   3) 50 to 59
   4) 40 to 49
   5) 30 to 39
   6) Under 30

2. What is your main objective for your investments?
   1) Generating retirement income now
   2) Large purchase within five years
   3) Savings for future retirement
   4) Savings for child's future education
   5) Charitable giving arrangement
   6) To leave an estate for my family and / or others
   Other _____

3. Over what period of time do you anticipate investments will remain in this plan?
   1) less than 5 years
   2) 5-15 years
   3) 16-25 years
   4) More than 25 years
   5) Perpetuity

4. Please indicate the approximate number of years until you anticipate beginning withdrawals.
   1) Immediately / Currently
   2) Within 5 years
   3) Between 5 and 10 years
   4) Between 10 and 15 years
   5) Between 15 and 20 years
   6) I do not anticipate making withdrawals for more than 20 years

5. If / when you begin withdrawals from your portfolio, what statement best describes your attitude towards your withdrawals:
   1) I wish to maximize my withdrawal amounts over my / our total expected investment horizon without a priority to preserve a remainder interest.
   2) I plan to withdraw amounts that will likely reduce the principal over time but wish to preserve some principal to pass to beneficiaries.

3) I plan to withdraw only amounts that would likely allow the principal to be preserved.
4) I plan to withdraw only amounts that would likely allow the principal to continue to grow over time.

6. How many months of cash reserves do you have?
    1) No cash reserves at all
    2) one to two months
    (3) three to six months
    4) seven to 12 months
    5) over 12 months

7. How predictable (or stable) and sufficient is your source of income?
    1) Unpredictable, making it difficult to budget or invest
    (2) Somewhat predictable, but can fluctuate from month-to-month
    3) Reasonably predictable, with some excess to invest from time-to-time
    4) Predictable and sufficient to allow for periodic investment
    5) Very predictable with large excess to invest on regular basis

8. Proper insurance protects you against negative events that may cause unexpected withdrawals from your investment assets. If you have appropriate insurance policies in place, you are able to be more aggressive in how you invest. Please check all of the following types of insurance coverage that you currently have in place and believe to be adequate:
    - Life Insurance
    - Property and Casualty Insurance
    - Health Insurance
    ○ Disability Insurance
    ○ Umbrella Policy
    ○ long-Term Care Insurance

9. Rank your understanding and comfort-level with investing and capital markets.
    1) No-experience and no comfort level in investing
    2) No experience, but some level of comfort in investing
    (3) Some experience, and interest in investing in markets
    4) Reasonable experience and comfort level with investing in markets
    5) Extensive background and understanding of investments and markets

10. which allocation below most closely matches your current investments?
    1) Don't know
    (2) 100% in savings or CDs
    3) 60% Bonds and 40% in Stocks
    4) 40% in Bonds and 60% in Stocks
    5) 100% in Stocks

11. What is the annualized rate of return you expect to achieve?
    1) I don't know
    (2) 2% to 5%
    3) 5% to 8%
    4) 8% to 10%
    5) Greater than 10%

12. Suppose that a substantial portion of your investment portfolio is invested in stocks. If you owned stocks or stock mutual funds during the 56% market decline of 2008 and into 2009, which of the following most closely describes the course of action you took or think you would have taken:
    1) Sold all of your stock holding to protect the portfolio from the risk of further downside
    2) Sold some stocks to partially protect the portfolio from the risk of further downside
    3) **Stayed the course and waited for the market to recover** ✓
    4) Bought more stock to take advantage of the perceived opportunity provided by lower stock prices

13. Inflation risk can result in the loss of purchasing power. Which statement below best describes your attitude with respect to your portfolio increasing in value above the rate of inflation?
    1) Not important, preservation of capital is top priority
    2) Somewhat important, preservation and income still outrank
    3) **Moderately important to have purchasing power increasing greater than the inflation rate** ✓
    4) Important, and understand that accepting increased market risk is required
    5) Vital, willing to accept higher risk to increase inflation-adjusted value of my investment portfolio

14. Please indicate your approximate family gross annual income.
    1) **Under $50k** ✓
    2) $50k to $100k
    3) $100k to $250k
    4) $250k to $500k
    5) $500k to $1M
    6) Over $1M

15. Of the Income listed above, what is the approximate percentage that you save or invest?
    1) **Under 10%** ✓
    2) 10% to 20%
    3) 20% to 30%
    4) More than 30%

16. Please indicate your approximate gross family net worth.
    1) **Under $500k** ✓
    2) $500k to $1M
    3) $1M to $2.5M
    4) $2.5M to $5M
    5) $5M to $10M
    6) Over $1M

17. How do you feel about fluctuations in the value of your portfolio?
    1) I want to minimize the possibility of loss in the value of my portfolio. I understand that I am sacrificing higher long-term returns by holding investments that reduce the potential for short-term loss and price fluctuation.
    2) **I can tolerate moderate losses in order to achieve potentially favorable returns.** ✓
    3) I can tolerate the risk of large tosses in my portfolio in order to increase the potential of achieving high returns.

Suitability
A Retail Responsibility

Mary Bennett had taught high school English for 30 years.

Her late husband, Dr. Harold Bennett, MD, had practiced orthopedic surgery up until the day of his death 3 months ago. Although his death had not been entirely unexpected—he had fought heart disease for a year—it had been very hard for Mary. It was especially difficult since they had no children, and Mary's older brother had passed away several years earlier.

In most marriages, the duties are divided along the lines of who is best able to handle a given task. For the Bennett's, Harold had always handled the money. While their combined incomes in most years had placed them in the upper middle earnings bracket, it was their frugality that made them millionaires. They had lived comfortably, though modestly, in the same house for nearly 25 years. While they often traveled, it was seldom for more than 2 weeks each summer, and it was always tourist class. They ate out once a week, bought their clothes at J.C. Penny's, and furnished their home from Sears. In short, it was not their income level so much as it was their spending level that allowed them to save and invest.

Since Mary's retirement, she had occupied herself with her garden, and with community service at the local library. Now that her husband had passed away, she found herself thrown into a number of activities in which she had little experience. Foremost among them was their investment portfolio. While Harold had setup a brokerage account about 10 years ago with Freedom Securities, he had not talked much about it over the past year. She wondered-whether his health had been worse than he wanted people to know.

She gathered together the cream-colored folders that Harold had used to organize their holdings. One contained a stack of monthly statements from Freedom. Another contained a few notes Harold had made regarding investment alternatives, and some brokerage research reports on a number of bonds. Mary noted that on the outside of that folder Harold had written the words "Safe—Income Producing."

She glanced at her watch, and picked up her purse. She had an appointment with Jack Camden down at the Freedom Securities offices to review her holdings. Jack had been the Broker managing their account for over a year, but Mary had never met him. She found a parking space right in front of the building, and went in.

Jack Camden was a pleasant, slightly portly fellow, wore a dark suit and an even darker blue shirt. He motioned for her to take a chair at the end of the desk. She judged him to be in his mid-30s, with black hair that was turning prematurely gray. He seemed quite capable, and when asked how long he had been in the investment business, answered: "about five years—a little over a year with Freedom."

Mary pulled out the most recent Account Statement from Freedom Securities—the one that listed her holdings—and asked Jack if he would help her understand what each entry meant. He began by going over the list of over-the-counter (OTC) stocks bought and sold over the past month, as well as the current OTC positions.

"What is an OTC stock," she asked?

Jack explained to her that these were shares of ownership that small companies traded in the Over-The-Counter market. "Each of these stocks is recommended as a BUY by the Freedom Securities research department. They have solid growth potential, and . . . "

"Do they pay interest?" she interrupted.

"No, no. These are stocks. Most of these don't even pay dividends."

She frowned. "How safe are they?" she asked.

Jack pointed out that stocks are not guaranteed investments; that there is a degree of price volatility with all stocks; and that these OTC issues are more volatile than most.

"Then how do I make money?"

"By selling a stock after it has gone up," he answered. "That is what we have been doing here," he noted, pointing to the section of her Statement where buys and sells were summarized. She saw three sells and two buys for the previous month, and seven OTC holdings in her portfolio at month end. The total dollar amount invested in the seven OTC names was about two-thirds of the value of all of her investments held with Freedom Securities.

The Account Statement also listed several bonds held, and the interest earned from those bonds. The Statement had a number of $50,000 under the heading "Margin," as well as an entry under the caption "interest Due."

"Does this mean I owe you money?" Mary inquired, pointing to the "Interest Due" box.

"We have leveraged your, portfolio a little, by drawing on your line of credit. It allows us to buy even more investments."

Mary knew that Harold had always avoided debt, and wondered why he would set up a line of credit with their Broker.

On the way home, she wondered about some of the investment strategies that Mr. Camden was pursuing. She had to admit, it looked like they were making money on the OTC stocks. Most of the sales were at prices above cost. But still she felt uncomfortable. Concluding that a second opinion might be helpful, she turned the car around and headed for the parking lot of Trinity State Bank. She had received a number of letters from the Bank touting their growing investment prowess, and Tim Henderson had been their banker for many years. Maybe he could help her feel more comfortable.

Tim was sitting at his desk when Mary poked her head through the door. He looked up and grinned. "Come in Mrs. Bennett," he said, standing to greet her. "How can I help my favorite customer today." He didn't greet most of the Bank's depositors that way. For one thing, he usually referred to those he knew by their first names. But Tim had been one of Mary's high school English students about 20 years earlier, and he could never quite bring himself to calling her Mary.

Mary explained her conversation with Jack Camden, and showed Tim the folders containing the Account Statements from Freedom and the notes Harold had made, Tim took several minutes to study the material before commenting. He did not want to make a pitch for Mary's investment account, but wondered if her portfolio was suitable for her circumstances.

"How long have you known Jack camden?" he asked.

"I met him for the first time today," was her reply.

"Has he ever called you to discuss your investment profile and goals?"

"He may have talked with Harold about those things, but I had never spoken to him before. What is an investment profile?" she asked.

"It is the information that an investment advisor would need before they could properly advise you on the appropriateness of various investment alternatives. Things such as your age and health, sources of earnings and income level, tax bracket, the explicit objectives of your investments in light of your needs and circumstances, your risk tolerance, expected duration of investments, and so forth."

"You see Mrs. Bennett, when a client relies upon a Broker to such an extent that the Broker is in a position to control the nature and frequency of the transactions in the clients account, that Broker assumes a responsibility. That responsibility is to make those investment recommendations that are suitable to that client, and to conduct transactions that are consistent with those recommendations without incurring excessive transaction costs."

"But Tim, how can he know what is suitable for me unless he asks?"

"That is my point. And his responsibility goes beyond merely asking. He must ensure that you understand the basic characteristics of your investment plan, and the appropriateness of that investment plan for you."

"It is possible that Mr. Camden visited with my husband about all this. It just doesn't sound like Harold to approve trades in small stocks when he seemed to be focused on safe, income producing investments. And I don't understand this borrowing on Margin. After all, I was retired and he was getting ready to stop working. What business do we have taking out new loans at our age?"

"Even if Harold had wanted to speculate and was aware of the risk, it does not release the Broker from his responsibility to determine suitability. "The issue is not whether the client considers the transactions in his account to be suitable." The test is whether the Broker fulfilled the obligation he assumed when he undertook to counsel the client: to make only such recommendations as would be consistent with and suitable to their needs. In this case, there is nothing to indicate that Harold had initiated any of these transactions, or that he was even aware of them. The truth is, you and Harold have relied on Mr. Camden to oversee your account."

"I'm not saying he's done a bad job," Mary broke in. "It looks like I've made money and the stocks that have been bought were all recommended by the Freedom Securities research department."

"A BUY recommendation by an equity research department does not constitute suitability," Tim replied. "A Broker cannot shift his responsibility as an investment counselor to his employer. It is Mr. Camdens' duty to make only such recommendations as are appropriate to the best interests of his clients. He may consider the recommendations of his research department in light of his clients' investment objectives and financial situation, but he may not tailor his clients investment objectives to the recommendations of his research department."

"Tim, do you think that having OTC stocks in my portfolio is suitable for me?" Mary asked.

"That's the right question," Tim answered. "The answer may be harder to come by. There is no doubt that, had you lost money in those shares, most observers would have said that highly volatile stocks were unsuitable recommendations for your portfolio. The world is full of second guessers who are quite willing to point out what the problems were <u>after</u> things go awry. The fact that you made money does not, however, render them suitable. I'd have to say that these are not the kind of investment you should have. Most definitely, you should not be buying them on margin!"

"Another thing that bothers me is the frequency of trades," Tim added. That's a lot of trading for any account—even one that should have an equity focus." He paused, looking at the Account Statements on his desk. When he spoke again, it was slowly and more deliberate.

"Suitability is a fundamental fiduciary duty. This responsibility is especially important because the knowledge and information of the professional investment manager may be greater than the knowledge and information of the client. This disparity places the individual client in a vulnerable position of trust. You rely on your investment advisor him to handle your account in such a way that your interests are served. And most brokers are very diligent in discharging this responsibility. But the reality is that the broker makes his money by selling products or executing security transactions. And the potential exists for him to make more money if he sells and trades more. That is a potential conflict of interest, and one that he should be particularly sensitive too."

Mary wasn't sure what to do. She felt much more comfortable with Tim Henderson, but maybe that was because she had known him for so long. He seemed to understand her better. On the other hand, Jack Camden had been making money in her investment portfolio, and seemed to know what he was doing. Yet, Mary couldn't help but wonder who it was that Jack was making money for. Had he placed his interests above that of his client?

SDH

****
"Even <u>I</u> don't wake up looking
like Cindy Crawford."
— Cindy Crawford, model
****

A State of Mind
Approaching Hard Decisions

At the base of each of our brains is a small organ called the amygdala, whose job it is to assess whether every incoming stimulus is a threat. If the answer is yes, the amygdala triggers an adrenaline response, flooding the cortex—the brains' rational part—with chemicals that partially block its function. It's a useful chemical response when the body is preparing its defenses against physical harm. However, the problem comes when the amygdala is triggered by an emotional or even an intellectual threat. Unable to distinguish between the physical threat and an emotional one, the brain flips over to its "fight or flight" mode at the very time it needs to rationally sort out additional options. The result is a form of conscious paralysis akin to the "deer in the headlights" syndrome. In this state, we are unable to think clearly and even our memory short-circuits. We are in the grip of what has been called the Pain Avoidance Model, and we want only to reduce the threat and return to our comfort zone.

What has this to do with investments? Everything.

Investment markets are, by their very nature, uncertain, volatile, and subject to unexpected influences from uncontrollable events. To participate in this environment by accepting some type of professional responsibility for other peoples money, adds still another dimension of risk: that of performing well under a variety of conditions. Occasionally, an investment may even go bad. Taken together, there is plenty for the amygdala to get excited about. Yet, that is the very time when clear thinking and deliberate action is most necessary.

Accordingly, one of the greatest challenges an investor faces is developing a mindset that will allow him to function rationally while in a panic. This quality of mind allows him to see things as they really are (not as he would like them to be) and afford a factual accounting of what is really going on.

The amygdala is not the only impediment to achieving this kind of Intellectual Integrity. All of us filter our environment through a screen of perceptions. What we think is happening is based largely on our interpretations, our biases, and on our point of view. At the same time, our reaction to our environment is similarly jaundiced by our individual and institutional character traits. These may include a lack of confidence, a reluctance to make painful decisions, or a value system that makes "rocking-the-boat" simply unacceptable. In short, seeing things as they really are and being able to respond as we should, are rare qualities.

In today's environment, a substantial portion of the challenge of seeing things as they really are, stems from the blinding rate of change occurring in nearly every corner of society. The old adage: "Things are more like they are today, then they ever were before", is painfully true. Where will the changes lead? How will things be different tomorrow? What does a change somewhere else mean for things here? All good questions—the answers to which are hard to see. Change is difficult for most of us to accept, especially when that change effects us directly, and more especially when that change threatens us.

Consider, for example, the case of retailing on the Internet. Catalogues have already taken a bite out of the consumer market held by the traditional store-front retailer. Now, look at the growing inroads made by a new kind of merchandiser—the Internet. At least one Website is even selling consumer products below cost, thereby planning to establish itself as the leading E-commerce portal. With growing recognition by the consumer, this audacious entrepreneur plans to make up its operating deficit by selling advertising space to manufacturers and suppliers. Since this marketer has no inventory (manufacturers will ship products directly to its customers) and no retail facility, overhead costs are minimal.

While some recognition of these changes are within tile grasp of many observers, if that observer is a traditional retailer occupying expensive commercial store-front space and carrying substantial fixed costs in facility and inventory, it may be more difficult to view the picture objectively. It may be even harder to act constructively. What would common sense dictate? Native good judgement seems illusive when it involves accepting pain.

Another example involves the portfolio manager who finds his investment falling in price. His returns are declining . . . his performance is going from bad to worse . . . investors are complaining . . . what to do? Again, relying on the dictates of good judgement is easier said than done. What would good judgement suggest in this instance? If the market is rotating away to other investments, then the question becomes one of relative value and time horizons. However, if the fall in price is the result of an individual selection that has failed to meet expectations, then the decision may involve a recognition that the investment was wrong. The pain involved in realizing a loss that accompanies an investment error is hard for most people to accept. As a result, it is not uncommon for the investor to hold that position indefinitely, in the hope that it will turn around, and in the fear that he will make another mistake if he sells too soon.

How then do we develop this prized quality of being able to see the world as it is.

It appears that one ingredient to this talent is the ability to accept, perhaps even endorse, those decisions that would put us out of our comfort zone—that might even be painful. We call these the "tough" decisions, and we typically delay them if possible or pass them to others to make. Even if delaying them now condemns us to worse pain down the road, we too often elect to avoid the pain now. It's just wired into every one of our heads.

Yet, there are those who seem able to absorb the threat, evaluate it dispassionately, structure a course to deal with it—and succeed. Harry Truman, Jack Welch, Warren Buffet, Peter Drucker . . . all appear to have grasped the Intellectual Integrity that allows them to see through the smoke that blinds most others. This ability is not a common trait. Certainly, our self-centered Western culture does not appear to be producing many such people. Quite the contrary we seem to be absorbed in a race to see how many different perceptions or points of view we can accommodate before anyone asks the question—which one is right . . . What is real?

Perhaps one of the more serious consequences of an inability to achieve this rational mindset is that it slows our learning. Consider what happens when a person is being corrected, their judgement is being challenged, or their view of the world (and possibly themselves) undergoes change. All of these events are sources of psychic pain, and their occurrence triggers the amygdala, causing the chemical response that prevents our rational minds from fully registering what is happening. If it prevents us from fully seeing our errors, how can we acknowledge our mistakes. And, if we can't acknowledge our mistakes, how can we learn?

The classic "fight or flight" response is: "It's not my fault!" This mindset does not even try to address the problem, but simply ducks the responsibility. As such, the learning process is slowed by our own reaction, and we cannot develop that balance in judgement—that Intellectual Integrity—that is so essential to seeing things realistically and responding correctly? On the other hand, those who have developed the mindset to more quickly adjust their judgement to realities, and those institutions who foster that mindset, accelerate the learning process by reducing the threat posed by fault.

This is doable. We are not condemned to be as we are. While the amygdala will send its signals to the cortex, the cortex also has the ability to send signals to the amygdala. The cortex can rationally influence the amygdala's instincts—like training a muscle—and limit the extent by which the chemical response to a situation overpowers and governs the rational response. The individual who achieves this improved level of control has developed a character trait that allows him to function with greater success in a changing world.

Any effort to train the amygdala will meet with greater success as we "de-personalize" the imput being received. If we take the ego . . . the "I" . . . out of the process, and focus as objectively as possible on the imput, we reduce the threat to us personally. A reduction in the perceived level of threat may help keep the amygdala calm and our perceptions more accurate.

One way to do this is by mentally deflecting the imput away from us and toward the organization of which we are a part. Recognizing that we are servants of an organization, and subordinating our own likes, wishes, and preferences to the goals and welfare of that organization, may help achieve this abstraction. If we have identified the goals and needs of the institution, and aligned our tasks accordingly, any imput will be perceived as less personal in nature, as it is directed at the welfare of the organization and not at us individually.

This new mindset can actually contribute to the learning process, as opposed to blocking it. If the needs of the institution are our first priority, we will be more inclined to ask: "What do we need to know or what do we need to do, to better meet the needs of the organization?" Our usual insecurities and weaknesses will be given a back seat, as we have the strength to ask what the realities are, and what we need to do to align ourselves to those realities.

In an investment context, this state of mind might be fostered by recognizing the market as an impersonal entity, which functions without regard for each of us. At any given time, the market will offer a price at which it will either buy your holding or sell you its. Its price quotes are not consistent. On the contrary, it may at times offer a very high price while at other times suggesting a very low price, with little apparent reasoning for the fluctuations. The market does not insist on a transaction, but simply provides a quote. Any transaction is up to you. If you are caught up in the mood of the market, or fall under its influence, you may find yourself reacting rather than acting. Maintaining your independence, and your emotional detachment from the market, can produce a mindset that is more suitable to an objective decision process. *In the end, the market doesn't care. It simply goes* on producing its quotes.

Facing things as they are, with the Intellectual Integrity to deal with them squarely, is a necessary prerequisite to an even grander state of mind—that of seeing things as they can be. The visionary who grasps trends, who identifies the likely course of events, who sees the possible, is in a position to manage far better than those who simply respond to events. Such managers possess greater confidence and greater credibility, and are able to make sometimes painful choices with greater courage, because they can see where those choices lead. Their view is not limited to the "here and now", but is anchored on a platform of current realities. The difference is their ability to see where those realities lead, and project the probabilities of the future.

This is the indispensable first quality of a leader. A guiding vision—a strongly defined sense of purpose—a clear idea of what needs to be done. These people are dreamers to be sure, but they are pragmatic dreamers. They have a strong point of view, and are willing to try and persuade others to their point of view. They are not afraid of the hard decisions, and have developed a consistent mindset that allows for all kinds of imput without derailing their fundamental goals. They engender trust because of their candor, the quality of their decisions, and the effectiveness of their implementation. Their confidence leads them to surround themselves with capable people who are empowered with the means of achievement. They keep always in their mind what Robert Lewis Stevenson said about doing the difficult: "Why not now, and where you stand."

SDH

****
The Greatest Reward Is Not What We Receive
For Our Labor,
But What We Become By It.
****

Growth Versus Value
A Stock Pickers Conundrum

How do you manage an equity portfolio?

Quite possibly the first question a stock investor may ask, it is often the most difficult to answer. Responding with "I buy low and sell high," or "I manage by my instincts," are not answers that inform, and most investors require a better understanding of your style or technique than those phrases provide. The serious investor will want to know—and you need for him to know—exactly what strategy you are pursuing. For both of you—it matters.

In reality, there are probably as many answers to this question as there are portfolio managers. However, investors have come to categorize most answers into two fundamental investment techniques—the Growth Strategy and the Value Strategy. Each strategy constitutes a decision making framework used to select stocks. Yet, they lead in very different directions.

Growth stock investing means searching for companies that are expected to grow faster than the economy at large. Growth investing is about identifying the next Microsoft or Cisco, in the belief that their faster growth will produce rising earnings, which in turn will lead to higher share prices. Approximately 40% of stock mutual funds tell their investors that they are pursuing a Growth strategy.

Value stock investing means finding companies that are selling for less than their intrinsic value. Value investing is about identifying the next Chrysler or Citibank, in the belief that the market will eventually recognize their true value, which will lead to higher share prices. Again, approximately 40% of stock mutual funds hold themselves out as Value investors.

The rationale behind pursuing a Growth investment strategy can be compelling. In most cases, a Growth stock has already exhibited strong revenue and earnings comparisons. Of course, while past growth can be measured pretty easily, the problem is figuring out how fast future growth will be and how long it will last. Nevertheless, it has not been unusual for Growth funds to post 5-year compound annual returns of ± 20% . In bullish years such as 1991, the <u>average</u> small-company Growth fund returned 58%. The key is in identifying companies such as Cisco, which went public in 1990 and grew by 156 times in the following 8 years.

The Value strategy can be a bit more complex. Typically, Value investors look for companies that have a low price/earnings ratio or a low price-to-book ratio. The rationale is that Value investing is less risky if the downside can be supported by the underlying value of the company's earnings or assets. Because the Value strategy is believed to be less volatile, the reward can be equally attractive if viewed from a long term perspective. From 1978 to 1998, small-company Value stocks delivered an average compound annual return above 20%, with 12% less volatility than the S&P 500.

Both strategies offer a consistent, disciplined approach, which is meaningful to an investor seeking to evaluate the merits of a money manager. Both have strengths and weaknesses. Perhaps the major drawback of the Growth strategy is its reliance on Growth—which must occur on a sustained basis and at levels which reach or exceed market expectations. Though the company may be posting very good comparisons in revenues and earnings, if the comparisons fall below expectations, considerable volatility in stock price may ensue. A second problem is the question of how much to pay for the growth potential. While Growth investing will usually test the upper ranges of most evaluation measures, the decision of how much of a premium is appropriate is sometimes hard to quantify.

Value investing has its share of pitfalls as well. Many times, the low price/earnings ratio is deserved, as the company has matured and may be in decline for one reason or another. Then too, while most valuation criteria are more easily quantified, they are subject to accounting anomalies. The market may put a low price on certain assets because they are worth less than book, or because they have value only if used by the company. How much are the assets really worth; begs the question—to whom?

In an effort to further understand the relative merits of Growth versus Value investing, consider the following scenarios. Based only your evaluation of current relative market conditions, and the information provided herein on each company, which names would you regard as Growth stocks, and which as Value stocks.

ARROWHEAD AEROSPACE INC.

Share Price	Current P/E	Next Year Estimated P/E	Book Value Per Share	Dividend Per Share
$24.25	25.0x	20.2x	$12.00	$0.36

Arrowhead was the winner in a tightly bid contract to develop and supply state-of-the-art navigation equipment to the U.S. Air Force. After experiencing lackluster earnings over the past several years as the result of high R&D expense, the Company can now look forward to at least 5 years of very strong earnings comparisons. The contract calls for delivery of the first 50 units next year, 100 units in year two, 200 units in year three, 400 units in year four, and 450 units in year five, for a total contract amount of 1200 units. With the majority of costs fixed, earnings are expected to advance from $0.97 per share this year to $1.20 next year, $1.65 in year two, $2.45 in year three, $4.00 in year four, and $4.25 in year five.

It is anticipated that the Air Force will look to update its navigation technology in about 5 years, possibly seeking a bid to contract the development of the next generation of navigation equipment. While Arrowhead is confident that it can compete successfully in this market, the technology involved is changing rapidly and there are many older and larger competitors.

BUTTONS & BOWS INC.

Share Price	Current P/E	Next Year Estimated P/E	Book Value Per Share	Dividend Per Share
$16.75	15.0x	14.6x	$13.50	$0.40

Buttons & Bows is a New England - based retailer that began offering sewing supplies through its storefront outlets in the mid-1950s. Over the years, the Company has grown into a major national chain, with over 900 sewing centers in 38 states. Most of the Company's outlets are located in downtown areas of smaller towns or in strip malls of mid-sized communities. Recently, Buttons & Bows has opened a number of retail centers in the major malls of larger cities, including Detroit, Milwaukee, Minneapolis, Seattle, and San Francisco. Early results from these newer mall-based outlets are mixed, with somewhat higher sales offset by significantly higher rents.

The Company has been managed by a succession of very conservative CEOs, and growth has historically been funded entirely from cash. The Company has no debt outstanding, though most of its retail sewing centers are located in leased facilities with long-term triple-net lease commitments. In addition to its entry into major city malls, the new management is looking to expand the Company's product image from a retail supplier of sewing supplies, to a sewing hobby center complete with classes and consulting services. This latter initiative will require some renovation of most outlets to create in-store work space. Management is considering the sale of additional common stock to raise the funds necessary to begin the renovation process.

CONSOLIDATED COMMUNICATIONS CORPORATION

Share Price	Current P/E	Next Year Estimated P/E	Book Value Per Share	Dividend Per Share
$176.50	32.9x	20.6x	$7.46	$0.00

Consolidated Communications Corporation (CCC) is a communications consulting and development company that advises clients on the best communications systems to meet their needs, and then coordinates the installation of those systems. The Company is at the forefront of communication technology, and seeks not only the most cost efficient system, but also the most effective system when viewed in terms of the evolving nature of the industry. Representing itself as a turn-key communications consultant, CCC has enjoyed overwhelming acceptance, and currently has more contracts pending than it can adequately service.

Earnings have advanced at a 51% compound annual rate over the past 3 years, and current street expectations call for even faster growth going forward. The net margin has risen in each of the past 3 years, from 11.5% to 15.7% to 20.1% in the most recent 12 months. Consensus expectations call for a 25% net margin this year. Given the surge in business, the Company is actively recruiting qualified personnel, and is having some difficulty filling all available positions. Yesterday, the President shocked the Management Committee by announcing that they would have to pass on some contract offers simply because they don't have the people to handle them.

As we can see from the above examples, identifying a company as a Growth vehicle or a Value vehicle is not always easy. There are subgrowth categories and subvalue categories, and there are instances where a metamorphosis takes place from one category to the other. A thoughtful manager may wish to place additional constraints on his investment discipline in an effort to guide him into fruitful investing. For example, a growth manager may wish to impose GARP—Growth At Reasonable Price—which weighs anticipated growth rates by the relative price of the shares. One Value investor may wish to focus on the prospects for the company's business, where as another may look only at the intrinsic worth of the underlying assets.

Whichever strategy or combination of strategies is pursued, it is vital that the manager remember that he is not investing in companies, he is ,investing in stocks. That's different. It is all too common for an analyst who spends considerable time evaluating the merits of a company, to develop an affinity for that company. Maybe it is the product or service being offered that he likes, or the facility that impresses him, or perhaps he has hit it off with management. Whatever the reason, he forgets that there is a price at which any stock should be sold, and there is a price at which any stock should be bought.

Ultimately, all equity investing is an effort to identify stocks that will experience an increase in price beyond what is currently being discounted by the market. Whether that increase is the result of growth in earnings or the realization of unrecognized value, it is essential that the market eventually come to share your evaluation. You may see substantial Growth potential or an abundance of Value, but if other investors don't share that view, your insights will remain sterile. Benjamin Graham and David Dodd said it best: "The market is not a weighing machine, on which the value of each issue is recorded by an exact and impersonal mechanism. Rather, the market is a voting machine, whereon countless individuals register choices which are the product partly of reason and partly of emotion."

SDH

****
We Are What We Repeatedly Do.
Excellence Is Not An Act . . . It Is A Habit.
****

In Search Of Alpha

Understanding Changes In Security Prices

Volatility in security prices stems from a host of factors, ranging from worldwide events to the success of an individual product or service. Efforts to understand the reasons for such volatility, and even quantify the nature of security price movements, have typically centered around two principle measurement devices. These are beta or the systematic volatility, and alpha or the unsystematic price movements.

The term beta comes from William Sharpe's Capital Asset Pricing Model. Beta is a coefficient that represents the sensitivity of a security (or an entire portfolio) to a market's aggregate return. Given that a market's overall return is always 1.00, a beta coefficient of 1.10, for example, would suggest a security that is 10% move volatile in price than the market as a whole . . . in both directions. Conversely, a beta of 0.85 identifies a security that is only 85% as volatile as the market; posting a price movement of 8.5% in a market that is up (or down) 10%. A negative beta indicates a security that inversely follows the market, that decreases in value if the market goes up, and vice versa.

The alpha measure attempts to identify that portion of a securities' return "which is uncorrelated to the market. The alpha variable is sometimes described as a "residual value" in that it reflects those factors unique to the security; which are independent of market movements and which may actually run counter to the direction and/or magnitude of overall market price trends.

The thoughtful analyst may ask: 'What proportion of a securities' price movement is the result of beta—the systematic sensitivity of the security to a change in the market, versus alpha—those unsystematic factors that are unique to the security. In search of the answer to this question, it is important to understand how beta and alpha are calculated.

Since beta is, in effect, the financial elasticity or the relative volatility of a security to the market, it is necessary that two sets of data be evaluated in its calculation. First, the price of the individual security needs to be tabulated, and second, the price of the market (represented by an index such as the S&P 500, for example) needs to be established. The market benchmark used should be representative of the individual security evaluated. Weekly price data for both sets of data would be satisfactory, since daily data tends to be a bit noisy, and monthly data is too infrequent. To be accurate, dividends should be included. The beta coefficient is simply the linear regression of these two sets of data. Charted, with the individual security in the y axis and and the market index in the x axis, we find the correlations throughout the time frame to be analyzed looking somewhat as shown on the following page.

A regression analysis of the data produces a straight line, with the slope of that line indicating the beta of the security. Several features of the above methodology render the beta number somewhat flawed.

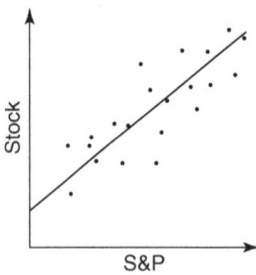

First, we see that beta is an average of a host of correlation points. Like all averages, it varies depending on the time span covered by the observations. Furthermore, the R-Square or fit of the line to the data samples varies considerably. Very seldom does the beta actually represent a precise relationship (most of the time it does not), but represents only an average of the relationships.

Second, since the correlation points represent historical relationships, the beta produced is a historical number. Yet, beta is typically used to forecast the anticipated reaction of a given asset to changes in the market. It is akin to viewing a future relationship by looking in the rear-view mirror. If the past is representative of the future, then the number might be a realistic estimate. If not . . .

Third, and of significant import for our purposes, the regression analysis undertaken captures price movements for all reasons, both systematic and unsystematic. In other words, whether the change in price is the result of a change in general interest rates, economic conditions, other other beta-type factors, or whether it results from a new management, a change in product costs, or other alpha-type factors, is not differentiated. In calculating beta, we have tried to identify a securities elasticity to movements in the market, but we have ended up capturing its elasticity to all conditions and events, whether stemming from market factors or induced by events quite apart from the market . . . which are unique to that individual security . . . which are alpha or unsystematic in nature.

If the beta calculation is simply a linear regression of past asset prices as a coefficient of market prices, how do we separate out the alpha. Much too often, we don't. One of the most often cited formula's for the calculation of alpha is called Jensen's alpha, named after Michael C. Jensen. Jensen's alpha is computed as:

$$Alpha = Actual\ Price - Expected\ Price$$

Jensen's alpha is simply the degree by which the actual return varies from the expected return as postulated by beta. It is the measure of return above or below the security market line . . . the measure of how much the asset price varies from betas' expectations. Alpha becomes a residual; the explanation of what is left after giving beta its dues. However, if historical beta includes the unspecified alphas of bygone days, this residual formula proves inadequate for the measurement of alpha.

Under the Capital Asset Pricing Theory, often referred to as the Law of One Price, beta-based asset allocation is the main driver of returns. This is because the alpha or unsystematic component can be minimized away in a broad diversification strategy. Accordingly, many investors, including institutional investors, focus mainly on the allocation decision, and do not engage in individual security selection. While the asset allocation decision may well be an active strategy based on a review of market conditions and anticipated trends, it relies for the most part on historical data, including the beta coefficient, for the allocation decision. What is needed is a means of identifying, and perhaps even postulating, tomorrow's asset prices, based on a prospective measure of alpha.

The identification of alpha would seem to be the primary goal in the securities selection effort. Unlike the beta number, which is an average of a series of historical comparisons, alpha attempts to identify, if not quantify, those unique factors and events that will affect the price of a security going forward. Alpha assumes that the security will continue to bob up and down on the lake of overall market conditions. However, the primary alpha question pertains to those events which are not a function of the market as a whole, but relate to individual circumstance, including product positioning, management, potential security mispricing, tactical timing, etc.

Certain of the disadvantages of beta can be addressed in this forward looking pursuit of alpha. In the first place, such an alpha would not be an average of a number of historical findings over a period. It is specific to events and conditions, and the time period encompassed by those events. Second, we are trying to know what the relative impact of those events and conditions will be going forward. Investors are much more concerned with the pricing of a security after they bought it, than before. The notion that we can catch a glimpse of tomorrows pricing by evaluating alpha, improves the investors' confidence in the prospects of the investment.

The search for alpha is not inexpensive, and requires considerable time and effort. The goal is to produce insight that will allow us to select Security A because of its unique advantages, over Security B, which does not possess such advantages. After all, superior investment performance comes from identifying those securities that outperform the average. If our efforts to identify the better performers fail, we would be better off using a passive management technique such as index investing, and save ourselves the time and effort of searching for alpha.

The search for alpha can take many forms and, whether we realize it or not, contributes greatly to the success of some of the investment techniques we hold dear. For example, the Efficient Market Hypothesis depends, for its efficiency, on a legion of investors actively gathering and analyzing information, which is then reflected in the price of a security. To the extent that this effort wanes, efficient pricing cannot be expected. Warren Buffett's Berkshire Hathaway is one of those investors, searching for alpha as a means of identifying and selecting specific long-term investment opportunities.

Most of what is called "Technical Analysis", is nothing more than looking over the shoulders of other investors, including those involved in the search for alpha, and interpreting their conclusions by observing security pricing and volume trends. Before demand and supply pressures are reflected in technical charges and graphs, someone has to enter buy and sell orders. Those entering such orders include the Medallion Fund, for example, which is analyzing investments in terms of mispricing and timing, and trading selected securities over shorter periods.

While one of the arguments cited in the Capital Asset Pricing Theory for beta alone is that we can diversify away alpha, we must ask the question: "Why would we want to diversity away alpha?" If we have the opportunity, through hard work and acquired insights, to identify that will allow us to select securities that outperform the averages, why would we want to content ourselves with a mediocre performance?

SDH

****

Laus Deo — Carpe Diem

****